Rational Expectations
and Econometric Practice

Rational Expectations
and Econometric Practice

Edited by
Robert E. Lucas, Jr.
University of Chicago
and
Thomas J. Sargent
*University of Minnesota
and Federal Reserve Bank
of Minneapolis*

The University of Minnesota Press
Minneapolis

Copyright © 1981 by the University of Minnesota
All rights reserved.
Published by the University of Minnesota Press,
2037 University Avenue Southeast, Minneapolis, MN 55414
Printed in the United States of America
Third printing, 1982

Library of Congress Cataloging in Publication Data

Main entry under title:
Rational expectations and econometric practice.
Bibliography: p.
    1. Econometrics — Addresses, essays, lectures.
2. Time-series analysis — Addresses, essays, lectures.
3. Monetary policy — Mathematical models — Addresses,
essays, lectures.   4. Economic policy — Mathematical
models — Addresses, essays, lectures.   I. Lucas,
Robert E.   II. Sargent, Thomas J.
HB139.R37   330'.028   80-24602
ISBN 0-8166-0916-0
ISBN 0-8166-0917-9 v. I (pbk.)
ISBN 0-8166-1071-1 v. II (pbk.)
ISBN 0-8166-1098-3 Set (pbk.)

To our parents

Contents

This Book Starts here

6. Macroeconomic Control Problems

PART 4 General Applications

20

Investigating Causal Relations by Econometric Models and Cross-Spectral Methods

C. W. J. Granger

There occurs on some occasions a difficulty in deciding the direction of causality between two related variables and also whether or not feedback is occurring. Testable definitions of causality and feedback are proposed and illustrated by use of simple two-variable models. The important problem of apparent instantaneous causality is discussed and it is suggested that the problem often arises due to slowness in recording information or because a sufficiently wide class of possible causal variables has not been used. It can be shown that the cross spectrum between two variables can be decomposed into two parts, each relating to a single causal arm of a feedback situation. Measures of causal lag and causal strength can then be constructed. A generalization of this result with the partial cross spectrum is suggested.

The object of this paper is to throw light on the relationships between certain classes of econometric models involving feedback and the functions arising in spectral analysis, particularly the cross spectrum and the partial cross spectrum. Causality and feedback are here defined in an explicit and testable fashion. It is shown that in the two-variable case the feedback mechanism can be broken down into two causal relations and that the cross spectrum can be considered as the sum of two cross spectra, each closely connected with one of the causations. The next three sections of the paper briefly introduce those aspects of spectral methods, model building, and causality which are required later. Section IV presents the results for the two-variable case and Section V generalizes these results for three variables.

I. Spectral Methods

If X_t is a stationary time series with mean zero, there are two basic spectral representations associated with the series: (i) the Cramer representation,

$$X_t = \int_{-\pi}^{\pi} e^{it\omega} \, dz_x(\omega),\tag{1}$$

[*Econometrica*, 1969, vol. 37, no. 3]

where $z_x(\omega)$ is a complex random process with uncorrelated increments so that

$$E[dz_x(\omega)\,\overline{dz_x(\lambda)}] = 0, \qquad \omega \neq \lambda,$$
$$= dF_x(\omega), \; \omega = \lambda; \tag{2}$$

(ii) the spectral representation of the covariance sequence

$$\mu_\tau^{xx} = E[X_t\bar{X}_{t-\tau}] = \int_{-\pi}^{\pi} e^{i\tau\omega}\, dF_x(\omega). \tag{3}$$

If X_t has no strictly periodic components, $dF_x(\omega) = f_x(\omega)\,d\omega$ where $f_x(\omega)$ is the power spectrum of X_t. The estimation and interpretation of power spectra have been discussed in Granger and Hatanaka (1964) and Nerlove (1964). The basic idea underlying the two spectral representations is that the series can be decomposed as a sum (i.e., integral) of uncorrelated components, each associated with a particular frequency. It follows that the variance of the series is equal to the sum of the variances of the components. The power spectrum records the variances of the components as a function of their frequencies and indicates the relative importance of the components in terms of their contribution to the overall variance.

If X_t and Y_t are a pair of stationary time series, so that Y_t has the spectrum $f_y(\omega)$ and Cramer representation

$$Y_t = \int_{-\pi}^{\pi} e^{it\omega}\, dz_y(\omega),$$

then the cross spectrum (strictly power cross spectrum) $Cr(\omega)$ between X_t and Y_t is a complex function of ω and arises both from

$$E[dz_x(\omega)\,\overline{dz_y(\omega)}] = 0, \qquad \omega \neq \lambda,$$
$$= Cr(\omega)\,d\omega, \; \omega = \lambda,$$

and

$$\mu_\tau^{xy} = E[X_t\bar{Y}_{t-\tau}] = \int_{-\pi}^{\pi} e^{i\tau\omega}Cr(\omega)\,d\omega.$$

It follows that the relationship between two series can be expressed only in terms of the relationships between corresponding frequency components.

Two further functions are defined from the cross spectrum as being more useful for interpreting relationships between variables: (i) the coherence,

$$C(\omega) = \frac{|Cr(\omega)|^2}{f_x(\omega)f_y(\omega)},$$

which is essentially the square of the correlation coefficient between corresponding frequency components of X_t and Y_t, and (ii) the phase,

$$\phi(\omega) = \tan^{-1}\frac{\text{imaginary part of } Cr(\omega)}{\text{real part of } Cr(\omega)},$$

which measures the phase difference between corresponding frequency components. When one variable is leading the other, $\phi(\omega)/\omega$ measure the extent of the time lag.

Thus, the coherence is used to measure the degree to which two series are related and the phase may be interpreted in terms of time lags.

Estimation and interpretation of the coherence and phase function are discussed in Granger and Hatanaka (1964, chaps. 5 and 6). It is worth noting that $\phi(\omega)$ has been found to be robust under changes in the stationarity assumption (Granger and Hatanaka 1964, chap. 9).

If X_t, Y_t, and Z_t are three time series, the problem of possibly misleading correlation and coherence values between two of them due to the influence on both of the third variable can be overcome by the use of partial cross-spectral methods.

The spectral, cross-spectral matrix $[f_{ij}(\omega)] = S(\omega)$ between the three variables is given by

$$E \begin{bmatrix} dz_x(\omega) \\ dz_y(\omega) \\ dz_z(\omega) \end{bmatrix} [\overline{dz_x(\omega)} \; \overline{dz_y(\omega)} \; \overline{dz_z(\omega)}] = [f_{ij}(\omega)] \, d\omega$$

where

$$f_{ij}(\omega) = f_x(\omega) \quad \text{when } i = j = x,$$
$$= Cr^{xy}(\omega) \text{ when } i = x, j = y,$$

etc.

The partial spectral, cross-spectral matrix between X_t and Y_t given Z_t is found by partitioning $S(\omega)$ into components:

$$S = \begin{bmatrix} S_{11} & S_{12} \\ S_{21} & S_{22} \end{bmatrix}.$$

The partitioning lines are between the second and third rows, and second and third columns. The partial spectral matrix is then

$$S_{xy,z} = S_{11} - S_{12} S_{22}^{-1} S_{21}.$$

Interpretation of the components of this matrix is similar to that involving partial correlation coefficients. Thus, the partial cross spectrum can be used to find the relationship between two series once the effect of a third series has been taken into account. The partial coherence and phase are defined directly from the partial cross spectrum as before. Interpretation of all of these functions and generalizations to the n-variable case can be found in Granger and Hatanaka (1964, chap. 5).

II. Feedback Models

Consider initially a stationary random vector $X_t = \{X_{1t}, X_{2t}, \ldots, X_{kt}\}$, each component of which has zero mean. A linear model for such a vector consists of a set of linear equations by which all or a subset of the components of X_t are "explained" in terms of present and past values of components of X_t. The part not explained by the model may be taken to consist of a white-noise random vector ε_t, such that

$$
\begin{aligned}
E[\varepsilon_t' \varepsilon_s] &= 0, \quad t \neq s, \\
&= I, \quad t = s,
\end{aligned}
\tag{4}
$$

where I is a unit matrix and 0 is a zero matrix.

Thus the model may be written as

$$
A_0 X_t = \sum_{j=1}^{m} A_j X_{t-j} + \varepsilon_t
\tag{5}
$$

where m may be infinite and the A's are matrices.

The completely general model as defined does not have unique matrices A_j as an orthogonal transformation. $Y_t = \Lambda X_t$ can be performed which leaves the form of the model the same, where Λ is the orthogonal matrix, i.e., a square matrix having the property $\Lambda \Lambda' = I$. This is seen to be the case as $\eta_t = \Lambda \varepsilon_t$ is still a white-noise vector. For the model to be determined, sufficient a priori knowledge is required about the values of the coefficients of at least one of the A's, in order for constraints to be set up so that such transformations are not possible. This is the so-called identification problem of classical econometrics. In the absence of such a priori constraints, Λ can always be chosen so that the A_0 is a triangular matrix, although not uniquely, thus giving a spurious causal-chain appearance to the model.

Models for which A_0 has nonvanishing terms off the main diagonal will be called "models with instantaneous causality." Models for which A_0 has no nonzero term off the main diagonal will be called "simple causal models." These names will be explained later. Simple causal models are uniquely determined if orthogonal transforms such as Λ are not possible without changing the basic form of the model. It is possible for a model apparently having instantaneous causality to be transformed using an orthogonal Λ to a simple causal model.

These definitions can be illustrated simply in the two variable case. Suppose the variables are X_t, Y_t. Then the model considered is of the form

$$
\begin{aligned}
X_t + b_0 Y_t &= \sum_{j=1}^{m} a_j X_{t-j} + \sum_{j=1}^{m} b_j Y_{t-j} + \varepsilon_t', \\[2mm]
Y_t + c_0 X_t &= \sum_{j=1}^{m} c_j X_{t-j} + \sum_{j=1}^{m} d_j Y_{t-j} + \varepsilon_t''.
\end{aligned}
\tag{6}
$$

If $b_0 = c_0 = 0$, then this will be a simple causal model. Otherwise it will be a model with instantaneous causality.

Whether or not a model involving some group of economic variables can be a simple causal model depends on what one considers to be the speed with which information flows through the economy and also on the sampling period of the data used. It might be true that when quarterly data are used, for example, a simple causal model is not sufficient to explain the relationships between the variables, while for monthly data a simple causal model would be all that is required. Thus, some nonsimple causal models may be constructed not because of the basic properties of the economy being studied but because of the data being used. It has been shown elsewhere (Granger 1963; Granger and Hatanaka 1964, chap. 7) that a simple causal mechanism can appear to be a feedback mechanism if the sampling period for the data is so long that details of causality cannot be picked out.

III. Causality

Cross-spectral methods provide a useful way of describing the relationship between two (or more) variables when one is causing the other(s). In many realistic economic situations, however, one suspects that feedback is occurring. In these situations the coherence and phase diagrams become difficult or impossible to interpret, particularly the phase diagram. The problem is how to devise definitions of causality and feedback which permits tests for their existence. Such a definition was proposed in earlier papers (Granger 1963; Granger and Hatanaka 1964, chap. 7). In this section, some of these definitions will be discussed and extended. Although later sections of this paper will use this definition of causality they will not completely depend upon it. Previous papers concerned with causality in economic systems (Basman 1963; Orcutt 1952; Simon 1953; Strotz and Wold 1960) have been particularly concerned with the problem of determining a causal interpretation of simultaneous equation systems, usually with instantaneous causality. Feedback is not explicitly discussed. This earlier work has concentrated on the form that the parameters of the equations should take in order to discern definite causal relationships. The stochastic elements and the natural time ordering of the variables play relatively minor roles in the theory. In the alternative theory to be discussed here, the stochastic nature of the variables and the direction of the flow of time will be central features. The theory is, in fact, not relevant for nonstochastic variables and will rely entirely on the assumption that the future cannot cause the past. This theory will not, of course, be contradictory to previous work but there appears to be little common ground. Its origins may be found in a suggestion by Wiener (1956). The relationship between the definition discussed here and the work of Good (1962) has yet to be determined.

If A_t is a stationary stochastic process, let $\bar{A}_t$ represent the set of *past* values $\{A_{t-j}, j = 1, 2, \ldots, \infty\}$ and $\bar{\bar{A}}_t$ represent the set of *past and present values* $\{A_{t-j}, j = 0, 1, \ldots, \infty\}$. Further let $A(k)$ represent the set $\{A_{t-j}, j = k, k + 1, \ldots, \infty\}$.

Denote the optimum, unbiased, least-squares predictor of A_t using the set of values B_t by $P_t(A \mid B)$. Thus, for instance, $P_t(X \mid \bar{X})$ will be the optimum predictor of X_t using only past X_t. The predictive error series will be denoted by $\varepsilon_t(A \mid B) = A_t - P_t(A \mid B)$. Let $\sigma^2(A \mid B)$ be the variance of $\varepsilon_t(A \mid B)$.

The initial definitions of causality, feedback, and so forth, will be very general in nature. Testable forms will be introduced later. Let U_t be all the information in the universe accumulated since time $t - 1$ and let $U_t - Y_t$ denote all this information *apart* from the specified series Y_t. We then have the following definitions.

DEFINITION 1: *Causality.* If $\sigma^2(X \mid U) < \sigma^2(X \mid \overline{U - Y})$, we say that Y is causing X, denoted by $Y_t \Rightarrow X_t$. We say that Y_t is causing X_t if we are better able to predict X_t using all available information than if the information apart from Y_t had been used.

DEFINITION 2: *Feedback.* If $\sigma^2(X \mid \bar{U}) < \sigma^2(X \mid \overline{U - Y})$, and $\sigma^2(Y \mid \bar{U}) < \sigma^2(Y \mid \overline{U - X})$, we say that feedback is occurring, which is denoted $Y_t \Leftrightarrow X_t$, i.e., feedback is said to occur when X_t is causing Y_t and also Y_t is causing X_t.

DEFINITION 3: *Instantaneous Causality.* If $\sigma^2(X \mid \bar{U}, \bar{\bar{Y}}) < \sigma^2(X \mid \bar{U})$, we say that instantaneous causality $Y_t \Rightarrow X_t$ is occurring. In other words, the current value of X_t is better "predicted" if the present value of Y_t is included in the "prediction" than if it is not.

DEFINITION 4: *Causality Lag.* If $Y_t \Rightarrow X_t$, we define the (integer) causality lag m to be the least value of k such that $\sigma^2[X \mid U - Y(k)] < \sigma^2[X \mid U - Y(k + 1)]$. Thus, knowing the values $Y_{t-j}, j = 0, 1, \ldots, m - 1$, will be of no help in improving the prediction of X_t.

The definitions have assumed that only stationary series are involved. In the nonstationary case, $\sigma(X \mid \bar{U})$ etc. will depend on time t and, in general, the existence of causality may alter over time. The definitions can clearly be generalized to be operative for a specified time t. One could then talk of causality existing at this moment of time. Considering nonstationary series, however, takes us further away from testable definitions and this tack will not be discussed further.

The one completely unreal aspect of the above definitions is the use of the series U_t, representing *all* available information. The large majority of the information in the universe will be quite irrelevant, i.e., will have no causal consequence. Suppose that all relevant information is numerical in nature and belongs to the vector set of time series $Y_t^D = \{Y_t^i, i \in D\}$ for some integer set D. Denote the set $\{i \in D, i \neq j\}$ by $D(j)$ and $\{Y_t^i, i \in D(j)\}$ by $Y_t^{D(j)}$, i.e., the full set of relevant information except one particular series. Similarly, we could leave out more than one series with the obvious notation. The previous definitions can now be used but with U_t replaced by Y_t and $U_t - Y_t$ by $Y^{D(j)}$. Thus, for example, suppose that the vector set consists only of two series, X_t and Y_t, and that all other information is irrelevant. Then $\sigma^2(X \mid \overline{X})$ represents the minimum predictive error variance of X_t using only past X_t and $\sigma^2(X \mid \overline{X}, \overline{Y})$ represents this minimum variance if both past X_t and past Y_t are used to predict X_t. Then Y_t is said to cause X_t if $\sigma^2(X \mid \overline{X}) > \sigma^2(X \mid \overline{X}, \overline{Y})$. The definition of causality is now relative to the set D. If relevant data has not been included in this set, then spurious causality could arise. For instance, if the set D was taken to consist only of the two series X_t and Y_t, but in fact there was a third series Z_t which was causing both within the enlarged set $D' = (X_t, Y_t, Z_t)$, then for the original set D, spurious causality between X_t and Y_t may be found. This is similar to spurious correlation and partial correlation between sets of data that arise when some other statistical variable of importance has not been included.

In practice it will not usually be possible to use completely optimum predictors, unless all sets of series are assumed to be normally distributed, since such optimum predictors may be nonlinear in complicated ways. It seems natural to use only linear predictors and the above definitions may again be used under this assumption of linearity. Thus, for instance, the best linear predictor of X_t using only past X_t and past Y_t will be of the form

$$P_t(X \mid \overline{X}, \overline{Y}) = \sum_{j=1}^{\infty} a_j X_{t-j} + \sum_{j=1}^{\infty} b_j Y_{t-j}$$

where the a_j's and b_j's are chosen to minimize $\sigma^2(X \mid \overline{X}, \overline{Y})$.

It can be argued that the variance is not the proper criterion to use to measure the closeness of a predictor P_t to the true value X_t. Certainly if some other criteria were used it may be possible to reach different conclusions about whether one series is causing another. The variance does seem to be a natural criterion to use in connection with linear predictors as it is mathematically easy to handle and simple to interpret. If one uses this criterion, a better name might be "causality in mean."

The original definition of causality has now been restricted in order to reach a form which can be tested. Whenever the word causality is used in later sections it will be taken to mean "linear causality in mean with respect to a specified set D."

It is possible to extend the definitions to the case where a subset of series D^* of D is considered to cause X_t. This would be the case if $\sigma^2(X \mid Y^D) < \sigma^2(X \mid Y^{D-D^*})$ and then $Y^{D^*} \Rightarrow X_t$. Thus, for instance, one could ask if past X_t is causing present X_t. Because new concepts are necessary in the consideration of such problems, they will not be discussed here in any detail.

It has been pointed out already (Granger 1963) that instantaneous causality, in which knowledge of the current value of a series helps in predicting the current value of a second series, can occasionally arise spuriously in certain cases. Suppose $Y_t \Rightarrow X_t$ with lag one unit but that the series are sampled every two time units. Then although there is no real instantaneous causality, the definitions will appear to suggest that such causality is occurring. This is because certain relevant information, the missing readings in the data, has not been used. Due to this effect, one might suggest that in many economic situations an apparent instantaneous causality would disappear if the economic variables were recorded at more frequent time intervals.

The definition of causality used above is based entirely on the predictability of some series, say X_t. If some other series Y_t contains information in past terms that helps in the prediction of X_t and if this information is contained in no other series used in the predictor, then Y_t is said to cause X_t. The flow of time clearly plays a central role in these definitions. In the author's opinion there is little use in the practice of attempting to discuss causality without introducing time, although philosophers have tried to do so. It also follows from the definitions that a purely deterministic series, that is, a series which can be predicted exactly from its past terms such as a nonstochastic series, cannot be said to have any causal influences other than its own past. This may seem to be contrary to common sense in certain special cases but it is difficult to find a *testable* alternative definition which could include the deterministic situation. Thus, for instance, if $X_t = bt$ and $Y_t = c(t + 1)$, then X_t can be predicted exactly by $b + X_{t-1}$ or by $(b/c)Y_{t-1}$. There seems to be no way of deciding if Y_t is a causal factor of X_t or not. In some cases the notation of the "simplest rule" might be applied. For example, if X_t is some complicated polynomial in t and $Y_t = X_{t+1}$, then it will be easier to predict X_t from Y_{t-1} than from past X_t. In some cases this rule cannot be used, as the previous example showed. In any case, experience does not indicate that one should expect economic laws to be simple in nature.

Even for stochastic series, the definitions introduced above may give apparently silly answers. Suppose $X_t = A_{t-1} + \varepsilon_t$, $Y_t = A_t + \eta_t$, and $Z_t = A_t + \gamma_t$, where ε_t, η_t, and γ_t are all uncorrelated white-noise series with equal variances and A_t is some stationary series. Within the set $D = (X_t, Y_t)$ the definition gives $Y_t \Rightarrow X_t$. Within the set $D' = (X_t, Y_t)$, it gives $Z_t \Rightarrow X_t$. But within the set $D'' = (X_t, Y_t, Z_t)$, neither Y_t nor Z_t causes X_t, although the sum of Y_t and Z_t would do so. How is one to decide if either Y_t or Z_t is a causal series for X_t? The answer, of course, is that neither is. The causal series is A_t and both Y_t and Z_t contain equal amounts of information about A_t. If the set of series within which causality was discussed was expanded to include A_t, then the above apparent paradox vanishes. It will often be found that constructed examples which seem to produce results contrary to common sense can be resolved by widening the set of data within which causality is defined.

IV. Two-Variable Models

In this section, the definitions introduced above will be illustrated using two-variable models and results will be proved concerning the form of the cross spectrum for such models.

Let X_t, Y_t be two stationary time series with zero means. The simple causal model is

$$X_t = \sum_{j=1}^{m} a_j X_{t-j} + \sum_{j=1}^{m} b_j Y_{t-j} + \varepsilon_t,$$

$$\tag{7}$$

$$Y_t = \sum_{j=1}^{m} c_j X_{t-j} + \sum_{j=1}^{m} d_j Y_{t-j} + \eta_t.$$

where ε_t, η_t are taken to be two uncorrelated white-noise series, i.e., $E[\varepsilon_t \varepsilon_s] = 0 = E[\eta_t \eta_s]$, $s \neq t$, and $E[\varepsilon_t \varepsilon_s] = 0$ all t, s. In (7) m can equal infinity but in practice, of course, due to the finite length of the available data, m will be assumed finite and shorter than the given time series.

The definition of causality given above implies that Y_t is causing X_t provided some b_j is not zero. Similarly X_t is causing Y_t if some c_j is not zero. If both of these events occur, there is said to be a feedback relationship between X_t and Y_t. It will be shown later that this new definition of causality is in fact identical to that introduced previously.

The more general model with instantaneous causality is

$$X_t + b_0 Y_t = \sum_{j=1}^{m} a_j X_{t-j} + \sum_{j=1}^{m} b_j Y_{t-j} + \varepsilon_t,$$

$$\tag{8}$$

$$Y_t + c_0 X_t = \sum_{j=1}^{m} c_j X_{t-j} + \sum_{j=1}^{m} d_j Y_{t-j} + \eta_t.$$

If the variables are such that this kind of representation is needed, then instantaneous causality is occuring and a knowledge of Y_t will improve the "prediction" or goodness of fit of the first equation for X_t.

Consider initially the simple causal model (7). In terms of the time shift operator U, that is, $UX_t = X_{t-1}$, these equations may be written

$$X_t = a(U)X_t + b(U)Y_t + \varepsilon_t,$$
$$Y_t = c(U)X_t + d(U)Y_t + \eta_t,$$

$$\tag{9}$$

where $a(U)$, $b(U)$, $c(U)$, and $d(U)$ are power series in U with the coefficient of U^0 zero, i.e., $a(U) = \sum_{j=1}^{m} a_j U^j$, etc.

Using the Cramer representations of the series, i.e.,

$$X_t = \int_{-\pi}^{\pi} e^{it\omega} \, dZ_x(\omega), \qquad Y_t = \int_{-\pi}^{\pi} e^{it\omega} \, dZ_y(\omega),$$

and similarly for ε_t and η_t, expressions such as $a(U)X_t$ can be written as

$$a(U)X_t = \int_{-\pi}^{\pi} e^{it\omega} a(e^{-i\omega}) \, dZ_x(\omega).$$

Thus, equations (9) may be written

$$\int_{-\pi}^{\pi} e^{it\omega} \{[1 - a(e^{-i\omega})] \, dZ_x(\omega) - b(e^{-i\omega}) \, dZ_y(\omega) - dZ_\varepsilon(\omega)\} = 0,$$

$$\int_{-\pi}^{\pi} e^{it\omega} \{-c(e^{-i\omega}) \, dZ_x(\omega) + [1 - d(e^{-i\omega})] \, dZ_y(\omega) - dZ_\eta(\omega)\} = 0,$$

from which it follows that

$$A \begin{bmatrix} dZ_x \\ dZ_y \end{bmatrix} = \begin{bmatrix} dZ_\varepsilon \\ dZ_\eta \end{bmatrix} \tag{10}$$

where

$$A = \begin{bmatrix} 1 - a & -b \\ -c & 1 - d \end{bmatrix}$$

and where a is written for $a(e^{-i\omega})$, etc., and dZ_x for $dZ_x(\omega)$, etc.

Thus, provided the inverse of A exists,

$$\begin{bmatrix} dZ_x \\ dZ_y \end{bmatrix} = A^{-1} \begin{bmatrix} dZ_\varepsilon \\ dZ_\eta \end{bmatrix}. \tag{11}$$

As the spectral, cross-spectral matrix for X_t, Y_t is directly obtainable from

$$E \begin{bmatrix} dZ_x \\ dZ_y \end{bmatrix} [\overline{dZ_x} \ \overline{dZ_y}],$$

these functions can quickly be found from (11) using the known properties of dZ_ε and dZ_η. One finds that the power spectra are given by

$$f_x(\omega) = \frac{1}{2\pi \Delta} (|1 - d|^2 \sigma_\varepsilon^2 + |b|^2 \sigma_\eta^2),$$

$$f_y(\omega) = \frac{1}{2\pi \Delta} (|c|^2 \sigma_\varepsilon^2 + |1 - a|^2 \sigma_\eta^2), \tag{12}$$

where $\Delta = |(1 - a)(1 - d) - bc|^2$. Of more interest is the cross spectrum which has the form

$$Cr(\omega) = \frac{1}{2\pi \Delta} [(1 - d)\bar{c}\sigma_\varepsilon^2 + (1 - \bar{a})b\sigma_\eta^2].$$

Thus, the cross spectrum may be written as the sum of two components

$$Cr(\omega) = C_1(\omega) + C_2(\omega), \tag{13}$$

where
$$C_1(\omega) = \frac{\sigma_\varepsilon^2}{2\pi\,\Delta}(1 - d)\bar{c}$$

and
$$C_2(\omega) = \frac{\sigma_\eta^2}{2\pi\,\Delta}(1 - \bar{a})b.$$

If Y_t is not causing X_t, then $b \equiv 0$ and so $C_2(\omega)$ vanishes. Similarly if X_t is not causing Y_t then $c \equiv 0$ and so $C_1(\omega)$ vanishes. It is thus clear that the cross spectrum can be decomposed into the sum of two components—one which depends upon the causality of X by Y and the other on the causality of Y by X.

If, for example, Y is not causing X so that $C_2(\omega)$ vanishes, then $Cr(\omega) = C_1(\omega)$ and the resulting coherence and phase diagrams will be interpreted in the usual manner. This suggests that in general $C_1(\omega)$ and $C_2(\omega)$ can each be treated separately as cross spectra connected with the two arms of the feedback mechanism. Thus, coherence and phase diagrams can be defined for $X \Rightarrow Y$ and $Y \Rightarrow X$. For example,

$$C_{\overrightarrow{xy}}(\omega) = \frac{|C_1(\omega)|^2}{f_x(\omega)f_y(\omega)}$$

may be considered to be a measure of the strength of the causality $X \Rightarrow Y$ plotted against frequency and is a direct generalization of coherence. We call $C_{\overrightarrow{xy}}(\omega)$ the causality coherence.

Further,

$$\phi_{\overrightarrow{xy}}(\omega) = \tan^{-1}\frac{\text{imaginary part of } C_1(\omega)}{\text{real part of } C_1(\omega)}$$

will measure the phase lag against frequency of $X \Rightarrow Y$ and will be called the causality phase diagram.

Similarly such functions can be defined for $Y \Rightarrow X$ using $C_2(\omega)$.

These functions are usually complicated expressions in a, b, c, and d; for example,

$$C_{\overrightarrow{xy}}(\omega) = \frac{\sigma_\varepsilon^4|(1 - d)c|^2}{(\sigma_\varepsilon^2|1 - d|^2 + \sigma_\eta^2|b|^2)(\sigma_\varepsilon^2|c|^2 + |1 - a|^2\sigma_\eta^2)}.$$

Such formulae merely illustrate how difficult it is to interpret econometric models in terms of frequency decompositions. It should be noted that $0 < |C_{\overrightarrow{xy}}(\omega)| < 1$ and similarly for $C_{\overrightarrow{yx}}(\omega)$.

As an illustration of these definitions, we consider the simple feedback system

$$\begin{aligned} X_t &= bY_{t-1} + \varepsilon_t, \\ Y_t &= cX_{t-2} + \eta_t, \end{aligned} \tag{14}$$

where $\sigma_\varepsilon^2 = \sigma_\eta^2 = 1$.

In this case $a(\omega) = 0$, $b(\omega) = be^{-i\omega}$, $c(\omega) = ce^{-2i\omega}$, and $d(\omega) = 0$. The spectra of the series $\{X_t\}$, $\{Y_t\}$ are

$$f_x(\omega) = \frac{1 + b^2}{2\pi|1 - bce^{-3i\omega}|^2}$$

and

$$f_y(\omega) = \frac{1 + c^2}{2\pi|1 - bce^{-3i\omega}|^2},$$

and thus are of similar shape.

The usual coherence and phase diagrams derived from the cross spectrum between these two series are

$$C(\omega) = \frac{c^2 + b^2 + 2bc \cos \omega}{(1 + b^2)(1 + c^2)}$$

and

$$\phi(\omega) = \tan^{-1} \frac{c \sin 2\omega - b \sin \omega}{c \cos 2\omega + b \cos \omega}.$$

These diagrams are clearly of little use in characterizing the feedback relationship between the two series.

When the causality-coherence and phase diagrams are considered, however, we get

$$C_{\overrightarrow{xy}}(\omega) = \frac{c^2}{(1 + b^2)(1 + c^2)}, \qquad C_{\overrightarrow{yx}}(\omega) = \frac{b^2}{(1 + b^2)(1 + c^2)}.$$

Both are constant for all ω, and, if $b \neq 0$, $c \neq 0$, $\phi_{\overrightarrow{xy}}(\omega) = 2\omega$ (time lag of two units),[1] $\phi_{\overrightarrow{yx}}(\omega) = \omega$ (time lag of one unit).

The causality lags are thus seen to be correct and the causality coherences to be reasonable. In particular, if $b = 0$ then $C_{\overrightarrow{yx}}(\omega) = 0$, i.e., no causality is found when none is present. (Further, in this new case, $\phi_{\overrightarrow{xy}}(\omega) = 0$.)

Other particular cases are also found to give correct results. If, for example, we again consider the same simple model (14) but with $\sigma_\varepsilon^2 = 1$, $\sigma_\eta^2 = 0$, i.e., $\eta_t \equiv 0$ for all t, then one finds $C_{\overrightarrow{xy}}(\omega) = 1$, $C_{\overrightarrow{yx}}(\omega) = 0$, i.e., X is "perfectly" causing Y and Y is not causing X, as is in fact the case.

If one now considers the model (8) in which instantaneous causality is allowed, it is found that the cross spectrum is given by

$$Cr(\omega) = \frac{1}{2\pi \Delta'}[(1 - d)(\bar{c} - c_0)\sigma_\varepsilon^2 + (1 - \bar{a})(b - b_0)\sigma_\eta^2] \qquad (15)$$

where $\Delta' = |(1 - a)(1 - d) - (b - b_0)(c - c_0)|^2$. Thus, once more, the cross spectrum can be considered as the sum of two components, each of

---

[1]A discussion of the interpretation of phase diagrams in terms of time lags may be found in Granger and Hatanaka (1964, chap. 5).

which can be associated with a "causality," provided that this includes instantaneous causality. It is, however, probably more sensible to decompose $Cr(\omega)$ into three parts, $Cr(\omega) = C_1(\omega) + C_2(\omega) + C_3(\omega)$, where $C_1(\omega)$ and $C_2(\omega)$ are as in (13) but with Δ replaced by Δ' and

$$C_3(\omega) = \frac{-1}{2\pi\,\Delta}[c_0(1 - d)\sigma_\varepsilon^2 + b_0(1 - a)\sigma_\eta^2] \tag{16}$$

representing the influence of the instantaneous causality.

Such a decomposition may be useful but it is clear that when instantaneous causality occurs, the measures of causal strength and phase lag will lose their meaning.

It was noted in Section II that instantaneous causality models such as (8) in general lack uniqueness of their parameters as an orthogonal transformation Λ applied to the variables leaves the general form of the model unaltered. It is interesting to note that such transformations do not have any effect on the cross spectrum given by (15) or the decomposition. This can be seen by noting that equations (8) lead to

$$A\begin{bmatrix} dz_x \\ dz_y \end{bmatrix} = \begin{bmatrix} dz_\varepsilon \\ dz_\eta \end{bmatrix}$$

with appropriate A. Applying the transformation Λ gives

$$\Lambda A\begin{bmatrix} dz_x \\ dz_y \end{bmatrix} = \Lambda\begin{bmatrix} dz_\varepsilon \\ dz_\eta \end{bmatrix}$$

so that

$$\begin{bmatrix} dz_x \\ dz_y \end{bmatrix} = (\Lambda A)^{-1}\Lambda\begin{bmatrix} dz_\varepsilon \\ dz_\eta \end{bmatrix}$$

$$= A^{-1}\begin{bmatrix} dz_\varepsilon \\ dz_\eta \end{bmatrix}$$

which is the same as if no such transformation had been applied. From its definition, Λ will possess an inverse. This result suggests that spectral methods are more robust in their interpretation than are simultaneous equation models.

Returning to the simple causal model (9),

$$X_t = a(U)X_t + b(U)Y_t + \varepsilon_t,$$
$$Y_t = c(U)X_t + d(U)Y_t + \eta_t,$$

throughout this section it has been stated that $Y_t \not\Rightarrow X_t$ if $b \equiv 0$. On intuitive grounds this seems to fit the definition of no causality introduced in Section III, within the set D of series consisting only of X_t and Y_t. If $b \equiv 0$ then X_t is determined from the first equation and the minimum variance of the predictive error of X_t using past X_t will be σ_ε^2. This variance cannot be reduced using past Y_t. It is perhaps worthwhile proving this result formally. In the general case, it is clear that $\sigma^2(X \mid \bar{X}, \bar{Y}) = \sigma_\varepsilon^2$, i.e., the variance of the predictive error of X_t, if both past X_t and past Y_t are used, will be σ_ε^2 from the top equation. If only past X_t is used to predict X_t, it is a well known result that the minimum variance of the predictive error is given by

$$\sigma^2(X \mid \bar{X}) = \exp \tfrac{1}{2}\pi \int_{-\pi}^{\pi} \log \tfrac{1}{2}\pi f_x(\omega)\, d\omega. \tag{17}$$

It was shown above in equation (12) that

$$f_x(\omega) = \frac{1}{2\pi \Delta}(|1 - d|^2\sigma_\varepsilon^2 + |b|^2\sigma_\eta^2)$$

where $\Delta = |(1 - a)(1 - d) - bc|^2$. To simplify this equation, we note that

$$\int_{-\pi}^{\pi} \log|1 - \alpha e^{i\omega}|^2\, d\omega = 0$$

by symmetry. Thus if,

$$f_x(\omega) = \alpha_0 \frac{\pi|1 - \alpha_j e^{i\omega}|^2}{\pi|1 - \beta_j e^{i\omega}|^2},$$

then $\sigma^2(X \mid \bar{X}) = \alpha_0$. For there to be no causality, we must have $\alpha_0 = \sigma_\varepsilon^2$. It is clear from the form of $f_x(\omega)$ that in general this could only occur if $|b| \equiv 0$, in which case $2\pi f_x(\omega) = \sigma_\varepsilon^2/|1 - a|^2$ and the required result follows.

V. Three-Variable Models

The above results can be generalized to the many-variables situation, but the only case which will be considered is that involving three variables.

Consider a simple causal model generalizing (7):

$$X_t = a_1(U)X_t + b_1(U)Y_t + c_1(U)Z_t + \varepsilon_{1,t},$$
$$Y_t = a_2(U)X_t + b_2(U)Y_t + c_2(U)Z_t + \varepsilon_{2,t},$$
$$Z_t = a_3(U)X_t + b_3(U)Y_t + c_3(U)Z_t + \varepsilon_{3,t},$$

where $a_1(U)$, etc., are polynomials in U, the shift operator, with the coefficient of U^0 zero. As before, $\varepsilon_{i,t}$, $i = 1, 2, 3$, are uncorrelated, white-noise series and denote the variance $\varepsilon_{i,t} = \sigma_i^2$.

Let $\alpha = a_1 - 1$, $\beta = b_2 - 1$, $\gamma = c_3 - 1$, and

$$A = \begin{bmatrix} \alpha & b_1 & c_1 \\ a_2 & \beta & c_2 \\ a_3 & b_3 & \gamma \end{bmatrix},$$

where $b_1 = b_1(e^{-i\omega})$, etc., as before. Using the same method as before, the spectral, cross-spectral matrix $S(\omega)$ is found to be given by $S(\omega) = A^{-1}k(A')^{-1}$ where

$$k = \begin{bmatrix} \sigma_1^2 & 0 & 0 \\ 0 & \sigma_2^2 & 0 \\ 0 & 0 & \sigma_3^2 \end{bmatrix}.$$

One finds, for instance, that the power spectrum of X_t is

$$f_x(\omega) = |\Delta|^{-2}[\sigma_1^2|\beta\gamma - c_2 b_3|^2 + \sigma_2^2|c_1 b_3 - \gamma b_1|^2 + \sigma_3^2|b_1 c_2 - c_1\beta|^2]$$

where Δ is the determinant of A.

The cross spectrum between X_t and Y_t is

$$C_r^{xy}(\omega) = |\Delta|^{-2}[\sigma_1^2(\beta\gamma - c_2 b_3)(\overline{c_2 a_3 - \gamma a_2}) + \sigma_2^2(c_1 b_3 - b_1\gamma)(\overline{\alpha\gamma - c_1 a_3}) \\ + \sigma_3^2(b_1 c_2 - c_1\beta)(\overline{c_1 a_2 - c_2\alpha})].$$

Thus, this cross spectrum is the sum of three components, but it is not clear that these can be directly linked with causalities. More useful results arise, however, when partial cross spectra are considered. After some algebraic manipulation it is found that, for instance, the partial cross spectrum between X_t and Y_t given Z_t is

$$C_r^{xy,z}(\omega) = -\frac{[\sigma_1^2\sigma_2^2 b_3 a_3 + \sigma_1^2\sigma_2^2\beta a_2 + \sigma_2^2\sigma_3^2 b_1\alpha]}{f_z'(\omega)}$$

where

$$f_z'(\omega) = \sigma_1^2|\beta\gamma - c_2 b_3|^2 + \sigma_2^2|c_1 b_3 - b_1\gamma|^2 + \sigma_3^2|b_1 c_2 - c_1\beta|^2.$$

Thus, the partial cross spectrum is the sum of three components

$$C_r^{xy,z}(\omega) = C_1^{xy,z} + C_2^{xy,z} + C_3^{xy,z}$$

where

$$C_1^{xy,z} = -\frac{\sigma_1^2\sigma_2^2 b_3 a_3}{f_z'(\omega)}, \text{ etc.}$$

These can be linked with causalities. The component $C_1^{xy,z}(\omega)$ represents the interrelationships of X_t and Y_t *through* Z_t, and the other two components are direct generalizations of the two causal cross spectra which arose in the two-variable case and can be interpreted accordingly.

In a similar manner one finds that the power spectrum of X_t, given Z_t is

$$f_{x,z}(\omega) = \frac{\sigma_1^2\sigma_2^2|b_3|^2 + \sigma_1^2\sigma_3^2|\beta|^2 + \sigma_2^2\sigma_3^2|b_1|^2}{f_z'(\omega)}.$$

The causal and feedback relationships between X_t and Y_t can be investigated in terms of the coherence and phase diagrams derived from the second and third components of the partial cross spectrum, i.e.,

$$\text{coherence } (\overrightarrow{xy}, z) = \frac{|C_2^{xy,z}|^2}{f_{x,y} f_{y,z}}, \text{ etc.}$$

VI. Conclusion

The fact that a feedback mechanism may be considered as the sum of two causal mechanisms and that these causalities can be studied by decomposing cross or partial cross spectra suggests methods whereby such mechanisms can be investigated. Hopefully, the problem of estimating the causal cross spectra will be discussed in a later publication. There are a number of possible approaches, and accumulated experience is needed to indicate which is best. Most of these approaches are via the model-building method by which the above results were obtained. It is worth investigating, however, whether a direct method of estimating the components of the cross spectrum can be found.

References

Basman, R. L. "The Causal Interpretation of Non-Triangular Systems of Economic Relations." *Econometrica* 31 (1963): 439–48.

Good, I. J. "A Causal Calculus, I, II." *British J. Philos. Soc.* 11 (1961): 305–18, and 12 (1962): 43–51.

Granger, C. W. J. "Economic Processes Involving Feedback." *Information and Control* 6 (1963): 28–48.

Granger, C. W. J., and Hatanaka, M. *Spectral Analysis of Economic Time Series.* Princeton, N.J.: Princeton Univ. Press, 1964.

Nerlove, M. "Spectral Analysis of Seasonal Adjustment Procedures." *Econometrica* 32 (1964): 241–86.

Orcutt, G. H. "Actions, Consequences and Causal Relations." *Rev. Econ. and Statis.* 34 (1952): 305–13.

Simon, H. A. "Causal Ordering and Identifiability." In *Studies in Econometric Method,* edited by W. C. Hood and T. C. Koopmans. Cowles Commission Monograph 14. New York, Wiley, 1953.

Strotz, R. H., and Wold, H. "Recursive versus Non-Recursive Systems: An Attempt at Synthesis." *Econometrica* 28 (1960): 417–27.

Wiener, N. "The Theory of Prediction." In *Modern Mathematics for Engineers,* Series 1, edited by E. F. Beckenbach. New York: McGraw-Hill, 1956.

21

Money, Income, and Causality

Christopher A. Sims

This study has two purposes. One is to examine the substantive question: Is there statistical evidence that money is "exogenous" in some sense in the money-income relationship? The other is to display in a simple example some time-series methodology not now in wide use. The main methodological novelty is the use of a direct test for the existence of unidirectional causality. This test is of wide importance, since most efficient estimation techniques for distributed lags are invalid unless causality is unidirectional in the sense of this paper. Also, the paper illustrates the estimation of long lag distributions without the imposition of the usual restrictions requiring the shape of the distribution to be rational or polynomial.

The main empirical finding is that the hypothesis that causality is unidirectional from money to income agrees with the postwar U.S. data, whereas the hypothesis that causality is unidirectional from income to money is rejected. It follows that the practice of making causal interpretations of distributed lag regressions of income on money is not invalidated (on the basis of this evidence) by the existence of "feedback" from income to money.

I. The Causal Ordering Question for Money and Income

It has long been known that money stock and current dollar measures of economic activity are positively correlated. There is, further, evidence that money or its rate of change tends to "lead" income in some sense.[1] A body

Work for this paper was carried out during my tenure as a research fellow at the National Bureau of Economic Research. Numerous members of the NBER staff provided support at various stages of the research. Special thanks are due to Philip Cagan, John Hause, Milton Friedman, the Columbia Monetary Economics Workshop, and a seminar at the Cowles Foundation, whose objections and advice have sharpened the paper's argument. Josephine Su carried out the computational work. H. I. Forman drew the charts.

[1] See Milton Friedman and Anna Schwartz (1963b), Friedman (1961), (1964).

[American Economic Review, 1972, vol. 62; no. 4]
© 1972 by The American Economic Association

of macroeconomic theory, the "Quantity Theory," explains these empirical observations as reflecting a causal relation running from money to income. However, it is widely recognized that no degree of positive association between money and income can by itself prove that variation in money causes variation in income. Money might equally well react passively and very reliably to fluctuations in income. Historically observed timing relations between turning points have also for some time been recognized not to be conclusive evidence for causal ordering. James Tobin and William Brainard and Tobin provide explicit examples of the possibilities for noncorrespondence between causal ordering and temporal ordering of turning points. People in close connection with the details of monetary policy know that some components of the money supply react passively to cyclical developments in the economy. Frank DeLeeuw and John Kalchbrenner, for example, argue that the monetary base (currency plus total reserves) is not properly treated as an exogenous variable in a regression equation because of the known dependence between certain of its components and cyclical factors.

Phillip Cagan uses an analysis of the details of money-supply determination to argue convincingly that the long-run relation between money supply and the price level cannot be due primarily to feedback from prices to money. His application of the same analytical technique to cyclical relations of money with income measures fails to yield a firm conclusion, however.

Friedman and Schwartz have argued on the basis of historical analysis that major depressions have been caused by autonomous movements in money stock.[2]

The issues between the monetarists and the skeptics are not easily defined on the basis of the literature cited in the preceding paragraphs. Probably few of the skeptics would deny *any* causal influence of money on income. But, on the other hand, leading exponents of the monetarist approach seem ready to admit that there is "clear evidence of the influence of business change on the quantity of money,"[3] at least for the mild cycles which have characterized the postwar United States.

Now if the consensus view that there is some influence of business conditions on money is correct, if this influence is of significant magnitude, and if current dollar GNP is a good index of business conditions,[4] then distributed lag regressions treating money as strictly exogenous are not causal relations. Since such regressions are now treated as causal relations by

[2]See Friedman and Schwartz (1963*b*), pp. 217–18 as reprinted in Friedman (1969).

[3]The quoted phrase is from Milton Friedman's introduction to Cagan, (1965; p. xxvi), and summarizes one of Cagan's main results.

[4]As I will argue below, it may be that the one-dimensional current dollar GNP index is so inadequate a measure of those aspects of business conditions which influence money supply that there is no feedback from current dollar GNP to money despite the existence of feedback from business conditions to money.

some economists, it is important to test the assumption of causal priority on which they rest.

As will be shown below, there is a natural analogue in a dynamic system to Wold's "causal chain" form for a static econometric model.[5] This analogue turns out to be exactly a model in which causation is unidirectional according to the criterion developed by C. W. J. Granger. But Wold's form is in general not testable in a static context; any multivariate set of data with a specified list of endogenous variables can be fit by a recursive model. The dynamic analogue is, however, easily testable: If and only if causality runs one way from current and past values of some list of exogenous variables to a given endogenous variable, then in a regression of the endogenous variable on past, current, and future values of the exogenous variables, the future values of the exogenous variables should have zero coefficients.

Application of this test to a two-variable system in a monetary aggregate and current dollar GNP with quarterly data shows clearly that causality does not run one way from GNP to money. The evidence agrees quite well with a null hypothesis that causality runs entirely from money to GNP, without feedback.

II. The Meaning of the Results

Before giving a rigorous explanation of the notion of causal direction and the detailed description of statistical results, it is worthwhile to consider in a nontechnical way what the results do and do not prove. That the test applied in this paper shows no feedback from y to x is a necessary condition for it to be reasonable to interpret a distributed lag regression of y on current and past x as a causal relation or to apply any of the common estimation methods involving use of lagged dependent variables or corrections for serial correlation. Hence the most conservative way to state the results for money and income is that they show it to be unreasonable to interpret a least-squares lag distribution for money on GNP as a causal relation, and that they provide no grounds for asserting that distributed lag regressions of GNP on money do not yield estimates of a causal relation. It is natural, and I believe appropriate, to phrase the result more positively: the data verify the null hypothesis that distributed lag regressions of GNP on money have a causal interpretation. However, it is possible to concoct models in which a money on GNP regression does not yield a causal relation and yet this paper's test would not detect feedback.

The test will fail to detect within-quarter feedback of a certain type. The "innovation" in the stochastic process x_t is that part of x_t which cannot be predicted from x_t's own past (i.e., the residual in a regression of x_t on its

---

[5]See Edmond Malinvaud (1965, pp. 511 ff.) for a description of causal chain models.

own past). If x_t and y_t are connected by two causal relations—one from x to y involving a distributed lag, and the other from y to x but with only the current innovation in y_t on the right-hand side—then the test used in this paper will not detect the y to x feedback.[6]

Where the data show negligible serial correlation, this failing of the test becomes important. For then y and x are their own innovations and one expects that causal relations may be purely contemporaneous. In the general case, with serially correlated data, the failing is not likely to be important. It can result in false conclusions only where there is a certain sort of exact relation between the lag distributions defining the causal structure and the autocorrelation functions of the error terms. With one important class of exceptions, there is seldom reason to suppose any relation at all between the causal structure and the properties of the error terms.

The exception arises for models in which some elements of optimal control enter. If one of the two relations in a bivariate system is chosen optimally, then the innovations in the variables become structural elements of the system. This fact is important for money and income, since it is easy to imagine that money may have been controlled to influence or to conform to income. It can be shown that in a bivariate system with optimal control of one variable, there will be in general two-way causality by the Granger criterion. The only exception is that if the information lag in the control process is just one period and if the criterion for control is minimal variance in, say, y, then causality will spuriously appear to run from y to x.[7] But then the only way optimal control would be likely to hide income-to-money feedback would be if income were controlled to hold down variance in money. This seems farfetched.

The fact that this paper finds no evidence of feedback from GNP to money is not direct evidence on the structure of money-supply determination. All that is necessary to allow interpretation of the money on GNP distributed lags as causal relations is the hypothesis that in this particular historical sample (1947–69), the determinants of money supply showed no *consistent* pattern of influence by GNP. Thus it would be enough if, for example, money supply were influenced quite differently by real and price components of GNP movements, so long as actual GNP movements were not dominated by one component or the other. Alternatively, a consistent pattern of feedback from GNP to money could have been swamped in this sample period by extraneous influences on money. The situation is analogous to that in a supply and demand estimation problem, where we have

[6]One elementary consequence is that it is possible for the test to show no feedback in either direction, despite the existence of well-defined lag distributions in both x on y and y on x regressions. This is the case where all the relation between y and x consists of contemporaneous correlation of their innovations.

[7]Proving this in any generality would require stretching the length and increasing the technical level of the paper. I expect to take up this point at greater length in a subsequent paper.

evidence that in a particular sample elements other than price dominated supply. Such evidence proves that in the sample the price-quantity relation traces the demand curve, but it does not in itself prove anything about the supply curve. Thus one can imagine that if heightened awareness of the importance of monetary policy makes money respond more consistently to the business cycle, single-equation estimates of the money-to-GNP relation will become unreliable.

Finally, we ought to consider whether the bivariate model underlying this paper could be mimicking a more complicated model with a different causal structure. The method of identifying causal direction employed here does rest on a sophisticated version of the post hoc ergo propter hoc principle. However, the method is not easily fooled. Simple linear structures with reversed causality like the one put forth by Tobin cannot be constructed to give apparent money-to-GNP causality. Complicated structures like that put forward by Brainard and Tobin (1968) in which both GNP and money are endogenous will, except under very special assumptions, yield a bivariate reduced form showing bidirectional causality. The special assumptions required to make endogenous money appear exogenous in a bivariate system must make money essentially identical to a truly exogenous variable. Thus, if money has in the sample been passively and quickly adjusted to match the animal spirits of bankers and businessmen, and if animal spirits is a truly exogenous variable affecting GNP with a distributed lag, then money might falsely appear to cause GNP. However, if there is substantial random error in the correspondence between animal spirits and money and that error has a pattern of serial correlation different from that of animal spirits itself, then the bivariate relation between money and GNP will appear to show bidirectional causality.[8]

An assumption that future values of money or income cause current values of the other, via economic actors' having forecasts of the future better than could be obtained from current and past money and GNP, will affect the apparent direction of causality. However, the effect is much more likely to make a truly unidirectional structure appear bidirectional than vice versa. For example, it is easy to see that if current money supply is determined in part by extraneous knowledge of GNP for several future quarters, past money could spuriously appear to affect current GNP. However, it is difficult to imagine in such a situation why past GNP and all the variation in future GNP which can be predicted from past GNP should *not* affect money. Without such an artificial assumption, one cannot explain a one-sided lag distribution of GNP on money by a "reversed-causation-with-accurate-anticipations" model.

---

[8]This point is not obvious, but to prove it would, as in the case of the previous point about optimal control, overextend the paper. The technically sophisticated reader may easily verify the proposition for himself.

III. Testing for the Direction of Causality

In a single, static sample, the "direction of causation" connecting two related groups of variables is ordinarily not identified.[9] That is, one can construct many different models of causal influence all of which are consistent with a given pattern of covariances amongst the variables. If one is willing to identify causal ordering with Wold's causal chain form for a multivariate model, and if enough identifying restrictions are available in addition to those specifying the causal chain form, one can test a particular causal chain ordering as a set of overidentifying restrictions. The conditions allowing such a test are seldom met in practice, however.

Granger has given a definition of a testable kind of causal ordering based on the notion that absence of correlation between *past* values of one variable X and that part of another variable Y which cannot be predicted from Y's own past implies absence of causal influence from X to Y. More precisely, the time-series Y is said to "cause" X relative to the universe U (U is a vector time-series including X and Y as components) if, and only if, predictions of $X(t)$ based on $U(s)$ for all $s < t$ are better than predictions based on all components of $U(s)$ except $Y(s)$ for all $s < t$.

We will give content to Granger's definitions by assuming all time series to be jointly covariance-stationary, by considering only linear predictors, and by taking expected squared forecast error as our criterion for predictive accuracy.

Consider the jointly covariance-stationary pair of stochastic processes X and Y. If X and Y are jointly purely linearly indeterministic (linearly regular in the terminology of Yu. S. Rozanov [1967]), then we can write

$$
\begin{aligned}
X(t) &= a^*u(t) + b^*v(t) \\
Y(t) &= c^*u(t) + d^*v(t)
\end{aligned}
\tag{1}
$$

where u and v are mutually uncorrelated white noise[10] processes with unit variance, a, b, c, and d all vanish for $t < 0$, and the notation

$$
g^*f(t) = \sum_{s=-\infty}^{\infty} g(s)f(t - s).
$$

The expression (1) is the moving average representation of the vector process $\begin{bmatrix} X \\ Y \end{bmatrix}$ and is unique up to multiplication by a unitary matrix.[11]

---

[9]It is my impression that many of the results in this section, even where they have not previously been given formal expression, are widely understood. E.g., Akaike (1967) clearly understands that a two-sided transfer function implies the existence of feedback.

[10]A "white noise" is a serially uncorrelated process.

[11]Actually, the statement that (1) is the moving average representation of $\begin{bmatrix} X \\ Y \end{bmatrix}$ is a condition for uniqueness. There will be forms of (1) for which a, b, c, and d are all 0 for $t < 0$ and u and v are white noises but do not yield moving average representations. These forms of (1) will not be unitary transformations of the moving average representation and can be distinguished from the true moving average representation by the fact that in a true moving average representation $a(0)u(t) + b(0)v(t)$ is the limiting forecast error in forecasting $X(t)$ from all past X and Y.

A useful result, not proved by Granger, is

THEOREM 1: Y does not cause X in Granger's definition if, and only if, a or b can be chosen identically 0.[12]

This result gives us another intuitive handle on Granger causality. If causality is from X to Y only, then of the two orthogonal white noises which make up X and Y, one is X itself "whitened" and the other is the error in predicting Y from current and past X, whitened. (A whitened variable is one which has been passed through a linear filter to make it a white noise.)

Granger has shown that if there is an autoregressive representation, given by

$$B^* \begin{bmatrix} X \\ Y \end{bmatrix}(t) = \begin{bmatrix} u \\ v \end{bmatrix}(t), \qquad (2)$$

$B(t) = 0$ for $t < 0$, u, v defined by (1), then the absence of causality running from Y to X is equivalent to the upper right-hand element of B being zero. That is, causality runs only from X to Y if past Y does not influence current X. From this point it is not hard to show:

THEOREM 2: When $\begin{bmatrix} X \\ Y \end{bmatrix}$ has an autoregressive representation, Y can be expressed as a distributed lag function of current and past X with a residual which is not correlated with any values of X, past or future, if, and only if, Y does not cause X in Granger's sense.

We can always estimate a regression of Y on current and past X. But only in the special case where causality runs from X to Y can we expect that no future values of X would enter the regression if we allowed them. Hence, we have a practical statistical test for unidirectional causality: Regress Y on past and future values of X, taking account by generalized least squares or prefiltering of the serial correlation in $w(t)$. Then if causality runs from X to Y only, future values of X in the regression should have coefficients insignificantly different from zero, as a group.

An implication of theorem 2 is that many commonly applied distributed lag estimation techniques are valid only if causality runs one way from independent to dependent variable. The condition that the independent variable X be "strictly exogenous," central to most statistical theory on time-series regression, is exactly the theorem 2 condition that $X(t)$ be uncorrelated with the residual $U(s)$ for any t, s. For example, quasi-differencing to eliminate serial correlation in residuals will produce inconsistent estimates without the one-way causality condition; and the "Koyck transformation" which is invoked to allow interpretation of regressions with autoregressive terms as estimates of infinite lag distributions depends on one-way causality. Hence in principle a large proportion of econometric studies involving distributed lags should include a preliminary test for direction of causality.

---

[12]Proofs of both theorems appear in the Appendix.

Remarks on Distributed Lag Methodology

Especially in a study of this kind, where we wish to make fairly precise use of F-tests on groups of coefficients, it is important that the assumption of serially uncorrelated residuals be approximately accurate. Therefore all variables used in regressions were measured as natural logs and prefiltered using the filter $1 - 1.5L + .5625L^2$; i.e., each logged variable $x(t)$ was replaced by $x(t) - 1.5x(t - 1) + .5625x(t - 2)$. This filter approximately flattens the spectral density of most economic time series, and the hope was that regression residuals would be very nearly white noise with this prefiltering.

Two problems are raised by this prefiltering. First, if the filter has failed to produce white noise residuals, it is quite unlikely to fail by leaving subtantial positive first-order serial correlation. Durbin-Watson statistics are therefore of little use in testing for lack of serial correlation, and tests based on the spectral density of the residuals were used instead. Second, as I pointed out in an earlier paper (1972), prefiltering may produce a per- verse effect on approximation error when lag distributions are subject to prior "smoothness" restrictions. Therefore, no Koyck, Almon, or rational lag restrictions were imposed a priori, and the length of the estimated lag distributions was kept generous.

In applying the F-tests for causal direction suggested in the previous section, one should bear in mind that the absolute size of the coefficients is important regardless of the F value. It is a truism too often ignored that coefficients which are "large" from the economic point of view should not be casually set to zero no matter how statistically "insignificant" they are. Thus, the fact that future values of the independent variable have coeffi- cients insignificantly different from zero only shows that unidirectional causality is possible. If the estimated coefficients on future values are as large or larger than those on past values, bidirectional causality may be very important in practice, despite insignificant F's. Moreover, small coef- ficients on future values of the independent variable may sometimes be safely ignored even when they are statistically significant. This is especially true in the light of my observation (1971) that nonzero coefficients on future values may be generated in discrete-time data from a "one-sided" continuous-time distributed lag.[13]

All the data used in the regressions presented in this paper were season- ally adjusted at the source. This creates potential problems of a sort which has not been widely recognized heretofore. Most seasonal adjustment pro- cedures in common use allow for a seasonal pattern which shifts slowly over time, and the rate at which the seasonal pattern is taken to shift varies

[13]The definition of causality given in the previous section generalizes easily to continuous time. One simply reinterprets (1) as a continuous-time relation, and "Y does not cause X" still corresponds to "b identically zero."

from one series to another. It can be shown[14] that in distributed lag regressions relating two variables which have been deseasonalized by procedures with different assumed rates of shift in the seasonal pattern, spurious "seasonal" variation is likely to appear in the estimated lag distribution. The lag distributions estimated in this paper are long enough and free enough in form that bias from this source should be obvious wherever it is important (and it is important in one regression). However, it would be better to start from undeseasonalized data, being sure that both variables in the relation are deseasonalized in the same way. A check along these lines, using frequency-domain procedures, was carried out for this paper and is mentioned in the discussion of results below.

IV. Time Domain Regression Results

The data used cover the period 1947–69, quarterly. Money was measured both as monetary base (MB)—currency plus reserves adjusted for changes in reserve requirements—and as $M1$—currency plus demand deposits. Figures for MB were taken from the series prepared by the Federal Reserve Bank of St. Louis and supplied to the National Bureau of Economic Research data bank. Results were similar for $M1$ and MB, so we sometimes use M or money to refer to both $M1$ and MB in what follows.

Regressions of the log of GNP (in current dollars) on future and lagged log M were significant, as were the reversed regressions of log M on future and lagged log GNP (see table 1). Table 2 reports tests for homogeneity between the pre-1958 and post-1958 sections of the sample. No significant differences between the subsamples appeared in the regressions. Future values of GNP were highly significant in explaining the M dependent

[14] I showed this in an earlier mimeographed version of this paper. A separate short paper on this topic is in preparation.

TABLE 1

Summary of *OLS* Regressions

	F for Independent Variables	$\bar{R}^2$	Standard Error of Estimate	Degrees of Freedom
$GNP = f(M1,$ 8 past lags)	1.89*	0.7927	0.01018	64
$GNP = f(M1,$ 4 future, 8 past lags)	1.37	0.7840	0.01040	60
$GNP = f(MB,$ 8 past lags)	2.24**	0.8004	0.00999	64
$GNP = f(MB,$ 4 future, 8 past lags)	1.61	0.7924	0.01019	60
$M1 = f(GNP,$ 4 future, 8 past lags)	11.25**	0.8385	0.00403	60
$MB = f(GNP,$ 4 future, 8 past lags)	5.89**	0.8735	0.00410	60

Note.—All regressions were fit to the period 1949III–1968IV. $M1$ is currency plus demand deposits. MB is monetary base as prepared by the Federal Reserve Bank of St. Louis. The F-tests shown are for the null hypothesis that all right-hand side variables except trend and seasonal dummies had zero coefficients. See also notes to table 4.

*Significant at 0.10 level.
**Significant at 0.05 level.

TABLE 2

F's FOR COMPARISONS OF SUBPERIODS
1948III–1957III vs. 1957IV–1968IV

Regression Equation	F	Degrees of Freedom
$GNP = f(M1,$ 8 past lags)	1.44	(14, 50)
$GNP = f(MB,$ 8 past lags)	0.64	(14, 50)
$M1 = g(GNP,$ 4 future, 8 past lags)	0.88	(18, 46)
$MB = f(GNP,$ 4 future, 8 past lags)	1.01	(18, 46)

NOTE.—Tests are for the null hypothesis that all coefficients (including trend and seasonals)
remained the same in both subsamples.

variable, but future values of M were not significant in explaining the
GNP dependent variable (see table 3). The largest individual coefficients
in each GNP on M regression occur on past lags, and the estimated shapes
for those regressions appear broadly reasonable on the assumption that
coefficients on future lags are small and coefficients on past lags are
nonzero and fairly smooth (see table 4 and figures 1 and 2).

These results allow firm rejection of the hypothesis that money is purely
passive, responding to GNP without influencing it. They are consistent
with the hypothesis that GNP is purely passive, responding to M according
to a stable distributed lag but not influencing M.

But let us note a few statistical caveats. Though the estimated distribution looks like what we expect from a one-sided true distribution, the
standard errors on the future coefficients are relatively high. These results
are just what a unidirectional causality believer would expect, but they are
not such as to necessarily force a believer in bidirectional causality to
change his mind. Also, seasonality problems are clearly present in the MB
on GNP regression. Seasonality effects appear to be less of a problem with
$M1$ than with MB.

DeLeeuw and Kalchbrenner (1969) have argued, in attacking the "reduced form" money vs. GNP regressions put out by the St. Louis Fed, that
the monetary base is not truly exogenous. We have discussed above the

TABLE 3

F-TESTS ON FOUR FUTURE
QUARTERS' COEFFICIENTS

Regression Equation	F
GNP on $M1$	0.36
GNP on MB	0.39
$M1$ on GNP	4.29**
MB on GNP	5.89**

NOTE.—All tests apply to regressions run over the full sample and are assumed distributed as $F(4, 60)$.
**Significant at 0.05 level.

TABLE 4

LAG DISTRIBUTIONS FROM TIME-DOMAIN REGRESSIONS

Coefficient	GNP on MB past only	GNP on MB with future	MB on GNP	GNP on M1 past only	GNP on M1 with future	M1 on GNP
Coefficient on lag of:						
−4	...	−0.65	.162	...	−.300	.050
−3	...	.290	−.013	...	.120	.117
−2	...	−.088	.105	...	.126	.069
−1	...	−.110	.179	...	.105	.125
0	.603	.532	.171	.570	.484	.181
1	.593	.507	.015	.370	.412	.089
2	.509	.515	.052	−.034	−.017	.116
3	−.029	.080	.264	.543	.582	.107
4	−.011	.023	.107	−.242	−.363	.027
5	−.865	−.822	−.009	−.178	−.147	.027
6	−.037	−.053	.016	−.180	−.136	.025
7	−.296	−.282	.147	−.157	−.139	.123
8	.072	.039	.130	−.326	−.405	.112
Standard errors of coefficients:						
Largest SE	.313	.338	.052	.293	.318	.051
Smallest SE	.272	.276	.045	.274	.294	.044
Sum of coefficients	.540	...	...	.365	...	...
Standard error of sum	.442	...	...	.523	...	...

NOTE.—Regressions were on *logs* of variables, prefiltered as explained in the text. Each regression included, in addition to the leading and lagging values of the independent variable for which coefficients are shown, a constant term, a linear trend term, and three seasonal dummies. Trends were in all cases significant. Seasonal dummies were insignificant. (The data were seasonally adjusted.)

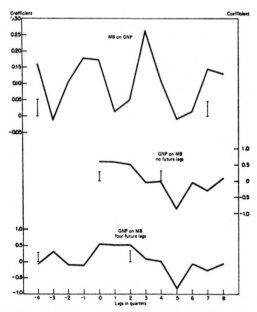

FIG. 1.—Lag distribution for *MB* and GNP. Smallest and largest standard errors are displayed as vertical lines above or below corresponding coefficients.

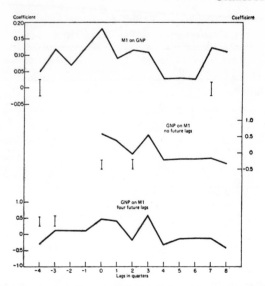

FIG. 2.—Lag distribution for $M1$ and GNP. Smallest and largest standard errors are displayed as vertical lines above or below corresponding coefficients.

substance of that argument. Suffice it to say here that they claim that one could make the monetary base more "exogenous" by extracting from it borrowed reserves and (possibly) cash in hands of the public. Attempts to use these adjusted MB series (one of them is actually unborrowed reserves) failed, in the sense that relations were less significant statistically and GNP on adjusted MB regressions did not show one-sided lag distributions.

The same regression equations used for GNP and M were estimated also with GNP replaced by the GNP deflator (PGNP) and then by real GNP (RGNP) with MB the money variable. Quantity theory even in its modern guise does not claim to have firm implications about the way income changes divide into real and price components, but it seemed useful to examine the possibility that monetary variables would predict the components separately as well as their product. Standard errors of the (logarithmic) equations regressing RGNP on MB were slightly larger than corresponding standard errors for current dollar GNP. Values of coefficients and F-statistics were much the same with RGNP as dependent variable as with GNP the dependent variable. Future lags were again highly significant for MB on GNP regressions and highly insignificant for the reversed relation. However, with RGNP, current plus eight past lagged values of MB were not as a group significantly different from zero at the .10 level. With PGNP, standard errors of estimate were small, but almost every F-test failed to attain significance, including the test on future lags in the MB on PGNP relation.

V. Tests for Serial Correlation in Residuals

Durbin-Watson statistics for all reported regressions are close to two. This is to be expected because of the prefiltering. The test on the cumulated periodogram of the residuals, described by James Durbin (1969), yields results in the indeterminate range for each regression.[15] The test on the cumulated periodogram is in principle capable of detecting departures from serial independence even when there is no first-order serial correlation, and in this sense is a stronger test than the Durbin-Watson for the case at hand.

The central difficulty here, though, is that a total of 17 of the available 78 degrees of freedom have been used up in the regression, so that the easily-computed bounds tests leave a wide range of indeterminacy. An alternative to the bounds tests is to use the likelihood ratio test for the null hypothesis that the periodogram of the residuals has constant expectation across a number of intervals. This test is described in Hannan (1960, p. 98).[16] In application to regression residuals this test is justified only when the number of observations is much larger than the number of independent variables, which is clearly not the case here. The statistics reported in table 5 would be distributed as chi-square with 7 degrees of freedom if asymptotic results applied, but the true significance levels of the test will be higher than the nominal ones. Even at nominal significance

[15]The test carried out was actually based on cumulation of the periodogram over 128 equally spaced points, instead of over the 39 harmonic frequencies as would be appropriate to get Durbin's test. This difference is, however, demonstrably asymptotically negligible (as sample size increases Durbin's test converges in distribution to any test based on more points than half the sample size) and seems unlikely to have been very important even at this particular sample size.

[16]Hannan's description includes Bartlett's small-sample correction to the likelihood ratio test. The results reported in table 5 do not include the Bartlett correction, since it was small.

TABLE 5

LIKELIHOOD-RATIO TESTS FOR
WHITE NOISE RESIDUALS

GNP on MB	GNP on M1	MB on GNP	M1 on GNP
13.02	19.01	11.04	12.64

Note.—.05 significance level for chi-squared with 7 degrees of freedom: 14.1. The statistics shown are each distributed asymptotically as chi-square with 7 degrees of freedom on the null hypothesis of white noise residuals. As noted in the text, the asymptotic distribution is probably not a good approximation to the true distribution here. For the GNP on M equations, residuals were taken from the form with no future lags. For the M on GNP equations, residuals were taken from the form including future lags.

levels, though, only the residuals from the regression of GNP on $M1$ are significantly "nonwhite" at a 5 percent level.

The conclusion from this list of approximate or inconclusive tests can only be that there is room for doubt about the accuracy of the F-tests on regression coefficients.

As a check on the least-squares results, these same regressions were estimated also using a frequency-domain procedure, Hannan's (1963) "inefficient" procedure.[17] This procedure has some disadvantages relative to least squares, but it has the two advantages that (1) it makes it computationally simple to estimate the variance-covariance structure of the residuals and use the estimate in constructing tests on the estimated regression coefficients, and (2) it makes it easy to deseasonalize raw data directly. Not all the tests for significance of groups of coefficients came out the same way at the same significance levels in the frequency-domain estimates, but the general agreement with the least-squares results was so close that there is no point in reproducing the frequency-domain results here.[18] Raw data for the monetary base was not readily available, but frequency-domain estimates using raw data on $M1$ and GNP, symmetrically deseasonalized, gave results very similar to those obtained with least squares on published deseasonalized data.

VI. The Form of the Lag Distribution

The lag distribution estimated here to relate GNP to M has only a loosely determined form because of the lack of prior restrictions on its shape. Still, it is worthwhile noting that it agrees in general shape with many previous estimates, and that it can be given an economic explanation. The distribution is positive at first, then becomes mostly negative beyond the fourth lag. The initial positive coefficients sum to a number greater than one, though the sum of all the coefficients is less than one. (Note, though, that the standard error on the sum of coefficients is very large; see table 4.) The pattern of a short-run elasticity exceeding unity and a long-run elasticity below unity agrees with the theoretical speculations of Friedman (1969, pp. 138–39) concerning the effects of a demand for money dependent on permanent rather than on current income. However, note that the contemporaneous quarter response is less than unitary, and that negative response does not set in for several quarters. To explain this, one must either introduce an averaging procedure into the other side of the equation,

[17]The theory of these estimates has been extended in Hannan (1967) and Wahba (1969). It is worthwhile noting that Wahba's proof that the Hannan inefficient estimates are "approximately" least-squares estimates is not a proof that the Hannan inefficient estimates have the same asymptotic distribution as least squares, and their asymptotic distributions are in fact different.

[18]The frequency-domain results were presented and discussed in an earlier mimeographed version of this paper.

making "permanent money" depend on permanent income, or one must introduce the possibility of transactional frictions which keep the economy off its demand curve for money in the short run. At least the latter of these elements is not novel. Alan Walters (1965) pointed out that over short enough time intervals people are likely to be off their demand curves. It seems only natural that, since individuals' money balances always fluctuate over short periods due to random timing of transactions, it should take time for changes in money balances to affect individuals' spending behavior.

VII. Conclusion

The main conclusions of the paper were summarized in the introduction. I repeat them more briefly here: In time-series regression it is possible to test the assumption that the right-hand side variable is exogenous; thus the choice of "direction of regression" need not be made entirely on a priori grounds. Application of this test to aggregate quarterly data on U.S. GNP and money stock variables shows that one clearly should not estimate a demand for money relation from these data, treating GNP as exogenous with money on the left-hand side; no evidence appears to contradict the common assumption that money can be treated as exogenous in a regression of GNP on current and past money.

Appendix

THEOREM 1: Y does not cause X in Granger's definition if, and only if, in the moving average representation

$$\begin{bmatrix} X(t) \\ Y(t) \end{bmatrix} = \begin{bmatrix} a & b \\ c & d \end{bmatrix}^{*} \begin{bmatrix} u \\ v \end{bmatrix}(t), \tag{A1}$$

a or b can be chosen to be identically zero.

PROOF: Following Rozanov we introduce the notation $H_z(t)$ to stand for the completion under the quadratic mean norm of the linear space of random variables spanned by $z(s)$ for $s \leq t$. Suppose b is zero. Clearly $X(t)$ then lies in $H_u(t)$. By the definition of a moving average (m.a.) representation, $H_{X,Y}(t)$ is identical to $H_{u,v}(t)$. But it follows from Rozanov's "Remarks" on pages 62–63 that if $H_u(t)$ and $H_X(t)$ are not identical, then with b zero the identity of $H_{X,Y}(t)$ and $H_{u,v}(t)$ fails. Therefore, $H_u(t)$ and $H_X(t)$ are identical. But then the projection of $X(t)$ on $H_{X,Y}(t-1)$ is in $H_X(t-1)$, which is to say that given past X, past Y does not help in predicting current X. One side of the double implication is proved.

In Granger's definition, Y not causing X is the same thing as the projection of $X(t+1)$ on $H_{X,Y}(t)$ lying in $H_X(t)$. Assuming this condition holds, define $u(t)$ as the difference between $X(t)$ and the projection of $X(t)$ on $H_X(t-1)$. Define $w(t)$ as the difference between $Y(t)$ and the projection of $Y(t)$ on $H_{X,Y}(t-1)$. Finally, define $v(t)$ as that part of $w(t)$ orthogonal to $u(t)$—i.e., the residual in a regression of $w(t)$ on $u(t)$. By definition, $u(t)$ and $w(t)$ and, therefore, $v(t)$ are uncorrelated with past values of each other. Also, $u(t)$ and $v(t)$ are contemporaneously uncorrelated and $H_{u,v}(t)$ is identical to $H_{X,Y}(t)$. Expressing $X(t)$ and $Y(t)$ in terms of the coordinates $u(s)$, $v(s)$, $s \leq t$, will give us a moving average representation of the form (A).

THEOREM 2: When $\begin{bmatrix} X \\ Y \end{bmatrix}$ has an autoregressive representation, Y can be expressed as a distributed lag function of current and past X with a residual which is not correlated with any $X(s)$, past or future if, and only if, Y does not cause X in Granger's sense.

PROOF: Suppose Y can be expressed as a distributed lag on X with a residual $w(t)$ independent of $X(s)$ for all s. Let $u(t)$ be the fundamental white noise process in the moving average representation of $X(t)$ alone and $v(t)$ be the fundamental white noise process in the m.a. representation of $w(t)$ alone. Write the assumed distributed lag relation

$$Y(t) = \mu^* X(t) + w(t) \tag{A2}$$

Then clearly

$$Y(t) = \mu^* a^* u(t) + d^* v(t), \tag{A3}$$

where $a^* u$ and $d^* v$ are the m.a. representations of X and w, respectively. The equation (A3) together with the m.a. representation of X are clearly in the form (A1) with $b \equiv 0$. Now we need only verify that u and v are jointly fundamental for X and Y, and for this we need only show that $H_{X,Y}(t)$ includes $H_{u,v}(t)$. $H_u(t)$ is in $H_X(t)$ by definition. $H_v(t)$ is in $H_w(t)$, which is in turn, by inspection of (A2), in $H_{X,Y}(t)$. One side of the double implication is proved. Suppose that we have the autoregressive representation

$$\begin{bmatrix} \alpha & \beta \\ \gamma & \delta \end{bmatrix} * \begin{bmatrix} X \\ Y \end{bmatrix}(t) = \begin{bmatrix} u \\ v \end{bmatrix}(t) \tag{A4}$$

and that the m.a. representation has the form (A1) with $b \equiv 0$. Let G be the matrix on the right-hand side of (A1) and H be the matrix on the left-hand side of (A4). Then almost everywhere $\tilde{G}^{-1} = \tilde{H}$. (The tilde denotes a Fourier transformation.) Since $\tilde{G}$ can be written in triangular form, $\tilde{H}$ (and thus H) can be written triangular also. But then we can substitute the first equation of (A4) into the second equation of (A1) to obtain

$$Y(t) = c^* \alpha^* X(t) + d^* v(t). \tag{A5}$$

Equation (A5) has the desired properties, since X can be expressed entirely in terms of u and v is uncorrelated with u.

References

Akaike, H. "Some Problems in the Application of the Cross-Spectral Method." In *Advanced Seminar on Spectral Analysis of Time Series,* edited by B. Harris. New York: 1967.

Brainard, W., and Tobin, J. "Pitfalls of Financial Model Building." *A.E.R. Proc.* 58 (May 1968): 99–122.

Cagan, P. *Determinants and Effects of Changes in the Stock of Money,* Studies in Business Cycles no. 13. New York: Nat. Bur. Econ. Res., 1965.

DeLeeuw, F., and Kalchbrenner, J. "Monetary and Fiscal Actions: A Test of Their Relative Stability—Comment," *Federal Reserve Bank St. Louis Rev.* 51 (April 1969): 6–11.

Durbin, J. "Tests for Serial Correlation in Regression Analysis Based on the Periodogram of Least Squares Residuals." *Biometrika* 56 (March 1969): 1–16.

Friedman, M. "The Lag in the Effect of Monetary Policy." *J.P.E.* 69 (October 1961): 447–66; reprinted in Friedman (1969).

———. "The Monetary Studies of the National Bureau," Nat. Bur. Econ. Res. *Annual Report* (1964); reprinted in Friedman (1969).

———. *The Optimum Quantity of Money and Other Essays.* Chicago: Aldine, 1969.

Friedman, M., and Schwartz, A. *Monetary History of the United States, 1867–1960.* Nat. Bur. Econ. Res. Studies in Business Cycles no. 12. Princeton: 1963. (*a*)

———. "Money and Business Cycles." *Rev. Econ. Statis.* 45, suppl. (February 1963): 32–64 (*b*); reprinted in Friedman (1969).

Granger, C. W. J. "Investigating Causal Relations by Econometric Models and Cross-Spectral Methods." *Econometrica* 37 (July 1969): 424–38.

Hannan, E. J. *Time Series Analysis.* London: 1969.

———. "Regression for Time Series." In *Time Series Analysis,* edited by M. Rosenblatt. New York: 1963.

———. "Estimating a Lagged Regression Relation," *Biometrika* 54 (1967): 409–18.

Malinvaud, E. *Statistical Methods of Econometrics.* Chicago: 1965.

Rozanov, Y. S. *Stationary Random Processes.* San Francisco: 1967.

Sims, C. A. "The Role of Approximate Prior Restrictions in Distributed Lag Estimation." *J. Amer. Statis. Assoc.* 67 (March 1972): 169–75.

———. "Discrete Approximation to Continuous-Time Distributed Lags in Econometrics." *Econometrica* 39 (May 1971): 545–63.

Tobin, J. "Money and Income: Post Hoc Ergo Propter Hoc?" *Q.J.E.* 84 (May 1970): 301–17.

Wahba, G. "Estimation of the Coefficients in a Multi-Dimensional Distributed Lag Model." *Econometrica* 37 (July 1969): 398–407.

Walters, A. "Professor Friedman on the Demand for Money." *J.P.E.* 73 (October 1965): 545–55.

22

Rational Expectations and the Dynamics of Hyperinflation

Thomas J. Sargent
Neil Wallace

This is a study of some theoretical difficulties and estimation problems that arise in economic models in which current expectations of future values of some of the endogenous variables enter in an essential way.[1] Such models are common, especially in monetary economics and macroeconomics. An example would be a model in which the public's expectations of future inflation influence aggregate demand, which together with aggregate supply helps determine the current actual rate of inflation. In order to keep the exposition simple and concrete, we shall center our discussion around Phillip Cagan's (1956) model of hyperinflation. This permits us to analyze all of the theoretical problems involved in larger models, and to illustrate some empirical methods for determining the validity of alternative methods of modeling the formation of expectations.

We are particularly interested in exploring the possibility of building and estimating a version of Cagan's model in which expectations are "rational." Expectations about a variable are said to be rational if they depend, in the proper way, on the same things that economic theory says actually determine that variable. By contrast, the usual method of modeling expectations involves supposing that they are formed by extrapolating past values of the variable being predicted, a scheme that usually, though not always, assumes that the people whose expectations count are ignorant of the economic forces governing the variable they are trying to predict.

We would like to thank Phillip Cagan and Christopher Sims for helpful comments on earlier versions of this paper. Sargent's work on this paper was partially financed by grants to the National Bureau of Economic Research from the Life Insurance Association of America and from the Alfred P. Sloan Foundation.

[1]The model studied by Walters (1971) bears a superficial resemblance to the one analyzed in this paper, but does not come to grips with the problem we are addressing. In Walters's model, current variables do not depend on currently held expectations about future values of any endogenous variables.

[*International Economic Review*, 1973, vol. 14, no. 2
© 1973 by *International Economic Review*

Section 1 contains our discussion of the alternative ways expectations might be assumed to be formed in Cagan's model, while Section 2 contains some empirical results reflecting on the adequacy of various of these alternatives. Our conclusions are contained in Section 3.

1. Models of Hyperinflation

Cagan's explanation of hyperinflation relies on a demand function for real balances of the form

$$\log \left(\frac{M}{P}\right)_t = \alpha\pi_t + \gamma Y + \psi + U_t, \quad \alpha < 0, \; \gamma > 0 \qquad (1)$$

where M is the demand for nominal balances, which Cagan assumes always equals the supply, P is the commodity price level, π_t is the public's expectation of the future rate of inflation, Y is real income, α, γ, and ψ are parameters, and U_t is a stochastic term with central tendency equal to zero. It is assumed that real income Y is constant over time. Cagan posited that the unobservable expectation π_t is a distributed lag of current and past actual rates of inflation, one with geometrically declining lag weights:

$$\pi_t = (1 - \lambda) \sum_{i=0}^{\infty} \lambda^i \log \frac{P_{t-i}}{P_{t-i-1}}, \qquad 0 \leq \lambda < 1. \quad (2)$$

Letting X_t denote $\log (P_t/P_{t-1})$ and using the lag operator L, which is defined by the operation $L^n X_t = X_{t-n}$, (2) can be written as

$$\pi_t = (1 - \lambda)\left[\sum_{i=0}^{\infty} (\lambda L)^i\right] X_t$$
$$= \frac{1 - \lambda}{1 - \lambda L} X_t. \qquad (3)$$

By taking the first difference of equation (1), we find that the rate of inflation is related to the rate of increase of the money supply by

$$\mu_t = X_t + \alpha(\pi_t - \pi_{t-1}) + U_t - U_{t-1}, \qquad (4)$$

where μ_t equals $\log (M_t/M_{t-1})$. Substituting (3) into (4), assuming that the appropriate lag-generating function is invertible, and solving for the rate of inflation X_t yields

$$X_t = \frac{\dfrac{1 - \lambda L}{1 + \alpha(1 - \lambda)}}{1 - \left[\dfrac{\lambda + \alpha(1 - \lambda)}{1 + \alpha(1 - \lambda)}\right]L} \mu_t - \frac{\left[\dfrac{1 - \lambda L}{1 + \alpha(1 - \lambda)}\right](1 - L)}{1 - \left[\dfrac{\lambda + \alpha(1 - \lambda)}{1 + \alpha(1 - \lambda)}\right]L} \qquad (5)$$

where we are assuming that $\|[\lambda + \alpha(1 - \lambda)]/[1 + \alpha(1 - \lambda)]\| < 1$. According to expression (5), the current rate of inflation can be viewed as determined by distributed lags of the change in the money supply and of the disturbance in the demand function for money, U_t.

Two implications of equation (5) are worthy of note. First, unless some special restrictions are placed on μ_t, the current rate of inflation X_t will be correlated with current and past values of the random disturbance U. Cagan implemented his model by substituting (2) into (1) to arrive at

$$\log\left(\frac{M}{P}\right)_t = \alpha(1 - \lambda) \sum_{i=0}^{\infty} \lambda^i X_{t-i} + \gamma Y + \psi + U_t, \qquad (1')$$

an equation whose parameters he estimated by the method of least squares. If there is correlation between X_t and current and past values of U, then this estimator is not statistically consistent.

Second, notice that Cagan's model is one in which expectations are not necessarily assumed to be "rational" in the sense of Muth (1961). That is, the public is assumed to form expectations of inflation according to (2), whereas the actual rate of inflation evolves according to equation (5). The prediction of future inflation generated by equation (5) might be different from the public's expectation of inflation. Unless some restrictions are placed on the stochastic process describing the μ's, the public's expectation of inflation may differ systematically from the forecast of inflation produced by the model. Thus, it is possible that the public is assumed not to be able to forecast inflation as well as does the model. In this sense, the model permits "irrational" expectations.

In order to explore the possibility of building and estimating a version of Cagan's model that incorporates "rational" expectations, it is necessary to be more specific about the horizon to which π_t corresponds. We make the simplest assumption, namely that the horizon is one period, π_t being the rate of inflation that the public expects, as of time t, to prevail between time t and time $t + 1$. Thus, π_t is the public's forecast of X_{t+1}. (It would clearly be possible to carry through our argument while assuming that the horizon appropriate to π_t is longer than one period.)

The assumption that expectations are rational is imposed by requiring that

$$\pi_t = \mathop{\mathsf{E}}_{t} X_{t+1}$$

where $\mathop{\mathsf{E}}_t X_{t+1}$ is the mathematical expectation of X_{t+1} formed using the model and information available as of time t. Then equation (4) becomes

$$X_t = \mu_t - \alpha \mathop{\mathsf{E}}_{t} X_{t+1} + \alpha \mathop{\mathsf{E}}_{t-1} X_t - U_t + U_{t-1}. \qquad (6)$$

Similarly, X_{t+1} is given by

$$X_{t+1} = \mu_{t+1} - \alpha \mathop{\mathsf{E}}_{t+1} X_{t+2} + \alpha \mathop{\mathsf{E}}_{t} X_{t+1} - U_{t+1} + U_t.$$

Taking expectations as of time t, we have

$$\mathop{E}_{t} X_{t+1} = \mathop{E}_{t} \mu_{t+1} - \alpha \mathop{E}_{t} X_{t+2} + \alpha \mathop{E}_{t} X_{t+1} - \mathop{E}_{t} U_{t+1} + U_{t}$$

or

$$\mathop{E}_{t} X_{t+1} = \frac{1}{1 - \alpha} \mathop{E}_{t} \mu_{t+1} - \frac{\alpha}{1 - \alpha} \mathop{E}_{t} X_{t+2} - \frac{1}{1 - \alpha} (\mathop{E}_{t} U_{t+1} - U_{t}). \qquad (7)$$

More generally, we have that

$$\mathop{E}_{t} X_{t+j} = \frac{1}{1 - \alpha} \mathop{E}_{t} \mu_{t+j} - \frac{\alpha}{1 - \alpha} \mathop{E}_{t} X_{t+j+1}$$

$$- \frac{1}{1 - \alpha} (\mathop{E}_{t} U_{t+j} - \mathop{E}_{t} U_{t+j-1}). \qquad (8)$$

By repeatedly substituting (8) into (7) we find that

$$\mathop{E}_{t} X_{t+1} = \frac{1}{1 - \alpha} \sum_{j=1}^{\infty} \left(\frac{-\alpha}{1 - \alpha} \right)^{j-1} \mathop{E}_{t} \mu_{t+j}$$

$$- \frac{1}{1 - \alpha} \sum_{j=1}^{\infty} \left(\frac{-\alpha}{1 - \alpha} \right)^{j-1} (\mathop{E}_{t} U_{t+j} - \mathop{E}_{t} U_{t+j-1}). \qquad (9)$$

Here we are imposing the terminal condition

$$\lim_{n \to \infty} \left(\frac{-\alpha}{1 - \alpha} \right)^{n-1} \mathop{E}_{t} X_{t+n} = 0.$$

Substituting equation (9) into equation (6) yields the following expression that describes the evolution of inflation:

$$X_t = \mu_t + \sum_{j=1}^{\infty} \left(\frac{-\alpha}{1 - \alpha} \right)^{j} \mathop{E}_{t} \mu_{t+j} - \sum_{j=1}^{\infty} \left(\frac{-\alpha}{1 - \alpha} \right)^{j} \mathop{E}_{t-1} \mu_{t+j-1}$$

$$- \sum_{j=1}^{\infty} \left(\frac{-\alpha}{1 - \alpha} \right)^{j} (\mathop{E}_{t} U_{t+j} - \mathop{E}_{t} U_{t+j-1}) \qquad (10)$$

$$+ \sum_{j=1}^{\infty} \left(\frac{-\alpha}{1 - \alpha} \right)^{j} (\mathop{E}_{t-1} U_{t+j-1} - \mathop{E}_{t-1} U_{t+j-2}) - U_t + U_{t-1}.$$

Writing down the corresponding expression for X_{t+1} and taking its expectation as of time t yields an expression identical to equation (9), which verifies that the public's expectation is indeed equivalent with the model's forecast of the rate of inflation one period hence. Notice that since $\alpha < 0$, we are assured that $0 < [-\alpha/(1 - \alpha)] < 1$, which makes it possible for the infinite sums in (9) and (10) to converge.

Equation (10) exhibits an important feature that characterizes all models in which expectations of future values of endogenous variables enter and in which those expectations are posited to be equivalent with the model's forecasts: the current values of some of the endogenous variables in such models will depend on the public's expectations of some of the "exogenous" variables from now until forever.[2] The reason for this outcome can be seen by inspecting equation (6). The current rate of inflation is influenced by the current forecast of inflation for next period. But next period's rate of inflation depends on next period's expectation of inflation two periods hence. An optimal forecasting scheme necessarily takes into account this dependence of current values on expectations of future values, which in turn depend on expectations of values even farther into the future, and so on, leading to a progression of infinite extent into the future. The current rate of inflation is then governed by the public's forecasts of the variables determining the subsequent rates of inflation, which in this case are the future rates of growth of the money supply and future disturbances in the demand function for money.

In order to complete our model of hyperinflation, it is necessary to supplement equation (10) with a description of how the public forms its expectations of subsequent rates of growth of the money supply. To accomplish this while remaining true to the objective of incorporating rational expectations in the model, it is necessary to write down an expression assumed to govern the actual evolution of the rate of increase in the money supply. The public can then be assumed to utilize this expression in forming its expectations of subsequent rates of growth in the money supply, thus guaranteeing that its expectations are consistent with the actual process governing the growth in money.

One tractable way of modeling the rate of growth in the money supply is to assume that it follows a purely autoregressive process, i.e.,

$$\mu_t = \sum_{i=1}^{\infty} w_i \mu_{t-i} + \tilde{\varepsilon}_t, \tag{11}$$

where the w_i's are constants and $\tilde{\varepsilon}_t$ is a serially uncorrelated random term with finite mean, which we take to be zero, and finite variance. The random variable $\tilde{\varepsilon}_t$ is assumed to be distributed independently of the U_t's that appear in the demand function for real balances. This specification implies that the rate of growth of the money supply is exogenous with respect to the rate of inflation.[3]

On the basis of equation (11), the public's expectation of future values

---

[2] See Wallace (1971) for a discussion of how this property of rational expectations is dealt with in a standard macroeconomic model.

[3] Lucas (1970) closes his model by assuming that government policy is governed by a purely autoregressive process.

of μ_t can be written down as the appropriate mathematical expectations as of time t. These expectations will have the forms

$$\underset{t}{\mathsf{E}}\,\mu_{t+j} = \sum_{i=0}^{\infty} v_{ij}\mu_{t-i} \qquad (12)$$

where the v_{ij}'s are functions of the w_i's that appear in (11). Substituting (12) into equation (10) yields

$$X_t = \mu_t + \sum_{j=1}^{\infty} \left(\frac{-\alpha}{1-\alpha}\right)^j \sum_{i=0}^{\infty} v_{ij}\mu_{t-i} - \sum_{j=1}^{\infty} \left(\frac{-\alpha}{1-\alpha}\right)^j \sum_{i=0}^{\infty} v_{ij}\mu_{t-i-1}$$

$$- \sum_{j=1}^{\infty} \left(\frac{-\alpha}{1-\alpha}\right)^j (\underset{t}{\mathsf{E}}\,U_{t+j} - \underset{t}{\mathsf{E}}\,U_{t+j-1})$$

$$+ \sum_{j=1}^{\infty} \left(\frac{-\alpha}{1-\alpha}\right)^j (\underset{t-1}{\mathsf{E}}\,U_{t+j-1} - \underset{t-1}{\mathsf{E}}\,U_{t+j-2}) - U_t + U_{t-1}.$$

This can be rewritten as

$$X_t = \sum_{i=0}^{\infty} Z_i \mu_{t-i} + \check{U}_t \qquad (13)$$

where

$$Z_0 = 1 + \sum_{j=1}^{\infty} \left(\frac{-\alpha}{1-\alpha}\right)^j v_{oj}$$

$$Z_i = \sum_{j=1}^{\infty} \left[\left(\frac{-\alpha}{1-\alpha}\right)^j (v_{ij} - v_{i+1,j})\right], \qquad\qquad i \geq 1,$$

$$\check{U}_t = -\sum_{j=1}^{\infty} \left(\frac{-\alpha}{1-\alpha}\right)^j (\underset{t}{\mathsf{E}}\,U_{t+j} - \underset{t}{\mathsf{E}}\,U_{t+j-1})$$

$$+ \sum_{j=1}^{\infty} \left(\frac{-\alpha}{1-\alpha}\right)^j (\underset{t-1}{\mathsf{E}}\,U_{t+j-1} - \underset{t-1}{\mathsf{E}}\,U_{t+j-2}) - U_t + U_{t-1}.$$

Equation (13) is a "reduced form" expressing the rate of inflation as a distributed lag of current and past rates of money creation. Since the $\bar{\varepsilon}$'s in (11) were assumed to be uncorrelated with the U's, it follows that the $\check{U}$'s are uncorrelated with the μ's in (13), thus confirming that it is legitimate to treat the rates of growth in the money supply as exogenous in (13). Hence, equation (13) can properly be estimated using least squares, the lack of correlation between the $\tilde{U}$'s and the μ's guaranteeing that the estimates will at least be consistent. Whether it would be possible to estimate the structural parameter α from the estimate of the reduced form coefficients would depend on precisely what form the autoregression in (11) was assumed to take, and on how much prior information about the autoregression coefficients was available. Unless the form of (11) were severely restricted, it would not be possible to estimate the structural parameter on the basis of the estimated reduced form parameters alone. However, the following two-stage estimator for α would be available: by least-squares estimate some versions of

$$\widehat{X}_{t+1} = \sum_{i=0}^{\infty} \widehat{h}_i \mu_{t-i};$$

then substitute $\widehat{X}_{t+1}$ for π_t and $\widehat{X}_t$ for π_{t-1} in equation (4) and estimate α by least squares. Since the μ_t's are valid instruments for π_t, being uncorrelated with the $\tilde{U}$'s, the estimator of α will be statistically consistent.

Assuming that the rate of increase in the money supply is governed by (11) thus enables us to complete a version of Cagan's model in which expectations are posited to be "rational." But there is reason to believe that (11) is not an adequate description of growth in the money supply in the context of this model. The model is designed to explain the behavior of inflation during periods of hyperinflation, periods in which the government is resorting to creation of money as the principal means of financing its expenditures. In order to keep real expenditures at the level it desires, the government is likely to respond to a decline in the purchasing power of money by increasing the rate at which it is adding to the stock of money. Such behavior makes the rate of increase in the money supply depend partly on the price level, thus setting up feedback from the public's expected rate of inflation, which helps determine the price level, to the rate of money creation. Such feedback must not occur if equation (11) is to be an adequate description of the money creation process. Using equation (11) to model the formation of expectations thus amounts to assuming that the public never really catches on to what the government is doing in financing its expenditures mainly by money creation.

Under certain conditions, it is possible to complete a version of Cagan's model in which the public understands that the government is printing money in order to finance most of its expenditures. This is well known for the case of a continuous-time, nonstochastic version of Cagan's model.[4] Thus, suppose that the demand for money is governed by

$$\frac{M(t)}{P(t)} = f[\pi(t)], \qquad\qquad f' < 0 \quad (14)$$

[4]E.g., see Friedman (1971).

where M, P, and π are now continuous functions of time. Suppose that there are no private bank deposits and that all money is non-interest-bearing debt of the government. Also suppose that the government finances all of its expenditures, which in real terms equal $G(t)$ at time t, by the creation of new money. Suppose the government wants to keep $G(t)$ constant over time at the rate G. The rate of money creation can be determined from the government's budget constraint,

$$\frac{\dot{M}(t)}{P(t)} = G, \tag{15}$$

where a dot above a variable denotes its derivative with respect to time. Equation (15) can be rewritten as

$$\frac{\dot{M}}{M} = \frac{P}{M} \cdot G.$$

Substituting (14) into the above equation gives

$$\frac{\dot{M}}{M} = \frac{G}{f(\pi)}, \tag{16}$$

which shows that the rate of money creation varies directly with the public's anticipated rate of inflation. Differentiating (14) with respect to time and rearranging gives

$$\frac{\dot{P}}{P} = \frac{\dot{M}}{M} - \frac{f'(\pi)}{f(\pi)}\dot{\pi}. \tag{17}$$

Now suppose we add the requirement that expectations be "rational," i.e.,

$$\pi = \frac{\dot{P}}{P}. \tag{18}$$

Equations (16), (17), and (18) form a system that governs the evolution of M, P, and π over time. The equilibrium of the system, if it exists, is easily found. Notice that if $\dot{\pi} = 0$ for all t, then

$$\frac{\dot{P}}{P} = \frac{\dot{M}}{M} = \frac{G}{f(\pi)}$$

or

$$\pi = \frac{G}{f(\pi)},$$

which is one equation in the unknown π. If this equation has a unique solution, then it determines π, which also equals $\dot{P}/P$ and $\dot{M}/M$. The equilibrium of the system is one in which P/P, π, and M/M are all unchanging over time.

The possibility that the public's expected rate of inflation influences the rate of money creation is an interesting one, for it turns out that such a mechanism is capable of providing a way of rationalizing the method of forming expectations about inflation that Cagan assumed. We have seen above that if the public's expectation of inflation is governed by Cagan's adaptive scheme, equation (2), then the actual inflation rate is described by equation (5), which can be rewritten as

$$\{1 + \alpha(1 - \lambda) - [\lambda + \alpha(1 - \lambda)]L\}X_t$$
$$= (1 - \lambda L)\mu_t - (1 - \lambda L)(1 - L)U_t. \quad (19)$$

To provide a rationalization of Cagan's model, we begin by supposing that the rate of money creation is governed by

$$\mu_t = \left(\frac{1 - \lambda}{1 - \lambda L}\right)X_t + \varepsilon_t \quad (20)$$

where ε_t is a serially uncorrelated random term. Substituting (20) into (19) yields

$$[\lambda + \alpha(1 - \lambda)](1 - L)X_t = (1 - \lambda L)[\varepsilon_t - (U_t - U_{t-1})].$$

This can be rewritten as

$$\left[1 - \frac{(1 - \lambda)L}{1 - \lambda L}\right]X_t = [\lambda + \alpha(1 - \lambda)]^{-1}[\varepsilon_t - (U_t - U_{t-1})]$$

or

$$X_t = \left(\frac{1 - \lambda}{1 - \lambda L}\right)X_{t-1} + [\lambda + \alpha(1 - \lambda)]^{-1}[\varepsilon_t - (U_t - U_{t-1})]. \quad (21)$$

Now suppose that U_t follows the Markov process[5] $U_t = U_{t-1} + \eta_t$, where η_t is a serially uncorrelated random term with mean zero and finite variance. On this assumption, equation (21) shows that the model's prediction of X_t as of time $t - 1$ is given by

$$\mathop{E}_{t-1} X_t = \left(\frac{1 - \lambda}{1 - \lambda L}\right)X_{t-1},$$

which is Cagan's adaptive expectations scheme. Then on the hypothesis that expectations are rational, (20) is equivalent with

$$\mu_t = \mathop{E}_t X_{t+1} + \varepsilon_t, \quad (22)$$

which can be regarded as a linear, discrete-time approximation to equation (16), one that captures the "feedback" from expected inflation to

---

[5]The residuals in Cagan's regressions, which are estimates of the U's, are highly serially correlated (see Cagan 1956 and Barro 1970). Barro reports Durbin-Watson statistics for Cagan's regressions ranging from .25 to .53. Thus, the assumption in the text appears to be an interesting one of which to investigate the implications.

money creation that will occur if the government is financing a roughly fixed rate of real expenditures by money creation.

Thus, we have been able to produce a set of restrictions on the U's and on the stochastic process governing the μ's that make Cagan's adaptive expectations scheme one that produces expectations that are identical to the model's predictions. The system that emerges is one in which at any given time the public expects a constant rate of inflation and a constant rate of money creation to prevail over the entire future. By equation (22), we have

$$\underset{t}{\mathsf{E}}\, \mu_{t+1} = \underset{t}{\mathsf{E}}\, X_{t+2},$$

or more generally

$$\underset{t}{\mathsf{E}}\, \mu_{t+j} = \underset{t}{\mathsf{E}}\, X_{t+j+1}.$$

But it is known that Cagan's adaptive expectation scheme has the property (see Muth 1960)

$$\underset{t}{\mathsf{E}}\, X_{t+j} = \underset{t}{\mathsf{E}}\, X_{t+1}, \qquad\qquad \text{all } j > 1.$$

Thus, it follows that

$$\underset{t}{\mathsf{E}}\, \mu_{t+j} = \underset{t}{\mathsf{E}}\, X_{t+j} = \underset{t}{\mathsf{E}}\, X_{t+1}, \qquad\qquad \text{for all } j > 1.$$

Notice that on our assumptions equation (9) becomes

$$\underset{t}{\mathsf{E}}\, X_{t+1} = \frac{1}{1-\alpha} \sum_{j=1}^{\infty} \left(\frac{-\alpha}{1-\alpha}\right)^{j-1} \underset{t}{\mathsf{E}}\, \mu_{t+j}$$

$$= \underset{t}{\mathsf{E}}\, \mu_{t+1} \frac{1}{1-\alpha} \sum_{j=1}^{\infty} \left(\frac{-\alpha}{1-\alpha}\right)^{j-1}$$

$$= \underset{t}{\mathsf{E}}\, \mu_{t+1}.$$

The system that we have set out resembles the continuous-time, non-stochastic system above in two ways. First, expectations of inflation influence the rate of money creation. Second, the equilibrium is one in which at each moment the public expects a single rate of inflation and money creation to prevail over the indefinite future. Moreover, the rate of money creation is expected to equal the rate of inflation.

This system is one in which expectations of money creation could equally well be formed as a distributed lag of past rates of money creation. Substituting (21) into (20) and rearranging gives

$$(1-L)\mu_t = \{[\lambda + \alpha(1-\lambda)]^{-1}(1-\lambda) + 1\}\varepsilon_t - \varepsilon_{t-1}$$
$$- [\lambda + \alpha(1-\lambda)]^{-1}(1-\lambda)(U_t - U_{t-1}).$$

This is a mixed moving average, autoregressive process which can be rewritten as

$$\mu_t = \left(\frac{1-\tau}{1-\tau L}\right)\mu_{t-1} + [\lambda + \alpha(1-\lambda)]^{-1}(1-\lambda)[\varepsilon_t - (U_t - U_{t-1})] + \varepsilon_t,$$

where τ is a parameter that depends on the ratio of the variance of ε_t to the variance of $(U_t - U_{t-1})$. On our assumptions, the least-squares forecast of μ_t is

$$\mathop{E}_{t-1}\mu_t = \left(\frac{1-\tau}{1-\tau L}\right)\mu_{t-1}.$$

The expected rate of inflation can also be written as the same function of past μ's.

Now suppose that we do not observe μ_t directly, but instead have data m_t which are polluted by errors of measurement, i.e.

$$m_t = \mu_t + s_t \tag{23}$$

where s_t is a serially uncorrelated random term that is distributed independently of ε_t and U_t. In this case, since μ is not observed while X is, the best way to forecast is to make use of equation (20) and to predict both money creation and inflation by distributed lags of past rates of inflation.

In summary, we have described two ways to build a model of hyperinflation in which expectations are rational. The first model consists of equations (11) and (13). In this system, μ_t and m_t are exogenous with respect to X, being uncorrelated with the random U's in the demand function for money that help determine X. In this system, money creation influences current and subsequent rates of inflation; but given lagged rates of money creation, past rates of inflation exert no influence on money creation. The system is one in which money creation "causes" inflation, in the sense of Granger (1969), while inflation does not "cause" money creation. In such a system, adaptive expectations schemes like Cagan's are not rational.

The second model is one in which Cagan's adaptive expectation mechanism is a rational one to employ. It consists of equations (10), (20), and (23). In this system, the best way to forecast the subsequent rates of money creation that appear in equation (10) is to extrapolate lagged rates of inflation. This in turn implies that inflation itself is best predicted by extrapolating lagged rates of inflation. This is a system in which both money creation and inflation are best predicted by extrapolating current and lagged rates of inflation and in which lagged rates of money creation add nothing to the predictions formed in this way. In this system, lagged inflation influences money creation, but lagged money creation does not appear to influence inflation once lagged rates of inflation are taken into account. A critical element in this system is the hypothesized feedback that occurs from expected inflation to money creation, a feedback that emerges because the government is attempting to finance a roughly constant rate of real expenditures principally by money creation.

2. Empirical Results

Our two models have very different implications about the structure of feedback between X and m. The model formed by (11) and (13) implies that m influences X with no feedback occurring from X to m. The model consisting of (10), (20), and (23) implies that X influences m but that there is no reverse feedback from m to X. More general models can be imagined in which mutual feedback from X to m and m to X occurs.[6] In this section, we apply statistical methods that are capable of determining which of these models best describes the data.

A test of the null hypothesis that there is no feedback from X_t to subsequent values of m can be carried out as follows.[7] Consider the following quite general representation of m_t:

$$m_t = \sum_{i=1}^{\infty} w_i m_{t-i} + \sum_{i=0}^{\infty} c_i X_{t-i} + e_t. \tag{24}$$

Here e_t is again a serially uncorrelated random variable assumed to have a finite variance and to be distributed independently of U in equation (1). Equation (11) is obviously a special case of (24), one with the c_i's all taken to be zero. Equation (20) is another special case of (24), one with the w_i's all taken to be zero. Equation (24) incorporates the possibility of feedback from the current rate of inflation to subsequent rates of money creation. To test the hypothesis that there is no feedback, we have to test the null hypothesis that all the c_i's are zero. This can be done by noticing the implications of the presence of nonzero c_i's in equation (20). Through equation (13), say, an increment in $\tilde{U}_t$ leads to an increase in X_t. But through equation (24), the increase in X_t causes changes in subsequent values of m_t, since the c_i's are not all zero. Thus nonzero c's imply nonzero correlations between the $\tilde{U}$'s and subsequent values of m. A test of the null hypothesis that the c's are zero can be carried out by estimating equation (13) by least squares, which on the null hypothesis produces consistent estimates of the parameters. Then correlations can be calculated between the residuals, which on the null hypothesis are consistent estimates of the true disturbances, and future values of m. Nonzero correlations lead to rejection of the hypothesis and imply that some of the c's are best taken not to be zero. As a practical matter, it is not necessary to carry out the test

---

[6]E.g., if to the system formed by (10), (20), and (23), we add the specification that we observe only $\tilde{X}$ which equals X plus measurement error, mutual feedback will in general characterize the relationship between $\tilde{X}$ and m.

[7]The test was proposed by Christopher Sims (1971).

in the two separate steps of estimating (13) and then correlating the residuals with future m's. Instead, the same thing is accomplished by adding future values of m directly to (13) and calculating a two-sided distributed lag regression

$$X_t = \sum_{i=-n}^{n} z_i m_{t-i} + e_t' \qquad (25)$$

where n is a parameter and e_t' is a statistical residual. Sizable coefficients on future values of m imply that some of the c's in (24) are not zero. Similarly, sizable coefficients on future values of X_t in the reverse distributed lag

$$m_t = \sum_{i=-n}^{n} h_i X_{t-i} + e_t'', \qquad (26)$$

where e_t'' is a statistical residual, permit the inference that there is feedback from the current rate of money creation to subsequent rates of inflation.

Estimating (25) and (26) by least squares unfortunately requires time series longer than most of those examined by Cagan. Only in the case of the German hyperinflation are data available over a long enough period.[8] For the German monthly data over the period March 1921 through May 1923, we have estimated (25) and (26) by least squares. The data have been "quasi-differenced," i.e. multiplied by $(1 - \hat{p}L)$ where $\hat{p}$ is the least-squares estimate of the first-order autoregression parameter of the residuals from (25) or (26) estimated by least squares for the levels of m_t and X_t. Each regression includes a trend term. Our estimates are recorded in tables 1 and 2. In each table we report the F-statistic pertinent for testing the null hypothesis that the coefficients on future values of the variable on the right side of the equation are zero. The F-statistic in table 1 is 38.4, well above the critical value of 5.56 at the 1 percent level of significance. This means that at the 1 percent level of significance we must reject the hypothesis that there is no feedback from current inflation to future rates of money creation.

On the other hand, the F-statistic in table 2, which reports the regression of money creation on inflation, is 4.8, a value that causes us to reject at the 95 percent confidence level the null hypothesis that there is no feedback from the rate of money creation to subsequent rates of inflation, but that fails to cause us to reject the null hypothesis at the 99 percent confidence level. The absolute values of the coefficients on future rates of inflation are only one-third to one-fourth of those on lagged rates of inflation. This is consistent with the presence of relatively weak feedback from money creation to inflation. The results imply that inflation strongly influences subse-

---

[8]The data, which are monthly, are to be found in Cagan's article (1956).

TABLE 1

Inflation Regressed on Money Creation
(Germany, April 1921–June 1923)

$$(1 - \hat{p}L)X_t = \sum_{i=-4}^{6} w_i(1 - \hat{p}L)m_{t-i}$$

$|i|$	Coefficients on Future Rates of Money Creation	Coefficients on Lagged Rates of Money Creation
0	. . .	1.2634(.2583)
1	1.5321(.2494)	−2.2126(.2630)
2	−.3920(.2397)	.5362(.2828)
3	−.4558(.1611)	−.2454(.2911)
4	.6625(.0942)	2.0478(.4346)
5	. . .	−1.7855(.6974)
6	. . .	−3.3095(.6005)

Note.—Constant = .0143(.0285); time = .0231(.0040); R_A^2 = .9770; D-W = 2.4123; F = 38.47; $F_{4,14}$(.05) = 3.34; $F_{4,14}$(.01) = 5.56. Estimated standard errors are in parentheses. The estimate $\hat{p}$ was obtained as the first-order serial regression coefficient for the residuals of equation (25) estimated by least squares; $\hat{p}$ = −.605.

quent rates of money creation, but that the influence of money creation on subsequent rates of inflation is harder to detect.

For the remaining six countries studied by Cagan, there are insufficient data to estimate (25) and (26) by ordinary least squares. There are available, however, alternative techniques that economize on data at the expense of introducing restrictions on the forms of distributed lag. It is convenient to adopt Klein's (1958) method of estimating distributed lags in which the coefficients (in positive lags) trail off or oscillate geometrically as the lag

TABLE 2

Money Creation Regressed on Inflation
(Germany, April 1921–June 1923)

$$(1 - \hat{p}L)m_t = \sum_{i=-4}^{6} z_i(1 - \hat{p}L)X_{t-i}$$

$|i|$	Coefficients on Future Rates of Inflation	Coefficients on Lagged Rates of Inflation
0	. . .	.1926(.0345)
1	−.0866(.0296)	.2120(.0524)
2	.0420(.0251)	.2234(.0548)
3	−.0398(.0220)	.1104(.0585)
4	.0379(.0217)	.2500(.0600)
5	. . .	.0291(.0632)
6	. . .	.0701(.0628)

Note.—Constant = −.0086(.0163); time = −.0009(.0028); R_A^2 = .8786; D-W = 1.9811; F = 4.77; $F_{4,14}$(.05) = 3.34; $F_{4,14}$(.01) = 5.56. Estimated standard errors are in parentheses. The estimate $\hat{p}$ was obtained as the first-order serial regression coefficient for the residuals of equation (26) estimated by least squares; $\hat{p}$ = .648.

increases. Thus, we have estimated the following particular forms of (25) and (26):

$$X_t = \gamma_0 + \gamma_1 \sum_{i=0}^{t-1} \delta^i m_{t-i} + \gamma_2 \delta^t + \gamma_3 m_{t+1} + \gamma_4 m_{t+2} + \gamma_5 t + e_t'' \qquad (25')$$

$$m_t = \alpha_0 + \alpha_1 \sum_{i=0}^{t-1} \phi^i X_{t-i} + \alpha_2 \phi^t + \alpha_3 X_{t+1} + \alpha_4 X_{t+2} + \alpha_5 t + e_t'. \qquad (26')$$

Quasi-differenced versions of equations (25') and (26') were estimated using the search procedure recommended by Hildreth and Lu (1960). The search over δ and ϕ was carried down to intervals of .01 over the interval $[-.99, .99]$.

The estimates of (25') and (26') are reported in tables 4 and 5, while table 3 reports F-statistics pertinent for testing the null hypothesis: $\gamma_3 = \gamma_4 = 0$ in (25'), and $\alpha_3 = \alpha_4 = 0$ in (26'). High values of the F-statistic lead to rejection of the null hypothesis.

For Germany, Austria, and Hungary I the F-statistics imply that at the 99 percent confidence level the null hypothesis that there is no feedback from X to m must be rejected. Only in the case of Greece are we forced to reject (at the 99 percent confidence level) the null hypothesis that there is no feedback from m to X. The regression for Austria yields very sizable coefficients on future value of X_t, indicating the likely presence of feedback from m to X despite the insignificance of the F-statistic at the 95 percent confidence level. In the cases of Russia, Poland, and Hungary II, the formal statistical tests permit us to reject neither of our two hypotheses at the 95 percent confidence level. Overall, the picture that emerges from tables 3, 4, and 5 is one in which the evidence for influence extending from X to m is rather stronger than for influence going the other direction.

As shown in Section 1, such a pattern of feedback could occur if expec-

TABLE 3

F-Statistics (X versus m)

Country	m Regressed on X	X Regressed on m	Degrees of Freedom	Critical Values of F	
				.05	.01
Germany	3.30	17.64**	24	3.40	5.61
Russia	<1	<1	15	3.68	6.36
Austria	2.89	15.53**	9	4.26	8.02
Hungary I	1.17	11.01**	9	4.26	8.02
Greece	7.68**	5.02*	12	3.88	6.93
Poland	<1	2.57	11	3.98	7.20
Hungary II	<1	<1	2	19.00	99.01

*Significant at .95 level of significance.
**Significant at .99 level of significance.

TABLE 4
INFLATION REGRESSED ON MONEY CREATION

$$(1 - \hat{p}L) \text{ applied to: } X_t = \gamma_0 + \gamma_1 \sum_{i=0}^{t-1} \delta^i m_{t-i} + \gamma_2 \delta^t + \gamma_3 m_{t+1} + \gamma_4 m_{t+2} + \gamma_5 t$$

Country	γ_0	γ_1	γ_2	δ	γ_3	γ_4	γ_5	D-W	R_A^2	$\hat{p}$
Germany: Nov. 1920–May 1923	-0.0712 (.1203)	-0.5107 (.1118)	0.0073 (.1905)	.68	2.1012 (.3060)	-.2633 (.2521)	0.0142 (.0102)	2.44	.8037	-.4585
Russia: Mar. 1922–Dec. 1923	-0.0906 (.1011)	-0.1110 (.1587)	0.5552 (.1683)	.58	0.1639 (.2084)	.2160 (.2142)	0.0199 (.0066)	1.89	.5308	.3920
Austria: Mar. 1921–May 1922	175.1205 (48.7372)	0.6694 (.2164)	-173.4718 (48.2640)	.99	1.4603 (.3106)	.6223 (.4176)	-1.8178 (.5063)	2.74	.9198	-.5278
Hungary I: Sept. 1922–Dec. 1923	0.2053 (.0920)	-0.3092 (.1597)	-0.1714 (.1529)	.55	1.8218 (.3581)	-.6498 (.3279)	-0.0002 (.0120)	2.87	.8338	-.3984
Greece: Mar. 1943–Sept. 1944	0.0090 (.0834)	-0.4184 (.3238)	0.0575 (.0471)	-.99	0.2765 (.3219)	.1356 (.1034)	0.0462 (.0119)	2.26	.9565	-.2145
Poland: June 1922–Nov. 1923	0.0276 (.0902)	1.0107 (.5618)	-0.0206 (.0738)	-.99	0.2431 (.5913)	.6045 (.4807)	-0.0122 (.0161)	1.99	.6715	.0223
Hungary II: Sept. 1945–May 1946	3470.5169 (610.6772)	1.1459 (.3285)	-3435.7382 (604.9208)	.99	1.6519 (.3336)	-.6487 (.1426)	-35.4153 (6.0521)	3.09	.9862	-.6612

NOTE.—The estimate $\hat{p}$ was obtained as the first-order serial regression coefficient for the residuals of equation (25') estimated by least squares.

TABLE 5
MONEY CREATION REGRESSED ON INFLATION

$(1 - \hat{p}L)$ applied to: $m_t = \alpha_0 + \alpha_1 \sum_{i=1}^{t-1} \phi^i X_{t-i} + \alpha_2 \phi^t + \alpha_3 X_{t+1} + \alpha_4 X_{t+2} + \alpha_5 t$

Country	α_0	α_1	α_2	ϕ	α_3	α_4	α_5	D-W	R_A^2	$\hat{p}$
Germany: Nov. 1920–May 1923	0.2037 (.0774)	.2717 (.0318)	-0.1693 (.0839)	.88	-.0779 (.0335)	.0448 (.0339)	-.0176 (.0056)	1.91	.9349	.1133
Russia: Mar. 1922–Dec. 1923	-30.5212 (40.0497)	.2083 (.0846)	30.6696 (39.9155)	.99	-.1051 (.1935)	.2591 (.1911)	.1939 (.3917)	2.39	.7082	-.3033
Austria: Mar. 1921–May 1922	60.6528 (15.8772)	.3031 (.0597)	-59.9510 (15.7376)	.99	.2676 (.0797)	.1586 (.0926)	-.6379 (.1562)	2.12	.8306	-.1010
Hungary I: Sept. 1922–Dec. 1923	-0.3974 (.0978)	.5816 (.0457)	0.5169 (.1107)	.80	.0198 (.0642)	.1269 (-.0783)	-.0282 (.0078)	2.67	.9572	-.4125
Greece: Mar. 1943–Sept. 1944	92.3591 (74.8968)	.3257 (.1872)	-91.4102 (74.2067)	.99	.2513 (.0681)	-.0010 (.0490)	-.9369 (.7435)	1.45	.9629	.3367
Poland: June 1922–Nov. 1923	13.0791 (32.2762)	.2688 (.0746)	-12.8325 (32.0157)	.99	.0039 (.0881)	.0346 (.0880)	-.1721 (.3180)	2.02	.8617	.0601
Hungary II: Sept. 1945–May 1946	-1.6880 (.6663)	.6186 (.1673)	1.2515 (.6138)	.34	.1366 (.1066)	-.0307 (.0378)	.2545 (.0735)	3.30	.9934	-.4339

NOTE.—The estimate $\hat{p}$ was obtained as the first-order serial regression coefficient for the residuals of equation (26') estimated by least squares.

tations of inflation were formed by extrapolating past rates of inflation while the government was expected to use money creation to finance a roughly constant rate of real government expenditures. In this regard, it is interesting to inspect table 6 and figure 1, which record for each country the statistic $(M_t - M_{t-1})/[1/2(P_t + P_{t-1})]$, which approximately equals the real resources commanded by creators of money in each period. With the exception of the last several observations, these data are generally without noticeable trends.[9] The assumption that the public expected the

[9]We do not take into account the changing importance of the private banking system in creating money over the courses of the various hyperinflations. A complete explanation of the apparent feedback from X to m during the various hyperinflations would probably assign a role to the behavior of the private banks.

TABLE 6

INDEX OF $(M_t - M_{t-1})/[1/2(P_t + P_{t-1})]$

Germany	Russia	Austria	Hungary I	Greece	Poland	Hungary II
0.26*	0.11†	1.07‡	1.04§	0.36‖	0.10#	0.31**
0.10	0.10	0.66	1.36	0.75	0.13	0.36
0.23	0.07	0.97	1.02	0.90	0.18	0.48
0.08	0.05	0.06	0.16	0.41	0.20	0.13
−0.09	0.06	0.97	0.29	0.62	0.22	0.05
0.10	0.08	0.92	−0.14	0.95	0.33	0.05
0.08	0.10	1.00	0.09	0.79	0.16	0.20
0.09	0.16	1.70	0.42	0.93	0.18	0.11
0.23	0.10	2.34	0.56	1.12	0.14	0.64
0.29	0.12	1.77	0.55	0.95	0.17	2.09
0.22	0.10	1.72	0.94	0.67	0.27	56.06
0.31	0.10	1.32	1.03	0.55	0.22	...
0.42	0.11	0.57	1.08	0.23	0.16	...
0.43	0.07	0.78	0.83	0.44	0.32	...
0.47	0.15	0.78	0.68	0.71	0.17	...
0.36	0.14	0.74	0.48	0.55	0.27	...
0.13	0.06	1.41	0.31	0.37	0.27	...
0.30	0.08	1.70	0.46	0.84	0.62	...
0.28	0.09	1.70	0.44	0.61	0.21	...
0.26	0.07	...	...	1.99	0.28	...
0.38	0.05	...	...	2.45	0.39	...
0.46	0.13	...	...	520.26	...	...
0.49	0.12	...	...	...	...	...
0.38	0.09	...	...	...	...	...
0.53	0.07	...	...	...	...	...
0.43	...	...	...	...	...	...
0.38	...	...	...	...	...	...
0.41	...	...	...	...	...	...
0.76	...	...	...	...	...	...
0.27	...	...	...	...	...	...
0.58	...	...	...	...	...	...
0.41	...	...	...	...	...	...
0.66	...	...	...	...	...	...
0.72	...	...	...	...	...	...
1.46	...	...	...	...	...	...
1.27	...	...	...	...	...	...
0.41	...	...	...	...	...	...
20.56	...	...	...	...	...	...

*Oct. 1929   †Feb. 1922   ‡Feb. 1921   §Aug. 1922   ‖Feb. 1943   #May 1922   **Aug. 1945

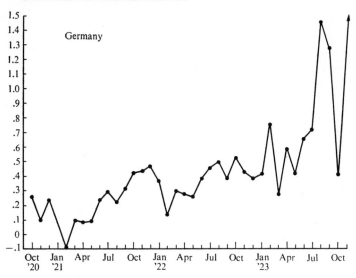

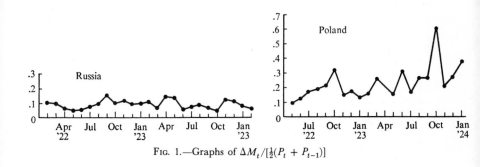

Fig. 1.—Graphs of $\Delta M_t / [\frac{1}{2}(P_t + P_{t-1})]$

government to keep its rate of real purchases roughly constant may thus not be a bad approximation.

Our explanation for the feedback from X to m tends to confirm the wisdom of Cagan's decision to model expectations by an extrapolation of lagged rates of inflation. Such a method of forming expectations seems to have been rational, since the data indicate that lagged rates of money creation exerted little influence on inflation beyond that already accounted for by lagged rates of inflation.

In Section 1 we mentioned that since Cagan's model implies that the disturbances in the demand function for money, equation (1), cause changes in the current price level, the current rate of inflation is likely not to be uncorrelated with the current disturbance U_t. The correlation between U and X implies that least-squares estimates of equation (1'), Cagan's equation, are not statistically consistent. It seems useful to investi-

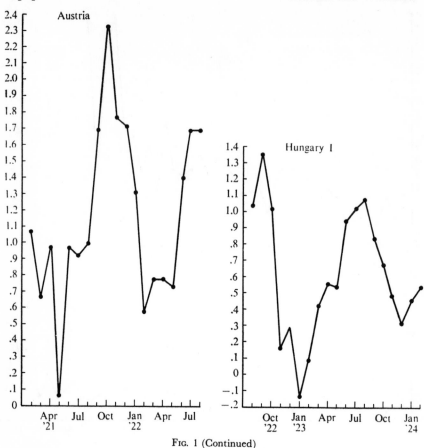

FIG. 1 (Continued)

gate the nature of the inconsistency, if only for a special case. We can do this for our "rational" version of Cagan's model that incorporates feedback from X to m, and that leads to the rate of inflation being governed by equation (21). Equation (21) can be rewritten as

$$[\lambda + \alpha(1 - \lambda)]X_t = (1 - L)^{-1}(1 - \lambda L)\varepsilon_t - (1 - \lambda L)U_t.$$

Inverting the above equation and solving for U_t gives

$$U_t = -\frac{\lambda + \alpha(1 - \lambda)}{1 - \lambda L}X_t + (1 - L)^{-1}\varepsilon_t, \qquad (27)$$

which summarizes the correlation between U_t and current and lagged X's. Now where (1′) is the correct model and where data are as abundant as

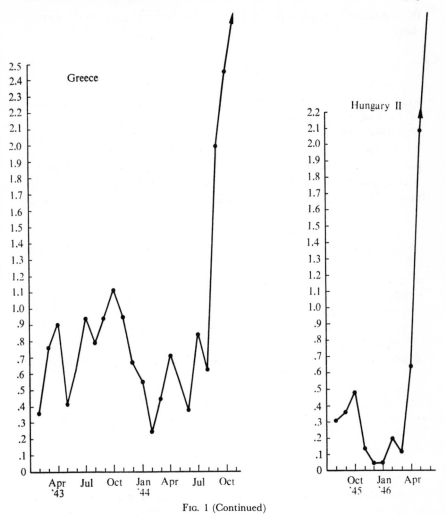

FIG. 1 (Continued)

necessary, consider using least squares to estimate the parameters of the equation

$$\left(\log_e \frac{M}{P}\right)_t = \sum_{i=0}^{\infty} h_i X_{t-i} + \psi + U_t \tag{28}$$

where $h_i = \alpha(1 - \lambda)\lambda^i$. Let us assume that the ε's in (27) are so small that they can be neglected, which amounts to ruling out "exogenous" changes in money creation, i.e., changes not governed by expected inflation. On this assumption, application of Theil's (1961) specification theorem shows that[10]

$$\text{plim } \widehat{h}_i = \alpha(1 - \lambda)\lambda^i - [\lambda + \alpha(1 - \lambda)]\lambda^i$$
$$= -\lambda\lambda^i \tag{29}$$

where $\widehat{h}_i$ is the least-squares estimate of h_i in (28), and where we have used (27) to obtain the regression of U_t on current and lagged X's. Equation (29) shows that least squares produces a consistent estimate of λ, but an inconsistent estimate of α, one whose probability limit does not even depend on α. The parameter α is usually estimated by taking note of the fact that $h_0 = \alpha(1 - \lambda)$ and estimating α by $\widehat{\alpha} = \widehat{h}_0/(1 - \widehat{\lambda})$ where hats denote least-squares estimates of the indicated parameters. Then (29) implies that

$$\text{plim } \widehat{\alpha} = \frac{-\lambda}{1 - \lambda}. \tag{30}$$

The implication is that, on the assumptions maintained here, λ can be reliably estimated by least squares, while the least-squares estimate of α conveys no information about α.

In the light of these calculations, it is interesting to review Cagan's (1956) and Barro's (1970) estimates of equation (1'), which we record in tables 7 and 8. We have recorded values of $-\widehat{\lambda}/(1 - \widehat{\lambda})$, so that the reader

---

[10]Substituting (27) into (1') and using the assumption that ε_t is zero for all t yields the following exact relationship between M/P and X:

$$\log\left(\frac{M}{P}\right)_t = \frac{\alpha(1 - \lambda) - [\lambda + \alpha(1 - \lambda)]}{1 - \lambda L}X_t + \gamma Y + \psi$$

or

$$\log\left(\frac{M}{P}\right)_t = -\lambda \sum_{i=0}^{\infty} \lambda^i X_{t-i} + \gamma Y + \psi.$$

Notice that (29) and (30) would continue to hold if the data on M_t were polluted by errors of measurement, so long as those errors were uncorrelated with current and lagged X's.

TABLE 7

CAGAN'S ESTIMATES OF α AND λ

Country	Time Period	$\widehat{\lambda}$	$\dfrac{-\widehat{\lambda}}{1 - \widehat{\lambda}}$	$\widehat{\alpha}$
Austria	Jan. 1921–Aug. 1922	.95	−19.5	−8.55
Germany	Sept. 1920–July 1923	.82	−4.5	−5.46
Greece	Jan. 1943–Aug. 1944	.86	−6.2	−4.09
Hungary	July 1922–Feb. 1924	.90	−9.5	−8.70
Hungary	July 1945–Feb. 1946	.86	−6.2	−3.63
Poland	Apr. 1922–Nov. 1923	.74	−2.9	−2.30
Russia	Dec. 1921–Jan. 1924	.70	−2.4	−3.06

SOURCE.—Cagan (1956), table 3.

TABLE 8

BARRO'S ESTIMATES OF α AND λ

Country	Time Period	$\hat{\lambda}$	$\dfrac{-\hat{\lambda}}{1 - \hat{\lambda}}$	$\hat{\alpha}$
Austria	Jan. 1921–Dec. 1922	.829	−4.85	−4.09
Germany	Jan. 1921–Aug. 1923	.824	−4.68	−3.79
Hungary	Oct. 1921–Feb. 1924	.861	−6.19	−5.53
Poland	Jan. 1922–Jan. 1924	.709	−2.44	−2.56

SOURCE.—Barro (1970), table 3.

can compare them with the estimates of α. Both Cagan's and Barro's estimates reveal a tendency for the absolute values of $\hat{\lambda}$ and $\hat{\alpha}$ to vary directly with one another. That is a pattern predicted by equation (30). In fact, $-\hat{\lambda}/(1 - \hat{\lambda})$ is often contained in the confidence interval around $\hat{\alpha}$ reported by Cagan and Barro. These results seem largely compatible with the view that the least-squares estimates of α convey little or no information about the population parameter α.

3. Conclusions

Cagan's adaptive mechanism for explaining expectations of inflation has sometimes been criticized as an *ad hoc* formulation that is inconsistent with the hypothesis that expectations are rational (e.g., Walters 1971). In this paper, we have showed that conditions exist under which adaptive expectations are fully rational. One essential condition is the presence of feedback from inflation to subsequent rates of money creation. Such feedback appears to have been present in at least several of the hyperinflations that we have studied. This might be explained by the government's resorting to money creation in order to finance its expenditures. Our empirical results indicate that to explain the hyperinflations it is not adequate to regard money creation as exogenous with respect to inflation. Instead, the monetary authorities seemed to make money creation respond directly and systematically to inflation, which was probably an important reason that the hyperinflations developed.

References

Barro, Robert J. "Inflation, the Payments Period, and the Demand for Money." *J.P.E.* 78 (November/December 1970): 1228–63.

Cagan, Phillip. "The Monetary Dynamics of Hyperinflation." In *Studies in the Quantity Theory of Money*, edited by Milton Friedman. Chicago: Univ. Chicago Press, 1956.

Friedman, Milton. "Government Revenue from Inflation." *J.P.E.* 79 (July/August 1971): 846–55.

Granger, C. W. J. "Investigating Causal Relations by Econometric Models and Cross-Spectral Methods." *Econometrica* 37 (July 1969): 424–38.

Hildreth, C., and Lu, J. Y. *Demand Relations with Autocorrelated Disturbances.* Technical Bulletin 276. East Lansing: Michigan State Univ., Agricultural Station, 1960.

Klein, L. R. "The Estimation of Distributed Lags." *Econometrica* 26 (October 1958): 553–61.

Lucas, Robert E., Jr. "Econometric Testing of the Natural Rate Hypothesis." Manuscript, October 1970.

Muth, John F. "Rational Expectations and the Theory of Price Movements." *Econometrica* 29 (July 1961): 315–35.

———. "Optimal Properties of Exponentially Weighted Forecasts." *J. Amer. Statis. Assoc.* 55 (June 1960): 299–306.

Sims, Christopher A. "Money, Income, and Causality." Manuscript, February 1971, Nat. Bur. Econ. Res.

Theil, H. *Economic Forecasts and Policy.* Amsterdam: North-Holland, 1961.

Wallace, Neil. "A Static Nonstationary Analysis of the Interaction Between Monetary and Fiscal Policy." Univ. Minnesota, Econ. Discussion Paper no. 9, August 1971.

Walters, A. A. "Consistent Expectations, Distributed Lags, and the Quantity Theory." *Econ. J.* 81 (June 1971): 273–81.

23

The Demand for Money during Hyperinflations under Rational Expectations

Thomas J. Sargent

This paper proposes methods for estimating the demand schedule for money that Cagan used in his famous study of hyperinflation (1956). Wallace and I (Sargent and Wallace 1973) pointed out that under assumptions that make Cagan's adaptive expectations scheme equivalent with assuming rational expectations, Cagan's estimator of α, which is the slope of the log of the demand for real balances with respect to expected inflation, is not statistically consistent. This is interesting in light of a paradox that emerged when Cagan used his estimates of α to calculate the sustained rates of inflation associated with the maximum flow of real resources that the creators of money could command by printing money. This "optimal" rate of inflation turns out to be $-1/\alpha$. For each of the seven hyperinflations, the reciprocal of Cagan's estimate of $-\alpha$ turned out to be less, and often very much less, than the actual average rate of inflation. The data are shown in table 1, which reproduces a table of Cagan's. Cagan's estimates imply that the creators of money expanded the money supply at rates that far exceeded the sustained rates which maximized the real revenues they could obtain. A natural first thing to consider in explaining this apparently irrational behavior by the creators of money is the possibility that it is a statistical artifact, namely, a consequence of using bad estimates of α.

This paper aims to complete a task begun by Wallace and me (Sargent and Wallace 1973), namely, the analysis of Cagan's model of hyperinflation under circumstances in which Cagan's "adaptive" scheme for forming expectations of inflation is equivalent with expectations that are "ra-

Research on this paper was supported by the Federal Reserve Bank of Minneapolis, which doesn't necessarily endorse the conclusions. Helpful comments on an earlier draft were received from Christopher Sims, Thomas Turner, John Geweke, Milton Friedman, Jacob Frenkel, Robert E. Lucas, Jr., and Rusdu Saracoglu. Rusdu Saracoglu performed the calculations using a computer program that he wrote for estimating bivariate mixed moving average, autoregressive models.

[*International Economic Review*, 1977, vol. 18, no. 1]

TABLE 1

	(1)	(2)	(3)
Austria	.117	12	47
Germany	.183	20	322
Greece	.244	28	365
Hungary I	.115	12	46
Hungary II	.236	32	19,800
Poland	.435	54	81
Russia	.327	39	57

Note.—Col. (1) $= -1/\hat{\alpha}$ (continuous compounding), rate per month that maximizes revenue of money creator; col. (2) $= (e^{-1/\alpha} - 1)$ 100 (neglects compounding); col. (3) = average actual rate of inflation per month.
Source.—Cagan (1956, fig. 9).

tional" in Muth's sense (1961). The model is a very simple simultaneous-equations model of the inflation-money creation process, one equation of which turns out to be identical with Cagan's simple portfolio equilibrium equation. As Wallace and I have argued, Cagan's use of single equations methods exposed him to the possibility of severe simultaneous-equations bias. The present paper uses the full information maximum likelihood estimator to obtain a consistent estimator of Cagan's model. It also obtains an expression for the statistical inconsistency of Cagan's estimator for his model under the circumstances in which adaptive expectations coincide with rational expectations.

One way of justifying imposing rational expectations on Cagan's model is that it enables one to specify a complete model of the inflation–money creation process in a very economical way. This is a virtue, since the time series from the hyperinflations are too short to permit estimating complicated parameterizations. But a more important reason for using the hypothesis of rational expectations to complete Cagan's model is that doing so delivers an econometric model that is seemingly consistent with the exogeneity (or "causal") structure exhibited by the money creation–inflation process during the seven hyperinflations studied by Cagan. Empirical tests by Wallace and me typically indicated substantial evidence of feedback from inflation to money creation, with markedly less feedback from money creation to inflation. Cagan's model under rational expectations predicts a particular extreme version of such a pattern: it predicts that inflation "causes" (in Granger's sense) money creation with no reverse feedback (or "causality") from money creation to inflation. Cagan's model with rational expectations thus seems to provide one way of explaining the Granger–causal structure exhibited in the data.

Cagan's paper is rightly regarded as one of the best pieces of empirical work ever done in economics. His model and his estimation method have been applied with apparent success to a number of additional countries experiencing high inflation rates, but rates falling short of those character-izing hyperinflations.[1] The key substantive conclusion that has been drawn from Cagan's study, and those subsequent studies as well, is that even in the apparently chaotic conditions of rampant inflation it is possi-ble to isolate a stable demand schedule for money having real balances varying inversely with the expected rate of inflation. In the light of the results of this paper, that conclusion must be severely modified. First, it is shown below that under conditions that make Cagan's model equivalent with assuming "rational" expectations, the slope parameter α is not econometrically identifiable. To identify α requires imposing a restriction on the covariance of the disturbances to the demand for money and to the supply of money. Neither economic theorizing nor intuition seems to pro-vide a ready restriction on that covariance. Proceeding on the "neutral" assumption that that covariance is zero, one can extract estimates of α. But even then, the estimates of α are characterized by large standard errors.

From a technical point of view, this paper is an exercise in applying vector time series models. The key references are Granger (1969), Sims (1972), Wilson (1973), Porter (1974), and Zellner and Palm (1974). The model studied here is an interesting one from the point of view of the vector time series model, since it is one in which inflation "causes" money creation in Granger's sense, although these two series are supposed to be perfectly in phase, so that neither one "leads" the other. The model thus provides an example that illustrates the difference between Granger's cau-sality and simple notions of the lead of one series over another. The model is also interesting because it illustrates the very important difference be-tween Granger causality and a separate notion of causality often used by economists, namely, that of invariance with respect to an intervention. The present model predicts that money "causes" inflation in the sense that a given change in the stochastic process or "feedback rule" governing the money supply will produce a determinate change in the stochastic process for inflation. The stochastic process for inflation is an invariant function of the stochastic process governing money creation. In Cagan's model with rational expectations imposed, inflation Granger-causes money creation with no reverse Granger causality from money to inflation because the system is operating under a particular money supply rule that in effect prevents the money supply from being of any use in predicting subsequent rates of inflation. If there is a change in monetary regime, that is, a switch in the money supply rule, the economic model predicts that the Granger-causality structure of the money-inflation process will change.

---

[1]Among such studies are some of those in Meiselman (1970).

I. The Model

Cagan's model of hyperinflation builds on a demand schedule for real balances of the form

$$m_t - p_t = \alpha \pi_t + u_t, \quad \alpha < 0 \tag{1}$$

where m is the log of the money supply (which is always equal to the log of the money demand); p is the log of the price level; π_t is the expected rate of inflation, i.e., the public's psychological expectation of $p_{t+1} - p_t$; and u_t is a random variable with mean zero. I have omitted a constant term from (1), though one would be included in empirical work. Cagan assumed that π_t was formed via the adaptive expectations scheme

$$\pi_t = \frac{1 - \lambda}{1 - \lambda L}(p_t - p_{t-1})$$

or

$$\pi_t = \frac{1 - \lambda}{1 - \lambda L}x_t \tag{2}$$

where $x_t = p_t - p_{t-1}$, the rate of inflation, and where L is the lag operator defined by $L^n x_t = x_{t-n}$.

Under rational expectations we require that

$$\pi_t = E_t x_{t+1}, \tag{3}$$

where $E_t x_{t+1}$ is the mathematical expectation of x_{t+1} conditional on information available as of time t.[2] Using (3) and recursions on (1), it is straightforward to show that under rational expectations we must have[3]

$$\pi_t = E_t x_{t+1} = \frac{1}{1 - \alpha} \sum_{j=1}^{\infty} \left(\frac{-\alpha}{1 - \alpha}\right)^{j-1} E_t \mu_{t+j}$$

$$- \frac{1}{1 - \alpha} \sum_{j=1}^{\infty} \left(\frac{-\alpha}{1 - \alpha}\right)^{j-1} (E_t u_{t+j} - E_t u_{t+j-1}) \tag{4}$$

---

[2] I assume that the information available consists (at least) of observations of current and past μ's and current and past x's. Thus $E_t x_{t+1} \equiv E[x_{t+1} | \mu_t, \mu_t, \ldots, x_t, x_{t-1}, \ldots]$. Similarly, where z_t is any arbitrary random variable, I will write $E_t z_{t+1}$ for $E[z_{t+1} | \mu_t, \mu_{t-1}, \ldots, x_t, x_{t-1}, \ldots]$.

[3] Substituting (3) into (1), first differencing, and shifting the time subscripts forward one period gives

$$\mu_{t+1} - x_{t+1} = \alpha E_{t+1} x_{t+2} - \alpha x_{t+1} + (u_{t+1} - u_t).$$

Taking expectations conditional on information available at time t gives

$$E_t x_{t+1} = \frac{1}{1 - \alpha} E_t \mu_{t+1} - \frac{\alpha}{1 - \alpha} E_t x_{t+2} - (E_t u_{t+1} - E_t u_t).$$

Recursion on the above difference equation shows that equation (4) is indeed a solution to that equation.

where $\mu_t = m_t - m_{t-1}$, the percentage rate of increase of the money supply. Equation (4) characterizes the (systematic part of the) stochastic process for inflation as a function of the (systematic part of the) stochastic process for money creation. The model asserts that (4) is invariant with respect to interventions in the form of changes in the stochastic process governing money creation. In this sense, since changes in the stochastic process for money creation are supposed to produce predictable changes in the stochastic process for inflation, money "causes" inflation.

For Cagan's adaptive expectation scheme (2) to be equivalent to rational expectations we require:

$$\frac{1-\lambda}{1-\lambda L}x_t = \frac{1}{1-\alpha}\sum_{j=1}^{\infty}\left(\frac{-\alpha}{1-\alpha}\right)^{j-1}E_t\mu_{t+j}$$

$$-\frac{1}{1-\alpha}\sum_{j=1}^{\infty}\left(\frac{-\alpha}{1-\alpha}\right)^{j-1}(E_tu_{t+j}-E_tu_{t+j-1}).$$ (5)

The necessary and sufficient condition for (5) to hold for all α and all t is

$$E_t\mu_{t+j} - E_t(u_{t+j}-u_{t+j-1}) = \frac{1-\lambda}{1-\lambda L}x_t.$$

For an arbitrary μ process, there exists a disturbance process u_t satisfying the above restriction, one in which $E_t(u_{t+j}-u_{t+j-1})$ is a complicated function of lagged x's and lagged μ's. From my point of view, however, the most fruitful conditions to impose are the following two that are sufficient (though clearly not necessary) to satisfy (5). The first condition is

$$u_t = u_{t-1} + \eta_t$$ (6)

where η_t is a serially uncorrelated random term with mean zero and variance σ_η^2; I assume that $E[\eta_t \,|\, \mu_{t-1}, \mu_{t-2}, \ldots, x_{t-1}, x_{t-2}, \ldots] = 0$. According to (6), u takes a random walk. Equation (6) implies that

$$E_tu_{t+j} = u_t, \quad j \geq 0$$

which implies that

$$E_tu_{t+j} - E_tu_{t+j-1} = 0 \quad \text{for all } j \geq 1.$$

The second of my pair of sufficient conditions for (5) is

$$E_t\mu_{t+j} = E_t\mu_{t+1} \quad \text{for } j > 1,$$ (7)

so that a constant rate of money creation is expected to occur over the entire future. Assuming (6) and (7) then implies that the appropriate version of (5) is[4]

$$\left(\frac{1-\lambda}{1-\lambda L}\right)x_t = E_t\mu_{t+1}\frac{1}{1-\alpha}\sum_{j=1}^{\infty}\left(\frac{-\alpha}{1-\alpha}\right)^{j-1}$$

or

$$\frac{1-\lambda}{1-\lambda L}x_t = E_t\mu_{t+1}. \tag{8}$$

A process that satisfies (8) is

$$\mu_t = \left(\frac{1-\lambda}{1-\lambda L}\right)x_t + \varepsilon_t(= E_t x_{t+1} + \varepsilon_t) \tag{9}$$

where ε_t is a serially uncorrelated random term with mean zero and variance σ_ε^2, and that satisfies

$$E(\varepsilon_t \mid x_{t-1}, x_{t-2}, \ldots, \mu_{t-1}, \mu_{t-2}, \ldots) = 0.$$

According to (9), the rate of money creation equals the expected rate of inflation plus a random term. Equation (9), which has been arrived at in a purely mechanical fashion by pursuing the implications of the assumption that Cagan's adaptive expectations scheme is rational, is nevertheless of interest as an hypothesis about the government's behavior. For example, if the government is creating money to finance a large part of a roughly fixed rate of real government purchases, then there is a presumption that inflation and expected inflation will feed back into money creation, an implication with which (9) is consistent. Thus, when π_t increases, causing $m_t - p_t$ to fall and thereby causing p_t to rise with a fixed m_t, money depreciates in value, prompting the creators of money to increase the rate of printing money in order to maintain their command over the flow of real resources (see Sargent and Wallace 1973). Alternatively, equation (9) is compatible with a "real bills" regime in which the monetary authority sets out to

[4]To see that process (9) satisfies (8), write (9) as

$$\mu_{t+1} = (1-\lambda)x_{t+1} + \frac{(1-\lambda)}{1-\lambda L}x_t + \varepsilon_{t+1}.$$

Taking expectations conditional on information available at t, we have

$$E_t\mu_{t+1} = (1-\lambda)E_t x_{t+1} + \frac{(1-\lambda)\lambda}{1-\lambda L}x_t.$$

But $E_t x_{t+1} = \frac{1-\lambda}{1-\lambda L}x_t$, so that we have

$$E_t\mu_{t+1} = [(1-\lambda) + \lambda]\left(\frac{1-\lambda}{1-\lambda L}\right)x_t$$

$$E_t\mu_{t+1} = \frac{1-\lambda}{1-\lambda L}x_t,$$

as required.

supply whatever money the public demands at some fixed nominal interest rate or some fixed real money supply. Equation (9) looks like a rule in which the monetary authority is attempting to peg the (rate of growth of the) real money supply. During the German hyperinflation, German monetary officials in effect repeatedly acknowledged that they were operating under a real-bills regime, acknowledgments made in efforts to argue that their actions were not causing the inflation but were merely responses to it.

The foregoing establishes that if equations (6) and (9) obtain, Cagan's adaptive expectations scheme is compatible with rational expectations and with the portfolio balance condition that he assumed. Under these assumptions, inflation and money creation form a bivariate stochastic process given by

$$\mu_t - x_t = \alpha(1 - L)\left(\frac{1 - \lambda}{1 - \lambda L}\right)x_t + \eta_t \qquad (10)$$

$$\mu_t = \left(\frac{1 - \lambda}{1 - \lambda L}\right)x_t + \varepsilon_t. \qquad (9)$$

Equation (10) was obtained by first differencing (1) and then substituting for π_t from (2) and for $u_t - u_{t-1}$ from (6). The process (10)–(9) can be rewritten as

$$(1 - L)x_t = [\lambda + \alpha(1 - \lambda)]^{-1}(1 - \lambda L)(\varepsilon_t - \eta_t) \qquad (11)$$

$$(1 - L)\mu_t = [(\lambda + \alpha(1 - \lambda))^{-1}](1 - \lambda)(\varepsilon_t - \eta_t) - \varepsilon_{t-1} + \varepsilon_t. \qquad (12)$$

Equations (11) and (12) can be derived directly from (10) and (9); alternatively, see Sargent and Wallace for a somewhat different but equivalent way of deriving (11) and (12).

The statistical model (11)–(12) was constructed in a fashion to guarantee the condition

$$E_t x_{t+1} = \frac{1 - \lambda}{1 - \lambda L}x_t$$

a condition that implies that λ does not Granger-cause x. For the above equation states that once lagged x's are taken into account, lagged μ's don't help predict current x, which is Granger's definition of μ's not causing x. It bears mentioning that the statistical model inherits its Granger-causal structure in large part from the particular conditions (6) and (7). The statistical model (11)–(12) is *not* invariant with respect to an intervention in the form of a change in the money supply rule. Rather, it is equation (4) that is supposed to be invariant with respect to interventions in the form of changes in monetary regime. According to (4), changes in the μ_t process—which show up in changes in the (functions) $E_t \mu_{t+j}$—result in changes in the systematic part of the inflation process, $E_t x_{t+1}$. Thus, one cannot expect the Granger-causal structure of the present model to survive interruptions in monetary regimes.

II. The Bias in Cagan's Estimator

A convenient way to evaluate the (asymptotic) bias in Cagan's estimator is first to obtain a bivariate Wold representation[5] for $(\Delta x_t, \Delta \mu_t)$. Write (11) and (12) as

$$(1 - L)x_t = \phi(1 - \lambda L)(\varepsilon_t - \eta_t) \tag{13}$$

$$(1 - L)\mu_t = \phi(1 - \lambda)(\varepsilon_t - \eta_t) + (1 - L)\varepsilon_t \tag{14}$$

where $\phi = [\lambda + \alpha(1 - \lambda)]^{-1}$. Next decompose ε_t according to

$$\varepsilon_t = E[\varepsilon_t | \varepsilon_t - \eta_t] + v_t$$

or

$$\varepsilon_t = \rho(\varepsilon_t - \eta_t) + v_t \tag{15}$$

where $E[v_t | \varepsilon_t - \eta_t] = 0$ and ρ is the regression coefficient of ε_t on $(\varepsilon_t - \eta_t)$. Substituting (15) into (14) gives

$$(1 - L)\mu_t = [\phi(1 - \lambda) + \rho(1 - L)](\varepsilon_t - \eta_t) + (1 - L)v_t. \tag{16}$$

Since v_t is orthogonal to $(\varepsilon_t - \eta_t)$ and is serially uncorrelated by construction (recall that $v_t = \varepsilon_t - \rho[\varepsilon_t - \eta_t]$, where ε_t and η_t are serially uncorrelated), it follows that (13) and (16) form a (triangular) bivariate Wold representation for $(\Delta x_t, \Delta \mu_t)$ with fundamental noises $(\varepsilon_t - \eta_t)$ and v_t. The existence of a triangular bivariate Wold representation verifies that Δx is econometrically exogenous with respect to $\Delta \mu$ and that $\Delta \mu$ does not cause Δx in Granger's sense (see Sims 1972). It also makes it very easy to determine the population projection of $\Delta \mu$ on current and past Δx's, from which the asymptotic bias in Cagan's estimator is calculable.

From (13) notice that

$$\varepsilon_t - \eta_t = \phi^{-1}\frac{(1 - L)}{1 - \lambda L}x_t. \tag{17}$$

To obtain the projection of $\Delta \mu_t$ against current and past (and future) Δx's, substitute (17) into (16) to get

$$(1 - L)\mu_t = [\phi(1 - \lambda) + (1 - L)\rho]\phi^{-1}\frac{(1 - L)}{1 - \lambda L}x_t + (1 - L)v_t.$$

Dividing through by $(1 - L)$ gives

$$\mu_t = \left[\frac{1 - \lambda}{1 - \lambda L} + \frac{(1 - L)\rho\phi^{-1}}{1 - \lambda L}\right]x_t + v_t$$

$$\mu_t = \left\{\frac{1 - \lambda + \rho[\lambda + \alpha(1 - \lambda)](1 - L)}{1 - \lambda L}\right\}x_t + v_t. \tag{18}$$

[5]The most readily accessible reference in economics on the multivariate Wold representation is Sims (1972), especially the appendix.

Recall from (13) that the v_t process is orthogonal to the x process. Therefore, equation (18) gives the projection of μ_t on x. Subtracting x_t from both sides gives the projection of $\mu_t - x_t$ against x_t:

$$\mu_t - x_t = \left\{ \frac{1 - \lambda + \rho[\lambda + \alpha(1 - \lambda)](1 - L) - (1 - \lambda L)}{1 - \lambda L} \right\} x_t + v_t$$

or

$$\mu_t - x_t = \frac{\{-\lambda + \rho[\lambda + \alpha(1 - \lambda)]\}(1 - L)}{(1 - \lambda L)} x_t + v_t. \qquad (19)$$

Operating on (19) with the "summation" operator $(1 - L)^{-1}$ gives

$$m_t - p_t = \frac{\{-\lambda + \rho[\lambda + \alpha(1 - \lambda)]\}}{1 - \lambda L} x_t + \xi_t \qquad (20)$$

where $\xi_t = \xi_{t-1} + v_t$. Equation (20) is the projection that Cagan estimated by (nonlinear) least-squares regression. Notice that the residuals in (20) follow a random walk. It is noteworthy in this regard that the residuals in Cagan's and Barro's estimates of (20) were highly serially correlated, Barro reporting very low values for Durbin-Watson statistics.

Now Cagan regarded the projection (20) as giving estimates of the equation

$$m_t - p_t = \frac{\alpha(1 - \lambda)}{1 - \lambda L} x_t + u_t. \qquad (21)$$

Least-squares regression consistently estimates the parameters of the population projection (20)—only those parameters are not in general the same ones Cagan took them to be. Comparison of (20) with (21) shows that Cagan's estimator of λ is consistent but that his estimator of α is not in general consistent, and will obey

$$\text{plim } \widehat{\alpha}(1 - \widehat{\lambda}) = \{-\lambda + \rho[\lambda + \alpha(1 - \lambda)]\}$$

which implies that

$$\text{plim } \widehat{\alpha} = \rho\alpha + (1 - \rho)\left(\frac{-\lambda}{1 - \lambda}\right). \qquad (22)$$

Notice that if $\rho = 0$, which will be true if $\varepsilon_t = 0$ for all t, (22) implies

$$\text{plim } \widehat{\alpha} = \frac{-\lambda}{1 - \lambda},$$

which is an expression that Wallace and I derived and used. On the other hand, if $\eta_t = 0$ for all t, so that there is no noise in the portfolio balance schedule, from (15) $\rho = 1$, which with (22) implies

$$\text{plim } \widehat{\alpha} = \alpha,$$

so that in this special case Cagan's estimator of α is consistent (and furthermore unbiased as it turns out, since $v_t = 0$ for all t).

On the special assumption $\sigma_{\varepsilon\eta} = 0$, we have

$$\rho = \frac{E[\varepsilon_t \cdot (\varepsilon_t - \eta_t)]}{E(\varepsilon_t - \eta_t)^2} = \frac{\sigma_\varepsilon^2}{\sigma_\varepsilon^2 + \sigma_\eta^2}.$$

Alternatively, multiplying (15) by η_t, taking expectations, and rearranging gives

$$\rho = \frac{\sigma_{v\eta}}{\sigma_\eta^2},$$

so that ρ is the regression coefficient of the residual v in the regression of
$(\mu - x)$ against current and past $(1 - L)x$ on the disturbance in the demand for money. If $v = \eta$, then $\rho = 1$.

An estimate of ρ could be obtained in the following way, again on the
special assumption $\sigma_{\varepsilon\eta} = 0$. Multiplying (15) by ε_t, taking expectations
and rearranging gives

$$\rho = 1 - \frac{\sigma_{v\varepsilon}}{\sigma_\varepsilon^2}.$$

The magnitude $\sigma_{v\varepsilon}/\sigma_\varepsilon^2$ is the regression coefficient of v on ε. The residual v
can be estimated by the residual in (the first difference of) Cagan's equa-
tion. The variable ε_t can be extracted using the methods described below
in Section IV. Then an estimate of ρ could be prepared using the above
equation. It would be possible to use that estimate of ρ to correct Cagan's
estimate of α by applying the formula

$$\text{plim } \widehat{\alpha} = \rho\alpha + (1 - \rho)\left(\frac{-\lambda}{1 - \lambda}\right).$$

The calculations in this section provide a useful exercise in interpreting
systems in which one variable (x) is econometrically exogenous with respect to (is not Granger-caused by) another variable (μ). In such a system,
as Sims's Theorem 2 assures us and as the preceding calculations verify,
the regression of μ on past, present, and future x's is one-sided on the
present and past. Thus, there exist representations (models) of the (μ, x)
process in which μ and $(\mu - x)$ are each one-sided linear functions of past
and present x's with disturbances that are orthogonal to past, present, and
future x's—so that in these relations x is strictly exogenous with respect to
μ and $(\mu - x)$, respectively. But the representation in which x is econometrically exogenous with respect to $(\mu - x)$—which is the relation that can be
consistently estimated by least squares or generalized least squares—is *not*
the demand function for money, which is the structural relation we are
interested in estimating. The reason is that in the structural relation (21),
u_t is not in general orthogonal to the x process. The upshot is that finding

that x is exogenous with respect to $(\mu - x)$ does not guarantee that the one-sided $(\mu - x)$ on x distributed lag regression which is estimable by single equation methods corresponds to the structural relation that we're interested in.

III. A Consistent Estimator

Equations (11) and (12) form a bivariate first-order moving average process in $(1 - L)\mu_t$ and $(1 - L)x_t$. Assuming that the white noises ε_t and η_t are jointly normally distributed, the likelihood function of a sample of length T observations, $t = 1, \ldots, T$, generated by (11)–(12) can be written down. To apply the method of maximum likelihood, it is most convenient to write the model in its vector autoregressive form. First note that from (9) we can write

$$\varepsilon_t = \mu_t - \frac{1 - \lambda}{1 - \lambda L} x_t. \tag{23}$$

Next from (11) we have

$$\varepsilon_t - \eta_t = \frac{[\lambda + \alpha(1 - \lambda)](1 - L)}{1 - \lambda L} x_t \tag{24}$$

Substituting (24) into (23) and rearranging gives

$$\eta_t = \mu_t - \left\{ \frac{1 - \lambda + [\lambda + \alpha(1 - \lambda)](1 - L)}{1 - \lambda L} \right\} x_t. \tag{25}$$

In vector notation equations (23) and (25) can be written

$$\begin{bmatrix} \varepsilon_t \\ \\ \eta_t \end{bmatrix} = \begin{bmatrix} -\dfrac{(1 - \lambda)}{1 - -L} & 1 \\ \\ -\dfrac{\{1 - \lambda + [\lambda + \alpha(1 - \lambda)](1 - L)\}}{1 - \lambda L} & 1 \end{bmatrix} \begin{bmatrix} x_t \\ \\ \mu_t \end{bmatrix}.$$

Multiplying both sides of the equation by $(1 - \lambda L)\, I$ where I is the 2×2 identity matrix, gives

$$\begin{bmatrix} (1 - \lambda L)\varepsilon_t \\ (1 - \lambda L)\eta_t \end{bmatrix} = \begin{bmatrix} -(1 - \lambda) & 1 - \lambda L \\ -\{1 - \lambda + [\lambda + \alpha(1 - \lambda)](1 - L)\} & 1 - \lambda L \end{bmatrix} \begin{bmatrix} x_t \\ \mu_t \end{bmatrix}$$

or

$$\begin{bmatrix} \varepsilon_t \\ \eta_t \end{bmatrix} - \lambda I \begin{bmatrix} \varepsilon_{t-1} \\ \eta_{t-1} \end{bmatrix} = \begin{bmatrix} -(1 - \lambda) & 1 \\ -[1 + \alpha(1 - \lambda)] & 1 \end{bmatrix} \begin{bmatrix} x_t \\ \mu_t \end{bmatrix}$$
$$+ \begin{bmatrix} 0 & -\lambda \\ \lambda + \alpha(1 - \lambda) & -\lambda \end{bmatrix} \begin{bmatrix} x_{t-1} \\ \mu_{t-1} \end{bmatrix}.$$

Let

$$G_0 = \begin{bmatrix} -(1 - \lambda) & 1 \\ -[1 + \alpha(1 - \lambda)] & 1 \end{bmatrix}.$$

Premultiplying the preceding equation by

$$G_0^{-1} = \begin{bmatrix} 1 & -1 \\ 1 + \alpha(1 - \lambda) & -(1 - \lambda) \end{bmatrix} / [\lambda + \alpha(1 - \lambda)]$$

gives

$$G_0^{-1}\begin{bmatrix} \varepsilon_t \\ \eta_t \end{bmatrix} - \lambda I G_0^{-1}\begin{bmatrix} \varepsilon_{t-1} \\ \eta_{t-1} \end{bmatrix} = \begin{bmatrix} x_t \\ \mu_t \end{bmatrix} + G_0^{-1}\begin{bmatrix} 0 & -\lambda \\ \lambda + \alpha(1 - \lambda) & -\lambda \end{bmatrix}\begin{bmatrix} x_{t-1} \\ \mu_{t-1} \end{bmatrix}$$

or

$$\begin{bmatrix} a_{1t} \\ a_{2t} \end{bmatrix} - \lambda I \begin{bmatrix} a_{1t-1} \\ a_{2t-1} \end{bmatrix} = \begin{bmatrix} x_t \\ \mu_t \end{bmatrix} + G_0^{-1}\begin{bmatrix} 0 & -\lambda \\ \lambda + \alpha(- \lambda) & -\lambda \end{bmatrix}\begin{bmatrix} x_{t-1} \\ \mu_{t-1} \end{bmatrix} \quad (26)$$

where

$$\begin{bmatrix} a_{1t} \\ a_{2t} \end{bmatrix} \equiv G_0^{-1}\begin{bmatrix} \varepsilon_t \\ \eta_t \end{bmatrix}.$$

Computing

$$G_0^{-1}\begin{bmatrix} 0 & -\lambda \\ \lambda + \alpha(1 - \lambda) & -\lambda \end{bmatrix}$$

explicitly and rearranging the above equation gives

$$\begin{bmatrix} x_t \\ \mu_t \end{bmatrix} = \begin{bmatrix} 1 & 0 \\ (1 - \lambda) & \lambda \end{bmatrix}\begin{bmatrix} x_{t-1} \\ \mu_{t-1} \end{bmatrix} + \begin{bmatrix} a_{1t} \\ a_{2t} \end{bmatrix} - \lambda I \begin{bmatrix} a_{1t-1} \\ a_{2t-1} \end{bmatrix}. \quad (27)$$

Equation (27) is a vector first order autoregression, first-order moving average process. The random variables a_{1t}, a_{2t} are the innovations in the x and μ processes, respectively. They are the one period-ahead forecasting errors for x_t and μ_t, respectively. The a's are related to the ε's and η's appearing in the structural equations of the model by

$$\begin{bmatrix} a_{1t} \\ a_{2t} \end{bmatrix} = G_0^{-1}\begin{bmatrix} \varepsilon_t \\ \eta_t \end{bmatrix}$$

$$\begin{bmatrix} a_{1t} \\ \\ a_{2t} \end{bmatrix} = \begin{bmatrix} \dfrac{1}{\lambda + \alpha(1 - \lambda)}(\varepsilon_t - \eta_t) \\ \\ \dfrac{1 - \lambda}{\lambda + \alpha(1 - \lambda)}(\varepsilon_t - \eta_t) + \varepsilon_t \end{bmatrix}. \quad (28)$$

Notice that the first equation of (27) can be written as

$$(1 - L)x_t = (1 - \lambda L)a_{1t}.$$

It is straightforward to write this in the autoregressive form

$$x_t = \left(\frac{1 - \lambda}{1 - \lambda L}\right)x_{t-1} + a_{1t}. \tag{29}$$

Since $E_{t-1}a_{1t} = 0$, we have

$$E_{t-1}x_t = \left(\frac{1 - \lambda}{1 - \lambda L}\right)x_{t-1}.$$

The second equation of (27) can be written as

$$(1 - \lambda L)\mu_t = (1 - \lambda)x_{t-1} + (1 - \lambda L)a_{2t}$$

But from (29) we have $(1 - \lambda)x_{t-1} = (1 - \lambda L)x_t - (1 - \lambda L)a_{1t}$, which when substituted into the above equation gives

$$(1 - \lambda L)\mu_t = (1 - \lambda L)x_t - (1 - \lambda L)a_{1t} + (1 - \lambda L)a_{2t}$$

or

$$\mu_t = x_t + a_{2t} - a_{1t}. \tag{30}$$

From (30), it follows that

$$E_{t-1}\mu_t = E_{t-1}x_t. \tag{31}$$

The triangular character of representation (27) demonstrates that μ does not "cause" in Granger's sense (i.e., help predict, once lagged own values are taken into account) the variable x. That is, x is econometrically exogenous with respect to μ.[6] On the other hand, x_t does cause the variable μ_t. Even stronger, the model implies that $E_{t-1}\mu_t = E_{t-1}x_t = (1 - \lambda)/(1 - \lambda L)x_{t-1}$ so that lagged μ's don't help predict μ once lagged x's are taken into account.[7] That x causes μ in Granger's sense is not to be confused with x's "leading" μ in any National Bureau sense. On the contrary,

---

[6] Sims (1972) proved the equivalence of Granger causality with econometric exogeneity.

[7] Wallace and I were mistaken when we asserted that "the system is one in which expectations of money creation could equally well be formed as a distributed lag of past rates of money creation," (1973, p. 337). It is true that

$$E[\mu_t | \mu_{t-1}, \ldots] = \frac{1 - \gamma}{1 - \gamma L}\mu_{t-1},$$

where γ is a parameter that depends on the ratio of the variance of ε_t to the variance of η_t. However, in the model $E[\mu_t | \mu_{t-1}, \ldots] \neq E[\mu_t | \mu_{t-1}, \ldots, x_{t-1}, \ldots]$. Instead, $E[\mu_t | \mu_{t-1}, \ldots, x_{t-1}, \ldots] = E[\mu_t | x_{t-1}, \ldots]$, which, of course, has a smaller prediction error variance than $E[\mu_t | \mu_{t-1}, \ldots]$. The erroneous statements on page 337 of Sargent and Wallace (1973) amount to an assertion that the Wold representation of the $x_t - \mu_t$ process contains only one noise, so that lagged values of *either* x or μ exhaust all information in the past values of x *and* μ useful for predicting *either* x or μ. That is wrong, as the triangular Wold representation derived in Section III of this paper verifies. The upshot of all this is that it was not necessary for Sargent and Wallace to posit measurement errors in the money supply to rationalize the empirical observation that x causes μ. That is already an implication of the system free of measurement errors.

according to (30), x_t and μ_t are "in phase" with one another, neither one leading the other. (The phase of their cross-spectrum equals zero at all frequencies.) Evidence that x leads μ would not be consistent with the model being studied here.

The vector autoregressive, moving average process (27) is in a form that can be estimated by the maximum likelihood estimator described by Wilson (1973). It is essential that the matrices multiplying current $\begin{bmatrix} a_{1t} \\ a_{2t} \end{bmatrix}$ and current $\begin{bmatrix} x_t \\ \mu_t \end{bmatrix}$ both be identity matrices in order to apply the method, so that each a_i process can be interpreted as the residual from a vector autoregression either for μ_t or x_t. This is by way of getting things in a form in which the likelihood function of $\begin{bmatrix} x_t \\ \mu_t \end{bmatrix}$ equals the likelihood function of $\begin{bmatrix} a_{1t} \\ a_{2t} \end{bmatrix}$.

Let

$$a_t = \begin{bmatrix} a_{1t} \\ a_{2t} \end{bmatrix},$$

and let D_a be the covariance matrix of a_t,

$$D_a = \begin{bmatrix} \sigma_{11} & \sigma_{12} \\ \sigma_{12} & \sigma_{22} \end{bmatrix} = E a_t a_t'.$$

The likelihood function of the sample $t = 1, \ldots, T$ can now be written as

$$L(\lambda, \sigma_{11}, \sigma_{12}, \sigma_{22} \mid \mu_t, x_t) = (2\pi^{-T}) |D_a|^{-T/2} \exp\left(-\frac{1}{2} \sum_{t=1}^{T} a_t' D_a^{-1} a_t \right) \quad (32)$$

Given initial values for (a_{10}, a_{20}) or equivalently for (ε_0, η_0), and given a value of λ, equation (26) or (27) can be used to solve for a_t, $t = 1, \ldots, T$. (I will take $a_{10} = a_{20} = 0$.)

Wilson notes that maximizing (32) is equivalent with minimizing with respect to λ the determinant of the estimated covariance matrix of the a_t's,

$$|\widehat{D}_a| \equiv |T^{-1} \sum_{t=1}^{T} \widehat{a}_t \widehat{a}_t'| \quad (33)$$

where the $\widehat{a}_t$'s are determined by solving (27) recursively and so depend on λ. The covariance matrix of the a_t's is estimated as

$$\widehat{D}_a = T^{-1} \sum_{t=1}^{T} \widehat{a}_t \widehat{a}_t'$$

evaluated at the value of λ that minimizes (33). The resulting estimates are known to be statistically consistent (see Wilson 1973).

Notice that α does not appear explicitly in the likelihood function, but only indirectly by way of the elements of D_a, namely, σ_{11}, σ_{12}, and σ_{22}. That this must be so can be seen by inspecting representation (27), in which λ appears explicitly but α does not. On the basis of the *four* parameters λ, σ_{11}, σ_{12}, and σ_{22} that are identified by (27), i.e., that characterize the likelihood function (32), we can think of attempting to estimate the *five* parameters of the model α, λ, σ_ε^2, σ_η^2, and $\sigma_{\varepsilon\eta}$. Not surprisingly, some of the parameters are underidentified. In particular, while λ and σ_ε^2 are identified, α, σ_η^2, and $\sigma_{\varepsilon\eta}$ are not separately identified. To see that α and $\sigma_{\varepsilon\eta}$ are not identified consider the following argument. From equation (28), we know that the identifiable parameters σ_{11}, σ_{12}, and σ_{22} are related to the structural parameters σ_ε^2, σ_η^2, $\sigma_{\varepsilon\eta}$, α, and λ by

$$\sigma_{11} = \left[\frac{1}{\lambda + \alpha(1 - \lambda)}\right]^2 (\sigma_\varepsilon^2 + \sigma_\eta^2 - 2\sigma_{\varepsilon\eta}) \tag{34}$$

$$\sigma_{12} = \frac{(1 - \lambda)}{[\lambda + \alpha(1 - \lambda)]^2}(\sigma_\varepsilon^2 + \sigma_\eta^2 - 2\sigma_{\varepsilon\eta}) + \frac{1}{\lambda + \alpha(1 - \lambda)}(\sigma_\varepsilon^2 - \sigma_{\varepsilon\eta}) \tag{35}$$

$$\sigma_{22} = \left\{\frac{(1 - \lambda)}{[\lambda + \alpha(1 - \lambda)]}\right\}^2 (\sigma_\varepsilon^2 + \sigma_\eta^2 - 2\sigma_{\varepsilon\eta}) + \sigma_\varepsilon^2$$
$$+ 2\left(\frac{1 - \lambda}{\lambda + \alpha(1 - \lambda)}\right)(\sigma_\varepsilon^2 - \sigma_{\varepsilon\eta}). \tag{36}$$

These equations imply

$$\sigma_{12} = (1 - \lambda)\sigma_{11} + \frac{1}{\lambda + \alpha(1 - \lambda)}(\sigma_\varepsilon^2 - \sigma_{\varepsilon\eta}) \tag{37}$$

$$\sigma_{22} = (1 - \lambda)^2 \sigma_{11} + \sigma_\varepsilon^2 + \frac{2(1 - \lambda)}{\lambda + \alpha(1 - \lambda)}(\sigma_\varepsilon^2 - \sigma_{\varepsilon\eta}). \tag{38}$$

Do there exist offsetting changes in α and $\sigma_{\varepsilon\eta}$ that leave both of these equations satisfied with σ_{11}, σ_{22}, and σ_{12} unchanged? That is, holding λ and σ_ε^2 constant, can we change α and $\sigma_{\varepsilon\eta}$ in offsetting ways that leave σ_{11}, σ_{12}, and σ_{22} constant? The answer is yes, as can be seen by differentiating (37) and (38) and setting $d\sigma_{12} = d\sigma_{11} = d\sigma_{22} = d\lambda = d\sigma_\varepsilon^2 = 0$:

$$0 = (1 - \lambda)[\lambda + \alpha(1 - \lambda)]^{-2}(\sigma_\varepsilon^2 - \sigma_{\varepsilon\eta})\,d\alpha$$
$$+ [\lambda + \alpha(1 - \lambda)]^{-1}\,d\sigma_{\varepsilon\eta} = 0 \tag{39}$$

$$0 = 2(1 - \lambda)^2[\lambda + \alpha(1 - \lambda)]^{-2}(\sigma_\varepsilon^2 - \sigma_{\varepsilon\eta})\,d\alpha$$
$$+ 2(1 - \lambda)[\lambda + \alpha(1 - \lambda)]^{-1}\,d\sigma_{\varepsilon\eta} = 0. \tag{40}$$

Dividing the second equation by $2(1 - \lambda)$ gives the first equation, which proves that if $d\alpha$ and $d\sigma_{\varepsilon\eta}$ obey equation (39), both equations (37) and (38) will remain satisfied. Thus, there exist offsetting changes in α and $\sigma_{\varepsilon\eta}$ that leave the identifiable parameters λ, σ_{11}, σ_{12}, and σ_{22} unaltered. It follows that $\sigma_{\varepsilon\eta}$ and α are not separately identifiable. It is evident from (27) or (32) that λ is identified. To see that σ_ε^2 is identifiable, simply recall that ε_t obeys the feedback rule

$$\mu_t = \frac{1 - \lambda}{1 - \lambda L} x_t + \varepsilon_t, \tag{9}$$

so that given λ, and samples of μ_t and x_t, σ_ε^2 is identifiable as the variance of the residual in the above equation.

To proceed to extract estimates of α it is necessary to impose a value of $\sigma_{\varepsilon\eta}$. I propose to impose the condition $\sigma_{\varepsilon\eta} = 0$, so that shocks to the money supply rule and shocks to portfolio balance are uncorrelated. It is straightforward to calculate

$$\begin{bmatrix} \sigma_\varepsilon^2 & \sigma_{\varepsilon\eta} \\ \sigma_{\varepsilon\eta} & \sigma_\eta^2 \end{bmatrix} = E \begin{bmatrix} \varepsilon_t \\ \eta_t \end{bmatrix} [\varepsilon_t \quad \eta_t] = G_0 D_a G_0'$$

$$= \begin{bmatrix} (1 - \lambda)^2\sigma_{11} + 2(1 - \lambda)\sigma_{12} + \sigma_{22}, \ (1 - \lambda)[1 + \alpha(1 - \lambda)]\sigma_{11} \\ \qquad\qquad\qquad - [2 - \lambda + \alpha(1 - \lambda)]\sigma_{12} + \sigma_{22} \\ (1 - \lambda)[1 + \alpha(1 - \lambda)]\sigma_{11} - [2 - \lambda + \alpha(1 - \lambda)]\sigma_{11} + \sigma_{22}, \\ \qquad [1 + \alpha(1 - \lambda)]^2\sigma_{11} - 2[1 + \alpha(1 - \lambda)]\sigma_{12} + \sigma_{22} \end{bmatrix}.$$

Imposing $\sigma_{\varepsilon\eta} = 0$, we have

$$0 = \sigma_{\varepsilon\eta} = (1 - \lambda)[1 + \alpha(1 - \lambda)]\sigma_{11} - [2 - \lambda + \alpha(1 - \lambda)]\sigma_{12} + \sigma_{22},$$

which implies that α is to be estimated by

$$\alpha = \frac{-\sigma_{11}}{(1 - \lambda)\sigma_{11} - \sigma_{12}} + \frac{(2 - \lambda)\sigma_{12}}{(1 - \lambda)[(1 - \lambda)\sigma_{11} - \sigma_{12}]} \tag{41}$$
$$- \frac{\sigma_{22}}{(1 - \lambda)[(1 - \lambda)\sigma_{11} - \sigma_{12}]}.$$

Let this estimator of α be

$$\widehat{\alpha} = g(\lambda, \sigma_{11}, \sigma_{12}, \sigma_{22}) = g(\theta)$$

where $\theta = (\lambda, \sigma_{11}, \sigma_{12}, \sigma_{22})$. Let Σ_θ be the estimated asymptotic covariance matrix of θ. Then the asymptotic variance of $\widehat{\alpha}$ will be estimated as

$$\operatorname{var} \widehat{\alpha} = \left(\frac{\partial g}{\partial \theta}\right)_{\widehat{\theta}} \Sigma_\theta \left(\frac{\partial g}{\partial \theta}\right)_{\widehat{\theta}}'$$

where $(\partial g/\partial \theta)_{\widehat{\theta}}$ is the (1×4) vector of partial derivatives of g with respect to θ evaluated at the maximum likelihood estimates $\widehat{\theta}$. The asymptotic covariance matrix of $(\lambda, \sigma_{11}, \sigma_{12}, \sigma_{22})$ is given by

$$\sum_{\theta} = \frac{1}{T} \begin{bmatrix} T\sigma_{\lambda}^2 & 0 & 0 & 0 \\ 0 & 2\sigma_{11}^2 & 2\sigma_{11}\sigma_{12} & 2\sigma_{12}^2 \\ 0 & 2\sigma_{11}\sigma_{12} & \sigma_{11}\sigma_{22} + \sigma_{12}^2 & 2\sigma_{12}\sigma_{22} \\ 0 & 2\sigma_{12}^2 & 2\sigma_{12}\sigma_{22} & 2\sigma_{22}^2 \end{bmatrix}$$

where $T\sigma_{\lambda}^2$ is estimated by

$$\sigma_{\lambda}^2 = \left[-\frac{\partial^2 \log L}{\partial \lambda^2} \right]_{\hat{\theta}}^{-1}$$

and where $\log L$ is the natural logarithm of the likelihood function (32). Notice that the maximum likelihood estimate of λ is asymptotically orthogonal to the estimates σ_{11}, σ_{12}, σ_{22}. The preceding formula for Σ_{θ} can be derived by applying results of Wilson (1973) and Anderson (1958, pp. 159–61). In the computations summarized below, the components σ_{11}, σ_{12}, and σ_{22} were estimated by

$$\hat{D}_a = \begin{pmatrix} \hat{\sigma}_{11} & \hat{\sigma}_{12} \\ \hat{\sigma}_{12} & \hat{\sigma}_{22} \end{pmatrix} = T^{-1} \sum_{t=1}^{T} \hat{a}_t \hat{a}_t',$$

the maximum likelihood estimator. The term

$$\left(-\frac{\partial^2 \log L}{\partial \lambda^2} \right)_{\hat{\theta}}$$

was estimated numerically in the course of minimizing (33) to obtain the maximum likelihood estimates.

It bears emphasizing that α is identifiable at all only on the basis of a restriction on $\sigma_{\varepsilon\eta}$, and that the estimator of α obtained by imposing $\sigma_{\varepsilon\eta} = 0$ depends sensitively on the covariance matrix of the errors in forecasting x_t and μ_t from the past. The estimates of α thereby obtained ought to be regarded as very delicate.

IV. An Alternative Estimator

If it is assumed that $\sigma_{\varepsilon\eta} = 0$, so that shocks to the demand for money and to the supply of money are uncorrelated, an instrumental variable estimator is available. From equations (30) and (29) we have that

$$E_{t-1}x_t = E_{t-1}\mu_t = \frac{1-\lambda}{1-\lambda L}x_{t-1},$$

and that

$$x_t - E_{t-1}x_t = a_{1t} = \frac{1}{\lambda + \alpha(1-\lambda)}(\varepsilon_t - \eta_t) \tag{42}$$

$$\mu_t - E_{t-1}x_t = a_{2t} = \frac{1-\lambda}{\lambda + \alpha(1-\lambda)}(\varepsilon_t - \eta_t) + \varepsilon_t. \tag{43}$$

Notice that

$$a_{2t} - (1 - \lambda)a_{1t} = \varepsilon_t. \tag{44}$$

This suggests the following procedure. Estimate by maximum likelihood the univariate first-order moving average process for Δx_t, i.e.,

$$(1 - L)x_t = (1 - \lambda L)a_{1t}$$

where $a_{1t} = [\lambda + \alpha(1 - \lambda)]^{-1}(\varepsilon_t - \eta_t)$ is "white." This will yield consistent estimates of λ and permit estimating the forecast errors. The forecasts $E_{t-1}x_t$ can be estimated from the above equation as

$$E_{t-1}x_t = x_{t-1} - \lambda a_{1t-1}.$$

Use of (44) shows that estimates of ε_t can be extracted according to

$$\varepsilon_t = (\mu_t - E_{t-1}x_t) - (1 - \lambda)(x_t - E_{t-1}x_t). \tag{45}$$

On the assumption that ε_t is uncorrelated with η_t, ε_t is a valid instrument for estimating equation (1): it is correlated with the regressors but orthogonal to the disturbance. Letting $\tilde{\varepsilon}_t$ be the estimates of ε_t obtained by applying (45), I propose fitting the first-stage regression

$$\hat{x}_t = \sum_{i=0}^{n} \hat{w}_i \tilde{\varepsilon}_{t-1}$$

where the hatted values denote least squares estimates. Then Cagan's equation (1) would be estimated by applying (nonlinear) least squares to the second-stage regression

$$m_t - p_t = \alpha \left(\frac{1 - \lambda}{1 - \lambda L} \right) \hat{x}_t + u_t - \frac{\alpha(1 - \lambda)}{1 - \lambda L} (\hat{x}_t - x_t). \tag{46}$$

This procedure yields consistent estimates of α and λ on the assumption that

$$\operatorname*{plim}_{T \to \infty} T^{-1} \sum_{t=1}^{T} \tilde{\varepsilon}_t \eta_t = 0,$$

a condition that the orthogonality of ε_t and η_t goes a long way toward delivering.

V. Testing the Model

Representation (27) shows that the model is a special case of the general vector first-order moving average, first-order autoregressive process

$$\begin{bmatrix} x_t \\ \mu_t \end{bmatrix} = \begin{bmatrix} c_{11} & c_{12} \\ c_{21} & c_{22} \end{bmatrix} \begin{pmatrix} x_{t-1} \\ \mu_{t-1} \end{pmatrix} + \begin{pmatrix} a_{1t} \\ a_{2t} \end{pmatrix} + \begin{pmatrix} b_{11} & b_{12} \\ b_{21} & b_{22} \end{pmatrix} \begin{pmatrix} a_{1t-1} \\ a_{2t-1} \end{pmatrix} \tag{27'}$$

where in (27) *seven* linear restrictions have been placed on the eight parameters $(c_{11}, c_{12}, c_{21}, c_{22}, b_{11}, b_{12}, b_{21}, b_{22})$ of (27′) so that the systematic part of (27) only involves the single parameter λ. The model (27) can be tested by relaxing some subset of the seven restrictions that were imposed on (27′) to get (27), maximizing the likelihood function under the less restrictive parameterization, and calculating the pertinent χ^2 statistic. Let $L(x_t, \mu_t; \theta_0)$ be the maximum of the likelihood function under parameterization (27), which is Cagan's model under rational expectations. Let $L(x_t, \mu_t; \theta, q)$ be the maximum of the likelihood function under (27′) with q of the seven restrictions in (27) being relaxed. Then

$$-2 \log \left[\frac{L(x_t, \mu_t; \theta_0)}{L(x_t, \mu_t; \theta, q)} \right]$$

is asymptotically distributed as $\chi^2(q)$. High values of the test statistic lead to rejection of representation (27). Below this test is implemented under several alternative relaxations of the restrictions on (27).

VI. Empirical Results

For Cagan's and Barro's data, respectively, tables 2 and 3 report the estimates obtained using the maximum likelihood estimator and the assumption that $\sigma_{\varepsilon\eta} = 0$. Asymptotic standard errors are in parentheses beneath each estimator. Cagan's and Barro's estimates are reported in tables 4 and 5 for convenience. For Cagan's data, the maximum likelihood estimator recovers estimates of α that are in most cases characterized by large stand-

TABLE 2

ESTIMATES FOR CAGAN'S DATA (Standard Errors in Parentheses)
(x and μ Are Deviations from Respective Means)

Country	$\hat{\lambda}$	$\hat{\alpha}$	$\hat{\sigma}_{11}$	$\hat{\sigma}_{12}$	$\hat{\sigma}_{22}$
Germany:					
Oct. 1920–July 1923	.6674	−5.973	.0625	.0158	.0091
	(.0533)	(4.615)	(.0147)	(.0048)	(.0022)
Austria:					
Feb. 1921–Aug. 1922	.7537	−.3113	.0385	.0148	.0085
	(.0589)	(1.5695)	(.0119)	(.0051)	(.0026)
Greece:					
Feb. 1943–Aug. 1944	.4587	−4.086	.0675	.0245	.0279
	(.0884)	(2.970)	(.0208)	(.0109)	(.0086)
Hungary I:					
Aug. 1922–Feb. 1924	.4183	−1.841	.0362	.0089	.0060
	(.0668)	(.3978)	(.0112)	(.0038)	(.0019)
Russia:					
Feb. 1922–Jan. 1924	.6259	−9.745	.0524	.0138	.0205
	(.0728)	(10.742)	(.0145)	(.0070)	(.0057)
Poland:					
May 1922–Nov. 1923	.5364	−2.529	.0566	.0149	.0089
	(.0722)	(.8562)	(.0175)	(.0059)	(.0027)

TABLE 3

Estimates for Barro's Data (Standard Errors in Parentheses)
(x and μ Are Deviations from Respective Means)

Country	$\widehat{\lambda}$	$\widehat{\alpha}$	$\widehat{\sigma}_{11}$	$\widehat{\sigma}_{12}$	$\widehat{\sigma}_{22}$
Austria:					
Apr. 1921–Dec. 1922	.6373	−3.979	.0584	.0161	.0081
	(.0739)	(2.805)	(.0172)	(.0056)	(.0024)
Germany:					
Feb. 1921–Aug. 1923	.5921	−2.344	.1806	.0653	.0263
	(.0510)	(1.223)	(.0445)	(.0165)	(.0065)
Hungary:					
Nov. 1921–Feb. 1924	.4323	−1.705	.0280	.0071	.0038
	(.0559)	(.2782)	(.0072)	(.0023)	(.0010)
Poland:					
Feb. 1922–Jan. 1924	.4790	−2.043	.0319	.0063	.0040
	(.0533)	(.3537)	(.0089)	(.0025)	(.0011)

ard errors. In particular, for the important German case, a case in which Cagan had apparently estimated α with a tight confidence band, my estimate of α has a big standard error, one nearly as big as the point estimate itself. Evidently, the estimate of α is not statistically significantly different from zero even at modest confidence levels, at least if we are willing to use the asymptotic (normal) distribution of the estimates.[8] For the Austrian and Russian cases, my estimate of α is smaller than its standard error. Only in the case of Hungary I, and to a lesser extent in the case of Poland, is the standard error of α small relative to the point estimate of α. Interestingly enough, for Hungary I my estimate of α of −1.84 is much smaller in absolute value than Cagan's estimate of −8.70. The reciprocal of +1.84 is .54, while the average monthly rate of inflation in the Hungary I case was .46. In the case of Hungary I, my estimate of α suggests that the paradox with which I began this paper, the apparent tendency of creators of money to print money "too fast," was not present. For what it is worth, then, my

[8] Actually, the normality of the asymptotic distribution is conjectural (see Porter 1974).

TABLE 4

Cagan's estimates of α, λ Together with Confidence Band for α

Country	$\widehat{\lambda}$	$\widehat{\alpha}$	(α_e, α_u)
Austria: Jan. 1921–Aug. 1922	.95	−8.55	−(4.43, 30.0)
Germany: Sept. 1920–July 1923	.82	−5.46	−(5.05, 6.13)
Greece: Jan. 1943–Aug. 1944	.86	−4.09	−(2.83, 32.5+)*
Hungary: July 1922–Feb. 1924	.90	−8.70	−(6.36, 42.2+)*
Hungary: July 1945–Feb. 1946	.86	−3.63	−(2.55, 4.73)
Poland: Apr. 1922–Nov. 1923	.74	−2.30	−(1.74, 3.94)
Russia: Dec. 1921–Jan. 1924	.70	−3.06	−(2.66, 3.76)

Note.—(α_e, α_u) = 90 percent confidence band calculated by Cagan using likelihood ratio method.
Source.—Cagan 1956, table 3.
*α_u actually exceeds right-hand figure in parentheses.

TABLE 5

BARRO'S ESTIMATES OF λ AND α

Country	$\hat{\lambda}$	$\hat{\alpha}^*$
Austria: Jan. 1921–Dec. 1922	.829	−4.09
		(−3.6, −4.5)
Germany: Jan. 1921–Aug. 1923	.824	−3.79
		(−3.3, −4.3)
Hungary: Oct. 1921–Feb. 1924	.861	−5.53
		(−4.6, −6.9)
Poland: Jan. 1922–Jan. 1924	.709	−2.56
		(−2.1, −3.3)

SOURCE.—Barrow 1970, table 3.
*95 percent confidence intervals in parentheses beneath each estimate.

estimate of α for Hungary I tends to explain away the paradox. For the other countries, the point estimates do not explain away the paradox. However, in each case, values of α that would cause the paradox to disappear do exist within confidence intervals of two standard errors on each side of the point estimate of α. This suggests that perhaps the paradox ought not to be taken as having been seriously confirmed since the estimates of α on which it is based seem so shaky.

Notice that my estimates of λ are always lower than Cagan's. That is an unexpected result, since according to the model, Cagan's estimate of λ and my maximum likelihood estimator are each consistent. The systematic difference in estimates as between the two estimators may reflect the inadequacy of the model.

For Barro's data, the maximum likelihood estimates are reported in table 3. For Austria and Germany, the estimated asymptotic standard errors of α are fairly large relative to the point estimates, while for Hungary I and Poland they are much smaller. As with Cagan's data, my estimate of α is much smaller than is Barro's for Hungary I. My estimate is somewhat smaller than Barro's for Poland. As with Cagan's data, my estimate of λ is always smaller than Cagan's.

The main conclusion that I draw from these estimates is that even under the restriction $\sigma_{\varepsilon\eta} = 0$, the slope parameter α is usually poorly estimated. When to this is added the observations that α is not even identifiable unless $\sigma_{\varepsilon\eta}$ is restricted and that economics does not seem to restrict $\sigma_{\varepsilon\eta}$, the uncertainty about α only increases. It seems correct to conclude that, with the possible exception of Hungary I, I have not been able to estimate very well the slope of the portfolio balance schedule.

This is not to say, however, that the model is necessarily defective. It is certainly conceivable that the model approximated reality quite well even though α cannot be estimated well or isn't even identifiable. As pointed out in Section VI, the proper way to test the model is to "overfit" the vector moving average, autoregressive representation (27), and to test

TABLE 6

PARAMETERIZATIONS FOR OVERFITTING

$$\begin{bmatrix} x_t \\ \mu_t \end{bmatrix} = C \begin{bmatrix} x_{t-1} \\ \mu_{t-1} \end{bmatrix} + \begin{bmatrix} a_{1t} \\ a_{2t} \end{bmatrix} + B \begin{bmatrix} a_{1t-1} \\ a_{2t-1} \end{bmatrix}$$

1. $C = \begin{bmatrix} c & 0 \\ (1-\lambda) & \lambda \end{bmatrix}$, $B = \begin{bmatrix} -\lambda & 0 \\ 0 & -\lambda \end{bmatrix}$

2. $C = \begin{bmatrix} 1 & c \\ 1-\lambda & \lambda \end{bmatrix}$, $B = \begin{bmatrix} -\lambda & 0 \\ 0 & -\lambda \end{bmatrix}$

3. $C = \begin{bmatrix} 1 & 0 \\ 1-\lambda & \lambda \end{bmatrix}$, $B = \begin{bmatrix} -\lambda & b \\ 0 & -\lambda \end{bmatrix}$

4. $C = \begin{bmatrix} c_1 & c_1 \\ 1-\lambda & \lambda \end{bmatrix}$, $B = \begin{bmatrix} -\lambda & 0 \\ 0 & -\lambda \end{bmatrix}$

5. $C = \begin{bmatrix} 1 & c \\ (1-\lambda) & \lambda \end{bmatrix}$, $B = \begin{bmatrix} -\lambda & b \\ 0 & -\lambda \end{bmatrix}$

6. $C = \begin{bmatrix} 1 & 0 \\ c_1 & c_2 \end{bmatrix}$, $B = \begin{bmatrix} -\lambda & 0 \\ 0 & -\lambda \end{bmatrix}$

whether the restrictions imposed by (27) are violated. For overfitting, I have estimated each of the six parameterizations reported in table 6. For each parameterization, the chi-square statistic described in Section VI was computed, and is reported in table 7 for Cagan's data and in table 8 for Barro's data. High values of the chi-square statistic lead to rejection of the null hypothesis that model (27) is adequate.

For Cagan's data, at the .95 confidence level, the model is rejected rela-

TABLE 7

CAGAN'S DATA RESULTS OF OVERFITTING: CHI-SQUARE STATISTICS

Country	Number					
	1 $\chi^2(1)$	2 $\chi^2(1)$	3 $\chi^2(1)$	4 $\chi^2(2)$	5 $\chi^2(2)$	6 $\chi^2(2)$
Germany:						
Oct. 1920–July 1923	0.52	1.12	2.06	0.95	3.37	2.14
Russia:						
Feb. 1922–Jan. 1924	0.21	3.05	2.84	3.90	7.79	0.97
Greece:						
Feb. 1943–Aug. 1944	1.04	1.53	0.25	4.14	1.87	0.40
Hungary I:						
Aug. 1922–Feb. 1924	4.13	7.57	3.13	7.57	7.62	0.24
Poland:						
May 1922–Nov. 1923	0.19	0.04	0.22	0.31	0.56	0.53
Austria:						
Feb. 1921–Aug. 1922	2.77	4.97	0.63	4.97	10.05	7.13

Significance levels: $\chi^2(1)_{.05} = 3.84$ $\chi^2(2)_{.05} = 5.99$
$\chi^2(1)_{.01} = 6.63$ $\chi^2(2)_{.01} = 9.21$

TABLE 8

BARRO'S DATA RESULTS OF OVERFITTING: CHI-SQUARE STATISTICS

	Parameterization					
	Number					
Country	1 $\chi^2(1)$	2 $\chi^2(1)$	3 $\chi^2(1)$	4 $\chi^2(2)$	5 $\chi^2(2)$	6 $\chi^2(2)$
Germany: Feb. 1921–Aug. 1923	1.272	0.382	0.3	3.5	0.33	$\approx$0.
Hungary I: Nov. 1921–Feb. 1924	5.424	7.6	1.232	7.63	8.49	0.39
Poland: Feb. 1922–Jan. 1924	1.58	0.528	0.184	0.528	0.66	8.8
Austria: Apr. 1921–Dec. 1922	0.502	3.11	0.006	3.97	3.13	$\approx$0.

Significance levels: $\chi^2(1)_{.05} = 3.84$ $\chi^2(2)_{.05} = 5.99$
$\chi^2(1)_{.025} = 5.02$ $\chi^2(2)_{.025} = 7.37$
$\chi^2(1)_{.01} = 6.63$ $\chi^2(2)_{.01} = 9.21$

tive to parameterization 5 for Russia, relative to parameterizations 1, 2, 4, and 5 for Hungary I, and relative to parameterizations 2, 5, and 6 for Austria. For Germany, Greece, and Poland, the model is not rejected relative to any of the six parameterizations at the .95 confidence level. For three of the hyperinflations, then, overfitting representation (27) does turn up evidence that would prompt rejection of the model. However, it surprised me just how adequately the model does seem to perform relative to the six parameterizations in table 6. Representation (27) is a very stark, highly restricted parameterization; indeed, the systematic part of the vector autoregression has only one parameter. I had expected the model to be rather decisively rejected by these overfitting tests. It is remarkable that the model seems to survive those tests for even three of the hyperinflations.

For Barro's data, at the .95 confidence level the chi-square statistics call for rejecting representation (27) relative to parameterizations (1), (2), (4), and (5) for Hungary I. The statistics do not call for rejection of (27) for Germany, Poland, or Austria.

Notice that for both Cagan's and Barro's data, the overfitting tests reject representation (27) for the case of Hungary I, a case for which my estimator of α obtained the tightest confidence band.

VII. Conclusions

This paper has applied maximum likelihood techniques to derive a consistent estimator of a bivariate, rational expectations version of Cagan's model of hyperinflation. The estimator, in principle, eliminates the simultaneous-equations, asymptotic bias that characterizes Cagan's estimator. Application of the maximum likelihood estimator typically yields "loose" estimates of the slope parameter of the demand schedule for money. The estimates are so loose that confidence bands of two standard errors on each side of them include values that would imply that the creators of money were inflating at rates that maximized their command over real resources, thus maybe resolving the "paradox" with which I began this paper. While perhaps this resolves the paradox, it does so in a destructive way, by suggesting that the demand for money in hyperinflation has not been isolated as well as might have been thought. This is not a very satisfactory state of affairs in which to leave the subject. In a subsequent paper, I intend to describe further efforts to isolate the demand schedule for money, using a technique which for special reasons cannot be applied to Cagan's model. Use of that technique will be shown to require abandoning the assumption of adaptive (geometric lag, unit-sum) expectations. The technique will be shown to break down under the singular circumstance that the model in the present paper is the correct one. However, the results of my "overfitting" tests, to the extent that they do not always emphatically reject the model in the present paper, suggest that the prospects for success are not great for using such a technique. It could just be true that the model in this paper is the "correct" one, so that even though the portfolio balance schedule was exactly the one Cagan assumed, the nature of the money supply regimes in effect during the hyperinflations makes difficult or impossible estimating the slope of that portfolio balance schedule.

References

Anderson, T. W. *An Introduction to Multivariate Statistical Analysis.* New York: Wiley, 1958.

Barro, Robert J. "Inflation, the Payments Period, and the Demand for Money." *J.P.E.* 78 (November/December 1970): 1228-63.

Cagan, Phillip. "The Monetary Dynamics of Hyperinflation." In *Studies in the Quantity Theory of Money,* edited by M. Friedman. Chicago: University of Chicago Press, 1956.

Granger, C. W. J. "Investigating Causal Relations by Econometric Models and Cross-Spectral Methods." *Econometrica* 37 (July 1969): 424-38.

Meiselman, David. *The Varieties of Monetary Experience.* Chicago: University of Chicago Press, 1970.

Muth, John F. "Rational Expectations and the Theory of Price Movements." *Econometrica* 29 (July 1961): 315-35.

Porter, Richard D. "Multiple Time Series Containing Unobserved Components." Manuscript, Board of Governors, Federal Reserve System, September 1974.

Sargent, Thomas J., and Wallace, Neil. "Rational Expectations and the Dynamics of Hyperinflation." *Internat. Econ. Rev.* 14 (June 1973): 328-50.

Sims, Christopher A. "Money, Income, and Causality." *A.E.R.* 62 (September 1972): 540-52.

Wilson, G. T. "The Estimation of Parameters in Multivariate Time Series Models." *J. Royal Statis. Soc. B,* 1973 (1), 76-85.

Zellner, A., and Palm, F. "Time Series Analysis and Simultaneous Equation Econometric Models." *J. Econometrics* 2 (May 1974): 17-54.

24

A Note on Maximum Likelihood Estimation of the Rational Expectations Model of the Term Structure

Thomas J. Sargent

The key implications of the rational expectations theory of the term structure of interest rates are that certain sequences of forward interest rates can be described as martingales. These implications are ones for which the most convenient and powerful tests of the theory can be made.[1] However, as Modigliani, Sutch and Shiller have emphasized, from the point of view of implementing the theory in the context of a macroeconometric model, it is not sufficient to represent the theory simply by its implications that those sequences of forward yields are martingales. To get the theory in a form that can be used in a macroeconometric model, Modigliani, Shiller, and Sutch in effect characterized the theory by its implications for the regression of long rates on current and past short-term rates. In addition to delivering something that might be used in a macroeconometric model, this approach can also be justified purely on the grounds that it provides a way of testing the theory on the basis of a much sparser data set than is required in order to test that the appropriate sequences of forward rates are martingales. That is, to test the model using the procedures to be discussed below, all that are required are suitable time series on a single long-term rate and a single short-term rate;[2] but to test some of the martingale implications directly requires time series over the entire term structure of rates.

This note is written by way of pursuing the general Modigliani, Sutch and Shiller approach. However, rather than follow Modigliani, Sutch,

The views expressed herein are solely those of the author and do not necessarily represent the views of the Federal Reserve Bank of Minneapolis or the Federal Reserve System. Research for this paper was supported by the Federal Reserve Bank of Minneapolis, which is not responsible for the conclusions. Robert Litterman ably performed the calculations. Comments from a referee are gratefully acknowledged.

[1] Some of these implications were spelled out by Roll (1970) and tested against data by Roll (1970) and Sargent (1972).

[2] Modigliani and Shiller (1973) made this point but did not formulate a formal econometric test.

[Journal of Monetary Economics, 1979, vol. 5]
© 1979 by North-Holland Publishing Company

and Shiller in focusing on the projection of long rates on current and past short rates, I will proceed by estimating the vector autoregression of long and short rates. This is a convenient representation for extracting predictions from the model, and also conserves all of the information required to compute the projection of one interest rate series on current and past (and maybe future) values of the other series. In particular, a compact formula is given for the restriction on the bivariate vector autoregression of the long-term rate and the short-term rate that is implied by the rational expectations theory. Then two procedures are given for estimating the vector autoregression under that restriction: the first being a two-step procedure that gives consistent but not fully efficient estimates under the restriction; the second being a maximum likelihood estimator. Some sample calculations are carried out and the pertinent likelihood ratio statistic is reported. The maximum likelihood algorithm used here would be a convenient one to use for estimating and testing rational expectations models of other relationships. The main purpose of this paper is to illustrate the feasibility of maximum likelihood estimation in the face of the complicated nonlinear restrictions implied by rational expectations in multi-period horizon models. To my knowledge, applications of this approach are not available in the literature.

Let R_{1t} be the one-period rate and R_{nt} be the n-period rate. I assume that the process of first differences $(\Delta R_{1t}, \Delta R_{nt})$ is a second-order jointly stationary, indeterministic stochastic process. Among other things, this means that the covariances between ΔR_{1t} and ΔR_{nt-s} exist and are independent of time t; it also means that the variances of ΔR_{1t} and ΔR_{nt} exist and do not depend on t. I will work with the mth-order bivariate autoregressive representation for the $(\Delta R_{1t}, \Delta R_{nt})$ process, the existence of which is implied by the preceding assumptions.[3] The theory imposes restrictions on this vector autoregression so long as agents have at least as much information as is contained in m lagged ΔR_{1t}'s and ΔR_{nt}'s, as will be proved by applying a variant of an argument of Shiller (1972).

I will represent the rational expectations theory of the term structure in the form[4]

$$R_{nt} = \frac{1}{n}(R_{1t} + E_t R_{1t+1} + \cdots + E_t R_{1t+n-1}), \tag{1}$$

[3] A nonrigorous discussion of vector autoregressions, vector stochastic processes, and some of their applications in macroeconomics is contained in Sargent (in press).

[4] Eq. (1) is only an approximation to the correct formula linking long with expected short rates. Modigliani and Shiller (1973) and Shiller (1972) recommend the alternative approximation

$$R_{nt} = (1 - \gamma) \sum_{j=0}^{\infty} \gamma^j E_t R_{1t+j},$$

where $\gamma = 1/(1 + r_0)$, r_0 being a "representative short-term rate," which Modigliani and Shiller recommend taking as the mean long-term rate. Modigliani and Shiller recommend that this approximation be used for very long-term rates.

where I will interpret $E_t x$ to mean the linear least-squares forecast of the random variable x based on information available at time t. I will assume that this information set includes at least (but possibly more than) current and all lagged values of both R_{1t} and R_{nt}. Let Ω_t be the information set that agents use at time t, so that $E_t x \equiv Ex|\Omega_t$. I assume that $\Omega_t \supset \Omega_{t-1} \supset \Omega_{t-2} \cdots$.

First differencing (1) gives

$$(R_{nt} - R_{nt-1}) = \frac{1}{n}[(R_{1t} - R_{1t-1}) + (ER_{1t+1}|\Omega_t - ER_{1t}|\Omega_{t-1})$$
$$+ \cdots + (ER_{1t+n-1}|\Omega_t - ER_{1t+n-2}|\Omega_{t-1})].$$

Let θ_{t-1} be any subset of Ω_{t-1}. Then use the law of iterated projections[5] to project both sides of the above equation on θ_{t-1} to get

$$E\,\Delta R_{nt}|\theta_{t-1} = \frac{1}{n}[E\,\Delta R_{1t}|\theta_{t-1} + E\,\Delta R_{1t+1}|\theta_{t-1}$$
$$+ \cdots + E\,\Delta R_{1t+n-1}|\theta_{t-1}]. \tag{2}$$

If we let $\theta_{t-1} = \{\Delta R_{1t-1}, \Delta R_{1t-2}, \ldots, \Delta R_{1t-m}, \Delta R_{nt-1}, \ldots, \Delta R_{nt-m}\}$, equation (2) implies a restriction across the systematic parts of the mth-order vector autoregression for $(\Delta R_{1t}, \Delta R_{nt})$. Let the mth-order vector autoregression for $\Delta R_{1t}, \Delta R_{nt}$ be

$$\Delta R_{1t} = \sum_{i=1}^{m} \alpha_i\,\Delta R_{1t-i} + \sum_{i=1}^{m} \beta_i\,\Delta R_{nt-i} + a_{1t},$$
$$\Delta R_{nt} = \sum_{i=1}^{m} \gamma_i\,\Delta R_{1t-i} + \sum_{i=1}^{m} \delta_i\,\Delta R_{nt-i} + a_{nt}, \tag{3}$$

where $\mathcal{E}a_{jt} \cdot \Delta R_{1t-i} = \mathcal{E}a_{jt}\,\Delta R_{nt-i} = 0$ for $j = 1, \ldots, n$ and $i = 1, \ldots, m$ ($\mathcal{E}$ is the mathematical expectation operator). The random variables a_{1t}, a_{nt} are the innovations in the $\Delta R_{1t}, \Delta R_{nt}$ processes, and are the one step-ahead prediction errors in linearly predicting ΔR_{1t} and ΔR_{nt}, respectively, on the basis of m observations of past ΔR_{1t}'s and ΔR_{nt}'s. Equation (3) can be written compactly as

$$x_t = Ax_{t-1} + a_t, \tag{4}$$

---

[5]Use of the law of iterated projections in this way is the argument of Shiller (1972) referred to earlier. The law of iterated projections states that $E(y|z) = E(E(y|x, z)|z)$, where x, y, z are random variables and E is the linear least-squares projection operator. The law is easily proved as a consequence of the fact that least-squares residuals are orthogonal to least-squares predictions.

where

$$x_t = \begin{bmatrix} \Delta R_{1t} \\ \Delta R_{1t-1} \\ \vdots \\ \Delta R_{1t-m+1} \\ \Delta R_{nt} \\ \Delta R_{nt-1} \\ \vdots \\ \Delta R_{nt-m+1} \end{bmatrix}, \qquad a_t = \begin{bmatrix} a_{1t} \\ 0 \\ 0 \\ \vdots \\ 0 \\ a_{nt} \\ 0 \\ 0 \\ \vdots \\ 0 \end{bmatrix},$$

$$A = \begin{bmatrix} \alpha_1 & \alpha_2 & \cdots & \alpha_m & \beta_1 & \beta_2 & \cdots & \beta_m \\ 1 & 0 & & 0 & 0 & 0 & & 0 \\ 0 & 1 & & 0 & 0 & 0 & & 0 \\ \vdots & & & & & & & \\ 0 & 0 & & 1 & 0 & 0 & 0 & 0 \\ \gamma_1 & \gamma_2 & & \gamma_m & \delta_1 & \delta_2 & \cdots & \delta_m \\ 0 & 0 & & 0 & 1 & 0 & & 0 \\ \vdots & & & & & & & \\ 0 & 0 & & 0 & 0 & 0 & \cdots 1 & 0 \end{bmatrix}.$$

Letting c be the $(1 \times 2m)$ row vector with one in the first column, zeroes elsewhere, and letting d be the $(1 \times 2m)$ row vector with one in the $(m + 1)$st column, zeroes elsewhere, we have $\Delta R_{1t} = cx_t$, and $\Delta R_{nt} = dx_t$. Using (4), we can write

$$\begin{aligned} x_{t+1} &= A^2 x_{t-1} + Aa_t + a_{t+1}, \\ x_{t+2} &= A^3 x_{t-1} + A^2 a_t + Aa_{t+1} + a_{t+2}, \\ &\vdots \\ x_{t+j} &= A^{j+1} x_{t-1} + A^j a_t + A^{j-1} a_{t+1} + \cdots + a_{t+j}. \end{aligned} \qquad (5)$$

Since a_{t+j} satisfies[6] $Ea_{t+k}|\theta_{t-1} = 0$ for $k = 0, 1, 2, \ldots$, we have from (5) that

$$Ex_{t+j}|\theta_{t-1} = A^{j+1} x_{t-1}. \qquad (6)$$

Now (4) implies that

$$\begin{aligned} \Delta R_{1t} &= cAx_{t-1} + a_{1t}, \\ \Delta R_{nt} &= dAx_{t-1} + a_{nt}. \end{aligned} \qquad (7)$$

[6]Technically, this holds only if $\mathcal{E}a_{jt}\Delta R_{1t-i} = \mathcal{E}a_{jt}\Delta R_{nt-i} = 0$ for $j = 1, n$, and $i = 1, 2, \ldots$. This amounts to the condition that the mth-order vector autoregression equals the infinite-order vector autoregression, so that coefficients on ΔR_1 and ΔR_n lagged more than m periods would be zero if they had been included in the population representation (3). Practically, the requirement amounts to choosing m large enough to account for the serial correlation and cross-serial correlation in the $(\Delta R_1, \Delta R_n)$ process.

But restriction (2) on the systematic part of the vector autoregression, together with (6), implies

$$\Delta R_{nt} = \frac{1}{n} c (A + A^2 + \cdots + A^n) x_{t-1} + a_{nt}. \tag{8}$$

Comparing (7) with (8), we see that the rational expectations theory imposes the following restriction across the nontrivial rows of A:

$$dA = \frac{1}{n} c (A + A^2 + \cdots + A^n). \tag{9}$$

Equation (9) is a compact representation of the restrictions that the rational expectations theory of the term structure imposes on the mth-order bivariate vector autoregression of the $(\Delta R_{1t}, \Delta R_{nt})$ process.[7]

I propose the following methods for estimating the vector autoregression for ΔR_{1t}, ΔR_{nt} under restriction (9). It is instructive first to consider a two-step procedure which potentially yields consistent, though not fully efficient estimates under the restriction. First, estimate by least squares the first row of A, i.e., estimate the first of equations (7). Then pursue the following iterative scheme for calculating the $(m + 1)$st row of A implied by this choice of the first row. First set the $(m + 1)$st row of A (i.e., the one corresponding to the autoregression for ΔR_{nt}) to a row of zeroes. Set the other rows of A at their known values. Call this preliminary estimate A_0. Then form a revised estimate of the $(m + 1)$st row of A according to

$$dA_1 = \frac{1}{n} c (A_0 + A_0^2 + \cdots + A_0^n).$$

In forming the other rows of A_1 leave the other rows of A at their initial values. Then recalculate A again, iterating on

$$dA_{i+1} = \frac{1}{n} c (A_i + A_i^2 + \cdots + A_i^n), \tag{10}$$

where A_i is the estimate of A on the ith iteration. At each step in forming A_{i+1}, all rows of A except the $(m + 1)$st are kept equal to the correspond-

---

[7]If we had used Modigliani and Shiller's formula (see note 4), restriction (9) would become

$$dA = (1 - \gamma) c A \sum_{j=0}^{\infty} \gamma^j A^j.$$

Assume that the eigenvalues of A are distinct, so that A can be written $A = P \Lambda P^{-1}$ where the columns of P are the eigenvectors of A while Λ is a diagonal matrix of eigenvalues of A. Then the above restriction can be written in the compact form.

$$dA = (1 - \gamma) c A P \left\{ \frac{1}{1 - \gamma \lambda} \right\} P^{-1},$$

assuming $\max|\gamma \lambda_i| < 1$, where $\{1/1 - \gamma \lambda\}$ is the diagonal matrix with $1/1 - \gamma \lambda_i$ in the (i, i) position. By making use of this formula, the algorithm proposed in the text can easily be modified for Modigliani and Shiller's formula.

ing rows of A_0. If it converges, this algorithm will find an A that satisfies restriction (9). Experience indicates that this scheme often converges, especially where the eigenvalues of A are well below unity. The elements of the first row of A are consistently estimated by least squares. The preceding algorithm, since it calculates the $(m + 1)$st row of A as a function of the first row of A, will produce consistent estimates of that $(m + 1)$st row under the usual regularity conditions.

The preceding algorithm in effect computes the γ's and δ's of (3) that satisfy (9) as functions of the α's and β's. Let us denote the solution to the iteration on (10) as the (set) function

$$(\gamma, \delta) = \phi(\alpha, \beta); \tag{11}$$

ϕ maps the α's and β's into a set of γ's and δ's that satisfy restriction (9). Our first estimator of the γ's and δ's is then simply $\phi(\alpha, \beta)$ evaluated with α and β being set at their least-squares estimates. Call this the "two-step estimator."

Under the hypothesis that (a_{1t}, a_{nt}) is bivariate normal, the likelihood function of a sample of (a_{1t}, a_{nt}) for $t = 1, \ldots, T$ is

$$L(\alpha, \beta, \gamma, \delta, V \,|\, \{\Delta R_{1t}\}, \{\Delta R_{nt}\})$$

$$= (2\pi)^{-T} |V|^{-T/2} \exp\left(-\frac{1}{2} \sum_{t=1}^{T} e_t' V^{-1} e_t\right), \tag{12}$$

where

$$e_t = \begin{bmatrix} a_{1t} \\ a_{nt} \end{bmatrix}, \qquad V = E e_t e_t'.$$

Maximizing (12) subject to (3) without any restrictions on the coefficients, i.e., taking the m α_i, β_i, γ_i, and δ_i's all as free parameters, is equivalent with estimating each equation of (3) by least squares.

Under the restriction (9), or equivalent (11), the likelihood function (12) becomes a function only of the α's and β's. As Wilson (1973) has noted, maximum likelihood estimates with an unknown V are obtained by minimizing with respect to the α's and β's the criterion

$$|\widehat{V}| = \left| \frac{1}{T} \sum_{t=1}^{T} e_t(\alpha, \beta) e_t(\alpha, \beta)' \right|, \tag{13}$$

where the e_t's (i.e., the a_{1t} and a_{nt}'s) are functions of the α's and β's (as well as the ΔR_{1t}'s and ΔR_{nt}'s) by virtue of their being calculated from (3) with (11) being imposed. A standard derivative free nonlinear minimization routine is capable of minimizing (13) numerically. The least-squares estimates of α and β would seem to be good starting values from which to pursue the nonlinear minimization. The maximum likelihood estimator of

V turns out to be

$$\widehat{V} = \frac{1}{T} \sum_{t=1}^{T} \widehat{e_t}\widehat{e_t'},$$

where the $\widehat{e_t}$'s are the estimated vectors of residuals.

Let L_u be the value of (12) at its unrestricted maximum while L_r is the value of (12) under the restriction (9). Then under the null hypothesis that the rational expectations model is correct,

$$-2 \log_e \left(\frac{L_r}{L_u}\right), \tag{14}$$

is asymptotically distributed as $\chi^2(q)$ where q is the number of restrictions imposed. In our case $q = 2m$, where m is the number of lags in the autoregression (3). High values of the likelihood ratio (14) lead to rejection of the restrictions (11) that are implied by the rational expectations theory of the term structure.[8]

Table 1 reports three sets of estimates of equation (3) for $m = 4$ where R_{nt} is taken as the rate on 5-year government bonds while R_{1t} is taken as the 3-month Treasury bill rate. The data are quarterly and point-in-time, first of month data for the first month of each quarter.[9] The data on the left-hand side variables of (3) span the period 1953 II–1971 IV. There are thus 71 observations on the disturbances, so that $T = 71$. The table reports estimates of (3) unconstrained (i.e., least-squares estimates of each equation of [3]), the two-step estimates which impose the rational expectations restrictions (11), and the maximum likelihood estimates that impose (11).

The likelihood ratio statistic pertinent for testing the null hypothesis that the rational expectations restrictions are correct is 8.58. Since the likelihood ratio statistic is distributed as chi-square with eight degrees of freedom, the marginal significance level is 0.3788. The likelihood ratio test thus does not provide any strong evidence for rejecting the rational expectations restrictions.

As indicated by the $|V|$ statistic, it is interesting that the two-step estimates provide a considerably poorer fit than do the maximum likelihood estimates.

---

[8]Using the calculations of Wilson (1973, p. 80), it is possible to show that the likelihood ratio (14) could be calculated from

$$T\{\log_e|V_r| - \log_e|V_u|\}$$

where V_r and V_u are the restricted and unrestricted estimates of V, respectively. In our case $T = 71$.

[9]The data were obtained from the Salomon Brothers publication *An Analytical Record*. Those data are monthly but are mid-month until 1959, at which time they are first of month. I linearly interpolated the earlier mid-month data in order to obtain approximate first of month series for the years 1953–58.

TABLE 1

ESTIMATES FOR A 5-YEAR GOVERNMENT BOND RATE AND 91-DAY TREASURY BILL RATE,
1953 II–1971 IV

j	1	2	3	4
Unrestricted estimates:				
α_j	−0.3663	−0.3235	0.1234	−0.0694
β_j	0.6373	0.4322	−0.3286	0.1703
γ_j	−0.2962	0.0203	0.2480	−0.1047
δ_j	0.2812	0.1200	−0.3934	0.0765
	$V = \begin{pmatrix} 0.3080 & 0.2072 \\ 0.2072 & 0.1924 \end{pmatrix}$,		$\lvert V \rvert = 0.01631$	
Two-step estimates:*				
γ_j	−0.0199	−0.0083	0.0016	−0.0021
δ_j	0.0285	0.0085	−0.0047	0.0053
	$V = \begin{pmatrix} 0.3080 & 0.2072 \\ 0.2072 & 0.2162 \end{pmatrix}$,		$\lvert V \rvert = 0.02364$	
Maximum likelihood estimates:				
α_j	−0.0717	−0.3660	−0.1465	0.0433
β_j	0.3700	0.3270	0.0995	0.0900
γ_j	−0.0183	−0.0154	−0.0033	0.0014
δ_j	0.0298	0.0172	0.0063	0.0029
	$V = \begin{pmatrix} 0.3362 & 0.2336 \\ 0.2336 & 0.2171 \end{pmatrix}$,		$\lvert V \rvert = 0.01840$	

Likelihood ratio statistic = 8.5816
Marginal significance level† = 0.3788

*α's and β's are the same as unrestricted estimates.

† Let X be a chi-square distributed random variable and let x be the test statistic. Then the marginal significance level is defined as $\mathrm{Prob}\{X > x\}$ under the null hypothesis.

Notice that the γ's and δ's estimated under the restriction (9) by both the two-step estimator and the maximum likelihood estimator are close to zero, so that with respect to the information in four lagged R_{1t}'s and R_{nt}'s, the long rate seems approximately described by a "weak" martingale.[10] That the restrictions given by the rational expectations theory of the term structure imply such an approximation for long rates under suitable regularity conditions was exploited earlier by Sargent (1976).

Modigliani and Sutch (1966) worked with a version of the theory in which only lagged short interest rates were included in the information set carried along in the model. As the argument leading to equation (2) shows, the rational expectations restrictions (2) are predicted to hold with θ_{t-1} being any subset of Ω_{t-1}, and in particular with θ_{t-1} being chosen in the

[10] The martingale property is a characteristic of conditional mathematical expectations. By a "weak" martingale I mean to denote a condition analogous to the martingale property ($\mathcal{E}_t x_{t+1} = x_t$, where $\mathcal{E}_t$ is mathematical expectation conditioned on some information set including at least x_t) holding for linear least-squares projections (i.e., the condition $E_t x_{t+1} = x_t$ where $E_t x_{t+1}$ is the linear least-squares projection of x_{t+1} based on information available at time t).

fashion of Modigiliani and Sutch, namely, $\theta_{t-1} = \{\Delta R_{1t-1}, \Delta R_{1t-2}, \ldots,$ $\Delta R_{1t-m}\}$. This specification of θ_{t-1} leads to the restriction on (3) that $\beta_i = \delta_i = 0, i = 1, \ldots, m$, where now the least-squares orthogonality conditions become $\mathcal{E}a_{jt} \Delta R_{1t-i} = 0$ for $j = 1, n,$ and $i = 1, \ldots, m$. With this restriction on the β's and δ's, (9) continues to represent the rational expectations restrictions across the α's and γ's. In fact, with the β_i's being zero, iterations on (10) are guaranteed to converge in one step. All of the estimation theory goes through as before.

Table 2 reports three sets of estimates with $\beta_i = \delta_i = 0, i = 1, \ldots, m$, with θ_{t-1} specified as $\{\Delta R_{1t-1}, \ldots, \Delta R_{1t-4}\}$. The likelihood ratio statistic pertinent for testing the null hypothesis that the rational expectations restrictions (9) are correct is only 3.0788. Since this statistic is distributed as chi-square with four degrees of freedom under the null hypothesis, the marginal significance level is 0.5447, which once again provides no strong evidence for rejecting the rational expectations restrictions.

It is interesting to test whether lagged ΔR_{nt}'s are usefully included in the information set θ_{t-1}. Comparing the unrestricted estimates in tables 1 and 2, i.e., the first sets of estimates, we note that the table 2 estimates are computed under a restriction on the table 1 specification. A likelihood ratio statistic for testing the null hypothesis that $\beta = \delta = 0$ can be computed as $T\{\log|V_r| - \log|V_u|\}$ where $|V_r|$ is the determinant of V estimated in table 2, while $|V_u|$ is the determinant in table 1. This statistic is distrib-

TABLE 2

ESTIMATES FOR A 5-YEAR GOVERNMENT BOND AND 91-DAY TREASURY BILL RATE, 1953 II–1971 IV ($\beta = \delta = 0$)

j	1	2	3	4
Unrestricted estimates:				
α_j	0.0847	−0.2229	0.0267	0.1492
γ_j	−0.1173	−0.0207	0.0808	0.0011
	$V = \begin{pmatrix} 0.3494 & 0.2311 \\ 0.2311 & 0.2089 \end{pmatrix}$,	$\|V\| = 0.01957$		
Two-step estimates:*				
γ_j	0.0020	−0.0024	0.0091	0.0077
	$V = \begin{pmatrix} 0.3494 & 0.2311 \\ 0.2311 & 0.2176 \end{pmatrix}$,	$\|V\| = 0.02258$		
Maximum likelihood estimates:				
α_j	0.2165	−0.2117	−0.0592	0.1540
γ_j	0.0055	−0.0065	0.0053	0.0086
	$V = \begin{pmatrix} 0.3603 & 0.2411 \\ 0.2412 & 0.2182 \end{pmatrix}$,	$\|V\| = 0.02044$		

Likelihood ratio test statistic = 3.0788
Marginal significance level† = 0.5447

*α's are the same as the unrestricted estimates.

† Let X be a chi-square distributed random variable and let x be the test statistic. Then the marginal significance level is defined as Prob$\{X > x\}$ under the null hypothesis.

uted as chi-square with eight degrees of freedom. The value of the test statistic turns out to be 12.94, which has a marginal significance level of 0.114. Computing the analogous test on the maximum likelihood restricted estimates (the third sets of estimates in tables 1 and 2) gives a likelihood ratio statistic of 7.438, which is distributed as chi-square with four degrees of freedom and so has a marginal significance level of 0.114. I would interpret these significance levels as being mildly though not spectacularly supportive of Modigliani and Sutch's choice of θ_{t-1}.

It should be emphasized that the theory predicts that none of the representations estimated in this paper will be invariant with respect to an intervention that alters the stochastic processes facing agents and thereby alters the second-order characteristics of the distributions of yields. For example, despite the moderate success of results that choose θ_{t-1} to be $\{\Delta R_{1t-1}, \Delta R_{1t-2}, \ldots\}$, it would not be appropriate to impose arbitrary alternative stochastic processes for the short rate (arguing that it is the monetary authority's instrument) and expect such term-structure relations to remain invariant.[11]

References

Granger, C. W. J. "Investigating Causal Relations by Econometric Models and Cross-spectral Methods." *Econometrica* (July 1969): 424–38.

Lucas, Robert E., Jr. "Econometric Policy Evaluation: A Critique." In *The Phillips Curve and the Labor Market*, edited by Karl Brunner and Allan Meltzer. Carnegie-Rochester Conferences on Public Policy, vol. 1, a supplementary series to the *J. Monetary Econ.* (1976).

Modigliani, Franco, and Shiller, Robert J. "Inflation, Rational Expectations, and the Term Structure of Interest Rates." *Economica* N.S. 40 (February 1973): 12–43.

Modigliani, Franco, and Sutch, Richard. "Innovations in Interest Rate Policy." *A.E.R. Papers and Proceedings* 61, no. 2 (May 1966): 178–97.

Roll, Richard. *The Behavior of Interest Rates.* New York: Basic Books, 1970.

———. "Rational Expectations and the Term Structure of Interest Rates." *J. Money, Credit and Banking* 4, no. 1 (February 1972): 74–97.

Sargent, Thomas J. "A Classical Macroeconometric Model for the United States." *J.P.E.* 84, no. 2 (April 1976): 207–37.

———. *Macroeconomic Theory.* New York: Academic Press, in press.

Shiller, Robert J. "Rational Expectations and the Structure of Interest Rates." Ph.D. dissertation, Massachusetts Inst. Tech., 1972.

Sims, Christopher A. "Money, Income, and Causality." *A.E.R.* 62, no. 4 (September 1972): 540–52.

Wilson, G. T. "The Estimation of Parameters in Multivariate Time Series Models." *J. Royal Statis. Soc.* B (1973): 76–85.

[11]This term-structure example can thus be added to the consumption, investment, and labor supply examples provided by Lucas (1976).

25

Estimation of Dynamic Labor Demand Schedules under Rational Expectations

Thomas J. Sargent

A dynamic linear demand schedule for labor is estimated and tested. The hypothesis of rational expectations and assumptions about the orders of the Markov processes governing technology impose overidentifying restrictions on a vector autoregression for straight-time employment, overtime employment, and the real wage. The model is estimated by the full-information maximum-likelihood method. The model is used as a vehicle for reexamining some of the paradoxical cyclical behavior of real wages described in the famous Dunlop–Tarshis–Keynes exchange.

Both Keynes (1939) and various classical writers asserted that real wages would move countercyclically as employers moved along downward-sloping demand schedules relating the employment-capital ratio to the real wage. Dunlop (1938) and Tarshis (1939) described evidence which they interpreted as failing to confirm a countercyclical pattern of real-wage movements. That and much subsequent evidence on the question, which is reviewed and extended by Bodkin (1969), consisted mostly of simple contemporaneous regressions between real wages and some measure of the stage of the business cycle. By and large that evidence was regarded as rejecting the view that the data can be described as observations falling along an aggregate demand schedule for employment. This view of the evidence in large measure stimulated attempts to describe aggregate employment and real wages by "disequilibrium models," the work of Barro and Grossman (1971) and Solow and Stiglitz (1968) being two prominent examples.

Work on this paper was supported by the Federal Reserve Bank of Minneapolis, which is not responsible for the conclusions. Robert Litterman very ably performed the rather involved calculations reported in this paper. Helpful comments from a referee are gratefully acknowledged. [John Kennan pointed out errors in the calculations in the original version of this paper. The present version corrects those errors; tables 5–13 have been corrected. The error was "minor" in the sense that most of the test statistics have been little affected by the corrections. I have made only the minimal changes in the text needed to square it with the corrected tables.]

[*Journal of Political Economy*, 1978, vol. 86, no. 6]

This paper aims to provide a framework for reexamining some of this evidence within the context of a stochastic and dynamic aggregate demand schedule for labor. The old evidence is simply not decisive because the view that the aggregate data lie along the type of demand schedule considered in this paper places no restrictions on the simple contemporaneous regressions in the studies summarized by Bodkin (1969); however, under certain conditions, that view does place restrictions on aggregate real wages and employment as a vector stochastic process. The plan of this paper is to extract and test these implications.

This paper starts from the findings of the recent paper by Salih Neftci (1978), which computed long two-sided distributed lags between aggregate employment and real wages for post-World War II data for the United States. Neftci found that there were complicated and economically significant dynamic interactions between real wages and employment and that there was much stronger evidence for Granger (1969) causality flowing from real wages to employment than for Granger causality in the reverse direction. Further, the influence of real wages on employment was predominantly negative.

To represent Neftci's findings in a slightly different form than he did, table 1 reports estimates of a fourth-order bivariate autoregression for quarterly aggregate measures of real wages w and employment n_1, both seasonally unadjusted. The theory of vector autoregressions and moving

TABLE 1

Vector Autoregressions for Seasonally Unadjusted Data
(1948I–1972IV)*

	Dependent Variable: n_{1t}		Dependent Variable: w_t	
	Coefficient	SE	Coefficient	SE
Constant	7.7038	2.7640	.17353	.1124
Trend	.0506	.0168	.00103	.0006
Fourth-quarter dummy	.5780	.4250	.02149	.0172
First-quarter dummy	−.9797	.3163	.03616	.0128
Second-quarter dummy	1.9887	.3883	.00646	.0158
n_{1t-1}	1.5946	.1075	−.00343	.0043
n_{1t-2}	−.9403	.2006	.00402	.0081
n_{1t-3}	.4128	.2001	−.00315	.0081
n_{1t-4}	−.1604	.1049	.00163	.0042
w_{t-1}	−1.5407	2.5467	.97586	.1036
w_{t-2}	2.0531	3.5659	−.02126	.1451
w_{t-3}	−4.5508	3.5039	.09912	.1426
w_{t-4}	1.4698	2.5500	−.13212	.1037
R^2	.9969	...	.99790	...
D–W	1.9835	...	2.04370	...
SE	.3677	...	.01500	...
Marginal significance level on lagged n's	.0000	...	.86900	...
Marginal significance level on lagged w's	.0910	...	.00000	...

* Observation period on left-hand-side variables.

TABLE 2

VECTOR-MOVING AVERAGE REPRESENTATION OF REAL WAGE AND AGGREGATE
EMPLOYMENT
(1948I-1972IV)*

Lag	1	2	3	4
0	.3697	0	0	.0150
1	.5897	−.00126	−.0231	.0146
2	.5946	−.00177	−.0287	.0140
3	.5464	−.00253	−.0840	.0149
4	.5025	−.00329	−.1553	.0139
5	.4444	−.00359	−.2103	.0130
6	.3741	−.00370	−.2580	.0123
7	.3080	−.00371	−.2983	.0115
8	.2520	−.00359	−.3262	.0108
9	.2048	−.00339	−.3426	.0102
10	.1661	−.00316	−.3493	.0096
11	.1357	−.00291	−.3480	.0091
12	.1125	−.00266	−.3406	.0086
13	.0950	−.00243	−.3285	.0081
14	.0820	−.00221	−.3135	.0076
15	.0724	−.00202	−.2966	.0071
16	.0652	−.00184	−.2789	.0067
17	.0597	−.00169	−.2611	.0063
18	.0554	−.00155	−.2436	.0059
19	.0519	−.00143	−.2269	.0055
20	.0488	−.00132	−.2110	.0051
21	.0460	−.00123	−.1962	.0048
22	.0434	−.00114	−.1824	.0045
23	.0410	−.00106	−.1696	.0042

NOTE.—Col. 1: Response of employment to 1 SD innovation in employment; col. 2: Response of real wage to 1 SD innovation in employment; col. 3: Response of employment to 1 SD innovation in real wage; col. 4: Response of real wage to 1 SD innovation in real wage. Correlation of innovations in employment and real wage is .2442.

* Observation period for left-hand-side variables. For method of construction of vector-moving average, see Appendix.

averages is reviewed briefly in the Appendix. The data are a straight-time wage index in manufacturing divided by the consumer price index, measured in 1967 dollars, and number of employees on nonagricultural payrolls, measured in millions of men. The data are described more in Section 3 below. The F-statistic pertinent for testing the null hypothesis that lagged real wages have zero coefficients in the vector autoregression for employment has a marginal significance level of .091. The F-statistic pertinent for testing the hypothesis that lagged levels of employment have zero coefficients in the vector autoregression for the real wage has a marginal significance level of .869.[1] This pattern is consistent with Neftci's finding much stronger evidence of Granger causality extending from real wages to employment than in the other direction.

Table 2 reports estimates of the moving average representation implied by the autoregressions in table 1. Table 2 depicts the matrix of responses to

[1] For data on the left-side variable extending from 1951I-1972IV, which more closely matches Neftci's period than mine, the marginal significance level for testing the null hypothesis that real wages do not Granger-cause employment is .0745, and for the null hypothesis that employment does not Granger-cause the real wage the marginal significance level is .5012. These autoregressions included constant, trend, and three seasonal dummies.

one-standard-deviation innovations in the real wage and employment respectively. A one-standard-deviation innovation in employment leads to a strong, sustained increase in employment and a small (relative to the response to its own innovation) sustained decrease in the real wage. A one-standard-deviation innovation in the real wage leads to a sustained and sizable decrease in employment and a sustained and sizable increase in the real wage. The response of employment to the real-wage innovation is of the same order of magnitude as it is to its own innovation, in contrast to the response of the real wage to the employment innovation. The magni-

TABLE 3

DECOMPOSITIONS OF VARIANCE OF FORECAST ERRORS*

| | VARIANCE OF k-STEP-AHEAD FORECAST ERROR | % VARIANCE IN k-STEP-AHEAD FORECAST ERROR EXPLAINED BY ORTHOGONALIZED INNOVATION IN: | |
		Employment	Real Wage
	Employment†		
Employment:			
$k = 1$	.1367	94.03	5.96
$k = 2$	.4783	95.24	4.75
$k = 3$	.8244	95.59	4.40
$k = 4$	1.1076	96.50	3.49
$k = 5$	1.3462	97.04	2.95
$k = 6$	1.5423	96.74	3.25
$k = 7$	1.7017	95.41	4.58
$k = 8$	1.8407	93.06	6.93
$k = 9$	1.9705	89.96	10.03
$k = 10$	2.0956	86.47	13.52
$k = 11$	2.2169	82.91	17.08
$k = 12$	2.3334	79.51	20.48
$k = 20$	2.9620	64.14	35.85
$k = 35$	3.2381	59.18	40.81
	Real Wage‡		
Real wage:			
$k = 1$	.00022	0	100.00
$k = 2$	.00043	.34	99.65
$k = 3$	.00062	.71	99.28
$k = 4$	.00083	1.25	98.74
$k = 5$	.00101	2.02	97.97
$k = 6$	.00117	2.78	97.21
$k = 7$	.00132	3.45	96.54
$k = 8$	.00145	4.04	95.95
$k = 9$	.00156	4.53	95.46
$k = 10$	.00166	4.91	95.08
$k = 11$	.00175	5.20	94.79
$k = 12$	.00183	5.41	94.58
$k = 20$	.00220	5.87	94.12
$k = 35$	.00238	5.91	94.08

* The orthogonalized innovation in employment here equals the innovation in employment, while the orthogonalized innovation in the real wage equals that part of the innovation in the real wage that is orthogonal to the innovation in employment.
† SE of orthogonalized innovation in employment = .01505.
‡ SE of orthogonalized innovation in real wage = .3586.

tude of the estimated response of employment to real-wage innovations seems of substantial economic significance.

Tables 3 and 4 report two alternative decompositions of the variances of the k-step-ahead forecast errors of the (n_1, w) process into parts attributable to variance in the "orthogonalized innovations" in employment and the real wage. As indicated in the Appendix, these decompositions are not unique, which accounts for the two tables. However, since the innovations in employment and the real wage in table 1 have only a moderate correla-

TABLE 4

Decompositions of Variance of Forecast Errors*

	Variance of k-step-ahead Forecast Error	% Variance in k-step-ahead Forecast Error Explained by Orthogonalized Innovation in:	
		Employment	Real Wage
	Employment†		
Employment:			
$k = 1$	.136	100.0	0
$k = 2$	.478	99.8	.10
$k = 3$	.824	99.8	.15
$k = 4$	1.107	99.2	.71
$k = 5$	1.346	97.7	2.27
$k = 6$	1.542	95.3	4.68
$k = 7$	1.701	92.0	7.92
$k = 8$	1.840	88.1	11.87
$k = 9$	1.970	83.8	16.16
$k = 10$	2.095	79.5	20.47
$k = 11$	2.216	75.4	24.52
$k = 12$	2.333	71.8	28.18
$k = 20$	2.962	56.6	43.38
$k = 35$	3.238	51.7	48.21
	Real Wage‡		
Real wage:			
$k = 1$	.00022	5.96	94.03
$k = 2$	.00043	4.34	95.65
$k = 3$	.00062	3.47	96.52
$k = 4$	.00083	2.74	97.25
$k = 5$	.00101	2.24	97.75
$k = 6$	.00117	1.95	98.04
$k = 7$	.00132	1.78	98.21
$k = 8$	.00145	1.67	98.32
$k = 9$	.00156	1.61	98.38
$k = 10$	.00166	1.56	98.43
$k = 11$	.00175	1.52	98.47
$k = 12$	.00183	1.48	98.51
$k = 20$	.00220	1.26	98.73
$k = 35$	.00238	1.17	98.82

* The orthogonalized innovation in the real wage here just equals the innovation in the real wage, while the orthogonalized innovation in employment equals that part of the employment innovation that is orthogonal to the innovation in the real wage.
† SE of orthogonalized innovation in employment = .0146.
‡ SE of orthogonalized innovation in real wage = .3697.

tion of .2442, the differences between the decompositions in tables 2 and 3 are bound to be modest, as they are. The tables reveal that a substantial percentage (40 or 48) of the 35-quarter-ahead forecast-error variance in employment (which approximates the steady-state variance in the indeterministic part of employment) is accounted for by innovations in the real wage. Only a small percentage (1 or 6) of the 35-quarter-ahead forecast-error variance in the real wage is accounted for by the innovation in employment.

Two characteristics of these results are particularly important for purposes of this study. First, there do appear to be some complicated dynamic interactions between aggregate employment and these real-wage data that might be susceptible to analysis with a dynamic model of the demand for employment. Second, these data seem to be consistent with the assumption that the real wage is not Granger-caused by employment. This assumption, which will be imposed below, substantially simplifies the modeling task.

The plan of this paper is to estimate a dynamic aggregative demand schedule for employment for postwar U.S. data. While the demand model makes employment depend inversely on the appropriate real wage, as does the static theory, a potentially rich dynamic structure is introduced into that dependence because firms are assumed to face costs of rapidly adjusting their labor force and so find it optimal to take into account future expected values of the real wage in determining their current employment. The model imposes overidentifying restrictions on a vector of stochastic processes composed of employment, a measure of overtime employment, and the real wage. The aim is to test the adequacy of these overidentifying restrictions.

The model is formed by blending the costly adjustment model of Lucas (1967), Treadway (1969), and Gould (1968) with Lucas's static model of overtime work and capacity (1970). The model is formulated so that it delivers linear decision rules relating the demand for straight-time employment and overtime employment each to the real-wage process. The model imposes the rational-expectations hypothesis, since firms are supposed to use the true moments of the real-wage process in forming forecasts. The rational-expectations hypothesis is a main source of the overidentifying restrictions imposed by the model.

In addition to providing some new evidence in the Dunlop-Tarshis tradition, this paper illustrates a technology for maximum-likelihood estimation of decision rules under the hypothesis that expectations are rational. That technology potentially has a variety of applications.[2]

---

[2]Applications of related methods are contained in Sargent (1977, 1978a). John Taylor (1978) uses a minimum-distance estimator to estimate a macroeconomic model subject to rational-expectations restrictions.

I. The Demand for Employment

The model is formed by taking Lucas's model of overtime work and capacity (1970) and amending it to permit potentially different adjustment costs to be associated with rapidly changing straight-time and overtime labor.[3] It is widely asserted that it is much cheaper to adjust the overtime labor force quickly than it is to adjust the straight-time labor force; consequently, it is alleged that overtime labor responds rapidly to the market signals that the firm receives, while the straight-time labor force responds more sluggishly. The model is designed to represent this phenomenon and to provide a framework for estimating its dimensions and testing it.

I shall work with a representative firm, although as I shall remark below, the model can handle certain kinds of diversity across firms. Following Lucas, suppose that the representative firm faces the instantaneous production function:

$$y(t + \tau) = f[n(t + \tau), k(t + \tau)], f_n, f_k, f_{nk} > 0; f_{nn}, f_{kk} < 0$$

$$t = 0, 1, 2, 3, \ldots$$

$$\tau \varepsilon [0, 1).$$

Here $y(t + \tau)$ is the rate of output per unit time at instant $t + \tau$, $n(t + \tau)$ is the number of employees at instant $t + \tau$, and $k(t + \tau)$ is the stock of capital at $t + \tau$. The length of the "day" is one, so that t indexes days and τ indexes moments within the day. The firm is assumed to have a constant capital stock over the day so that $k(t + \tau) = k(t) \equiv k_t$ for $\tau \varepsilon [0, 1)$. The firm is assumed to be able to hire workers for a straight-time shift of fixed length $h_1 < 1$ at the real wage w_t during day t. During the overtime shift of length $h_2 = 1 - h_1$, the firm can hire all the labor it wants during day t at the real wage pw_t, where $p \approx 1.5$ is an overtime premium. Thus, for the first h_1 moments of day t the firm must pay workers w_t, while for the remaining h_2 moments it must pay pw_t. Confronted with these market opportunities, it is optimal for the firm to choose to set $n(t + \tau) = n_{1t}$ for $\tau \varepsilon [0, h_1]$ and $n(t + \tau) = n_{2t}$ for $\tau \varepsilon (h_1, 1)$. That is, it is optimal for the firm to choose a single level of straight-time employment n_{1t} during t and a single level of overtime employment of n_{2t} during the day t.

The firm's output over the "day" is then

$$y_t = \int_0^1 y(t + \tau) \, d\tau$$

$$= h_1 f(n_{1t}, k_t) + h_2 f(n_{2t}, k_t).$$

[3] Restrictions on the production function required to permit Lucas's static model to account for the cyclical behavior of labor productivity and real average hourly earnings were discussed by Sargent and Wallace (1974). Adding differential costs for adjusting straight-time and overtime labor would widen the class of production functions that could lead to procyclical movements of average hourly earnings and labor productivity.

I take several steps to specialize this setup further. First, to simplify things, I assume that capital is constant over time so that k_t can be dropped as an argument from $f(\cdot, \cdot)$. (In the econometric work below, steps are taken to detrend the data prior to estimation partly in order to minimize the damage caused by this approximation.) Second, I assume a quadratic production function and write instantaneous output on the first and second shifts as

$$f(n_{1t}, k) = (f_0 + a_{1t})n_{1t} - (f_1/2)n_{1t}^2$$
$$f(n_{2t}, k) = (f_0 + a_{2t})n_{2t} - (f_1/2)n_{2t}^2$$

where $f_0, f_1 > 0$, and where a_{1t} and a_{2t} are exogenous stochastic processes affecting productivity of straight-time and overtime employment. I assume that $Ea_{1t} = Ea_{2t} = 0$. The stochastic processes a_{1t} and a_{2t} will be required to satisfy certain regularity conditions to be specified below.

The firm is assumed to bear daily costs of adjusting its straight-time labor force of $(d/2)(n_{1t} - n_{1t-1})^2$ and to bear daily costs of adjusting its overtime labor force of $(e/2)(n_{2t} - n_{2t-1})^2$. It is widely believed that it is substantially more expensive to adjust the straight-time labor force so that $d \gg e$. The firm faces an exogenous stochastic process for the real wage (w_t). The firm's straight-time and overtime wage bills are, respectively, $w_t h_1 n_{1t}$ and $p w_t h_2 n_{2t}$.

The firm chooses contingency plans for n_{1t} and n_{2t} to maximize its expected real present value:[4]

$$
\begin{aligned}
v_t = E_t \sum_{j=0}^{\infty} b^j [& (f_0 + a_{1t+j} - w_{t+j})h_1 n_{1t+j} - (f_1/2)h_1 n_{1t+j}^2 \\
& - \frac{d}{2}(n_{1t+j} - n_{1t+j-1})^2 + (f_0 + a_{2t+j} - p w_{t+j})h_2 n_{2t+j} \\
& - (f_1/2)h_2 n_{2t+j}^2 - \frac{e}{2}(n_{2t+j} - n_{2t+j-1})^2] \\
& f_0, f_1, d, e > 0, p > 1, 0 < b < 1,
\end{aligned}
\tag{1}
$$

where n_{1t-1} and n_{2t-1}, as well as the stochastic processes for w, a_1, and a_2, are given to the firm. Here b is a real discount factor that lies between zero and one. The operator E_t is defined by $E_t x \equiv Ex | \Omega_t$, where x is a random

---

[4]Optimization problems of this form are discussed by Holt, Modigliani, Muth, and Simon (1960), Graves and Telser (1972), and Kwakernaak and Sivan (1972). The treatment here closely follows that of Sargent (1978b). It would be straightforward to carry along n firms, each facing the same wage process and operating under the same functional form for its objective function (1), yet each having different values for the parameters f_0, f_1, d, and e. It would then be straightforward to aggregate the Euler equations and their solutions (7). Thus, assuming a representative firm is only a convenience, as the model admits a tidy theory of aggregation.

variable, E is the mathematical expectation operator, and Ω_t is an information set available to the firm at time t. I assume that Ω_t includes at least $\{n_{1t-1}, n_{2t-1}, a_{1t}, a_{1t-1}, \ldots, a_{2t}, a_{2t-1}, \ldots, w_t, w_{t-1}, \ldots\}$. The firm is assumed to maximize (1) by choosing stochastic processes for n_1 and n_2 from the set of stochastic processes that are (nonanticipative) functions of the information set Ω_t. (Below, I will further restrict the class of stochastic processes over which the optimization is carried out.) I assume that the stochastic processes w_t, a_{1t}, and a_{2t} are of exponential order less than $1/b$, which means that for some $K > 0$ and some x such that $1 \le x < 1/b$, $|E_t w_{t+j}| < K(x)^{j+t}$, $|E_t a_{1t+j}| < K(x)^{j+t}$, $|E_t a_{2t+j}| < K(x)^{j+t}$, for all t and all $j \ge 0$. I further assume that all random variables have finite first- and second-order moments.

First-order necessary conditions for the maximization of (1) consist of a set of "Euler equations" and a pair of transversality conditions.[5] The Euler equations for $\{n_{1t}\}$ and $\{n_{2t}\}$ are

$$bE_{t+j}n_{1t+j+1} + \phi_1 n_{1t+j} + n_{1t+j-1} = (h_1/d)(w_{t+j} - a_{1t+j} - f_0)$$
$$j = 0, 1, 2, \ldots,$$
$$bE_{t+j}n_{2t+j+1} + \phi_2 n_{2t+j} + n_{2t+j-1} = (h_2/e)(pw_{t+j} - a_{2t+j} - f_0)$$
$$j = 0, 1, 2, \ldots, \tag{2}$$

where

$$\phi_1 = -[(f_1 h_1/d) + (1 + b)]$$
$$\phi_2 = -[(f_1 h_2/e) + (1 + b)]. \tag{3}$$

The transversality conditions are

$$\lim_{T \to \infty} b^T E_t n_{1t+T} = \lim_{T \to \infty} b^T E_t n_{2t+T} = 0. \tag{4}$$

To solve the Euler equations for the optimum contingency plans, first obtain the factorizations

$$\left(1 + \frac{\phi_1}{b}z + \frac{1}{b}z^2\right) = (1 - \delta_1 z)(1 - \delta_2 z), \tag{5}$$

$$\left(1 + \frac{\phi_2}{b}z + \frac{1}{b}z^2\right) = (1 - \mu_1 z)(1 - \mu_2 z). \tag{6}$$

Given the assumptions about the signs and magnitudes of the parameters composing b, ϕ_1, and ϕ_2, it follows that factorizations exist with $0 < \delta_1 < 1 < (1/b) < \delta_2$ and $0 < \mu_1 < 1 < (1/b) < \mu_2$. It then follows that solutions of the Euler equations that satisfy the transversality conditions and

---

[5] See Sargent (1978*b*), chaps. 9 and 14.

the initial conditions are given by[6]

$$n_{1t} = \delta_1 n_{1t-1} - (\delta_1 h_1/d) \sum_{i=0}^{\infty} \left(\frac{1}{\delta_2}\right)^i E_t(w_{t+i} - a_{1t+i} - f_0), \qquad (7a)$$

$$n_{2t} = \mu_1 n_{2t-1} - (\mu_1 h_2/e) \sum_{i=0}^{\infty} \left(\frac{1}{\mu_2}\right)^i E_t(pw_{t+i} - a_{2t+i} - f_0). \qquad (7b)$$

It can be verified directly that these solutions satisfy the Euler equations and the transversality conditions. The polynomial equation (5) implicitly defines δ_1 and δ_2 as functions of $(f_1 h_1/d)$. By studying this polynomial,[7] it is possible to show that δ_1 is a decreasing function of $(f_1 h_1/d)$ and that $(1/\delta_2) = b \delta_1$. It follows that δ_1 and $(1/\delta_2)$ both increase with increases in the adjustment-cost parameter d. Reference to equation (7a) then shows that increases in the adjustment-cost parameter d, by increasing δ_1 and $(1/\delta_2)$, decrease the speed with which the firm responds to the real-wage and productivity signals that it receives. Similarly, μ_1 and $(1/\mu_2)$ are decreasing functions of $(f_1 h_2/e)$ and $(1/\mu_2) = b\mu_1$.

Equations (7a) and (7b) are decision rules for setting n_{1t} and n_{2t} as linear functions of n_{1t-1}, n_{2t-1}, and the conditional expectations $E_t w_{t+i}$, $E_t a_{1t+i}$, and $E_t a_{2t+i}$, $i = 0, 1, 2, \ldots$. However, in general, these conditional expectations are nonlinear functions of the information in Ω_t. Given particular stochastic processes for w_t, a_{1t}, and a_{2t}, equations (7a) and (7b) can be solved for decision rules expressing n_{1t} and n_{2t} as, in general, nonlinear functions of Ω_t.

For the purposes of empirical work, it is convenient to restrict ourselves to the class of decision rules that are linear functions of Ω_t. The optimal linear decision rules can be obtained by replacing the conditional mathematical expectations in (7a) and (7b) with the corresponding linear least-squares projections on the information set Ω_t. Accordingly, *henceforth, in all forecasting formulas, I will replace the mathematical expectation operator E by the linear least-squares projection operator $\widehat{E}$.*[8]

To derive from (7a) and (7b) explicit decision rules for n_{1t} and n_{2t} as functions of Ω_t, it is necessary further to restrict the stochastic processes w_t, a_{1t}, and a_{2t}. I assume that a_{1t} and a_{2t} are each first-order Markov processes for which

$$\begin{aligned} \widehat{E}_t a_{1t+i} &= \rho_1^i a_{1t} \quad i \geq 0 \\ \widehat{E}_t a_{2t+i} &= \rho_2^i a_{2t} \quad i \geq 0, \end{aligned} \qquad (8)$$

---

[6]See Sargent (1978b).

[7]See Sargent (1978b). The solution (7) clearly exhibits the certainty-equivalence or separation property. That is, the same solution for n_{1t} and n_{2t} would emerge if we maximized the criterion formed by replacing $(a_{1t+j}, a_{2t+j}, w_{t+j})$ by $(E_t a_{1t+j}, E_t a_{2t+j}, E_t w_{t+j})$ and dropping the operator E_t from outside the sum in (1).

[8]In the statistical literature the linear least-squares projection operator $\widehat{E}$ is often referred to as the "wide sense expectation" operator.

where $|\rho_1| < 1/b$, $|\rho_2| < 1/b$. That is, I assume that a_{1t} and a_{2t} are generated by the stochastic processes

$$
\begin{aligned}
a_{1t} &= \rho_1 a_{1t-1} + \tilde{\xi}_{1t}, \\
a_{2t} &= \rho_2 a_{2t-1} + \tilde{\xi}_{2t},
\end{aligned}
\tag{9}
$$

where $\tilde{\xi}_{1t}$ and $\tilde{\xi}_{2t}$ are least-squares residuals with finite variances and $\widehat{E}\tilde{\xi}_{1t}|\Omega_{t-1} = \widehat{E}\tilde{\xi}_{2t}|\Omega_{t-1} = 0$. Although (9) permits $\tilde{\xi}_{1t}$ and $\tilde{\xi}_{2t}$ to be arbitrarily correlated contemporaneously, it does in effect rule out correlation between them at any nonzero lags. I assume that w_t is an nth-order Markov process

$$
w_t = v_0 + v_1 w_{t-1} + v_2 w_{t-2} + \cdots + v_n w_{t-n} + \xi_{3t}, \tag{10}
$$

where ξ_{3t} is a least-squares disturbance that satisfies $\widehat{E}_{t-1}\xi_{3t} \equiv \widehat{E}\xi_{3t}|\Omega_{t-1} = 0$. The condition that $\widehat{E}\xi_{3t}|\Omega_{t-1} = 0$ means that ξ_{3t} is serially uncorrelated and that w_t is not caused in Granger's (1969) sense, by n_1 or n_2. That the lack of Granger causality from n_1 or n_2 to w is a workable approximation for the data to be studied here is supported by the empirical results of Neftci (1978), which are summarized above. It is convenient to represent the nth-order process (10) as the $(n + 1)$-vector first-order Markov process, $x_t = A x_{t-1} + \varepsilon_t$, where

$$
x_t = \begin{bmatrix} w_t \\ w_{t-1} \\ w_{t-2} \\ \vdots \\ w_{t-n} \\ 1 \end{bmatrix} \qquad \varepsilon_t = \begin{bmatrix} \xi_{3t} \\ 0 \\ 0 \\ \vdots \\ 0 \\ 0 \end{bmatrix}
$$

$$
A = \begin{bmatrix}
v_1 & v_2 & \cdots & & v_n & v_0 \\
1 & 0 & & & 0 & 0 \\
0 & 1 & & & 0 & 0 \\
\vdots & \vdots & & & & \\
0 & 0 & \cdots & 1 & 0 & 0 \\
0 & 0 & \cdots & 0 & 0 & 1
\end{bmatrix}.
$$

We can write,

$$
\begin{aligned}
x_{t+1} &= A x_t + \varepsilon_{t+1} \\
x_{t+2} &= A^2 x_t + \varepsilon_{t+2} + A\varepsilon_{t+1} \\
&\vdots \\
x_{t+j} &= A^j x_t + \varepsilon_{t+j} + A\varepsilon_{t+j-1} + \cdots A^{j-1}\varepsilon_{t+1}.
\end{aligned}
$$

Since $\widehat{E}_t \varepsilon_{t+k} = 0$ for $k \geq 1$, we have $\widehat{E}_t x_{t+j} = A^j x_t$. Assume that the eigenvalues of A are distinct so that A can be written as $A = P\Lambda P^{-1}$, where the columns of P are the eigenvectors of A and Λ is the diagonal matrix whose elements are the eigenvalues of A.[9] Then we have $\widehat{E}_t x_{t+j} = P\Lambda^j P^{-1} x_t$. Finally, let c be the $1 \times (n+1)$ row vector $(1, 0, 0, \ldots, 0)$ so that $w_t = c x_t$. We thus have that

$$\widehat{E}_t w_{t+j} = c P \Lambda^j P^{-1} x_t. \tag{11}$$

Substituting from (8) and (11) into (7a) gives[10]

$$n_{1t} = \delta_1 n_{1t-1} - \frac{\delta_1 h_1}{d} c P \sum_{i=0}^{\infty} \left(\frac{1}{\delta_2} \Lambda \right)^i P^{-1} x_t$$

$$+ \frac{\delta_1 h_1}{d} \left[f_0 \Big/ \left(1 - \frac{1}{\delta_2} \right) \right] + \frac{\delta_1 h_1}{d} \left[1 \Big/ \left(1 - \frac{\rho_1}{\delta_2} \right) \right] a_{1t}.$$

Let λ_i be the iith element of Λ. Since $\delta_2 = (1/\delta_1 b)$, we have that $|\lambda_i / \delta_2| = |\lambda_i \delta_1 b| < 1$ by virtue of the assumption that w_t is of exponential order less than $1/b$, that is, that $|\lambda_i \cdot b| < 1$. Then the infinite sum above converges and we can write

$$n_{1t} = \delta_1 n_{1t-1} - \frac{\delta_1 h_1}{d} c P (I - \delta_2^{-1} \Lambda)^{-1} P^{-1} x_t$$

$$+ \frac{\delta_1 h_1}{d} \left[f_0 \Big/ \left(1 - \frac{1}{\delta_2} \right) \right] + \frac{\delta_1 h_1}{d} \left[1 \Big/ \left(1 - \frac{\rho_1}{\delta_2} \right) \right] a_{1t}. \tag{12}$$

Let us write (12) as[11]

$$n_{1t} = \delta_1 n_{1t-1} + \alpha_1 w_t + \alpha_2 w_{t-1} + \cdots + \alpha_n w_{t-n+1} + \alpha_0$$

$$+ \frac{\delta_1 h_1}{d} \left(\frac{f_0}{1 - \delta_1 b} \right) + a'_{1t}, \tag{13}$$

where

$$(\alpha_1, \alpha_2, \ldots, \alpha_n, \alpha_0) = -\frac{\delta_1 h_1}{d} c P (I - \delta_1 b \Lambda)^{-1} P^{-1}$$

$$a'_{1t} = \frac{\delta_1 h_1}{d} \left(\frac{1}{1 - \rho_1 \delta_1 b} \right) a_{1t}. \tag{14}$$

---

[9]The assumption that w_t is of exponential order less than $(1/b)$ implies that the max $|\lambda_i| < (1/b)$, where λ_i is the ith element of Λ.

[10]Here I am using that

$$\left(\sum_{t=0}^{\infty} \left(\frac{1}{\delta_2} \right)^i \rho_1^i \right) a_{1t} = \left[1 \Big/ \left(1 - \frac{\rho_1}{\delta_2} \right) \right] a_{1t}$$

since $|\rho_1| < 1/b$ and $|\delta_2| > 1/b$, so that the infinite sum converges.

[11]Engineers directly obtain solutions of the form (13) by solving matrix Riccati equations, e.g., see Kwakernaak and Sivan (1972). In their jargon, our system is *not* "controllable" but is "stabilizable" and "detectable" so that convergence of iterations on the Riccati equation is assured. The stabilizability of our system depends on $\{a_{1t}\}$, $\{a_{2t}\}$, and $\{w_t\}$ being of exponential order less than $(1/b)$.

Proceeding in the same way, we can write the decision rule for n_{2t} as

$$n_{2t} = \mu_1 n_{2t-1} + \beta_1 w_t + \beta_2 w_{t-1} + \cdots + \beta_n w_{t-n+1} + \beta_0$$
$$+ \frac{\mu_1 h_2}{e}\left(\frac{f_0}{1 - \mu_1 b}\right) + a'_{2t}, \tag{15}$$

where

$$(\beta_1, \beta_2, \ldots, \beta_n, \beta_0) = -p\frac{\mu_1 h_2}{e}cP(I - \mu, b\Lambda)^{-1}P^{-1},$$
$$a'_{2t} = \frac{\mu_1 h_2}{e}\left(\frac{1}{1 - \rho_2 \mu_1 b}\right)a_{2t}. \tag{16}$$

Equations (14) and (16) succinctly summarize how the distributed lag coefficients, the α's and β's, reflect the combination of forecasting (through the parameters of P and Λ) and optimization (through the parameters d, δ, and μ) elements. Clearly, the decision rules (13) and (15) are not invariant with respect to changes in the stochastic process for real wages (10), a general characteristic of optimum decision rules whose far-reaching implications for econometric policy evaluation have been stressed by Robert E. Lucas, Jr. (1976).

Since I will fit the model to data that are deviations from means and trends, I shall henceforth drop the constants from (13), (15), and (10). Substitute (10) for w_t and subtract $\rho_1 a'_{1t-1}$ from both sides of (13) to get

$$n_{1t} = (\delta_1 + \rho_1)n_{1t-1} - \rho_1 \delta_1 n_{1t-2} + (\alpha_2 + \alpha_1 v_1 - \alpha_1 \rho_1)w_{t-1}$$
$$+ (\alpha_3 + \alpha_1 v_2 - \alpha_2 \rho_1)w_{t-2} + \cdots + (\alpha_n + \alpha_1 v_{n-1} - \alpha_{n-1}\rho_1)w_{t-n+1}$$
$$+ (\alpha_1 v_n - \alpha_n \rho_1)w_{t-n} + [\alpha_1 \xi_{3t} + (a'_{1t} - \rho_1 a'_{1t-1})]. \tag{17}$$

From our earlier assumptions, $\widehat{E}_{t-1}[\alpha_1 \xi_{3t} + (a'_{1t} - \rho_1 a'_{1t-1})] = 0$, so that (17) is the (vector) autoregression for n_{1t}. In particular, we have

$$\widehat{E}_{t-1}n_{1t} = (\delta_1 + \rho_1)n_{1t-1} - \rho_1 \delta_1 n_{1t-2} + (\alpha_2 + \alpha_1 v_1 - \rho_1 \alpha_1)w_{t-1}$$
$$+ (\alpha_3 + \alpha_1 v_2 - \alpha_2 \rho_1)w_{t-2}$$
$$+ \cdots + (\alpha_n + \alpha_1 v_{n-1} - \alpha_{n-1}\rho_1)w_{t-n+1}$$
$$+ (\alpha_1 v_n - \alpha_n \rho_1)w_{t-n}. \tag{18}$$

Similarly, we have for n_{2t}

$$n_{2t} = (\mu_1 + \rho_2)n_{2t-1} - \rho_2 \mu_1 n_{2t-2} + (\beta_2 + \beta_1 v_1 - \beta_1 \rho_2)w_{t-1}$$
$$+ (\beta_3 + \beta_1 v_2 - \beta_2 \rho_2)w_{t-2}$$
$$+ \cdots + (\beta_n + \beta_1 v_{n-1} - \beta_{n-1}\rho_2)w_{t-n+1}$$
$$+ (\beta_1 v_n - \beta_n \rho_2)w_{t-n} + [\beta_1 \xi_{3t} + (a'_{2t} - \rho_2 a'_{2t-1})]. \tag{19}$$

We can now write the complete three-variate vector autoregression for n_{1t}, n_{2t}, w_t as

$$
\begin{aligned}
n_{1t} = {}& (\delta_1 + \rho_1)n_{1t-1} - \rho_1\delta_1 n_{1t-2} + (\alpha_2 + \alpha_1 v_1 - \alpha_1\rho_1)w_{t-1} \\
& + (\alpha_3 + \alpha_1 v_2 - \alpha_2\rho_1)w_{t-2} \\
& + \cdots + (\alpha_n + \alpha_1 v_{n-1} - \alpha_{n-1}\rho_1)w_{t-n+1} \\
& + (\alpha_1 v_n - \alpha_n\rho_1)w_{t-n} + u_{1t}
\end{aligned}
\tag{20a}
$$

$$
\begin{aligned}
n_{2t} = {}& (\mu_1 + \rho_2)n_{2t-1} - \rho_2\mu_1 n_{2t-2} + (\beta_2 + \beta_1 v_1 - \beta_1\rho_2)w_{t-1} \\
& + (\beta_3 + \beta_1 v_2 - \beta_2\rho_2)w_{t-2} \\
& + \cdots + (\beta_n + \beta_1 v_{n-1} - \beta_{n-1}\rho_2)w_{t-n+1} \\
& + (\beta_1 v_n - \beta_n\rho_2)w_{t-n} + u_{2t}
\end{aligned}
\tag{20b}
$$

$$
w_t = v_1 w_{t-1} + v_2 w_{t-2} + \cdots + v_n w_{t-n} + u_{3t},
\tag{20c}
$$

where

$$
u_t \equiv \begin{bmatrix} u_{1t} \\ u_{2t} \\ u_{3t} \end{bmatrix} \equiv \begin{bmatrix} \alpha_1\xi_{3t} + (a'_{1t} - \rho_1 a'_{1t-1}) \\ \beta_1\xi_{3t} + (a'_{2t} - \rho_2 a'_{2t-1}) \\ \xi_{3t} \end{bmatrix} = \begin{bmatrix} n_{1t} - \widehat{E}_{t-1}n_{1t} \\ n_{2t} - \widehat{E}_{t-1}n_{2t} \\ w_t - \widehat{E}_{t-1}w_t \end{bmatrix}.
$$

Here u_t is the vector of innovations, that is, errors in predicting (n_{1t}, n_{2t}, w_t) from past information. There are $(3n + 4)$ regressors in (20), that is, w_{t-1}, $\ldots$, w_{t-n}, each of which appear three times, and n_{1t-1}, n_{1t-2}, n_{2t-1}, and n_{2t-2}, each of which appears once. The free parameters of the model are f_1, d, e, ρ_1, ρ_2, v_1, $\ldots$, v_n, so that there are $(n + 5)$ parameters to be estimated. As it turns out, the model is overidentified for $n > 1$.

Collecting the equations that summarize the restrictions that the model imposes on the vector autoregression (20), we have

$$
\phi_1 = -\left[\frac{f_1 h_1}{d} + (1 + b)\right]
$$

$$
\phi_2 = -\left[\frac{f_1 h_2}{e} + (1 + b)\right]
$$

$$
\left(1 + \frac{\phi_1}{b}z + \frac{1}{b}z^2\right) = (1 - \delta_1 z)(1 - \delta_2 z)
$$

$$
\left(1 + \frac{\phi_2}{b}z + \frac{1}{b}z^2\right) = (1 - \mu_1 z)(1 - \mu_2 z)
\tag{21}
$$

$$
(\alpha_1, \alpha_2, \ldots, \alpha_n, \alpha_0) = -\frac{\delta_1 h_1}{d}cP(I - \delta_1 b\Lambda)^{-1}P^{-1}
$$

$$
(\beta_1, \beta_2, \ldots, \beta_n, \beta_0) = -p\frac{\mu_1 h_2}{e}cP(I - \mu_1 b\Lambda)^{-1}P^{-1}
$$

$$
A = P\Lambda P^{-1}.
$$

Estimates of the free parameters $\theta = (f_1, d, e, \rho_1, \rho_2, v_1, \ldots, v_n)$ are obtained by using the method of maximum likelihood to estimate the vector autoregression (20a), (20b), and (20c), subject to (21).[12] Let $\widehat{u}_t = (\widehat{u}_{1t}, \widehat{u}_{2t}, \widehat{u}_{3t})'$ be the sample residual vector associated with the parameter values θ. Under the assumption that u_t is a trivariate normal vector with $Eu_t u_t' = V$, the likelihood function of a sample of observations on the residuals extending over $t = 1, \ldots, T$ is

$$L(\theta) = (2\pi)^{-(1/2)3T}|V|^{-T/2} \exp\left(-\frac{1}{2}\sum_{t=1}^{T} \widehat{u}_t' V^{-1} \widehat{u}_t\right). \qquad (22)$$

As shown by Wilson (1973) and Bard (1974), maximum-likelihood estimates of θ with V unknown can be obtained by minimizing $|\widehat{V}|$ with respect to θ, where $\widehat{V}$ is the sample covariance matrix of u_t,

$$\widehat{V} = \frac{1}{T}\sum_{t=1}^{T} \widehat{u}_t \widehat{u}_t'.$$

The matrix $\widehat{V}$ is the maximum-likelihood estimator of V (see Wilson [1973] or Bard [1974, pp. 62–66]).[13] The value of the likelihood function turns out to be $\log L(\theta) = -(1/2)mT \log (2\pi) - (1/2)T\{\log|\widehat{V}| + m\}$, where m is the number of variates, equal to three in the present model.

Now consider the unconstrained version of the vector autoregression (20) in which each of the $(3n + 4)$ regressors has its own free parameter. Let L_u be the value of the likelihood function at its unrestricted maximum, that is, the maximum obtained by permitting each of the $(3n + 4)$ regressors to have its own free parameter. Let L_r be the value of the likelihood under the restrictions (21). Then $-2 \log_e(L_r/L_u)$ is asymptotically distributed as $\chi^2(q)$ where $q = (3n + 4) - (n + 5)$ is the number of restrictions imposed by the theory. High values of the likelihood ratio lead to rejection of the restrictions that the theory imposes on the vector autoregression. Using the calculations of Wilson (1973, p. 80) or Bard (1974), it can be shown that the likelihood ratio is equal to $T\{\log_e|\widehat{V}_r| - \log_e|\widehat{V}_u|\}$, where $\widehat{V}_r$ and $\widehat{V}_u$ are the restricted and unrestricted estimates of V, respectively.

I also used a likelihood-ratio statistic to test the constrained vector autoregression ([20a], [20b], and [20c]) against a second and even less

---

[12]The parameters f_0 and v_0 are dropped because the data are in the form of deviations from means and trend terms. The parameters b, p, h_1, and h_2 will be fixed a priori.

[13]The likelihood function was maximized by using a derivative-free hill-climbing method with a Davidon-Fletcher-Powell algorithm for updating the Hessian. The complicated nature of the restrictions (21) led me to opt for a derivative-free method over an algorithm that required even analytical first derivatives. My attempts numerically to calculate asymptotic standard errors from the inverse of the information matrix were unsuccessful as one or two diagonal elements turned out to be negative.

constrained alternative, namely, an unconstrained trivariate vector auto-regression with n lagged values of n_1, n_2, and w on the right-hand side of each equation. Let $\hat{V}_u$ be the estimated sample covariance matrix of the residuals in the unrestricted vector autoregression. Then the appropriate likelihood-ratio statistic is given by $T\{\log_e|\hat{V}_r| - \log_e|\hat{V}_u|\}$. Since the unconstrained parameterization now has $9n$ free parameters, the likelihood ratio is asymptotically distributed as χ^2 with $\{9n - (n + 5)\}$ degrees of freedom.

II. Alternative Estimation Strategies

It should be stressed that the vector autoregression ([20a], [20b], and [20c]) which builds in the cross-equation restrictions implied by the model has been obtained under the assumption (8) that the productivity shocks a_{1t} and a_{2t} are first-order Markov processes. The forms of the vector auto-regressions ([20a], [20b], and [20c]) would be altered had we assumed other forms for the a_{1t} and a_{2t} processes, as the reader can verify by calculations paralleling those above.

An alternative estimation strategy is available that avoids the necessity to make specific assumptions about the forms of the stochastic processes for the disturbances a_{1t} and a_{2t}, only requiring that these processes be covariance stationary. The alternative estimator requires instead that the w_t process be strictly econometrically exogenous with respect to n_{1t} and n_{2t}, in particular requiring that $Ew_t a_{1s} = Ew_t a_{2s} = 0$ for all t and s. Under that assumption, the model (7a) and (7b) can readily be shown to place restrictions on the projections of n_{1t} and n_{2t}, respectively, on the entire $\{w_s\}$ process. The structure of those restrictions parallels those worked out by Sargent (1978a) for a consumption function example. An asymptotically efficient estimator such as "Hannan's efficient estimator," which allows for complicated serial-correlation patterns in the disturbances, could then be applied to estimating the projections with and without the restrictions imposed by the model.

This alternative estimation strategy gets along with much weaker assumptions about the serial-correlation properties of the disturbance processes $\{a_{1t}\}$ and $\{a_{2t}\}$ at the cost of making somewhat more stringent assumptions about the exogeneity of w_t, that is, about the correlation between w_t and the a_{js}'s. The original estimator proposed that operates on (20a), (20b), and (20c) does assume that $\{w_t\}$ is a process that is *not* caused in Granger's (1969) sense by n_{1t} or n_{2t}, that is, that $\hat{E}(w_t|w_{t-1}, w_{t-2}, \ldots, n_{1t-1}, n_{1t-2}, \ldots, n_{2t-1}, n_{2t-2}, \ldots) = \hat{E}(w_t|w_{t-1}, w_{t-2}, \ldots)$. Now Sims's (1972) theorems assure us that if w_t is *not* Granger-caused by n_{1t} or n_{2t}, then there exists a statistical representation in which w_t is strictly econometrically exogenous with respect to n_{1t} or n_{2t}. However, this statistical representation need not correspond with the appropriate economic behavioral relationship. It is possible for n_{1t} or n_{2t} to fail to cause w_t, and yet for "instantaneous causality" to flow from n_{1t} or n_{2t} to w_t so that w_t is not strictly exogenous in the appropriate model. See Sargent (1977a) for an example of this phenomenon within the context of Cagan's model of hyperinflation. The "autoregressive estimator" based on (20a), (20b), and (20c) permits arbitrary correlation between the innovations to n_{1t} or n_{2t} and w_t and makes no assumption about which pattern of instantaneous causality explains those correlations. On the other hand, the alternative "projection estimator" attributes all of those correlations to the workings of the demand schedules for n_{1t} and n_{2t}, ([7a] and [7b]). For the present application, I prefer the estimator that makes the weaker assumption about the correlations between innovations to employment and the real wage.

The reader by now will have understood that optimizing, rational-expectations models do not entirely eliminate the need for side assumptions not grounded in economic theory. Some arbitrary assumptions about the nature of the serial-correlation structure of the disturbances and/or about strict econometric exogeneity are necessary in order to proceed with estimation.

Perhaps I should conclude this section by pointing to another source of arbitrariness, namely, the latitude at our disposal in specifying the firm's optimization problem. For example, adding terms like $-(d_2/2)(n_{1t} - 2n_{1t-1} + n_{t-2})^2$ to the firm's daily profits would lead to Euler equations that are fourth-order stochastic difference equations and would lead to decision rules that depend on two lagged values of employment. Such specifications would seem plausible and would lead to materially different restrictions than those above on vector autoregressions (or projections of n on w, as the case may be). There are clearly limits set by the requirements of econometric identification on our ability to estimate such complicated adjustment-cost parameterizations. Identification problems in such models have as yet received little attention at a general level.

The general theme of this section has been to issue a warning that rational-expectations, optimizing models will not be able to save us entirely from the ad hoc assumptions and interpretations made in applied work. However, this is not to deny that the rational-expectations hypothesis seems promising as a device for organizing restrictions on parameterizations of econometric models.

III. Parameter Estimates

The model was estimated using quarterly data on total civilian employment and a straight-time real-wage index, with the period of observation extending from 1947I through 1972IV, of which n observations at the beginning of the sample are lost when the order of the wage autoregression is set at n. The variable n_{1t} was in the first instance measured by the seasonally adjusted BLS series "Employees on Nonagricultural Payrolls, Private and Government." To get a measure of n_{2t}, the following procedure was used. I defined the variable $\bar{h}_t$ to be average weekly hours, a series measured by the seasonally adjusted BLS series "Average Weekly Hours in Manufacturing." I then estimated total man-hours by $\bar{h}_t n_{1t}$. Finally, I measured n_{2t} by $n_{2t} = \bar{h}_t n_{1t} - h_1 n_{1t}/h_2$, where h_1 and h_2 were set a priori at 37 and 17, respectively.[14] The real wage w_t was measured by deflating the seasonally unadjusted BLS series "Average Hourly Earnings: Straight-Time Manufacturing Production Workers" by the seasonally unadjusted consumer price index (1967 = 100).

I also created seasonally unadjusted measures of n_{1t} and n_{2t} by taking as a measure of n_{1t} the seasonally unadjusted BLS series "Employees on Private Nonagricultural Payrolls" and then using the preceding procedure to create estimates of n_{2t} by using the seasonally unadjusted average weekly hours series. The data are quarterly averages of monthly data. Notice that h_1 and h_2 are constants that are independent of time.

For reasons developed in Sargent (1976), I would argue that seasonally unadjusted data are the ones that ought to be used. Briefly, this view follows from the assumption that agents are themselves observing and responding to the seasonally unadjusted variates, so that the cross-equation restrictions delivered by the model pertain to the seasonally unadjusted data. Seasonal adjustment of the data could cause rejection of the cross-equation rational-expectations restrictions when they are in fact true. However, arguments have been made against this position in advocacy of seasonally adjusted data in exactly the present context (see Sims [1976]). For this reason, I report some results for both seasonally adjusted and unadjusted data.

I begin by describing the estimates obtained using the seasonally adjusted employment series together with the seasonally unadjusted real-wage series. (Later I will describe the results obtained with the seasonally unadjusted series for all variables.) Before estimating the model, the data on n_{1t} and n_{2t} were each detrended by regressing them on a constant, linear trend and trend squared, and then using the residuals from those regressions as the data for estimating the model.[15] The data on w_t were formed

[14]That these values for h_1 and h_2 do not add to unity, as in the theoretical presentation of the model, amounts only to a harmless renormalization. I guessed at these values for h_1 and h_2. The guess for h_1 measured in hours per week seemed reasonable after having inspected the time series for average weekly hours. For purposes of constructing the data on n_{2t}, the choice of both h_1 and h_2 matters. For the purpose of estimating the demand functions, given the data on n_1 and n_2, only the ratio of h_1 to h_2 matters, as proportional changes in d and e can cancel the effects of proportionate increases in h_1 and h_2.

[15]With the seasonally unadjusted employment data, I first regressed each of n_{1t}, n_{2t}, and w_t against a constant, trend, trend squared, and three seasonal dummies and used the residuals from those regressions as the data.

as the residuals from a regression on a constant, linear trend, trend squared, and three seasonal dummies. Two reasons can be given for detrending in this way prior to fitting the model. First, the model ignores the effects of capital on employment, except to the extent that these can be captured by the productivity processes a_{1t} and a_{2t}. Second, the theory predicts that any deterministic components of the employment and real-wage processes will not be related by the same distributed lag model as are their indeterministic parts. Detrending prior to estimation is a device designed to isolate the indeterministic components. The real wage is measured in 1967 dollars, while employment is measured in millions of men.

Table 5 reports estimates of the model for $n = 4$ for the seasonally adjusted data. The free parameters were f_1, d, e, ρ_1, ρ_2, v_1, v_2, v_3, and v_4 with b being fixed at .95, h_1 at 37, h_2 at 17, and the premium p at 1.5. Since $n = 4$, for the more constrained of our two alternative hypotheses, the likelihood-ratio statistic is asymptotically distributed as χ^2 with $q = (3n + 4) - (n + 5) = 7$ degrees of freedom. The likelihood ratio is 9.57, which has a "marginal confidence level" of .786. The marginal confidence level is defined as follows. Let X be a χ^2 random variable with q degrees of freedom. Let x be the value of the likelihood-ratio statistic. Then the marginal confidence level is defined as $\text{Prob}\{X < x\}$ under the null

TABLE 5

SEASONALLY ADJUSTED DATA, FIRST SOLUTION OF LIKELIHOOD EQUATIONS ($n = 4$)
(1948I–1972IV)*

$f_1 = .5325$	$v_1 = .9554$	$KS(n_1)\dagger = .0755$
$d = 2367.87$	$v_2 = .0033$	$KS(n_2) = .0766$
$e = 122.737$	$v_3 = .0754$	$KS(w) = .0309$
$\rho_1 = .5957$	$v_4 = -.1849$	
$\rho_2 = .2052$		
$\delta_1 = .9322$	$\mu_1 = .7790$	
$\alpha_1 = -.0685$	$\beta_1 = -.5120$	
$\alpha_2 = .0046$	$\beta_2 = .0160$	
$\alpha_3 = .0054$	$\beta_3 = .0233$	
$\alpha_4 = .0112$	$\beta_4 = .0701$	

$$V = \begin{pmatrix} .9171E - 01 & .1982E + 00 & .1297E - 02 \\ & .7705E + 00 & .2075E - 02 \\ & & .1949E - 03 \end{pmatrix}$$

$$B^{-1}VB^{-1\prime} = \begin{pmatrix} .9189E - 01 & .1990E + 00 & .1311E - 02 \\ & .7727E + 00 & .2175E - 02 \\ & & .1949E - 03 \end{pmatrix}$$

$|\widehat{V}_r| = .5494E - 05$, $|\widehat{V}_u| = .4993E - 05$ $|\widetilde{V}_u| = .34743E - 05$

$T\{\log |\widehat{V}_r| - \log |\widehat{V}_u|\} = 9.5686$ $T\{\log |\widehat{V}_r| - \log |\widetilde{V}_u|\} = 45.8263$

Marginal confidence level $= .7856$ Marginal confidence level $= .9867$

*Period of observation on the dependent variables.

† $KS(n_1)$, $KS(n_2)$, and $KS(w)$ denote Kolmogorov-Smirnov statistics on cumulated periodograms of innovations of n_1, n_2, and w, respectively.

hypothesis. High values of the confidence level lead to rejecting the hypothesis. The likelihood-ratio statistic in this case indicates that the hypothesis cannot be rejected at marginal significance levels below .20. However, versus the less-constrained alternative hypothesis, the marginal confidence level is .9867, which indicates that the data do contain substantial evidence against the hypothesis. Notice the different lag shapes and the magnitudes of the distributed lag coefficients of straight-time employment and overtime employment in the real wage, the α's and β's, respectively. Overtime employment is estimated to be more responsive to the real wage. Further, the straight-time adjustment cost parameter d is estimated to be much larger than the overtime adjustment cost parameter e. That is why n_{1t} depends more strongly on n_{1t-1} than n_{2t} does on n_{2t-1}, that is, why δ_1 is estimated to exceed μ_1.

Since the likelihood ratio test assumes that the u's are serially uncorrelated, table 5 also reports three statistics, $KS(n_1)$, $KS(n_2)$, and $KS(w)$, which are Kolmogorov-Smirnov statistics from the cumulated periodograms for u_1, u_2, and u_3, that is, for the estimated innovations for n_1, n_2, and w, respectively, implied by the vector autoregression constrained by the model. The Kolmogorov-Smirnov statistic recorded is the maximum absolute deviation of the cumulated periodogram of the disturbance from its theoretical value under the assumption that the disturbances are serially uncorrelated. Durbin (1969) reports tables for the distribution of this statistic, though they are not applicable where lagged dependent variables are included as regressors, as in the present case. It is nevertheless of some comfort that the Kolmogorov-Smirnov statistics in table 5 and in subsequent tables do not signal dangerous levels of serial correlation. Notice that the Kolmogorov statistics are greater for the n_1 and n_2 innovations than for the w innovation. This is symptomatic of the fact that the model fits an nth-order Markov process in w but only permits two lagged own-values to enter the autoregressions for n_1 and n_2, thereby leaving it more likely that the model will neglect some higher-order serial correlation for n_1 and n_2. This pattern for the Kolmogorov-Smirnov statistics repeats itself in the subsequent tables.

Table 5 also reports the estimated covariance matrix of the innovations $V = Eu_t u_t'$. Recall that

$$\begin{bmatrix} u_{1t} \\ u_{2t} \\ u_{3t} \end{bmatrix} = \begin{bmatrix} 1 & 0 & \alpha_1 \\ 0 & 1 & \beta_1 \\ 0 & 0 & 1 \end{bmatrix} \begin{bmatrix} \xi_{1t} \\ \xi_{2t} \\ \xi_{3t} \end{bmatrix} \equiv B\xi_t$$

where $\xi_{1t} = a'_{1t} - \rho_1 a'_{1t-1}$, $\xi_{2t} = a'_{2t} - \rho_2 a'_{2t-1}$, and where

$$B = \begin{bmatrix} 1 & 0 & \alpha_1 \\ 0 & 1 & \beta_1 \\ 0 & 0 & 1 \end{bmatrix}, \qquad \xi_t = \begin{bmatrix} \xi_{1t} \\ \xi_{2t} \\ \xi_{3t} \end{bmatrix}.$$

Then, since $\xi_t = B^{-1}u_t$, the covariance matrix of ξ_t can be estimated from $E\xi_t\xi_t' = B^{-1}VB^{-1'}$, an estimate of which is also reported in table 5. The correlation between the innovations to a_{1t}', and to a_{2t}', that is, ξ_{1t} and ξ_{2t}, is estimated to be .747. The correlation between the innovations to a_{1t}' and w_t, that is, ξ_{1t} and ξ_{3t}, is .3097, while that between ξ_{2t} and ξ_{3t} is .1772. I had expected ξ_{1t} and ξ_{2t} to be even more highly correlated than they are.

As it happens, the estimates reported in table 5 correspond to the higher of two local maxima of the likelihood function which I found. The parameter estimates associated with the lower of these two local maxima are reported in table 6. In view of the form of the vector autoregression ([20a], [20b], and [20c]), it is not at all surprising that the likelihood function should exhibit multiple maxima. In particular, notice that the coefficients in (20a), (20b), and (20c) on n_{1t-1}, n_{1t-2}, n_{2t-1}, n_{2t-2} are, respectively, $(\delta_1 + \rho_1)$, $-\delta_1\rho_1$, $(\mu_1 + \rho_2)$, and $-\mu_1\rho_2$. If it were not for the constraints across μ_1 and the β's and across δ_1 and the α's and the appearance of ρ_1 and ρ_2 elsewhere on the right-hand side of (20a), (20b), and (20c), the parameters δ_1, ρ_1, μ_1, and ρ_2 would not be identified, since it would be impossible to distinguish the effects of δ_1 from ρ_1 and the effects of μ_1 from ρ_2. The presence of lagged w's on the right-hand side of (20a), (20b), and (20c) and the aforementioned constraints resolve this identification problem but leave a vestige of it in the form of probable multiple peaks in the likelihood function with small samples. Comparing the parameter esti-

TABLE 6

Second Solution of Likelihood
Equations Seasonally Adjusted Data,
$(n = 4)$ (1948I–1972IV)*

$f_1 = 19.80$	$\rho_1 = .9372$	$v_1 = .9542$
$d = 2377.90$	$\rho_2 = .7800$	$v_2 = .0052$
$e = 104.02$	$\mu_1 = .2002$	$v_3 = .0743$
$\delta_1 = .5886$		$v_4 = -.1867$
$\alpha_1 = -.0195$	$\beta_1 = -.0600$	$KS(n_1) = .0759$
$\alpha_2 = .00013$	$\beta_2 = -.00014$	$KS(n_2) = .0772$
$\alpha_3 = .00033$	$\beta_3 = -.00044$	$KS(w) = .0309$
$\alpha_4 = .00203$	$\beta_4 = .00213$	

$$V = \begin{pmatrix} .9220E - 01 & .2000E + 00 & .1298E - 02 \\ & .7747E + 00 & .2077E - 02 \\ & & .1949E - 03 \end{pmatrix}$$

$$B^{-1}VB^{-1'} = \begin{pmatrix} .9225E - 01 & .2002E + 00 & .1301E - 02 \\ & .7749E + 00 & .2089E - 02 \\ & & .1949E - 03 \end{pmatrix}$$

$|\widehat{V}_r| = .5497E - 05$, $|\widehat{V}_u| = .4993E - 05$
$T\{\log|\widehat{V}_r| - \log|\widehat{V}_u|\} = 9.6253$
Marginal confidence level = .7892

*Period of observation on the dependent variables.

mates in tables 5 and 6 shows that table 5 is a low (ρ_1, ρ_2)-high (δ_1, μ_1) solution, while table 6 reports the low (δ_1, μ_1)-high (ρ_1, ρ_2) solution. Notice that for the table 6 estimates, $\rho_1 + \delta_1 = 1.526$ and $\rho_1 \delta_1 = .552$, while for the table 5 estimates, $\rho_1 + \delta_1 = 1.528$ while $\rho_1 \delta_1 = .555$.

Figures 1 and 2 depict two views of the log likelihood surface as a function of δ_1 and ρ_1. The log likelihood surface has a ridge and is characterized by two local maxima. Figure 3 depicts iso-likelihood contours in the (δ_1, ρ_1) plane. These figures emphasize the weakness of the identification of (δ_1, ρ_1) and of (μ_1, ρ_2).

The presence of multiple maxima of the likelihood function means that caution is called for in interpreting the test statistics reported, since the asymptotic distribution on which the test is computed does not predict multiple maxima for the likelihood function and so does not provide a very good approximation for the sample size that we are studying. The presence of multiple maxima of the likelihood function also argues for starting the nonlinear estimation from several different initial parameter estimates. I followed this practice in each case reported below.

Table 7 reports the estimates for the seasonally unadjusted data with $n = 4$. The estimates indicate $d \gg e$ and are qualitatively similar to those described above. For testing the model versus the more constrained of the two alternative hypotheses, the marginal confidence level is .56. Versus the less constrained alternative, the marginal confidence level is .67. These

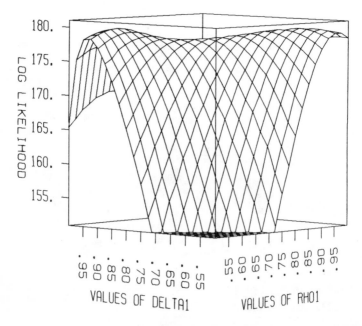

Fig. 1—Likelihood surface

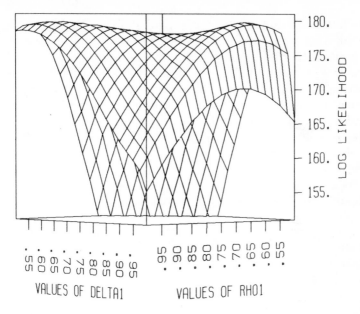

VALUES OF DELTA1   VALUES OF RHO1

Fig 2.—Likelihood surface

TABLE 7
SEASONALLY UNADJUSTED DATA $(n = 4)$ (1948I–1972IV)*

$f_1 = .4709$
$d = 3266.00$
$e = 78.60$
$\rho_1 = .3967$
$\rho_2 = .1006$
$\delta_1 = .9487$
$\alpha_1 = -.0498$
$\alpha_2 = -.0023$
$\alpha_3 = .0035$
$\alpha_4 = .0088$

$v_1 = .9167$
$v_2 = .0185$
$v_3 = .0997$
$v_4 = -.1969$

$\mu_1 = .7429$
$\beta_1 = -.6739$
$\beta_2 = .0044$
$\beta_3 = .0187$
$\beta_4 = .0936$

$KS(n_1) = .0679$
$KS(n_2) = .0735$
$KS(w) = .0253$

$$V = \begin{pmatrix} .1404E + 00 & .2664E + 00 & .1150E - 02 \\ & .8155E + 00 & .9539E - 03 \\ & & .1945E - 03 \end{pmatrix}$$

$$B^{-1}VB^{-\prime} = \begin{pmatrix} .1405E + 00 & .2672E + 00 & .1159E - 02 \\ & .8169E + 00 & .1085E - 02 \\ & & .1945E - 03 \end{pmatrix}$$

$|\widehat{V}_r| = .7848E - 05, |\widehat{V}_u| = .7324E - 05$
$T\{\log |\widehat{V}_r| - \log |\widehat{V}_u|\} = 6.9043$
Marginal confidence level = .5611

$|\widetilde{V}_u| = .58289E - 05$
$T\{\log |\widehat{V}_r| - \log |\widetilde{V}_u|\} = 29.7430$
Marginal confidence level = .6742

*Period of observation on the dependent variables.

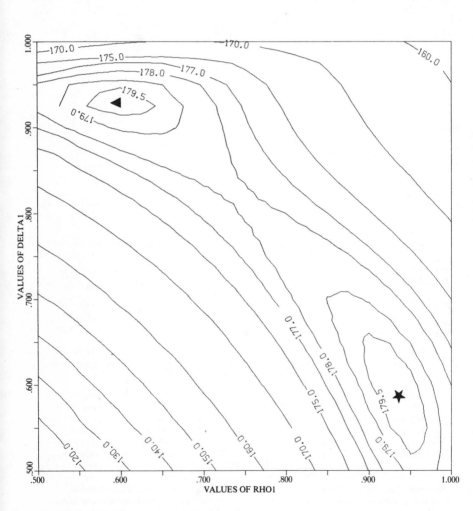

VALUE
AT PEAKS
★ 179.88384
▲ 179.91114

Fig. 3 — Iso-likelihood contours

TABLE 8

Seasonally Unadjusted Data $(n = 8)$ $(1949I-1972IV)$*

$f_1 = .2859$	$v_1 = .9048$	$v_5 = .0296$
$d = 3266.29$	$v_2 = .0751$	$v_6 = .0856$
$e = 75.6755$	$v_3 = .1132$	$v_7 = -.1441$
$\rho_1 = .5601$	$v_4 = -.2533$	$v_8 = .0173$
$\rho_2 = .1724$		
$\delta_1 = .9633$	$\mu_1 = .7932$	$KS(n_1) = .0697$
$\alpha_1 = -.0547$	$\beta_1 = -.8794$	$KS(n_2) = .0769$
$\alpha_2 = .0017$	$\beta_2 = -.0166$	$KS(w) = .0352$
$\alpha_3 = .0059$	$\beta_3 = .0441$	
$\alpha_4 = .0126$	$\beta_4 = .1580$	
$\alpha_5 = -.0000$	$\beta_5 = -.0130$	
$\alpha_6 = .0016$	$\beta_6 = .0087$	
$\alpha_7 = .0064$	$\beta_7 = .0868$	
$\alpha_8 = -.0009$	$\beta_8 = -.0114$	

$$V = \begin{pmatrix} .9532E - 01 & .2139E + 00 & .1190E - 02 \\ & .7932E + 00 & .2350E - 02 \\ & & .1797E - 03 \end{pmatrix}$$

$$B^{-1}VB^{-1\prime} = \begin{pmatrix} .9545E - 01 & .2150E + 00 & .1200E - 02 \\ & .7975E + 00 & .2508E - 02 \\ & & .1797E - 03 \end{pmatrix}$$

$|\widehat{V}_r| = .4915E - 05, |\widehat{V}_u| = .3948E - 05$ $\qquad$ $|\widetilde{V}_u| = .339897E - 05$

$T\{\log |\widehat{V}_r| - \log |\widehat{V}_u|\} = 21.0198$ $\qquad$ $T\{\log |\widehat{V}_r| - \log |\widetilde{V}_u|\} = 35.4066$

Marginal confidence level $= .8638$ $\qquad$ Marginal confidence level $= .0063$

Hansen Test Statistic for Strict Exogeneity $= 5.2284$
Marginal confidence level of Hansen statistic $= .9266$

*Period of observation on the dependent variables.

results indicate that the sample does not contain strong evidence against the hypothesis.

Table 8 reports estimates of the model for the seasonally unadjusted data with $n = 8$. The likelihood-ratio statistic for testing against the more constrained alternative hypothesis is now distributed asymptotically as χ^2 with 15 degrees of freedom under the null hypothesis that the model is correct. Once again, both likelihood ratios indicate that the sample does not contain too much evidence against the model.[16] For the seasonally

[16]Table 8 also reports a test statistic that Lars Hansen has proposed for testing the null hypothesis that $E\xi_{1t}\xi_{3t} = E\xi_{2t}\xi_{3t} = 0$. This null hypothesis, that the innovations to a'_{1t} and a'_{2t} both are orthogonal to the innovation to w_t, is a sufficient condition that w_t is strictly econometrically exogenous in the labor-demand schedules as represented in (13) and (15). These orthogonality conditions are sufficient for strict exogeneity of w_t in (13) and (15), *given* the assumption that w_t is not Granger caused by n_1 or n_2. The test statistic is a quadratic form in the estimated covariance matrix $B^{-1}VB^{-1\prime}$ and is asymptotically distributed as chi-square with two degrees of freedom. The marginal confidence level of the test statistic is .927, which indicates that the data contain somewhat moderate, but not spectacular, evidence against the null hypothesis of strict exogeneity of $\{w_t\}$ in (13) and (15). The test statistic is described in Hansen and Sargent (1978). [This note was added while revising the paper for this volume.]

unadjusted data with $n = 8$, table 9 reports the maximum-likelihood estimates of the vector autoregression (20a), (20b), and (20c), both unconstrained and constrained by the restrictions of the model (21). The constrained and unconstrained estimates are close except in one respect: The model-constrained vector autoregressions for n_1 and n_2 have coefficients on lagged w's that are generally much smaller in absolute value than their unconstrained counterparts. This pattern is also reflected in tables 10 through 14. Table 10 shows the vector moving average representation implied by the model-constrained estimates while table 11 shows a decomposition of variance of the 35-quarter-ahead forecast-error variance. Tables 12 and 13 show the corresponding moving average representation and decomposition of variance for the unconstrained estimates that are reported in table 9. Comparison of tables 10 and 12, on one hand, and tables 11 and 13, on the other, indicates that while the constrained model captures the same response of n_1 and n_2 to their own innovations that is depicted in the unconstrained estimates, the constrained model substantially underestimates the responses of n_1 and n_2 to innovations in w. The moving

TABLE 9
Vector Autoregressions ($n = 8$) Seasonally Unadjusted Data
(1949I–1972IV)

	Unconstrained	Constrained by (21)
(20a):		
n_{1t-1}	1.5405	1.5234
n_{1t-2}	−.5672	−.5395
w_{t-1}	−.5019	−.0172
w_{t-2}	−2.3065	.0009
w_{t-3}	.3722	.0031
w_{t-4}	−1.2789	.0067
w_{t-5}	5.9131	−.0000
w_{t-6}	−.1290	.0008
w_{t-7}	−5.6493	.0034
w_{t-8}	1.0665	−.0005
(20b):		
n_{2t-1}	1.0056	.9656
n_{2t-2}	−.1858	−.1367
w_{t-1}	−.9141	−.6606
w_{t-2}	10.9315	−.0191
w_{t-3}	−9.6982	.0509
w_{t-4}	−5.0961	.1825
w_{t-5}	21.3571	−.0150
w_{t-6}	−10.1041	.0101
w_{t-7}	−2.3063	.1003
w_{t-8}	−2.5990	−.0132
(20c):		
w_{t-1}	.8999	.9048
w_{t-2}	.0401	.0751
w_{t-3}	.1254	.1132
w_{t-4}	−.2676	−.2533
w_{t-5}	.0965	.0296
w_{t-6}	.0917	.0856
w_{t-7}	−.2225	−.1441
w_{t-8}	.0348	.0173

TABLE 10

Moving Average Representation Implied by Model for
Seasonally Unadjusted (Table 8) Estimates

Lag	n_1	w	n_2
Response to a one-standard-deviation innovation in n_1:			
0.	.4202	0	0
1.	.6401	0	0
2.	.7485	0	0
3.	.7948	0	0
4.	.8069	0	0
5.	.8005	0	0
6.	.7840	0	0
7.	.7625	0	0
8.	.7385	0	0
9.	.7137	0	0
10.	.6887	0	0
11.	.6641	0	0
12.	.6401	0	0
13.	.6168	0	0
14.	.5943	0	0
15.	.5725	0	0
16.	.5515	0	0
17.	.5313	0	0
18.	.5118	0	0
19.	.4930	0	0
20.	.4749	0	0
21.	.4574	0	0
22.	.4406	0	0
23.	.4244	0	0
24.	.4088	0	0
25.	.3938	0	0
26.	.3794	0	0
27.	.3654	0	0
28.	.3520	0	0
29.	.3391	0	0
30.	.3266	0	0
31.	.3146	0	0
Response to a one-standard-deviation innovation in w:			
0.	0	.0143	0
1.	−.0002	.0129	−.0094
2.	−.0006	.0127	−.0179
3.	−.0009	.0141	−.0239
4.	−.0012	.0116	−.0270
5.	−.0014	.0101	−.0279
6.	−.0015	.0100	−.0272
7.	−.0015	.0070	−.0247
8.	−.0014	.0052	−.0213
9.	−.0013	.0037	−.0173
10.	−.0011	.0015	−.0129
11.	−.0009	.0002	−.0087
12.	−.0007	−.0008	−.0048
13.	−.0005	−.0020	−.0013
14.	−.0003	−.0025	.0016
15.	−.0002	−.0028	.0039
16.	−.0000	−.0031	.0055
17.	.0001	−.0029	.0065
18.	.0002	−.0027	.0069
19.	.0002	−.0024	.0069
20.	.0002	−.0020	.0065
21.	.0002	−.0015	.0058
22.	.0002	−.0011	.0049
23.	.0002	−.0007	.0039
24.	.0002	−.0003	.0029

TABLE 10 (*Continued*)

25.	.0001	.0000	.0019
26.	.0001	.0003	.0010
27.	.0000	.0005	.0002
28.	−.0000	.0006	−.0005
29.	−.0000	.0007	−.0009
30.	−.0001	.0007	−.0013
31.	−.0001	.0007	−.0015

Response to a one-standard-deviation innovation in n_2:

0.	0	0	1.0385
1.	0	0	1.0028
2.	0	0	.8263
3.	0	0	.6608
4.	0	0	.5251
5.	0	0	.4167
6.	0	0	.3306
7.	0	0	.2622
8.	0	0	.2080
9.	0	0	.1650
10.	0	0	.1309
11.	0	0	.1038
12.	0	0	.0824
13.	0	0	.0653
14.	0	0	.0518
15.	0	0	.0411
16.	0	0	.0326
17.	0	0	.0259
18.	0	0	.0205
19.	0	0	.0163
20.	0	0	.0130
21.	0	0	.0102
22.	0	0	.0081
23.	0	0	.0064
24.	0	0	.0051
25.	0	0	.0041
26.	0	0	.0032
27.	0	0	.0026
28.	0	0	.0020
29.	0	0	.0016
30.	0	0	.0013
31.	0	0	.0010

Correlation matrix of innovations:

	n_1	w	n_2
n_1	1.00	.220	.775
w		1.000	.144
n_2			1.000

average representation implied by the model-constrained estimates have one-standard-deviation wage innovations giving rise to much smaller movements in n_1 and n_2 than are those associated with one-standard-deviation own innovations in n_1 and n_2. Contrast this with the relatively sizable responses of n_1 and n_2 to real-wage innovations in the unconstrained estimates. The decompositions of variance in tables 11 and 13 indicate the extent to which the constrained model attributes less of a role to real-wage innovations in driving n_1 and n_2.

Notice how both tables 10 and 12 show n_2 responding more quickly to an own innovation than does n_1.

TABLE 11

Variance Decompositions for Forecast Errors
Implied by Model (Tables 8 and 9 Estimates)
Seasonally Unadjusted Data

	n_1	w	n_2
$x = n_1$	95.2	4.79	0
$x = w$	0	100.	0
$x = n_2$	58.39	1.56	40.05

Note.— Percentage of 35-step-ahead forecast error variance in x accounted for by "orthogonalized innovations" in n_1, w, n_2. Orthogonalization order: w, n_1, n_2. Orthogonalization order refers to the procedure described in the Appendix of defining an orthogonal u process from $u_t = Fε_t$. If the orthogonalization order is n_1, w, n_2, then the "orthogonalized n_1 innovation" is simply the n_1 innovation; the "orthogonalized w innovation" is the part of the w innovation orthogonal to the n_1 innovation; the "orthogonalized n_2 innovation" is the part of the n_2 innovation that is orthogonal to both the n_1 and w innovations.

The estimates in tables 10–13 came from the data that are residuals from regressions on constant, trend, trend squared, and three seasonal dummies. Table 14 is the counterpart of table 13 where trend squared has been omitted. The effect of dropping trend squared is to increase somewhat the percentage of the variance of the 35-quarter-ahead prediction error in n_1 or n_2 that is explained by innovations in the real wage. The results in table 14 are presented to form a bridge to the estimates of Neftci and those summarized in the introduction, which included trend but not trend-squared terms.

The vector autoregressions summarized in tables 9–14 all impose the extensive zero restrictions incorporated in (20a), (20b), and (20c), for example, lagged n_2's do not appear in the autoregression for n_1. Tables 15 and 16 report summary statistics for fourth-order vector autoregressions with no such zero restrictions built in, that is, four lags of each variable appear in the autoregression for each of n_1, n_2, and w. A constant, trend, and three seasonal dummies are also included in the regressions. Table 15 reports marginal significance levels appropriate for testing the null hypothesis that n_1 or n_2 or w fails to Granger-cause each of the other variables. These F-statistics are consistent with Neftci's results and indicate stronger evidence for Granger causality flowing from w to n_1 and n_2 than from n_1 or n_2 to w. However, the statistics also indicate Granger causality from n_1 to n_2 and from n_2 to n_1, patterns which are ruled out by the model (20a), (20b), (20c), and (21). The data indicate dynamic interactions between n_1 and n_2 that the model in its present form cannot account for. The decompositions of variance of 35-quarter-ahead forecast errors in table 16 once again reinforce Neftci's findings in confirming that substantial percentages of the variance in employment forecasting errors are attributable to innovations in the real wage.

TABLE 12

MOVING AVERAGE REPRESENTATION IMPLIED BY MAXIMUM LIKELIHOOD
ESTIMATES OF VECTOR AUTOREGRESSION, UNCONSTRAINED
SEASONALLY UNADJUSTED DATA (1948I–1972IV)

Lag	n_1	w	n_2
Response to a one-standard-deviation innovation in n_1:			
0.	.3917	0	0
1.	.6034	0	0
2.	.7073	0	0
3.	.7474	0	0
4.	.7502	0	0
5.	.7318	0	0
6.	.7018	0	0
7.	.6660	0	0
8.	.6280	0	0
9.	.5896	0	0
10.	.5522	0	0
11.	.5162	0	0
12.	.4820	0	0
13.	.4497	0	0
14.	.4194	0	0
15.	.3910	0	0
16.	.3645	0	0
17.	.3397	0	0
18.	.3166	0	0
19.	.2950	0	0
20.	.2749	0	0
21.	.2562	0	0
22.	.2387	0	0
23.	.2224	0	0
24.	.2073	0	0
25.	.1931	0	0
26.	.1800	0	0
27.	.1677	0	0
28.	.1563	0	0
29.	.1456	0	0
30.	.1357	0	0
31.	.1264	0	0
Response to a one-standard-deviation innovation in w:			
0.	0	.0143	0
1.	−.0072	.0128	−.0130
2.	−.0503	.0121	−.0092
3.	−.1038	.0132	−.1421
4.	−.1794	.0102	−.3371
5.	−.1807	.0091	−.1859
6.	−.1412	.0096	−.1814
7.	−.1645	.0059	−.2162
8.	−.1888	.0042	−.2261
9.	−.2178	.0027	−.3018
10.	−.2583	.0000	−.3350
11.	−.2744	−.0009	−.2937
12.	−.2873	−.0019	−.2974
13.	−.3078	−.0033	−.2748
14.	−.3135	−.0035	−.2345
15.	−.3158	−.0037	−.2133
16.	−.3138	−.0040	−.1676
17.	−.2991	−.0035	−.1157
18.	−.2826	−.0031	−.0817
19.	−.2637	−.0027	−.0391
20.	−.2388	−.0019	−.0034
21.	−.2146	−.0013	.0200
22.	−.1896	−.0008	.0453

TABLE 12 (*Continued*)

23.	−.1636	−.0001	.0613
24.	−.1406	.0003	.0678
25.	−.1195	.0006	.0730
26.	−.1002	.0010	.0707
27.	−.0848	.0011	.0637
28.	−.0719	.0012	.0562
29.	−.0616	.0012	.0449
30.	−.0545	.0011	.0327
31.	−.0494	.0010	.0216

Response to a one-standard-deviation innovation in n_2:

0.	0	0	.9921
1.	0	0	.9977
2.	0	0	.8190
3.	0	0	.6382
4.	0	0	.4896
5.	0	0	.3738
6.	0	0	.2849
7.	0	0	.2171
8.	0	0	.1653
9.	0	0	.1259
10.	0	0	.0959
11.	0	0	.0731
12.	0	0	.0556
13.	0	0	.0424
14.	0	0	.0323
15.	0	0	.0246
16.	0	0	.0187
17.	0	0	.0143
18.	0	0	.0109
19.	0	0	.0083
20.	0	0	.0063
21.	0	0	.0048
22.	0	0	.0037
23.	0	0	.0028
24.	0	0	.0021
25.	0	0	.0016
26.	0	0	.0012
27.	0	0	.0009
28.	0	0	.0007
29.	0	0	.0005
30.	0	0	.0004
31.	0	0	.0003
32.	0	0	.0002
33.	0	0	.0002
34.	0	0	.0001

Correlation matrix of innovations:

	n_1	w	n_2
n_1	1.00	.2176	.7526
w		1.0000	.1716
n_2			1.0000

In summary, while the model usually passes the likelihood-ratio tests I have calculated, it does seem to do violence to two aspects of the data. First, the model generates estimates that seem to understate the magnitude of the inverse influence exerted by the real wage on employment. Second, a priori the model neglects dynamic interactions between n_1 and n_2 that seem to be there. On the first point, the maximum-likelihood estimates of

TABLE 13

Decomposition of Variance of Forecast Error for Unconstrained Estimates, Seasonally Unadjusted Data (1948I–1972IV)

	n_1	w	n_2
Orthogonalization order* $= n_1, w, n_2$:			
$x = n_1$	82.03	17.97	0
$x = w$	4.74	95.26	0
$x = n_2$	43.59	20.25	36.16
Orthogonalization order $= n_1, n_2, w$:			
$x = n_1$	82.03	17.97	.003
$x = w$	4.74	95.25	.01
$x = n_2$	45.59	20.48	35.94
Orthogonalization order $= w, n_1, n_2$:			
$x = n_1$	91.58	8.42	0
$x = w$	0	100	0
$x = n_2$	44.79	19.05	36.16

Note.—Percentage of 35-step-ahead forecast error variance in x accounted for by "orthogonalized innovations" in n_1, w, n_2.

*Orthogonalization order refers to the procedure described in the appendix of defining an orthogonal u process from $u_t = Fe_t$. If the orthogonalization order is n_1, w, n_2, then the "orthogonalized n_1 innovation" is simply the n_1 innovation; the "orthogonalized w innovation" is the part of the w innovation orthogonal to the n_1 innovation; the "orthogonalized n_2 innovation" is the part of the n_2 innovation that is orthogonal to both the n_1 and w innovations.

TABLE 14

Decomposition of Variance of Forecast Errors, Seasonally Unadjusted Data (1948I–1972IV)

	n_1	w	n_2
Orthogonalization order* $= n_1, w, n_2$:			
$x = n_1$	50.74	49.26	0
$x = w$	3.58	96.42	0
$x = n_2$	45.68	24.71	29.62
Orthogonalization order $= n_1, n_2, w$:			
$x = n_1$	50.74	49.23	.03
$x = w$	3.58	96.36	.06
$x = n_2$	45.68	24.31	30.01
Orthogonalization order $= w, n_1, n_2$:			
$x = n_1$	64.66	35.34	0
$x = w$	0	100	0
$x = n_2$	46.80	23.59	29.62

Note.—Percentage of 35-step-ahead forecast error variance in x accounted for by "orthogonalized innovations" in n_1, w, n_2. Data are residuals from regressions on constant, trend, and three seasonal dummies, with no trend-squared terms, in contradistinction to the table 13 results.

* Orthogonalization order refers to the procedure described in the Appendix of defining an orthogonal u process from $u = Fe_t$. If the orthogonalization order is n_1, w, n_2, then the "orthogonalized n_1 innovation" is simply the n_1 innovation; the "orthogonalized w innovation" is the part of the w innovation orthogonal to the n_1 innovation; the "orthogonalized n_2 innovation" is the part of the n_2 innovation that is orthogonal to both the n_1 and w innovations.

TABLE 15

Summary Statistics for Fourth-Order Vector
Autoregressions for (n_1, n_2, w)
Seasonally Unadjusted Data*
(1948I–1972IV)

Marginal Significance Levels† Pertinent for
Testing Null Hypothesis That Lagged n_1 or n_2 or
w's Have Zero Coefficients in Autoregression for x

	n_1	n_2	w
$x = n_1$	.0000	.0000	.2000
$x = n_2$	.0395	.0000	.0446
$x = w$	.6857	.6128	.0000

* Regressions included a constant, trend, and three seasonal dummies.
† Where f is the calculated value of the pertinent F-statistic, the
marginal significance level is defined as prob$\{F > f\}$ under the null
hypothesis.

TABLE 16

Decomposition of Variance of Forecast Error
Implied by Vector Autoregression for (n_1, n_2, w)
Seasonally Unadjusted Data
(1948I–1972IV)

	n_1	w	n_2
Orthogonalization order* = n_1, w, n_2:			
$x = n_1$	21.82	48.74	29.44
$x = w$	.76	98.39	.85
$x = n_2$	23.64	16.25	60.25
Orthogonalization order = w, n_1, n_2:			
$x = n_1$	26.90	43.66	29.44
$x = w$	2.11	97.03	.85
$x = n_2$	20.82	18.93	60.24

Note.—Percentage of 35-quarter ahead forecast error variance in x
accounted for by "orthogonalized innovation" in n_1, w, n_2.
* Orthogonalization order refers to the procedure described in the
Appendix of defining an orthogonal u process from $u_t = F\varepsilon_t$. If the
orthogonalization order is n_1, w, n_2, then the "orthogonalized n_1 innovation" is simply the n_1 innovation; the "orthogonalized w innovation"
is the part of the w innovation orthogonal to the n_1 innovation; the
"orthogonalized n_2 innovation" is the part of the n_2 innovation that is
orthogonal to both the n_1 and w innovations.

the parameters d and e, which also influence the response to w of n_1 and n_2, respectively, seem mainly to have been chosen to permit the model to capture the response of n_1 and n_2 to their own innovations. As a by-product, this involved understating the responses of n_1 and n_2 to w, which seems less costly in terms of the likelihood function than misstating the response to own innovations. Perhaps a richer specification of the Markov processes for a_{1t} and a_{2t}, say permitting them to be second-order processes, would permit enough flexibility to remedy this feature. Permitting the Markov processes for a_{1t} and a_{2t} to depend on lagged cross terms a_2 and a_1, respectively, would provide one way to remedy the second deficiency of the model, for it would potentially permit dynamic interactions between n_1 and n_2 of the kind revealed by table 15. Another way to account for those dynamic interactions would be to let costs of adjustment for n_1 depend on the level of n_2, and vice versa. This could be done while remaining within the linear-quadratic framework of this paper. However, extensions in each of these directions, while feasible, are costly both in the sense that they reduce the degree of overidentification of the model and in the sense that they make maximum-likelihood estimation more expensive.

IV. Conclusions

The simple contemporaneous correlations that formed the evidence in the original Dunlop-Tarshis-Keynes exchange and also in much of the follow-up empirical work done to date are not sufficient to rule on the question of whether the time series are compatible with a model in which firms are always on their demand schedules for employment. This is true according to virtually any dynamic and stochastic theory of the demand for employment. In this paper, I have tried to indicate one way in which the time-series evidence can be brought to bear on the question in the context of a simple dynamic, stochastic model. The empirical results are moderately comforting to the view that the employment-real-wage observations lie along a demand schedule for employment. It is important to emphasize that this view has content (i.e., imposes overidentifying restrictions) because I have a priori imposed restrictions on the orders of the adjustment-cost processes and on the Markov processes governing disturbances. At a general level without such restrictions, it is doubtful whether the equilibrium view has content.

Appendix
Vector Autoregressions and Moving Averages

Let x_t be an $(n \times 1)$ vector jointly covariance stationary, linearly indeterministic stochastic process. The mth-order vector *autoregression* for this process is

$$x_t = \alpha + \sum_{j=1}^{m} A_j x_{t-j} + \varepsilon_t^m, \tag{A1}$$

where ε_t^m is an $(n \times 1)$ vector of least-squares disturbances. Here α is an $(n \times 1)$ vector and the A_j's are $n \times n$ matrices that under mild regularity conditions are uniquely determined by the population orthogonality conditions $E\varepsilon_t^m = 0$ and $E\varepsilon_t^m x'_{t-j} = 0_{n \times n}, j = 1, 2, \ldots, m$. The ε_t^m process is termed the process of innovations, the parts of x_t that cannot be predicted linearly from m lagged x_t's; ε_t^m is the process of one-step-ahead prediction errors. If $m = \infty$, the orthogonality conditions imply that $E\varepsilon_t^m \varepsilon_{t-s}^{m'} = 0$ for $s \neq 0$, having the practical implication that if m is taken to be big enough, as we shall assume, the ε_t^m vector is serially uncorrelated. If we solve the vector difference equation (A1) for x_t backward in terms of the ε process and ignore transient terms, we get the vector *moving average* representation

$$x_t = \alpha' + \sum_{j=0}^{\infty} C_j \varepsilon_{t-j}^m \tag{A2}$$

where α' is an $(nx1)$ vector of constants, where C_j is an (nxn) matrix and $C_0 \equiv I$. The matrix Fourier transforms of the A_j's and C_j's are related by

$$(I - A_1 e^{-iw} - \cdots - A_m e^{-iwm})^{-1} = \sum_{j=0}^{\infty} C_j e^{-iwj}.$$

The $(nx1)$ vector process ε_t^m is composed of disturbances that are mutually orthogonal at all nonzero lags and leads (by the orthogonality conditions), but

$$E\varepsilon_t^m \varepsilon_t^{m'} = \sum$$

is not in general diagonal. To illustrate how to construct a moving average representation with a disturbance process that is orthogonal contemporaneously as well as at all lags, let $n = 2$ and consider the transformation

$$\begin{pmatrix} \varepsilon_{1t}^m \\ \varepsilon_{2t}^m \end{pmatrix} = \begin{pmatrix} 1 & 0 \\ \rho & 1 \end{pmatrix} \begin{pmatrix} u_{1t} \\ u_{2t} \end{pmatrix} = Fu_t,$$

where $\rho = E\varepsilon_{1t}^m \varepsilon_{2t}^m / E(\varepsilon_{1t}^m)^2$. Here we are choosing $u_{1t} = \varepsilon_{1t}^m$ and are decomposing ε_{2t}^m by the least-squares projection equation $\varepsilon_{2t}^m = \rho \varepsilon_{1t}^m + u_{2t}$ where the least-squares orthogonality condition $Eu_{2t}\varepsilon_{1t}^m = 0$ implies that $\rho = E\varepsilon_{1t}^m \varepsilon_{2t}^m / E(\varepsilon_{1t}^m)^2$. Here u_{2t} is the part of ε_{2t}^m that is orthogonal to ε_{1t}^m. By construction, u_{1t} and u_{2t} are orthogonal. Therefore, a new moving average representation in terms of mutually orthogonal disturbances at all lags is given by

$$x_t = \alpha' + \sum_{j=0}^{\infty} C_j Fu_{t-j}$$

$$= \alpha' + \sum_{j=0}^{\infty} D_j u_{t-j},$$

where $D_j = C_j F$. Of course, there is more than one such choice of u_t processes that does the job. For example, in the $n = 2$ example, we could have selected $u_{1t} = \varepsilon_{2t}^m$ and then chosen u_{2t} as the part of ε_{1t}^m that is orthogonal to ε_{2t}^m. In the text, for the $n = 2$ case, I have calculated moving average representations for both of the ways of choosing u_t discussed above. More generally any choice of $u_t = F^{-1}\varepsilon_t^m$ that makes $Eu_t u_t' = F^{-1}\Sigma F'^{-1}$ a diagonal matrix can be used to deliver a moving average representation in terms of a u process that is orthogonal contemporaneously as well as at all leads and lags.

In the $n = 2$ case, the first-mentioned way of defining u_t is equivalent with changing the form of the vector autoregression (A1) by adding current x_{1t} to the right-hand side of the autoregression for x_{2t} and then solving the vector-difference equation for a moving average representation in terms of the vector of residuals from this pair of autoregressions. The second-mentioned way of defining u_t amounts to changing the form of the vector autoregression (A1) by adding current x_{2t} to the right-hand side of the autoregression for x_{1t} (leaving current x_{1t} excluded from the autoregression for x_{2t}) and calculating the moving average in terms of the residuals from these equations.

The k-step-ahead error in forecasting x_t linearly from its own past is given by

$$x_t - \widehat{E}_{t-k}x_t = C_0\varepsilon_t^m + \cdots + C_{k-1}\varepsilon_{t-k-1}^m$$
$$= D_0 v_t + \cdots + D_{k-1}u_{t-k+1},$$

where $\widehat{E}_{t-k}x_t$ is the linear least-squares forecast of x_t given $x_{t-k}, x_{t-k-1}, \ldots$ From the extensive orthogonality conditions built in, we have that the covariance matrix of k-step-ahead prediction errors is $E(x_t - \widehat{E}_{t-k}x_t)(x_t - \widehat{E}_{t-k}x_t)' = D_0\widehat{E}u_t u_t' D_0' + \cdots + D_{k-1}Eu_t u_t' D_{k-1}'$. By calculating the diagonal terms in this formula, we achieve a decomposition of the variance k-step-ahead prediction error into the parts attributable to variance in the n components of u_t. For every choice of u_t process, there is such a decomposition of variance.

Under certain regularity conditions, least-squares estimates of the vector autoregression (A1) are known to be statistically consistent (Anderson and Taylor [1976] and Ljung [1976]). For a more extensive discussion of vector stochastic processes and some macroeconomic applications, see Sargent (1978b).

References

Anderson, T. W., and Taylor, John B. "Conditions for Strong Consistency of Least Squares Estimates in Linear Models." Technical Report no. 213, Stanford Univ. Inst. Math. Studies Soc. Sci., August 1976.

Bard, Yonathan. *Nonlinear Parameter Estimation.* New York: Academic Press, 1974.

Barro, Robert J., and Grossman, H. I. "A General Disequilibrium Model of Income and Employment." *A.E.R.* 61 (March 1971): 82–93.

Bodkin, Ronald G. "Real Wages and Cyclical Variations in Employment: An examination of the Evidence." *Canadian J. Econ.* 2 (August 1969): 353–74.

Dunlop, John T. "The Movement of Real and Money Wage Rates." *Econ. J.* 48 (September 1938): 413–34.

Durbin, J. "Tests for Serial Correlation in Residual Analysis Based on the Periodogram of Least-Squares Residuals." *Biometrika* 56 (March 1969): 1–15.

Gould, John P. "Adjustment Costs in the Theory of Investment of the Firm." *Rev. Econ. Studies* 35 (January 1968): 47–55.

Granger, C. W. J. "Investigating Causal Relations by Econometric Models and Cross-spectral Methods." *Econometrica* 37, no. 3 (July 1969): 424–38.

Graves, R., and Telser, L. *Functional Analysis in Mathematical Economics: Optimization over Infinite Horizons.* Chicago: Univ. Chicago Press, 1972.

Hansen, Lars Peter, and Sargent, Thomas J. "Techniques for the Application of Rational Expectations Models to Economic Time Series." Manuscript. Minneapolis: Federal Reserve Bank of Minneapolis, July 1978.

Holt, Charles C.; Modigliani, F.; Muth, T. F.; and Simon, H. A. *Planning Production, Inventories, and Work Force.* Englewood Cliffs, N.J.: Prentice-Hall, 1960.

Keynes, John Maynard. "Relative Movements of Real Wages and Output." *Econ. J.* 49 (March 1939): 34–51.

Kwakernaak, Huibert, and Sivan, Raphael. *Linear Optimal Control Systems.* New York: Wiley Interscience, 1972.

Ljung, L. "Consistency of the Least Squares Identification Method." *IEEE Transactions on Automatic Control* (October 1976), pp. 779–81.

Lucas, Robert E. "Adjustment Costs and the Theory of Supply." *J.P.E.* 75, no. 4, pt. 1 (August 1967): 321–34.

———. "Capacity, Overtime, and Empirical Production Functions." *A.E.R.* Papers and Proc. 60, no. 2 (May 1970): 23–27.

———. "Econometric Policy Evaluation: A Critique." In *The Phillips Curve and Labor Markets,* edited by Karl Brunner and Allan H. Meltzer. The Carnegie-Rochester Conferences on Public Policy, a Suppl. Series to the *J. Monetary Econ.,* vol. 1. Amsterdam: North-Holland, 1976.

Neftci, Salih N. "A Time Series Analysis of the Real Wages–Employment Relationship." *J.P.E.* 86, no. 2, pt. 1 (April 1978): 281–91.

Phelps, Edmund S. "A Note on Short-Run Employment and Real Wage Rate under Competitive Commodity Markets." *Internat. Econ. Rev.* 10, no. 2 (June 1969): 220–32.

Sargent, Thomas J. "'Comment' on Seasonal Adjustment and Multiple Time Series Analysis by Kenneth Wallis." Paper presented at NBER/Bureau of Census Conference on Seasonal Adjustment of Economic Time Series, Washington, September 9–10, 1976.

———. "The Demand for Money during Hyperinflations under Rational Expectations: I." *Internat. Econ. Rev.* 18 (February 1977): 59–82.

———. "Rational Expectations, Econometric Exogeneity, and Consumption." *J.P.E.* 86, no. 4 (August 1978): 673–700. (*a*).

———. *Notes on Macroeconomic Theory.* New York: Academic Press, 1978, in press. (*b*)

Sargent, Thomas J., and Wallace, Neil. "The Elasticity of Substitution and Cyclical Behavior of Productivity, Wages, and Labor's Share." *A.E.R.* Papers and Proc. 64 (May 1974): 257–63.

Sims, Christopher A. "Money, Income, and Causality." *A.E.R.* 62, no. 4 (September 1972): 540–52.

———. "Response to Sargent's Comment on Wallis' Paper." Manuscript. Univ. Minnesota, November 1976.

Solow, Robert M., and Stiglitz, J. E. "Output, Employment, and Wages in the Short Run." *Q.J.E.* 82 (November 1968): 537–60.

Tarshis, Lorie. "Changes in Real and Money Wages." *Econ. J.* 49 (March 1939): 150–54.

Taylor, John B. "Estimation and Control of a Macroeconomic Model with Rational Expectations." Manuscript. Columbia Univ., February 1978.

Treadway, Arthur B. "On Rational Entrepreneurial Behavior and the Demand for Investment." *Rev. Econ. Studies* 36, no. 106 (April 1969): 227–39.

Wilson, G. T. "The Estimation of Parameters in Multivariate Time Series Models," *J. Royal Statis. Soc.* ser. B, no. 1 (1973), pp. 76–85.

26

Stochastic Implications of the Life Cycle–Permanent Income Hypothesis: Theory and Evidence

Robert E. Hall

Optimization of the part of consumers is shown to imply that the marginal utility of consumption evolves according to a random walk with trend. To a reasonable approximation, consumption itself should evolve in the same way. In particular, no variable apart from current consumption should be of any value in predicting future consumption. This implication is tested with time-series data for the postwar United States. It is confirmed for real disposable income, which has no predictive power for consumption, but rejected for an index of stock prices. The paper concludes that the evidence supports a modified version of the life cycle–permanent income hypothesis.

As a matter of theory, the life cycle–permanent income hypothesis is widely accepted as the proper application of the theory of the consumer to the problem of dividing consumption between the present and the future. According to the hypothesis, consumers form estimates of their ability to consume in the long run and then set current consumption to the appropriate fraction of that estimate. The estimate may be stated in the form of wealth, following Modigliani, in which case the fraction is the annuity value of wealth, or as permanent income, following Friedman, in which case the fraction should be very close to one. The major problem in empirical research based on the hypothesis has arisen in fitting the part of the model that relates current and past observed income to expected future income. The relationship almost always takes the form of a fixed distributed lag, though this practice has been very effectively criticized by Robert Lucas (1976). Further, the estimated distributed lag is usually puzzlingly short. Equations purporting to embody the life cycle–permanent income principle

This research was supported by the National Science Foundation. I am grateful to Marjorie Flavin for assistance and to numerous colleagues for helpful suggestions.

[*Journal of Political Economy*, 1978, vol. 86, no. 6]
© 1978 by The University of Chicago. 0022-3808/78/8606-0005$01.44

are actually little different from the simple Keynesian consumption function where consumption is determined by contemporaneous income alone.

Much empirical research is seriously weakened by failing to take proper
account of the endogeneity of income when it is the major independent
variable in the consumption function. Classic papers by Haavelmo (1943)
and Friedman and Becker (1957) showed clearly how the practice of
treating income as exogenous in a consumption function severely distorts
the estimated function. Even so, regressions with consumption as the dependent variable continue to be estimated and interpreted within the life cycle–
permanent income framework.[1]

Though in principle simultaneous-equations econometric techniques can
be used to estimate the structural consumption function when its major
right-hand variable is endogenous, these techniques rest on the hypothesis
that certain observed variables, used as instruments, are truly exogenous
yet have an important influence on income. The two requirements are often
contradictory, and estimation is based on an uneasy compromise where the
exogeneity of the instruments is uncertain. Furthermore, the hypothesis of
exogeneity is untestable.

This paper takes an alternative econometric approach to the study of
the life cycle–permanent income hypothesis by asking exactly what can be
learned from a consumption regression where it is conceded from the outset
that none of the right-hand variables is exogenous. This proceeds from a
theoretical examination of the stochastic implications of the theory. When
consumers maximize expected future utility, it is shown that the conditional
expectation of future marginal utility is a function of today's level of consumption alone—all other information is irrelevant. In other words, apart
from a trend, marginal utility obeys a random walk. If marginal utility is a
linear function of consumption, then the implied stochastic properties of
consumption are also those of a random walk, again apart from a trend.
Regression techniques can always reveal the conditional expectation of
consumption or marginal utility given past consumption and any other past
variables. The strong stochastic implication of the life cycle–permanent
income hypothesis is that only consumption lagged one period should have a
nonzero coefficient in such a regression. This implication can be tested
rigorously without any assumptions about exogeneity.

Testing of the theoretical implication proceeds as follows: The simplest
implication of the hypothesis is that consumption lagged more than one
period has no predictive power for current consumption. A more stringent
testable implication of the random-walk hypothesis holds that consumption
is unrelated to *any* economic variable that is observed in earlier periods. In
particular, lagged income should have no explanatory power with respect
to consumption. Previous research on consumption has suggested that

[1] Examples are Darby 1972 and Blinder 1977.

lagged income might be a good predictor of current consumption, but this hypothesis is inconsistent with the intelligent, forward-looking behavior of consumers that forms the basis of the permanent-income theory. If the previous value of consumption incorporated all information about the well-being of consumers at that time, then lagged values of actual income should have no additional explanatory value once lagged consumption is included. The data support this view—lagged income has a slightly negative co-efficient in an equation with consumption as the dependent variable and lagged consumption as an independent variable. Of course, contemporaneous income has high explanatory value, but this does not contradict the principal stochastic implication of the life cycle–permanent income hypothesis.

As a final test of the random-walk hypothesis, the predictive power of lagged values of corporate stock prices is tested. Changes in stock prices lagged by a single quarter are found to have a measurable value in predicting changes in consumption, which in a formal sense refutes the simple random-walk hypothesis. However, the finding is consistent with a modification of the hypothesis that recognizes a brief lag between changes in permanent income and the corresponding changes in consumption. The discovery that consumption moves in a way similar to stock prices actually supports this modification of the random-walk hypothesis since stock prices are well known to obey a random walk themselves.

The paper concludes with a discussion of the implications of the pure life cycle–permanent income hypothesis for macroeconomic forecasting and policy analysis. If every deviation of consumption from its trend is unexpected and permanent, then the best forecast of future consumption is just today's level adjusted for trend. Forecasts of future changes in income are irrelevant, since the information used in preparing them is already incorporated in today's consumption. In a forecasting model, consumption should be treated as an exogenous variable. For policy analysis, the pure life cycle–permanent income hypothesis supports the modern view that only unexpected changes in policy affect consumption—everything known about future changes in policy is already incorporated in present consumption. Further, unexpected changes in policy affect consumption only to the extent that they affect permanent income, and then their effects are expected to be permanent. Policies that have a transitory effect on income are incapable of having a transitory effect on consumption. However, none of the findings of the paper implies that policies affecting income have no effect on consumption. For example, a permanent tax reduction generates an immediate increase in permanent income and thus an immediate increase in consumption. But the evidence that policies act only through permanent income certainly complicates the problem of formulating countercyclical policies that act through consumption.

I. Theory

Consider the conventional model of life-cycle consumption under uncertainty: maximize $E_t \sum_{\tau=0}^{T-t} (1 + \delta)^{-\tau} u(c_{t+\tau})$ subject to $\sum_{\tau=0}^{T-t} (1 + r)^{-\tau} (c_{t+\tau} - w_{t+\tau}) = A_t$. The notation used throughout the paper is:

E_t = mathematical expectation conditional on all information available in t;

δ = rate of subjective time preference;

r = real rate of interest ($r \geq \delta$), assumed constant over time;

T = length of economic life;

$u()$ = one-period utility function, strictly concave;

c_t = consumption;

w_t = earnings;

A_t = assets apart from human capital.

Earnings, w_t, are stochastic and are the only source of uncertainty. In each period, t, the consumer chooses consumption, c_t, to maximize expected lifetime utility in the light of all information available then. The consumer knows the value of w_t when choosing c_t. No specific assumptions are made about the stochastic properties of w_t except that the conditional expectation of future earnings given today's information, $E_t w_{t+\tau}$, exists. In particular, successive w_t's are not assumed to be independent, nor is w_t required to be stationary in any sense. [2]

The principal theoretical result, proved in the Appendix, is the following:

Theorem.—Suppose the consumer maximizes expected utility as stated above. Then $E_t u'(c_{t+1}) = [(1 + \delta)/(1 + r)] u'(c_t)$.

The implications of this result are presented in a series of corollaries.

Corollary 1.—No information available in period t apart from the level of consumption, c_t, helps predict future consumption, c_{t+1}, in the sense of affecting the expected value of marginal utility. In particular, income or wealth in periods t or earlier are irrelevant, once c_t is known.

Corollary 2.—Marginal utility obeys the regression relation, $u'(c_{t+1}) = \gamma u'(c_t) + \varepsilon_{t+1}$, where $\gamma = (1 + \delta)/(1 + r)$ and ε_{t+1} is a true regression disturbance; that is, $E_t \varepsilon_{t+1} = 0$.

Corollary 3.—If the utility function is quadratic, $u(c_t) = -\frac{1}{2}(\bar{c} - c_t)^2$ (where $\bar{c}$ is the bliss level of consumption), then consumption obeys the exact regression, $c_{t+1} = \beta_0 + \gamma c_t - \varepsilon_{t+1}$, with $\beta_0 = \bar{c}(r - \delta)/(1 + r)$. Again, no variable observed in period t or earlier will have a nonzero coefficient if added to this regression.

Corollary 4.—If the utility function has the constant elasticity of substitution form, $u(c_t) = c_t^{(\sigma-1)/\sigma}$, then the following statistical model describes the evolution of consumption: $c_{t+1}^{-1/\sigma} = \gamma c_t^{-1/\sigma} + \varepsilon_{t+1}$.

---

[2] An illuminating analysis of the behavior of consumption when income is stationary appears in Yaari (1976). Further aspects are discussed by Bewley (1976).

Corollary 5.—Suppose that the change in marginal utility from one period to the next is small, both because the interest rate is close to the rate of time preference and because the stochastic change is small. Then consumption itself obeys a random walk, apart from trend.[3] Specifically, $c_{t+1} = \lambda_t c_t + \varepsilon_{t+1}/u''(c_t)$ + higher-order terms where λ_t is $[(1 + \delta)/(1 + r)]$ raised to the power of the reciprocal of the elasticity of marginal utility

$$\lambda_t = \left(\frac{1 + \delta}{1 + r}\right)^{u'(c_t)/c_t u''(c_t)}$$

The rate of growth, λ_t, exceeds one because u'' is negative. It may change over time if the elasticity of marginal utility depends on the level of consumption. However, it seems likely that constancy of λ_t will be a good approximation, at least over a decade or two. Further, the factor $1/u''(c_t)$ in the disturbance is of little concern in regression work—it might introduce a mild heteroscedasticity, but it would not bias the results of ordinary least squares. From this point on, ε_t will be redefined to incorporate $1/u''(c_t)$ where appropriate.

This line of reasoning reaches the conclusion that the simple relationship $c_t = \lambda c_{t-1} + \varepsilon_t$ where ε_t is unpredictable at time $t - 1$, is a close approximation to the stochastic behavior of consumption under the life cycle–permanent income hypothesis. The disturbance, ε_t, summarizes the impact of all new information that becomes available in period t about the consumer's lifetime well-being. Its relation to other economic variables can be seen in the following way. First, assets, A_t, evolve according to $A_t = (1 + r)(A_{t-1} - c_{t-1} + w_{t-1})$. Second, let H_t be human capital, defined as current earnings plus the expected present value of future earnings: $H_t = \Sigma_{\tau=0}^{T-t} (1 + r)^{-\tau} E_t w_{t+\tau}$ where $E_t w_t = w_t$. Then H_t evolves according to $H_t = (1 + r)(H_{t-1} - w_{t-1}) + \Sigma_{\tau=0}^{T-t} (1 + r)^{-\tau}(E_t w_{t+\tau} - E_{t-1} w_{t+\tau})$. Let η_t be the second term, that is, the present value of the set of changes in expectations of future earnings that occur between $t - 1$ and t. Then by construction, $E_{t-1} \eta_t = 0$. Still, the first term in the expression for H_t may introduce a complicated intertemporal dependence into its stochastic behavior; only under very special circumstances will it be a random walk. The implied stochastic equation for total wealth is $A_t + H_t = (1 + r)(A_{t-1} + H_{t-1} - c_{t-1}) + \eta_t$. The evolution of total wealth then depends on the relationship between the new information about wealth, η_t, and the induced change in consumption as measured by ε_t. Under certainty equivalence, justified either by quadratic utility or by the small size of ε_t, the relationship is simple: $\varepsilon_t = [1 + \lambda/(1 + r) + \cdots + \lambda^{T-t}/(1 + r)^{T-t}]\eta_t = \alpha_t \eta_t$. This is the modified annuity value of the increment in wealth. The

---

[3] Granger and Newbold (1976) present much stronger results for a similar problem but assume a normal distribution for the disturbance.

modification takes account of the consumer's plans to make consumption grow at proportional rate λ over the rest of his life. Then the stochastic equation for total wealth is $A_t + H_t = (1 + r)(1 - \alpha_{t-1})(A_{t-1} + H_{t-1}) + \eta_t$, which is a random walk with trend.

Consumers, then, process all available information each period about current and future earnings. They convert data on earnings, which may have large, predictable movements over time, into human capital, which evolves according to a combination of a highly predictable element associated with the realization of current earnings and an unpredictable element associated with changing expectations about future earnings. Taking account as well of financial assets accumulated from past earnings, consumers determine an appropriate current level of consumption. As shown at the beginning of this section, this implies that marginal utility evolves as a random walk with trend. As a result of consumers' optimization, wealth also evolves as a random walk with trend. Although it is tempting to summarize the theory by saying that consumption is proportional to wealth, wealth is a random walk, and so consumption is a random walk, this is not accurate. Rather, the underlying behavior of consumers makes both consumption and wealth evolve as random walks.

All of the theoretical results presented in this section rest on the assumption that consumers face a known, constant, real interest rate. If the real interest rate varies over time in a way that is known for certain in advance, the results would remain true with minor amendments—mainly, λ_t would vary over time on this account. The importance of known variations in interest rates depends on the elasticity of substitution between the present and future. If that elasticity is low, the influence would be unimportant. On the other hand, if the real interest rate applicable between periods t and $t + 1$ is uncertain at the time the consumption decision in period t is made, then the theoretical results no longer apply. However, there seems no strong reason for this to bias the results of the statistical tests in one direction or another.

II. Tests to Distinguish the Life Cycle–Permanent Income Theory from Alternative Theories

The tests of the stochastic implications of the life cycle–permanent income hypothesis carried out in this paper all have the form of estimating a conditional expectation, $E(c_t \mid c_{t-1}, x_{t-1})$, where x_{t-1} is a vector of data known in period $t - 1$, and then testing the hypothesis that the conditional expectation is actually not a function of x_{t-1}.[4] In all cases, the conditional expecta-

---

[4] The nature of the hypothesis being tested and the statistical tests themselves are essentially the same as in the large body of research on efficient capital markets (see Fama 1970). Sims (1978) treats the statistical problem of the asymptotic distribution of the regression coefficients of x_{t-1} in this kind of regression, with the conclusion that the standard formulas are correct.

tion is made linear in x_{t-1}, so the tests are the usual F-tests for the exclusion of a group of variables from a regression. Again, regression is the appropriate statistical technique for estimating the conditional expectation, and no claim is made that the true structural relation between consumption and its determinants is revealed by this approach.

What departures from the life cycle–permanent income hypothesis will this kind of test detect? There are two principal lines of thought about consumption that contradict the hypothesis. One holds that consumers are unable to smooth consumption over transitory fluctuations in income because of liquidity constraints and other practical considerations. Consumption is therefore too sensitive to current income to conform to the life cycle–permanent income principle. The second holds that a reasonable measure of permanent income is a distributed lag of past actual income, so the consumption function should relate actual consumption to such a distributed lag. A general consumption function embodying both ideas might let consumption respond with a fairly large coefficient to contemporaneous income and then have a distributed lag over past income. Such consumption functions are in widespread use and fit the data extremely well. But their estimation involves the very substantial issue that income and consumption are jointly determined. Estimation by least squares provides no evidence whether the observed behavior is consistent with the life cycle–permanent income hypothesis or not. Simultaneous estimation could provide evidence, but it would rest on crucial assumptions of exogeneity. Regressions of consumption on lagged consumption and lagged income *can* provide evidence without assumptions of exogeneity, as this section will show.

Consider first the issue of excessive sensitivity of consumption to transitory fluctuations in income, which has been emphasized by Tobin and Dolde (1971) and Mishkin (1976). The simplest alternative hypothesis supposes that a fraction of the population simply consumes all of its disposable income, instead of obeying the life cycle–permanent income consumption function. Suppose this fraction earns a proportion μ of total income, and let $c_t' = \mu y_t$ be their consumption. The other part of consumption, say c_t'', follows the rule set out earlier: $c_t'' = \lambda c_{t-1}'' + \varepsilon_t$. The conditional expectation of total consumption, c_t, given its own lagged value, and, say, two lagged values of income, is $E(c_t \mid c_{t-1}, y_{t-1}, y_{t-2}) = E(c_t' \mid c_{t-1}, y_{t-1}, y_{t-2}) + E(c_t'' \mid c_{t-1}, y_{t-1}, y_{t-2}) = \mu E(y_t \mid c_{t-1}, y_{t-1}, y_{t-2}) + \lambda(c_{t-1} - \mu y_{t-1})$. Suppose that disposable income obeys a univariate autoregressive process of second order, so $E(y_t \mid c_{t-1}, y_{t-1}, y_{t-2}) = \rho_1 y_{t-1} + \rho_2 y_{t-2}$. Then $E(c_t \mid c_{t-1}, y_{t-1}, y_{t-2}) = \lambda c_{t-1} + \mu(\rho_1 - \lambda) y_{t-1} + \mu \rho_2 y_{t-2}$. The life cycle–permanent income hypothesis will be rejected unless $\rho_1 = \lambda$ and $\rho_2 = 0$, that is, unless disposable income and consumption obey exactly the same stochastic process. If they do, permanent income and observed income are the same thing, and the liquidity-constrained fraction of the population is obeying the hypothesis anyway, so the hypothesis is confirmed. The proposed test involving regressing c_t on c_{t-1}, y_{t-1}, and y_{t-2} will reject the life cycle–permanent income hypothesis in favor of the simple liquidity-constrained model whenever the latter is materially different from the former.

The distributed lag approximation to permanent income was first suggested by Friedman (1957, 1963) and has figured prominently in consumption functions ever since. Distributed lags are not necessarily incompatible with the life cycle–permanent income hypothesis—if income obeys a stable stochastic process, there should be a structural relation between the innovation in income and consumption (Flavin 1977).[5] Still, the theory of the consumer presented earlier rules out any extra predictive value of a distributed lag of income (excluding contemporaneous income) in a regression that contains lagged consumption. If consumers use a nonoptimal distributed lag in forming their estimates of permanent income, then this central implication of the life cycle–permanent income hypothesis is false. This proposition is easiest to establish for the simple Koyck or geometric distributed lag, $c_t = \alpha \sum_{i=0}^{\infty} \beta^i y_{t-i}$ or $c_t = \beta c_{t-1} + \alpha y_t$. Suppose, as before, that y_t obeys a second-order autoregressive process, $E(y_t \mid c_{t-1}, y_{t-1}, y_{t-2}) = \rho_1 y_{t-1} + \rho_2 y_{t-2}$. Then the conditional expectation is $E(c_t \mid c_{t-1}, y_{t-1}, y_{t-2}) = \beta c_{t-1} + \alpha \rho_1 y_{t-1} + \alpha \rho_2 y_{t-2}$. As long as income is serially correlated ($\rho_1 \neq 0$ or $\rho_2 \neq 0$), this conditional expectation will not depend solely on c_{t-1} and the pure life cycle–permanent income hypothesis will be refuted. Discussion of the peculiarities of the case of uncorrelated income seems unnecessary since income is in fact highly serially correlated. With this slight qualification, the proposed test procedure will always detect a Koyck lag if it is present and thus refute the life cycle–permanent income hypothesis.

It is possible to show that the test also applies to the general distributed lag model used by Modigliani (1971) and others. If the lag in the underlying structural consumption function is nonoptimal, lagged income will have additional predictive power for current consumption beyond that of lagged consumption, so the life cycle–permanent income hypothesis will be rejected. Data generated by consumers who use an optimal distributed lag of current and past income in making consumption decisions will not cause rejection. This shows the crucial distinction between structural models which include contemporaneous income and the test regressions of this paper where the principle of the tests involves the inclusion of lagged variables alone.

This section has shown that simple tests of the predictive power of variables other than lagged consumption can detect departures from the pure life cycle–permanent income hypothesis in the two directions that have been widely suggested in previous research on consumption. Both excessive sensitivity to current income because of liquidity constraints and non-

---

[5] Lucas (1976) argues convincingly that the stochastic process for income will shift if policy rules change.

TABLE 1

REGRESSION RESULTS FOR THE BASIC MODEL, 1948–77

$$c_t^{-1/\sigma} = \gamma c_{t-1}^{-1/\sigma} + \varepsilon_t$$

Equation	σ	Constant	γ	SE	R^2	D-W Statistic
1.0	.2	. . .	.983 (.003)	.000735	.9964	2.06
1.2	1.0	. . .	.996 (.001)	.00271	.9985	1.83
1.3	− 1.0	−.014	1.011 (.003)	.0146	.9988	1.70

NOTE.—The numbers in parentheses in these and subsequent regressions are standard errors.

optimal distributed lag behavior will give additional predictive power to lagged income beyond that of lagged consumption in a regression for current consumption. The discussion of this section focused on the possible role of lagged income because that role is so closely related to alternative theories of consumption. Valid tests can be performed with any variable that is known in period $t - 1$ or earlier. The additional tests presented in the next section use extra lagged values of consumption and lagged values of common stock prices. Both variables have plausible justifications, but are less closely related to competing theories of consumption.

III. The Data and Results for the Basic Model

The most careful research on consumption has distinguished between the investment and consumption activities of consumers by removing investment in consumer durables and adding the imputed service flow of the stock of durables to consumption. For the purposes of this paper, however, it is more satisfactory simply to examine consumption of nondurables and services. All of the theoretical foundations of the aggregate consumption function apply to individual categories of consumption as well. Dropping durables altogether avoids the suspicion that the findings are an artifact of the procedure for imputing a service flow to the stock of durables. The data on consumption used throughout the study, then, can be defined exactly as consumption of nondurables and services in 1972 dollars from the U.S. National Income and Product Accounts divided by the population. All data are quarterly.

Table 1 presents the results of fitting the basic regression relation between current and lagged marginal utility predicted by the pure life cycle–permanent income theory. Equations 1.1 and 1.2 are for the constant-elasticity utility function, with $\sigma = 0.2$ and 1.0, respectively. Equation 1.3 is for the quadratic utility function exactly, or for any utility function approximately, and is simply a regression of consumption on its own lagged value and a constant. All three equations show that the predictive value of

510 ROBERT E. HALL

lagged marginal utility for current marginal utility is extremely high; that is, the typical information that becomes available in each quarter, as measured by ε_t, has only a small impact on consumption or marginal utility. Of course, this is no more than a theoretical interpretation of the well-known fact that consumption is highly serially correlated. The close fit of the regressions in table 1 is not itself confirmation of the life cycle–permanent income hypothesis, since the hypothesis makes no prediction about the variability of permanent income and the resultant variance of ε_t. The theory is compatible with any amount of unexplained variation in the regression.

There is no usable statistical criterion for choice among the three equations in table 1. The transformation of the dependent variable rules out the simple principle of least squares. Under the assumption of a normal distribution for ε_t, there is a likelihood function with an extra term, the Jacobian determinant, to take account of the transformation. However, for this sample, it proved to be an increasing function of σ for all values, so no maximum-likelihood estimator is available. This seems to reflect the operation of corollary 5—the ε_t's are small enough that any specification of marginal utility is essentially proportional to consumption itself, and the effective content of the life cycle–permanent income theory is to make consumption itself evolve as a random walk with trend. From this point on, the paper will discuss only equation 1.3 and its extensions to other variables.

The principal stochastic implication of the life cycle–permanent income hypothesis is that no other variables observed in quarter $t - 1$ or earlier can help predict the residuals from the regressions in table 1. Before formal statistical tests are used, it is useful to study the residuals themselves. The pattern of the residuals is extremely similar in the three regressions, but the residuals themselves are easiest to interpret for equation 3, where they have the units of consumption per capita in 1972 dollars. These residuals appear in table 2.

The standard error of the residuals in 14.6, so roughly six of the observations should exceed 29.2 in magnitude. There are in fact six. Three are drops in consumption, and of these, one coincides with the standard dating of recessions: 1974:4. Five milder recessions contribute drops of less than two standard deviations: 1949:3, 1953:4, 1958:1, 1960:3, and 1970:4. The other major decline in consumption is associated with the Korean War, in 1950:4. Most of the drops in consumption occurred quickly, in one or two quarters. The only important exception was in the period from 1973:4 to 1975:1, when six straight quarters of consecutive decline took place. On the expansionary side, there is little consistent evidence of any systematic tendency for consumption to recover in a regular pattern after a setback. The largest single increase occurred in 1965:4. This, together with three successive increases in 1964, accounts for all of the increase in consumption relative to trend associated with the prolonged boom of the mid- and late sixties.

TABLE 2

Residuals from Regression of Consumption on Lagged Consumption, 1948–77 ($)

1948:		1956:		1964:		1972:	
1....	.5	1....	2.8	1....	17.8	1....	20.0
2....	8.0	2....	−10.1	2....	20.0	2....	32.7
3....	−15.5	3....	−6.1	3....	14.6	3....	8.4
4....	3.5	4....	1.2	4....	−4.4	4....	21.1
1949:		1957:		1965:		1973:	
1....	−8.6	1....	−10.8	1....	5.8	1....	8.0
2....	−8.5	2....	−6.1	2....	5.2	2....	−15.6
3....	−27.2	3....	2.4	3....	10.2	3....	3.0
4....	−.1	4....	−13.6	4....	38.7	4....	−32.8
1950:		1958:		1966:		1974:	
1....	5.6	1....	−29.1	1....	−1.3	1....	−27.3
2....	23.8	2....	8.3	2....	3.7	2....	−23.4
3....	15.5	3....	14.3	3....	−1.9	3....	−16.6
4....	−31.0	4....	−1.9	4....	−12.4	4....	−42.8
1951:		1959:		1967:		1975:	
1....	16.0	1....	15.1	1....	10.2	1....	−5.8
2....	−24.8	2....	3.8	2....	2.0	2....	25.6
3....	9.0	3....	−2.7	3....	−2.8	3....	−21.3
4....	−6.1	4....	1.1	4....	−7.5	4....	.9
1952:		1960:		1968:		1976:	
1....	−15.1	1....	−5.6	1....	15.6	1....	24.4
2....	18.0	2....	8.8	2....	7.9	2....	8.3
3....	10.0	3....	−24.3	3....	22.2	3....	2.3
4....	8.6	4....	−10.1	4....	−8.1	4....	30.4
1953:		1961:		1969:		1977:	
1....	−1.6	1....	1.8	1....	.8	1....	−1.8
2....	−1.0	2....	10.1	2....	−5.3		
3....	−22.1	3....	−16.9	3....	−2.4		
4....	−27.0	4....	15.8	4....	.3		
1954:		1962:		1970:			
1....	−.1	1....	−1.7	1,....	4.0		
2....	−2.4	2....	3.4	2....	−12.3		
3....	11.9	3....	−.8	3....	−.3		
4....	7.4	4....	.6	4....	−21.5		
1955:		1963:		1971:			
1....	6.1	1....	−8.4	1....	1.5		
2....	7.0	2....	−1.3	2....	−2.4		
3....	−.8	3....	11.7	3....	−14.6		
4....	22.3	4....	−6.3	4....	−6.6		

The data contain no obvious refutation of the unpredictability of the residuals from the basic model, but, just as a study of stock prices will never convince the "chartist" that it is futile to try to predict their future, the confirmed believer in regular fluctuations in consumption will not be swayed by the data alone. More powerful methods for summarizing the data are required.

IV. Can Consumption Be Predicted from Its Own Past Values?

The simplest testable implication of the pure life cycle–permanent income hypothesis is that only the first lagged value of consumption helps predict current consumption. This implication would be refuted if consumption had a definite cyclical pattern described by a difference equation of second or higher order.[6] Intelligent consumers ought to be able to offset any such cyclical pattern and restore the noncyclical optimal behavior of consumption predicted by the hypothesis. The following regression tests this implication by adding additional lagged values of consumption to equation 1.3:

$$c_t = 8.2 + 1.130c_{t-1} - 0.040c_{t-2} + 0.030c_{t-3} - 0.113c_{t-4};$$
$$(8.3) \quad (0.092) \qquad (0.142) \qquad (0.142) \qquad (0.093)$$
$$R^2 = .9988; \quad s = 14.5; \quad \text{D-W} = 1.96.$$

The contribution of the extra lagged values is to increase the accuracy of the forecast of current consumption by about 10 cents per person per year. The F-statistic for the hypothesis that the coefficients of c_{t-2}, c_{t-3}, and c_{t-4} are all zero is 1.7, well under the critical point of the F-distribution of 2.7 at the 5 percent level. Only very weak evidence against the pure life cycle–permanent income hypothesis appears in this regression. In particular, there are no definite signs that consumption obeys a second-order difference equation capable of generating stochastic cycles. In this respect, consumption differs sharply from other aggregate economic measures, which do typically obey second-order autoregressions.

V. Can Consumption Be Predicted from Disposable Income?

If lagged income has substantial predictive power beyond that of lagged consumption, then the life cycle–permanent income hypothesis is refuted. As discussed in Section II, this evidence would support the alternative views that consumers are excessively sensitive to current income, or, more generally, that they use an ad hoc, nonoptimal distributed lag of past income in making consumption decisions.

Table 3 presents a variety of regressions testing the predictive power of real disposable income per capita, measured as current dollar disposable income from the national accounts divided by the implicit deflator for consumption of nondurables and services and divided by population. Equation 3.1 shows that a single lagged level of disposable income has essentially no predictive value at all. The coefficient of y_{t-1} is slightly negative, but this is easily explained by sampling variation alone. The F-statistic for the exclusion of all but the constant and c_{t-1} is 0.1, far below the critical F of 3.9. Equation 3.2 tries a year-long distributed lag estimated without constraint. The first lagged value of disposable income has a slight positive coefficient, but this is more than outweighed by the three negative coefficients for the longer lags. The long-run "marginal propensity to consume," measured by the sum of the coefficients, is actually negative, though again this could easily result from sampling variation. The F-statistic for the joint predictive value of all four lagged income variables is 2.0, somewhat less than the critical value of 2.4 at the 5 percent level. Note

---

[6] Fama (1970) calls the similar test for asset prices a "weak form" test.

TABLE 3

Equations Relating Consumption to Lagged Consumption and Past Levels of Real Disposable Income

Equation No. and Equation	R^2	s	D-W	F	F^*
3.1 .... $c_t = -16 + 1.024\, c_{t-1} - .010\, y_{t-1}$ (11) (.044) (.032)	.9988	14.7	1.71	.1	3.9
3.2 .... $c_t = -23 + 1.076\, c_{t-1} + .049\, y_{t-1} - .051\, y_{t-2}$ (11) (.047) (.043) (.052) $-.023\, y_{t-3} - .024\, y_{t-4}$ (.051) (.037)	.9989	14.4	2.02	2.0	2.4
3.3 .... $c_t = -25 + 1.113\, c_{t-1} + \sum_{i=1}^{12} \beta_i y_{t-1} \quad \Sigma\beta_i = .077$ (11) (.054) (.040)	.9988	14.6	1.92	2.0	2.7

that the pure life cycle–permanent income hypothesis would be rejected if the size of the test were 10 percent or higher.

Equation 3.3 fits a 12-quarter Almon lag to see if a long distributed lag can compete with lagged consumption as a predictor for current consumption. Again, the sum of the lag coefficients is slightly negative, now almost significantly so. The F-statistic for the hypothesis of no contribution from the complete distributed lag on income is again close to the critical value.

The sample evidence of the relation between consumption and lagged income seems to say the following: There is a statistically marginal and numerically small relation between consumption and very recent levels of disposable income. The sum of the lag coefficients is slightly negative. Further, there is no evidence at all supporting the view that a long distributed lag covering several years helps to predict consumption. This evidence casts just a little doubt on the life cycle–permanent income hypothesis in its purest form but is not at all destructive to a somewhat more flexible interpretation of the hypothesis, to be discussed shortly.

VI. Wealth and Consumption

Of the many alternative variables that might be included on the right-hand side of a regression to test the pure life cycle–permanent income hypothesis, some measure of wealth is one of the leading candidates. Theory and prevailing practice agree that contemporaneous wealth has a strong influence on consumption, so lagged wealth is a logical variable to test. Again, the hypothesis implies that wealth measured in earlier quarters should have no predictive value with respect to this quarter's consumption. All information contained in lagged wealth should be summarized in lagged consumption.

Reliable quarterly data on property values are not available for most categories of property. For one major category, however, essentially perfect data are available at any frequency, namely, the market value of corporate stock. Tests of the random-walk hypothesis do not require a comprehensive wealth variable, so a test based on stock prices is appropriate, even though the resulting equation does not describe the structural relation between wealth and consumption. The tests reported here are based on Standard and Poor's comprehensive index of the prices of stocks deflated by the implicit deflator for nondurables and services and divided by population. This variable will be called s. It makes a statistically unambiguous contribution to prediction of current consumption:

$$c_t = -22 + 1.012c_{t-1} + 0.223s_{t-1} - 0.258s_{t-2} + 0.167s_{t-3} - 0.120s_{t-4}$$
$$(8) \quad (0.004) \quad (0.051) \quad (0.083) \quad (0.083) \quad (0.051)$$
$$R^2 = .9990; \quad SE = 14.4; \quad D\text{-}W = 2.05.$$

The F-statistic for the hypothesis that the coefficients of the lagged stock prices are all zero is 6.5, well above the critical value of 2.4 at the 5 percent

level. Further, each coefficient considered separately is clearly different
from zero according to the usual t-test. However, the improvement in the
predictive power of the regression, while statistically significant, is not
numerically large. The standard error of the regression is about 20 cents
per person per year smaller in this equation compared with the basic model
of equation 1.3 ($\$14.40$ against $\$14.60$). Most of the predictive value of the
stock price comes from the *change* in the price in the immediately preceding
quarter. A smaller contribution is made by the change in the price 3
quarters earlier. Use of the Almon lag technique for both levels and differences in the stock price failed to turn up any evidence of a longer distributed
lag.

VII. Implications of the Empirical Evidence

The pure life cycle–permanent income hypothesis—that c_t cannot be predicted by any variable dated $t - 1$ or earlier other than c_{t-1}—is rejected
by the data. The stock market is valuable in predicting consumption 1
quarter in the future. Most of the predictive power comes from Δs_{t-1}. But
the data seem entirely compatible with a modification of the hypothesis
that leaves its central content unchanged. Suppose that consumption does
depend on permanent income, and that marginal utility indeed does evolve
as a random walk with trend, but that some part of consumption takes time
to adjust to a change in permanent income. Then any variable that is
correlated with permanent income in $t - 1$ will help in predicting the
change in consumption in period t, since part of that change is the lagged
response to the previous change in permanent income. Both the finding that
consumption is only weakly associated with its own past values and that
immediate past values of changes in stock prices have a modest predictive
value are compatible with this modification of the life cycle–permanent
income hypothesis.

Whatever problems remain in the consumption function, there seems
little reason to doubt the life cycle–permanent income hypothesis. Within
a framework in which permanent income is treated as an unobserved
variable the data seem fully compatible with the hypothesis, provided a
short lag between permanent income and consumption is recognized. Of
course, acceptance of the hypothesis does not yield a complete consumption
function, since no equation for permanent income has been developed. The
evidence against the ad hoc distributed-lag model relating permanent income
to actual income seems fairly strong. The task of further research is to
create a more satisfactory model for permanent income, one that recognizes
that consumers appraise their economic well-being in an intelligent way
that involves looking into the future.

It is important not to treat any of the equations of this paper as structural
relations between consumption and the variables that are used to predict it.

For example, table 3 should not be read as implying that income has a negative effect on consumption. The effect of a particular change in income depends on the change in permanent income it induces, and this can range anywhere from no effect to a dollar-for-dollar effect, depending on the way that consumers evaluate the change. In any case, the regressions understate the true structural relation between the change in income and the change in consumption because they omit the contemporaneous part of the relation.

VIII. Implications for Forecasting and Policy Analysis

Under the pure life cycle–permanent income hypothesis, a forecast of future consumption obtained by extrapolating today's level by the historical trend is impossible to improve. The results of this paper have the strong implication that beyond the next few quarters consumption should be treated as an exogenous variable. There is no point in forecasting future income and then relating it to income, since any information available today about future income is already incorporated in today's permanent income. Forecasts of consumption next quarter can be improved slightly with current stock prices, but no further improvement can be achieved in this way in later quarters.

With respect to the analysis of stabilization policy, the findings of this paper go no further than supporting the view that policy affects consumption only as much as it affects permanent income. In the analysis of policies that are known to leave permanent income unchanged, consumption may be treated as exogenous. Further, only *new* information about taxes and other policy instruments can affect permanent income. Beyond these general propositions, the policy analyst must answer the difficult question of the effect of a given policy on permanent income in order to predict its effect on consumption. Regression of consumption on current and past values of income are of no value whatsoever in answering this question.

Appendix

1. *Theorem*

If a consumer maximizes $E_t \sum_{t=0}^{T} (1 + \delta)^{-t} u(c_t)$, subject to $\sum_{t=0}^{T} (1 + r)^{-t}(c_t - w_t)$ $= A_0$, sequentially determining c_t at each t, then $E_t u'(c_{t+1}) = [(1 + \delta)/(1 + r)]$ $\times u'(c_t)$.

Proof.—At time t, the consumer chooses c_t so as to maximize $(1 + \delta)^{-t} u(c_t) +$ $E_t \sum_{\tau=t+1}^{T} (1 + \delta)^{-t} u(c_\tau)$ subject to $\sum_{\tau=t}^{T} (1 + r)^{(t-\tau)}(c_\tau - w_\tau) = A_t$. The optimal sequential strategy has the form $c_\tau = g_\tau(w_\tau, w_{\tau-1}, \dots, w_0, A_0)$. Consider a variation from this strategy: $c_t = g_t(w_t, \dots) + x$: $c_{t+1} = g_{t+1}(w_{t+1}, w_t, \dots) - (1 + r)x$.

Note that the new consumption strategy also satisfies the budget constraint. Now consider $\max_x \{(1 + \delta)^{-t} u(g_t + x) + E_t [(1 + \delta)^{-t-1} u(g_{t+1} - (1 + r)x) + \sum_{\tau=t+2}^{T} (1 + \delta)^{-\tau} u(g_\tau)]\}$.

The first-order condition is $(1 + \delta)^{-t} u'(g_t + x) - E_t (1 + \delta)^{-t-1}(1 + r)$ $u'(g_{t+1} - (1 + r)x) = 0$ as asserted.

2. *Proof of Corollary 5*

Recall that $u'(c_{t+1}) = [(1 + \delta)/(1 + r)]u'(c_t) + \varepsilon_{t+1}$ and $\lambda_t = [(1 + \delta)/(1 + r)]^{u'(c_t)/[c_t u''(c_t)]}$. Expand the implicit equation for c_{t+1} in a Taylor series at the point $\lambda_t = 1$ $(r = \delta)$ and $\varepsilon_{t+1} = 0$: $c_{t+1} = c_t + (\lambda_t - 1)(\partial c_{t+1}/\partial \lambda_t) + \varepsilon_{t+1}(\partial c_{t+1}/\partial \varepsilon_{t+1})$ + higher-order terms. At the point $\lambda_t = 1$ and $\varepsilon_{t+1} = 0$, c_{t+1} equals c_t, and it is not hard to show that $\partial c_{t+1}/\partial \lambda_t = c_t$ and $\partial c_{t+1}/\partial \varepsilon_{t+1} = 1/u''(c_t)$. Thus $c_{t+1} = c_t + (\lambda_t - 1)c_t + \varepsilon_{t+1}/u''(c_t) = \lambda_t c_t + \varepsilon_{t+1}/u''(c_t)$, as asserted.

References

Bewley, Truman. "The Permanent Income Hypothesis: A Theoretical Formulation." Mimeographed. Cambridge, Mass.: Harvard Univ., Dept. Econ., September 1976.

Blinder, Alan. "Temporary Taxes and Consumer Spending." Mimeographed. Jerusalem: Inst. Advanced Studies, April 1977.

Darby, Michael R. "The Allocation of Transitory Income among Consumers' Assets." *A.E.R.* 62 (December 1972): 928–41.

Fama, Eugene F. "Efficient Capital Markets: A Review of Theory and Empirical Work." *J. Finance* 25 (May 1970): 383–417.

Flavin, Marjorie. "The Adjustment of Consumption to Changing Expectations about Future Income." Unpublished paper, Massachusetts Inst. Tech., February 1977.

Friedman, Milton. *A Theory of the Consumption Function*. Princeton, N.J.: Princeton Univ. Press, 1957.

————. "Windfalls, the 'Horizon,' and Related Concepts in the Permanent-Income Hypothesis." In *Measurement in Economics: Studies in Mathematical Economics and Econometrics in Memory of Yehuda Grunfeld*, edited by Carl Christ et al. Stanford, Calif.: Stanford Univ. Press, 1963.

Friedman, Milton, and Becker, Gary S. "A Statistical Illusion in Judging Keynesian Models." *J.P.E.* 65, no. 1 (February 1957): 64–75.

Granger, C. W. J., and Newbold, P. "Forecasting Transformed Series." *J. Royal Statis. Soc.* ser. B, 38, no. 2 (1976): 189–203.

Haavelmo, Trygve. "The Statistical Implications of a System of Simultaneous Equations." *Econometrica* 11 (January 1943): 1–12.

Lucas, Robert E., Jr. "Econometric Policy Evaluation: A Critique." In *The Phillips Curve and Labor Markets*, edited by Karl Brunner and Allan H. Meltzer. Carnegie-Rochester Conference Series on Public Policy. Amsterdam: North-Holland; New York: American Elsevier, 1976.

Mishkin, Frederic. "Illiquidity, Consumer Durable Expenditure, and Monetary Policy." *A.E.R.* 66 (September 1976): 642–54.

Modigliani, Franco. "Monetary Policy and Consumption." In *Consumer Spending and Monetary Policy: The Linkages*. Conference Series No. 5. Boston: Federal Reserve Bank of Boston, 1971.

Sims, Christopher A. "Least Squares Estimation of Autoregressions with Some Unit Roots." Discussion Paper no. 78–95, Univ. Minnesota, Center Econ. Res., March 1978.

Tobin, James, and Dolde, Walter. "Wealth, Liquidity, and Consumption." In *Consumer Spending and Monetary Policy: The Linkages*. Conference Series No. 5. Boston: Federal Reserve Bank of Boston, 1971.

Yaari, Menahem E. "A Law of Large Numbers in the Theory of Consumer's Choice under Uncertainty." *J. Econ. Theory* 12 (April 1976): 202–17.

PART 5 Testing for Neutrality

27

A Classical Macroeconometric Model for the United States

Thomas J. Sargent

A statistical definition of the natural unemployment rate hypothesis is advanced and tested. A particular illustrative structural macroeconomic model satisfying the definition is set forth and estimated. The model has "classical" policy implications, implying a number of neutrality propositions asserting the invariance of the conditional means of real variables with respect to the feedback rule for the money supply. The aim is to test how emphatically the data reject a model incorporating rather severe classical hypotheses.

This paper estimates a small, linear, classical macroeconometric model for the postwar United States. One reason for estimating the model is to produce a simple device capable of generating unconditional forecasts of key economic aggregates such as the unemployment rate, the price level, and the interest rate. But a more important reason is that as part of the estimation process the hypotheses underlying the model are subjected to empirical testing. Since these hypotheses are very "classical" and sharply at variance with Keynesian macroeconomics, it would be useful to know at what confidence levels the data reject them.

The present model is considerably more monetarist than is the St. Louis model.[1] Indeed, as interpreted and manipulated by its builders, the St. Louis model is incapable of rationalizing prominent monetarist positions. In particular, it implies that simple x percent growth rules for money can generally be improved upon by adopting rules with feedback from past endogenous variables to current money.[2] By way of contrast,

This paper was financed by the Federal Reserve Bank of Minneapolis, which does not necessarily endorse the opinions expressed. Thomas Turner, Paul Anderson, and Salih Neftci performed the calculations.

[1] See Andersen and Carlson 1970.

[2] Cooper and Fischer (1974) have made this point.

[*Journal of Political Economy*, 1976, vol. 84, no. 2]

the present model is one in which an x percent growth rule for the money supply seems not to be dominated by any rule with feedback.[3]

The deterministic (nonrandom) classical model, the static analysis of which is enshrined in macroeconomics textbooks, has never been taken seriously, because its predictions seem so terribly at variance with the data. In particular, it is hard to explain the observed persistent movements in employment and unemployment with the textbook classical model. How meaningfully integrating random. disturbances into the classical model would affect the analysis is a matter about which there is presently little agreement. On the one hand, in his American Economic Association presidential address, James Tobin (1972) seemed to assert that the presence of random disturbances in demand and supply schedules so alters the character of the general system that it sets up an exploitable trade-off between unemployment and inflation even in a system where all agents optimize. On the other hand, Robert Lucas (1972b) has analyzed a general equilibrium system in which agents cope optimally with the existence of uncertainty. While there exist "nonneutralities" in that system, there are no nonneutralities that the government can either exploit or offset by way of countercyclical policy.

This paper formulates, tests, and estimates a version of the classical model that has its origin in hypotheses that place severe restrictions on the random behavior of unemployment, output, and the interest rate. The model implies that those three "real" variables are econometrically exogenous with respect to variables measuring monetary and fiscal policies. As a consequence, government manipulations of monetary and fiscal policy variables have no predictable effects on unemployment, output, or the interest rate and hence are useless for pursuing countercyclical policy. Such implications are in the nature of neutrality results, albeit ones that require drawing some fairly fine econometric distinctions. The key elements of the model that provide the sources of the restrictions on the stochastic nature of output, unemployment, and interest are: (a) a drastic version of the natural unemployment rate hypothesis; (b) the expectations theory of the term structure of interest rates, and (c) the assumption that the public's expectations are "rational."

The chief novelty of this paper is its formulation of a drastic, statistical definition of the natural unemployment rate hypothesis. That definition is not dependent on any particular macroeconomic structural model, being compatible with a variety of structures one could imagine. The particular structural model presented in this paper is intended only as an illustrative example that satisfies this definition of the natural-rate hypothesis. This particular structure does, however, illustrate some of the

---

[3] Models with this property have previously been analyzed by Sargent (1973) and Sargent and Wallace (1975).

strong classical properties that will be possessed by models that satisfy the definition of the natural-rate hypothesis advanced here. A major aim of the paper is to indicate how this definition of the natural-rate hypothesis can be tested and to present some test results.

This paper is organized as follows. In section I a prototype of the model is described. However, no attempt is made here to rationalize in a deep way the equations comprising the model. Section I is designed to display the system briefly and to establish its classical nature. Section II then provides a definition of the natural-rate hypothesis that is the cornerstone of the model. Statistical tests of the hypothesis are described. Section II also describes how the rational-expectations theory of the term structure of interest rates is implemented in the model and how its central implications can be tested. Section III implements the econometric tests described in Section II. Finally, Section IV contains estimates of the complete model. The casual reader not interested in econometrics can read only Sections I and IV and find there estimates of the model and a description of how it works.

I. Overview of the Model

I begin by describing a simple prototype of the model. It differs from the model finally estimated in some minor ways but illustrates well the mechanics of the model.

The prototype consists of the following five equations:

$$Un_t = \gamma(p_t - E_{t-1}p_t) + \sum_{i=1}^{n_1} \lambda_i Un_{t-i} + u_{1t}, \tag{1.1}$$

where $\gamma < 0$ (a Phillips curve);

$$n_{ft} = \beta(p_t - E_{t-1}p_t) + dUn_t + \sum_{i=1}^{n_2} w_i n_{ft-i} + u_{2t}, \tag{1.2}$$

where $\beta > 0$, and $d < 0$ (a labor force participation equation);

$$y_t = \alpha_0 t + \alpha_1(n_{ft} - Un_t + pop_t) + u_{3t}, \tag{1.3}$$

where $\alpha_1 \simeq 1$ (a production function);

$$R_t = R_{t-1} + \xi(Z_t - E_{t-1}Z_t) + u_{4t} \tag{1.4}$$

(a martingale equation for the long-term interest rate); and

$$m_t - p_t = b_1 R_t + b_2 y_t + b_3(m_{t-1} - p_{t-1}) + u_{5t}, \tag{1.5}$$

where $b_1 < 0$ and $b_2, b_3 > 0$ (a portfolio-balance schedule). The variables are defined as: Un_t = unemployment rate; p_t = log of GNP deflator;

n_{ft} = log of labor force participation rate; y_t = log of real GNP; pop_t = log of population; R_t = long-term interest rate; m_t = log of money supply; Z_t = a vector of exogenous variables in the "IS" curve, including tax rates and government purchases; u_{jt} = mutually and serially independent random terms with zero means, so that $E_{t-1}u_{jt} = 0$, $j = 1, \ldots, 5$; and $E_{t-1}X_t$ = the mathematical expectation of X_t conditioned on information available at time $t - 1$. The variables Z_t, pop_t, and m_t are taken as exogenous.

Equation (1.1) is a Phillips curve that posits an inverse supply-side relationship between unemployment and the unexpected part of the current price level. The public's psychological expectation about the price level is supposed to be "rational," meaning that it equals $E_{t-1}p_t$. The equation embodies the natural unemployment rate hypothesis, since it asserts that unemployment does not depend on the anticipated part of the rate of inflation. Equation (1.1) is essentially Lucas's (1973) formulation of the Phillips curve.

Equation (1.2) is a labor force participation equation positing that the participation rate depends directly on the unexpected part of the price level and inversely on the unemployment rate (the "discouraged worker effect"). The presence of unemployment and the unexpected part of prices in equations describing labor force participation is not unusual (e.g., see Wachter [1972] and the work cited by him).

Upon noting that the log of employment approximately equals $(n_{ft} - Un_t + pop_t)$, equation (1.3) is seen to be a Cobb-Douglas production function that excludes capital. The regressions reported by Bodkin and Klein (1967) and Lucas (1970) suggest that little violence is done to the data by omitting capital from equation (1.3). That is, time-series regressions of the log of output against the logs of capital and employment typically display constant or increasing returns to employment and zero or slightly negative returns to capital. For my purposes, excluding capital from equation (1.3) permits the construction of a model in which there is no need to account for capital accumulation.

Equation (1.4) posits that the long-term interest rate is a martingale. Fiscal policy and other aggregate-demand variables influence the long rate in two ways. First, the unexpected components of Z_t influence the "innovation" in the long rate, that is, the part of the long rate that cannot be predicted from the past. Second, the foreseen or expected part of Z_t is already reflected in R_{t-1} and affects R_t in precisely the same way it affects R_{t-1}.

Equation (1.5) is a standard portfolio-balance schedule.

The model is five equations in the five endogenous variables Un_t, n_{ft}, Y_t, R_t, and p_t. The exogenous variables are Z_t, pop_t, and m_t.

To complete the model, the stochastic processes governing the exogenous variables m_t, Z_t, and pop_t must be specified. I will assume the autoregressive schemes

$$m_t = \sum_{i=1}^{n_3} \xi_i m_{t-i} + \varepsilon_{1t}, \tag{1.6a}$$

$$Z_t = \sum_{i=1}^{n_4} \psi_i Z_{t-i} + \varepsilon_{2t}, \tag{1.6b}$$

and

$$pop_t = \sum_{i=1}^{n_5} \omega_i pop_{t-i} + \varepsilon_{3t}, \tag{1.6c}$$

where the ξ_i's, ψ_i's, and ω_i's are parameters, and the ε_t's are serially independent random variables with means of zero; they are assumed to be distributed independently of the u's in the structural equations (1.1)–(1.5). To solve the model and to forecast with it, expected values of the exogenous variables, for example, $E_{t-1}m_t$ and $E_t m_{t+1}$, are required. These expected values are calculated using the autoregressions above for the exogenous variables. This is partly by way of imposing rationality, since the expected price $E_{t-1}p_t$ turns out to depend on $E_{t-1}m_t$, $E_{t-1}Z_t$, and $E_{t-1}pop_t$. Rationality amounts to requiring that the public's expectations of the exogenous variables m_t, Z_t, and pop_t equal the mathematical expectations computed from the appropriate objective probability distributions, that is, the autoregressions above.

The model has a standard aggregate-demand and -supply representation in the p, y plane. Substituting equations (1.1) and (1.2) into (1.3) gives the aggregate-supply schedule

$$y_t = \alpha_0 t + \alpha_1 pop_t + [\alpha_1 \beta + (\alpha_1 d - \alpha_1)\gamma](p_t - E_{t-1}p_t)$$

$$+ (\alpha_1 d - \alpha_1) \sum_{i=1}^{n_1} \lambda_i Un_{t-i} + \alpha_1 \sum_{i=1}^{n_2} w_i n_{ft-i}$$

$$+ (\alpha_1 d - \alpha_1)u_{1t} + \alpha_1 u_{2t} + u_{3t}.$$

Since $\alpha_1 \beta_1 + (\alpha_1 d - \alpha_1)\gamma > 0$, the aggregate-supply schedule is upward sloping in the p–y plane.

Substituting equation (1.4) into (1.5) gives the aggregate-demand schedule $p_t = m_t - b_1 R_{t-1} - b_1 \xi(Z_t - E_{t-1}Z_t) - b_2 y_t - b_3(m_{t-1} - p_{t-1}) - b_1 u_{4t} - u_{5t}$, which slopes downward in the p, y plane. Increases in m_t and in the aggregate-demand innovations $\xi(Z_t - E_{t-1}Z_t)$ cause the demand schedule to shift outward. The equilibrium p, y combination is determined at the intersection of the demand and supply curves.

While the model is clearly simultaneous in determining the current values of the five endogenous variables, for generating forecasts it is recursive. The one-period-ahead forecast of Un_t is determined by taking expectations in equation (1.1) conditional on data known at $t - 1$:

$$E_{t-1}Un_t = \sum_{i=1}^{n_1} \lambda_i Un_{t-i}, \qquad (1.1')$$

which follows since $E_{t-1}(p_t - E_{t-1}p_t) = E_{t-1}p_t - E_{t-1}p_t = 0$. The forecast of n_{f_t} is then given from equation (1.2) as

$$E_{t-1}n_{f_t} = dE_{t-1}Un_t + \sum_{i=1}^{n_2} w_i n_{f_{t-i}}.$$

Then from equation (1.3) we have the forecast of the log of GNP as $E_{t-1}y_t = \alpha_0 t + \alpha_1(E_{t-1}n_{f_t} - E_{t-1}Un_t + E_{t-1}pop_t)$. From equation (1.4) the forecast of the long-term interest rate is simply $E_{t-1}R_t = R_{t-1}$, which follows since $E_{t-1}(Z_t - E_{t-1}Z_t) = 0$. Finally, from the portfolio-balance schedule, the forecast of p_t is $E_{t-1}p_t = E_{t-1}m_t - b_1 E_{t-1}R_t - b_2 E_{t-1}y_t - b_3(m_{t-1} - p_{t-1})$. To compute the forecasts of the endogenous variables, the forecasts $E_{t-1}m_t$ and $E_{t-1}pop_t$ of the exogenous variables are required.

The predictions of the model are obviously classical in spirit. The predictions of the "real" variables are all independent of the prediction of the money supply, which only influences the predicted price level. For predicting the long-term interest rate, predictions of the fiscal and other aggregate-demand variables add no information to that in the current long rate since they are already properly embedded in the current long-term rate. Finally, the model implies that the monetary authority does not have the option of pegging the nominal interest rate R_t via some feedback rule by letting the money supply be whatever it must to guarantee portfolio balance at that interest rate.[4] For suppose that the authority were to attempt to peg the interest rate via the feedback rule

$$R_t = F\theta_{t-1}, \qquad (1.7)$$

where θ_{t-1} is a vector of observations on endogenous and exogenous variables dated $t - 1$ and earlier, and F is a vector of parameters conformable with θ_{t-1}. The predictions of R_t from equations (1.4) and (1.7) are clearly in general inconsistent, so that the interest rate is overdetermined. Thus, this model is characterized by Wicksell's classical overdeterminacy of the interest rate (and indeterminacy of the price level) under a pegged interest rate.

It bears emphasizing that, while for prediction the model has a very classical recursive structure, it is a simultaneous model when it comes to determining current variables. Thus, money is not a "veil" in the model,

---

[4] This is one of the options analyzed for a stochastic Keynesian model by William Poole (1970).

since (random) increases in money can be shown to stimulate both GNP and the price level. So will (random) increases in the aggregate-demand Z's. But it turns out that in this model it is best to predict as if money were a veil. The fact that variables are determined jointly simply cannot be exploited in prediction; neither can it be exploited for control.

I have indicated that to generate forecasts of the endogenous variables the exogenous variables should be set equal to the forecasts $E_t m_{t+1}$, $E_t Z_{t+1}$, and $E_t pop_{t+1}$, which are to be computed from the autoregressions (eqq. [1.6a]–[1.6c]) that actually govern those exogenous variables. It seems that something more is possible in the way of forecasting, but it turns out not to be useful to the policymaker. In particular it is possible to use the model to "predict" values of the endogenous variables in $t + 1$, conditional on alternative assumed values for the exogenous variables m_{t+1}, Z_{t+1}, and pop_{t+1}, *given* values of $E_t m_{t+1}$, $E_t Z_{t+1}$, and $E_t pop_{t+1}$. For example, for a given $E_t m_{t+1}$, different values of m_{t+1} will be associated with different values of the *real* variables output and unemployment. The larger $m_{t+1} - E_t m_{t+1}$ is, the larger will be the "predicted" value of output and the lower the "predicted" value of unemployment. But such "conditional" forecasts are of no use in forming policy. For example, it will not work to use the model to "forecast" unemployment for alternative values of m_{t+1}, given $E_t m_{t+1}$, and then to set m_{t+1} in order to achieve the unemployment rate desired by the monetary authority. Expecting that to work amounts to assuming that the public would continue to form its expectations about m_{t+1} by using equation (1.6a) even if the authority adopted the new and different rule for setting m implicit in the procedure above. That violates the assumption that expectations are rational. What affects unemployment and output is the gap between m_{t+1} and $E_t m_{t+1}$, and there is no way that the authority can expect to set this gap at some desired nonzero level.

This completes the overview of the model. I now turn to the task of setting forth more precisely the nature of the key hypotheses underlying the model. In the process, statistical tests of those hypotheses will be described and implemented.

II. The Stochastic Model of Unemployment and Interest Rates

This section sets forth and describes tests of a naive but powerful formulation of the hypothesis that there is a natural rate of unemployment. The hypothesis formulated here is much stricter than the usual statement of the natural-rate hypothesis, which posits that the government can persistently depress the unemployment rate below the "natural rate" only at the cost of accepting an accelerating inflation. In contrast, the present formulation implies that there is *no* way that the government can operate so that it can expect to depress the unemployment rate below the natural rate, even in the short run. Among other things, that implies that policy-makers face no "cruel choice" between inflation and unemployment over *any* relevant time frame.

The tests of the natural-rate hypothesis implemented here differ substantially from the usual one, which involves testing the hypothesis that certain sums of distributed-lag weights are unity or zero. This usual test has been harshly criticized on theoretical grounds[5] and furthermore is subject to the purely econometric objection that economic time-series data usually yield very little information about "long-run" magnitudes such as the sum of distributed-lag weights.[6] The tests implemented here do not seem to depend on estimating any such long-run properties of lag distributions.

The present statement of the natural-rate hypothesis is compatible with, but somewhat stronger than, the one presented and tested by Lucas. The strategy that I use to test the hypothesis is more naive and purely "statistical" than was Lucas's (1973) procedure, which involved actually estimating a concrete structural model.

The Natural-Rate Hypothesis

I begin with the univariate Wold representation of the unemployment rate, Un_t. Wold showed that if a variable, for example, Un_t, is an indeterministic, covariance-stationary process, it can be represented as a one-sided moving average of "white noise":

$$Un_t = \sum_{j=0}^{\infty} a_j u_{t-j}, \qquad \sum_{j=0}^{\infty} a_j^2 < \infty, \qquad (2.1)$$

where the u's are serially uncorrelated with mean zero and finite variance σ^2. The model in equation (2.1) is obviously intended to apply to deviations of unemployment from its mean and any deterministic components. To make things simpler without really altering the essentials, I shall assume that the u's and the other white noises to be introduced below are serially independent.[7] I also assume that the roots of

$$\sum_{j=0}^{\infty} a_j \lambda^j = 0$$

[5] See Sargent 1971 and Lucas 1972a.

[6] See Sims 1972a. A lag distribution that embodies a wrong prior restraint on the sum of the lag weights but is sufficiently flexible can usually achieve a fit arbitrarily close to what could be achieved if the erroneous constraint on the sum of the lag weights were removed. (This assumes that the spectral density of the independent variable has no spike at zero frequency.)

[7] Dropping the assumption that the u's and other white noises are serially independent but only serially uncorrelated would necessitate replacing conditional mathematical expectations with linear least-squares forecasts in the subsequent argument. With that replacement the argument would go through. The statistical tests reported in the next section only utilize the assumption that the various white noises are serially uncorrelated.

lie outside the unit circle, so that Un_t possesses the autoregressive representation

$$Un_t = \sum_{j=1}^{\infty} g_i Un_{t-j} + u_t. \tag{2.2}$$

Even with these restrictions, equation (2.1) is a very general representation of a covariance-stationary, indeterministic process, the a_j's being chosen to enable the covariogram of $\sum a_j u_{t-j}$ to match that of Un_j. So far, then, I have not restricted the process for the unemployment rate very much.

Let the vector θ_t be the set of observations on all variables observed as of time t or earlier; θ_t includes observations on current and past GNP, interest rates, prices, and any other things, including unemployment itself, thought potentially to contribute to predicting unemployment. The following statement of the natural-rate hypothesis can now be advanced: the unemployment rate Un_t is said to obey the natural-rate hypothesis if in its (univariate) Wold representation (eq. [2.1]), the innovation u_t obeys

$$E(u_t|\theta_{t-1}) = 0, \tag{2.3}$$

so that the innovation in the unemployment rate is statistically independent of each component of θ_{t-1} and so cannot be predicted on the basis of the information in θ_{t-1}. This means that taking into account components of θ_{t-1} other than lagged Un_t's does not, on the least-squares criterion, improve the forecast of Un_t that can be made on the basis of lagged Un's alone. The least-squares forecast of Un_t on the basis of $Un_{t-1}, Un_{t-2}, \ldots$, call it $\hat{Un}_t$, is given by

$$\hat{Un}_t = \sum_{i=1}^{\infty} g_i Un_{t-i} = \sum_{j=1}^{\infty} a_j u_{t-j}.$$

On our assumption that the u's are serially independent, $\hat{Un}_t = E(Un_t|Un_{t-1}, Un_{t-2}, \ldots) = E(Un_t|u_{t-1}, u_{t-2} \ldots)$.

The statement that the best forecast of u_t conditional on all past data is simply its unconditional mean of zero amounts to a very strict version of the natural-rate hypothesis. For θ_{t-1} includes past values of monetary and fiscal policy variables. Such variables are asserted to offer no aid in predicting the unemployment rate, once lagged unemployment rates are taken into account. Furthermore, equation (2.3) implies that the current value of any control variable determined via a deterministic feedback rule on θ_{t-1} is also of no use in predicting the unemployment rate. For example, suppose that the logarithm of the money supply at t, m_t, is determined according to the deterministic, very general feedback rule

$$m_t = f(\theta_{t-1}), \tag{2.4}$$

where f is some (perhaps very complicated) function that determines the monetary authority's feedback rule. Then the above version of the natural-rate hypothesis implies that once lagged Un's are taken into account, current m_t is of no use in predicting Un_t, so that $E(Un_t \mid m_t, Un_{t-1}, Un_{t-2}, \ldots) = E(Un_t \mid Un_{t-1}, Un_{t-2}, \ldots)$. This holds regardless of the nature of the function f or the particular parameter values characterizing f. Now feedback rules of the form of equation (2.4) form the class of rules for government-policy variables that control theory indicates to be optimal ones for macroeconometric models (fixed-coefficient stochastic-difference equations). The statement above of the natural-rate hypothesis implies that the choice of f has no effect on the mean of the unemployment rate, conditional on past data. This is a very strong implication about the conditional mean of the unemployment rate, one that denies, for example, that policymakers have any scope to trade a lower expected unemployment rate for a higher expected rate of inflation.[8] By way of contrast, the existing macroeconometric models, as usually manipulated, all imply that the parameters of f and the feedback rules for other government-policy variables *do* help determine the conditional mean of the unemployment rate, and that policymakers must face up to a hard choice between the unemployment rate and the inflation rate they can expect to achieve.

It is important to note that the definition above of the natural-rate hypothesis does not rule out the possibility that there are correlations between the unemployment rate and other variables such as prices or wages or the money supply. It does imply, however, that any such correlations that exist cannot be exploited in predicting the unemployment rate. To take an example, Lucas's model of the Phillips curve is

$$Un_t = \sum_{i=1}^{\infty} g_i Un_{t-1} + g_0(X_t - EX_t|\theta_{t-1}) + u_t',$$

where X_t is the price level at time t, $EX_t|\theta_{t-1}$ is the mathematical expectation of the price level at t, conditional on information available at time $t - 1$, and u_t' is a well-behaved disturbance term, one that satisfies $Eu_t'|\theta_{t-1} = 0$.[9] The equation above posits a correlation between the innovations of Un_t and X_t; but notice that

$$E(Un_t|\theta_{t-1}) = \sum_{i=1}^{\infty} g_i Un_{t-1},$$

[8] It does not necessarily follow that the distribution of the innovation in unemployment is independent of the feedback rule for policy—only that its conditional mean is. The empirical tests reported in this paper are of neutrality-in-conditional-means propositions. Stronger neutrality propositions, asserting invariance of the entire probability distribution of some real economic variables with respect to the policy rule, obtain in some macroeconomic models (see, e.g., Sargent and Wallace 1975).

[9] The notations $E_{t-1}X_t$ and $EX_t \mid \theta_{t-1}$ are alternatives denoting the same concept, so that $E_{t-1} X_t \equiv EX_t \mid \theta_{t-1}$.

so that such a correlation does not help in predicting the unemployment rate. Obviously, the same sort of result would obtain were X_t interpreted as a vector of exogenous and endogenous variables.

As another example of correlation between unemployment and another variable that does not aid in forecasting unemployment, consider the system

$$Un_t = \sum_{i=1}^{m} g_i Un_{t-i} + u_t$$

$$X_t = \sum_{i=1}^{n} \lambda_i X_{t-i} + \sum_{i=1}^{q} \gamma_i Un_{t-i} + \varepsilon_t,$$

where the g's, λ's, and γ_i's are parameters, and u_t and ε_t are mutually uncorrelated and serially independent random variables with finite variances. In this system, unemployment helps predict X, even taking lagged X's into account; but once lagged Un's are taken into account, lagged values of X are of no aid in predicting unemployment.

Testing the Hypothesis

Granger (1969) and Sims (1972b) have described the statistical theory that can be used to construct tests of the natural-rate hypothesis as formulated above. According to Granger, ". . . We say that Y_t is *causing* X_t if we are better able to predict X_t using all available [past] information than if the information apart from [past] Y_t had been used" (p. 428). The formulation above of the natural-rate hypothesis thus posits that the unemployment rate is *caused*, in Granger's sense, by *no* other variables. From Granger's paper, a direct statistical test of that hypothesis is available. Consider the unemployment rate Un_t and some other variable Y_t. Using the method of least squares, estimate the linear regression of Un_t on lagged Un's and lagged Y's as

$$\hat{U}n_t = \sum_{j=1}^{m} \hat{\alpha}_j Un_{t-j} + \sum_{j=1}^{n} \hat{\beta}_j Y_{t-j}, \tag{2.5}$$

where the $\hat{\alpha}_j$'s and $\hat{\beta}_j$'s are least-squares estimates. On the null hypothesis that Y does *not* cause Un, the parent parameters $\beta_j, j = 1, \ldots, n$, equal zero. The natural-rate hypothesis can then be tested by testing the null hypothesis $\beta_j = 0$ (when $j = 1, \ldots, n$), for various choices of Y. Alternatively, lagged values of several variables can be added to the right side of equation (2.5). On the natural-rate hypothesis, all such variables bear zero coefficients.

An alternative way of testing the natural-rate hypothesis as posed here is to employ the test for Granger causality proposed by Sims (1972b). Assume that Un and some other series Y are jointly covariance stationary and that they are purely indeterministic. Then the generalization of Wold's representation theorem to n dimensions implies that Un_t and Y_t have the moving-average representation

$$Un_t = \sum_{i=0}^{\infty} a_i \varepsilon_{t-i} + \sum_{i=0}^{\infty} b_i \eta_{t-i} \qquad (2.6a)$$

$$Y_t = \sum_{i=0}^{\infty} c_i \varepsilon_{t-i} + \sum_{i=0}^{\infty} d_i \eta_{t-i}, \qquad (2.6b)$$

where ε and η are serially uncorrelated and mutually uncorrelated with finite variances; equations (2.6a) and (2.6b) are very general representations of the two processes Un_t and Y_t, the a's, b's, c's, and d's being chosen to make the cross-covariogram between the moving sums on the left-hand sides of the two equations match that between Un and Y. Sims showed that Y does not cause Un in Granger's sense if and only if either all of the a_i's or all of the b_i's in those equations are zero.[10] On the basis of this result, Sims showed that Y_t could be expressed as a one-sided distributed lag of Un_t with a disturbance uncorrelated with past, future, and current Un's if and only if Y fails to "cause" Un. Sims's test for exogeneity of Un is to regress Y on past, present, and future Un's and then to test the null hypothesis that coefficients on future Un's are zero. That is, by least-squares estimate,

$$Y_t = \sum_{i=-n}^{n} \gamma_i Un_{t-i} + e_t,$$

where e_t is a residual. On the null hypothesis that Y does not cause Un, $\gamma_i = 0$ for $i < 0$.

The Interest Rate

The equation for the long-term interest rate is motivated by the rational-expectations version of the expectations theory of the term structure.[11] Let R_{nt} be the yield to maturity on an n-period bond at time t, where n is large in relation to unit increments in t. I approximate the rational-expectations theory of the term structure as asserting

$$R_{nt} = \frac{1}{n}(R_{1t} + E_t R_{1\,t+1} + \ldots + E_t R_{1\,t+n-1}), \qquad (2.7)$$

---

[10] This is a very important result, since it establishes the coincidence between Granger causality and the econometrician's definition of statistical exogeneity. (It is assumed that the process $[Un_t/Y_t]$ possesses an autoregressive representation.)

[11] For expositions of the rational-expectations theory of the term structure and evidence that it performs acceptably well, see Shiller (1972) and Modigliani and Shiller (1973).

so that the n-period rate is an average of the current short rate R_{1t} and expected future short rates $E_t R_{1t+j}, j = 1, \ldots, n - 1$. Expectations about future short rates are assumed to be rational. Subtracting R_{nt} from R_{nt+1} gives $R_{nt+1} - R_{nt} = \eta_{nt+1} + (1/n)(E_t R_{1t+n} - R_{1t})$, where $\eta_{nt+1} = (1/n)[(R_{1t+1} - E_t R_{1t+1}) + (E_{t+1} R_{1t+2} - E_t R_{1t+2}) + \ldots + (E_{t+1} R_{1t+n-1} - E_t R_{1t+n-1})]$. The term η_{nt+1} is of the nature of an "innovation" and as an implication of rationality obeys $E_t \eta_{nt+1} = 0$. Furthermore, for large n and well-behaved (i.e., flat enough) yield curves, $(1/n)(E_t R_{1t+n} - R_{1t}) \simeq 0$. Consequently, for large n, there obtains the approximation

$$E_t R_{nt+1} = R_{nt}, \tag{2.8}$$

which says that the n-period rate is a martingale process.

Suppose that the reduced form for the short-term interest rate is $R_{1t} = \beta Z_t$, where β is conformable to Z_t and where Z_t is a vector of exogenous variables including government expenditures, tax rates, the money supply, and other determinants of the real rate of interest and the expected rate of inflation. That gives us $E_t R_{1t+j} = \beta E_t Z_{t+j}$. Then equation (2.7) becomes $R_{nt} = (1/n)\beta(Z_t + E_t Z_{t+1} + \ldots + E_t Z_{t+n-1})$. So we have

$$R_{nt+1} - R_{nt} = (1/n)\beta[(Z_{t+1} - E_t Z_{t+1}) + (E_{t+1} Z_{t+2} - E_t Z_{t+2}) + \ldots$$
$$+ (E_{t+1} Z_{t+n-1} - E_t Z_{t+n-1})] + (1/n)\beta(E_t Z_{t+n} - Z_t). \tag{2.9}$$

Supposing that Z_t is a vector autoregressive process, it is easy to show that[12]

$$(E_{t+1} Z_{t+j} - E_t Z_{t+j}) = \Gamma_{j-1}(Z_{t+1} - E_t Z_{t+1}), \tag{2.10}$$

where Γ_{j-1} is a square matrix conformable with Z, one whose elements are functions of the parameters of the autoregression for Z. Substituting equation (2.10) into (2.9), we obtain $R_{nt+1} - R_{nt} = (1/n)\beta(I + \Gamma_1 + \Gamma_2 + \ldots + \Gamma_{n-2})(Z_{t+1} - E_t Z_{t+1}) + (1/n)\beta(E_t Z_{t+n} - Z_t)$. Upon imposing our flat-yield-curve approximation $(1/n)(E_t Z_{t+n} - Z_t) = 0$, the equation above becomes

$$R_{nt+1} - R_{nt} = \xi(Z_{t+1} - E_t Z_{t+1}), \tag{2.11}$$

where $\xi = (1/n)\beta(I + \Gamma_1 + \ldots + \Gamma_{n-2})$. This is a version of equation (1.5). As before, we have the implication of equation (2.8), $E_t R_{nt+1} = R_{nt}$.

According to equation (2.8), a regression of $R_{nt+1} - R_{nt}$ against any

---

[12] This is an implication of Wold's chain rule of forecasting (see, e.g., Shiller 1972 and Modigliani and Shiller 1973).

variables dated t or earlier ought to have coefficients of zero. For example, a regression of $R_{nt+1} - R_{nt}$ against prices or rates of inflation dated t or earlier ought to have zero regression coefficients. The reason is that R_{nt} already has built into it expectations of inflation over almost all of the horizon for R_{nt+1} and that any revisions in those expectations between t and $t + 1$ cannot be predicted on the basis of information available at time t, by virtue of the rationality of those expectations.

Another way to test equation (2.7) is to note that it implies that R_{nt} is not caused by any variable. That can be tested by fitting two-sided distributed lags of causal candidates against R_{nt} and testing the null hypothesis that the coefficients on future R_n's are zero.

For my purposes, the important implication of the theory is that R_n cannot be predicted better by taking into account other variables, once lagged values of R_n have been taken into account. So it would be perfectly acceptable to modify equation (2.8) to read

$$E_t R_{nt+1} = \sum_{i=0}^{n} w_i R_{nt-i}, \qquad (2.8')$$

which carries the crucial implication that R_{nt} is caused by no other variables. Equation (2.8') should perhaps be preferred over equation (2.8) according to certain theories about the liquidity premiums that allegedly infest the term structure.[13]

The assertion that other variables such as monetary aggregates and fiscal-policy variables contain no information (over and above that contained in lagged values of the long rate) that can be used to predict the long rate is one that contradicts the implications of all existing macroeconometric models, as they are usually manipulated.[14] Stochastic simulations of these models will in general generate data for which a variety of monetary, fiscal, and other variables "cause" the long rate and thereby aid in its prediction.

---

[13] A more adequate approximation than eq. (2.8) is available, one that does not ignore the term $1/n(E_t R_{1t+n} - R_{1t})$. Notice that the term-structure eq. (2.7) implies that

$$E_t n R_{nt+1} = (n + 1)R_{n+1,t} - R_{1t}. \qquad (2.8'')$$

Equation (2.8'') implies that R_n is caused by (i.e., not exogenous with respect to) R_{n+1} and R_1 but is *not* caused by (i.e., is exogenous with respect to) any other variables once R_{n+1} and R_1 are taken into account. Equation (2.8'') shares the classical character of the less adequate approximation equation (2.8). Essentially, (2.8'') asserts that as a block the term structure of interest rates is statistically exogenous or not caused by other variables. This is enough to preserve the classical nature of the model but is weaker than requiring the interest rate on bonds of a given maturity to be statistically exogenous with respect to all other variables.

[14] The St. Louis model is no exception.

Observations on the Tests

The restrictions imposed by the statistical models for unemployment and the interest rate outlined here are stricter than what is really necessary to deliver the classical policy implications of the model. Thus, suppose that X_t is a vector of "real" economic aggregates at time t including variables such as real GNP, unemployment, layoffs, interest rates, and so on; X_t excludes variables measuring the composition of output, such as aggregate consumption and investment and outputs of particular commodities. Let g_t be a list of monetary and fiscal-policy variables at time t. Then a model in general will have classical policy implications if it satisfies

$$E(X_t | X_{t-1}, X_{t-2}, \cdots ; g_{t-1}, g_{t-2}, \ldots) = E(X_t | X_{t-1}, X_{t-2}, \ldots), \quad (2.12)$$

so that as a block the aggregate real variables X are statistically exogenous with respect to (not caused by, in Granger's sense) the variables in g. For a system satisfying equation (2.12), movements in the components of g do not have predictable effects on subsequent values of the real variables in X. So equation (2.12) exhibits the same sort of neutrality of certain real variables with respect to monetary and fiscal policy as does the model in Section I.

While the model of Section I is an example of a system satisfying equation (2.12), (2.12) is more general. There are systems satisfying equation (2.12) that violate the hypothesis for the unemployment rate and the interest rate described here in Section II which are key hypotheses underlying the model of Section I. Thus, equation (2.12) does *not* imply $E(Un_t | Un_{t-1}, Un_{t-2}, \cdots ; g_{t-1}, g_{t-2}, \ldots) = E(Un_t | Un_{t-1}, Un_{t-2}, \ldots)$, even though Un_t is a component of X_t. A simple example that illustrates this is a system satisfying equation (2.12) in which, say, layoffs help cause unemployment. Suppose that some components of g_t are set via a feedback rule on layoffs. Then even though g does not cause (help predict) Un when lagged unemployment *and* lagged layoffs are taken into account, components of g will help predict unemployment when only lagged unemployment is taken into account. This is because g contains some information about lagged layoffs. This is a "spurious" type of causality from g to Un in which an omitted variable (layoffs) is causing both g and Un (see Granger 1969); when layoffs are omitted, g only appears to cause Un because it is standing in for the omitted lagged-layoff rates.

The possibility of such spurious apparent causality running from components of g to Un is noteworthy, since the statement above of the natural-rate hypothesis is so very strict. In particular, it rules out even the possibility that other real variables (the components of X in eq. [2.12]) cause unemployment. This seems too drastic, since it is easy to imagine structures in which there is extensive causality from, say, GNP and layoffs to unemployment that satisfy equation (2.12) and so are basically classical in nature. For such a system, our tests might well reject the very strict version of the natural-rate hypothesis adopted above.

While failure of monetary and fiscal-policy variables to cause unemployment and other real variables is sufficient to deliver classical policy implications, it is not really necessary. One can imagine structures in which policy variables cause (help predict) unemployment and other real variables, but in which switching from one deterministic rule for setting the policy variable to another leaves the stochastic behavior of unemployment unchanged. As an example, consider the structural system

$$Un_t = \sum_{i=1}^{n_1} \lambda_i Un_{t-i} + \beta_0(m_t - E_{t-1}m_t) + \beta_1(m_{t-1} - E_{t-2}m_{t-1}) + u_t$$

$$(2.13)$$

and

$$m_t = \sum_{i=1}^{n_2} \delta_i m_{t-i} + \varepsilon_t, \qquad (2.14)$$

where ε_t and u_t are random variables, and $E_{t-1}\varepsilon_t = E_{t-1}u_t = 0$. For the structure above, it is easy to calculate

$$E(Un_t|Un_{t-1}, \ldots, m_{t-1}, m_{t-2}, \ldots) = \sum_{i=1}^{n_1} \lambda_i Un_{t-i} + \beta_1(m_{t-1}$$
$$- \sum_{i=1}^{n_2} \delta_i m_{t-i-1}).$$

It follows that m helps predict (causes) Un_t. But notice that according to equation (2.13) switching from one deterministic rule for m (i.e., a rule for which $m_t = E_{t-1}m_t$) to any other deterministic rule will leave the stochastic behavior of unemployment unaltered. Even though m causes unemployment in this system, it is true that one deterministic rule is as good as any other, so that there is no scope for countercyclical policy by way of "leaning against the wind."

The preceding observations suggest reasons for believing that this paper tests versions of classical hypotheses that are really stronger than what is necessary to deliver classical policy conclusions, so that the tests seem biased against the natural-rate hypothesis and other classical hypotheses. However, it is important to note that the tests are not uniformly biased against classical hypotheses, since it is possible to concoct nonclassical systems that will mimic the classical characteristics that my tests look for. Thus, the tests might be fooled into failing to reject the natural-rate hypothesis in a system for which that hypothesis is false. Suppose that the true reduced form for Un_t is

$$Un_t = \sum_{i=1}^{2} \lambda_i Un_{t-1} + \alpha_0 m_t + \varepsilon_t, \tag{2.15}$$

where $E(\varepsilon_t | Un_{t-1}, \ldots, m_t, m_{t-1}) = 0$ and where the λ's and α's are fixed parameters. Suppose that the authority sets m_t according to the deterministic feedback rule

$$m_t = \sum_{i=1}^{2} \delta_i Un_{t-i}.$$

Then clearly

$$E(Un_t | Un_{t-1}, Un_{t-2}, \ldots ; m_t, m_{t-1}) = \sum_{i=1}^{2} (\lambda_i + \alpha_0 \delta_i) Un_{t-i},$$

Here Un is not caused by m, in Granger's sense, because the authority, by making m_t an exact function of past Un's, eliminates any value from the m series for predicting Un.

While the tests might be fooled by such a structure, that structure itself seems unlikely to me. In particular, if the reduced form were equation (2.15) and the authority were to set m_t by a feedback only on lagged Un's, and not also on other variables, presumably the authority would want to minimize the variance of Un_t, which it could accomplish by eliminating any serial correlation in Un_t. That is, in our example, it could minimize the variance in Un by setting $\lambda_1 + \alpha_0 \delta_1 = 0, \lambda_2 + \alpha_0 \delta_2 = 0$. Then the variance of unemployment would equal the variance of ε_t. But in reality, variables like unemployment and the deviation of GNP from trend are highly serially correlated. That makes it hard to believe that any failure of, say, m to cause Un is due to the authority's manipulating m in response to past movements in Un, since that requires imputing to the authority a perverse objective, that is, one tolerating much serial correlation and variance in Un.

III. Empirical Results

Tables 1–6 report the results of performing tests along the lines proposed by Granger and Sims for quarterly data on the dependent variables spanning the period 1952 II–1972 III. The unemployment rate for all civilian workers is used for Un, while Moody's Baa corporate bond index is taken for the long-term interest rate R. The variables used as candidates for the "causal" variables Y are the logarithm of the money supply, currency plus demand deposits, (m); the federal, state, and local government surplus on the national-income-accounts basis in 1958 dollars (*surp*); the logarithms of the GNP deflator (*p*); a straight-time wage index in manufacturing (*w*); federal, state, and local purchases of goods and services in 1958 dollars (*g*); and federal, state, and local purchases in current dollars (*g*$).[15]

Each of the series has been seasonally adjusted by taking the Fourier transform of the series, setting its real and imaginary parts to zero in a band of width $\pi/12$ about the seasonal frequencies, and then taking the inverse Fourier transform to obtain a seasonally adjusted series.[16] This method has the virtue of applying a seasonal-adjustment filter with the same frequency-response function to each series, thereby avoiding the distortions in estimating distributed lags between variables that can be caused where the series have been adjusted asymmetrically (see Sims 1974 and Wallis 1974). Furthermore, the method reduces the spectral power of the series to zero at the seasonal frequencies, which Sims (1974) has argued helps eliminate bias in the form of seasonal patterns showing up in estimated distributed-lag coefficients.

Table 1 reports the results of implementing Granger's test for causality between *Un* and each of the *Y* candidates listed above. For each *Y*, the test is run in both directions: first *Un* is regressed on lagged *Un*'s and lagged *Y*'s to permit testing the null hypothesis that *Y* does not cause *Un* (i.e., that the coefficients on lagged *Y*'s are zero), then *Y* is regressed on lagged *Y*'s and lagged *Un*'s to permit testing the null hypothesis that *Un* does not cause *Y* (i.e., that the coefficients on lagged *Un*'s are zero). Regressions in both directions include a constant and a linear trend. The regressions include four lagged values of the dependent variable and six lagged values of the other variable. The *F*-statistic pertinent for

[15] The wage is an index of the straight-time manufacturing wage (*w*), which is seasonally adjusted and reported on a monthly basis in *Employment and Earnings* (Department of Labor, Bureau of Labor Statistics). The civilian unemployment rate (*Un*) seasonally unadjusted, on a monthly basis, was taken from *Employment and Earnings*. For population I used the civilian noninstitutional population aged 16 and over, constructed by subtracting armed forces numbers from the total population aged 16 and over. The noninstitutional population aged 16 and over was interpolated from annual figures compiled by the Current Population Survey and reported in table 1, Bureau of Labor Statistics *Handbook of Labor Statistics*, 1973. Armed forces numbers were obtained by averaging monthly numbers reported in *Employment and Earnings*. The civilian labor force aged 16 years and older was taken from *Employment and Earnings* and divided by pop_t to obtain the labor force participation rate. The money supply (*m*) is $M1$, currency plus adjusted demand deposits taken from the *Federal Reserve Bulletin*. The Baa rate (*R*) was obtained from Moody's Investor's Service. For *R*, *w*, and *Un*, the monthly figures were averaged to obtain quarterly figures. The GNP deflator (*p*); federal, state, and local purchases in current dollars (*g*$); and federal, state, and local purchases in 1958 dollars (*g*) were all taken from the National Income Accounts; the federal, state, and local government surplus in current dollars was also taken from the National Income Accounts and then divided by the GNP deflator to obtain the surplus in 1958 dollars (*surp*).

[16] A deterministic trend was extracted before taking the Fourier transform and then added back in after taking the inverse transform. The degrees of freedom for the *F*-statistics have been adjusted for the loss of degrees of freedom due to setting the seasonal bands to zero. The appropriate correction is described by Sims (1974).

TABLE 1

REGRESSION OF $Y(t) = \sum_{s=1}^{4} \alpha(s)Y(t-s) + \sum_{l=1}^{6} \beta(l)X(t-l) + \delta_1 t + \delta_0$

1952II–1972III

Y	X	$\alpha(1)$	$\alpha(2)$	$\alpha(3)$	$\alpha(4)$	$\beta(1)$	$\beta(2)$	$\beta(3)$	$\beta(4)$	$\beta(5)$	$\beta(6)$	δ_1	δ_0	$\bar{R}^2$	SE of Est. Adj.	D-W	F-Statistic on All β $F(6, 60)$
Un	m	1.317 (10.25)	−0.541 (−2.64)	−0.029 (−0.14)	0.113 (0.94)	−14.244 (−1.89)	7.787 (0.57)	7.578 (0.53)	−24.943 (−1.75)	26.849 (1.85)	−0.862 (−0.10)	−0.010 (−1.32)	−9.526 (−1.86)	.918	0.346	1.973	2.627*
m	Un	1.279 (9.75)	−0.367 (−1.60)	0.022 (0.09)	0.063 (0.44)	−0.002 (−0.88)	0.003 (0.82)	0.0005 (0.13)	0.00002 (0.01)	−0.002 (−0.56)	−0.0009 (−0.44)	0.0002 (1.33)	0.022 (0.26)	.999	0.006	1.991	1.506
Un	$surp$	1.435 (10.84)	−0.540 (−2.33)	−0.121 (−0.52)	0.134 (1.02)	−0.020 (−1.32)	0.035 (1.58)	−0.035 (−1.56)	0.029 (1.33)	−0.002 (−0.07)	−0.007 (−0.57)	−0.0004 (−0.21)	0.439 (2.36)	.906	0.372	1.995	0.954
$surp$	Un	1.143 (8.60)	−0.399 (−2.02)	0.149 (0.75)	−0.248 (−1.90)	−0.319 (−0.26)	0.268 (0.13)	−0.848 (−0.40)	2.875 (1.36)	−3.330 (−1.73)	1.979 (1.77)	−0.017 (−1.04)	−3.200 (−1.84)	.814	3.323	1.992	1.034
Un	g	1.498 (11.99)	−0.641 (−2.87)	−0.027 (−0.12)	0.057 (0.40)	0.814 (0.75)	−1.085 (−0.82)	−0.037 (−0.03)	1.152 (0.88)	−1.336 (−1.14)	0.143 (0.20)	0.002 (0.28)	2.036 (0.44)	.902	0.380	1.917	0.489
g	Un	0.685 (5.20)	−0.042 (−0.27)	0.069 (0.46)	−0.110 (−0.96)	−0.016 (−1.10)	−0.004 (−0.15)	0.024 (0.88)	−0.065 (−2.42)	0.034 (1.31)	0.004 (0.22)	0.003 (3.28)	1.840 (3.30)	.960	0.043	1.979	4.564**
Un	$g\$$	1.506 (12.28)	−0.614 (−2.76)	−0.134 (−0.57)	0.147 (1.09)	0.204 (0.07)	−4.415 (−0.95)	7.494 (1.73)	0.211 (0.05)	−6.820 (−1.61)	3.455 (1.56)	−0.002 (−0.19)	−0.052 (−0.02)	.908	0.368	2.056	1.145
$g\$$	Un	1.135 (9.84)	−0.066 (−0.37)	0.099 (0.57)	−0.292 (−2.99)	−0.014 (−2.87)	0.021 (2.45)	−0.006 (−0.63)	−0.008 (−0.86)	0.004 (0.43)	−0.003 (−0.55)	0.002 (3.99)	0.530 (3.84)	.999	0.014	1.806	2.504*
p	Un	1.469 (11.55)	−0.610 (−2.73)	−0.120 (−0.54)	0.132 (1.04)	−15.845 (−1.34)	22.334 (1.23)	−0.608 (−0.03)	−12.832 (−0.71)	14.059 (0.85)	−3.717 (−0.34)	−0.018 (−1.48)	−14.386 (−1.43)	.906	0.372	2.063	0.936
Un	p	1.090 (8.42)	0.003 (0.02)	0.034 (0.17)	−0.120 (−0.87)	0.0004 (0.31)	−0.002 (−0.94)	0.002 (0.78)	−0.002 (−0.88)	0.001 (0.54)	−0.0004 (−0.31)	0.00002 (0.20)	−0.026 (−0.30)	.999	0.004	2.019	1.222
w	Un	1.238 (8.02)	−0.437 (−1.94)	−0.204 (−0.92)	0.122 (0.95)	−18.346 (−1.76)	25.905 (1.81)	−20.746 (−1.44)	20.274 (1.46)	1.146 (0.08)	1.050 (0.10)	−0.084 (−2.44)	−2.469 (−2.36)	.917	0.350	2.027	2.371*
Un	w	1.066 (7.05)	−0.347 (−1.66)	0.431 (2.03)	−0.074 (−0.43)	−0.003 (−1.50)	0.00007 (0.02)	0.00001 (0.00)	0.004 (1.08)	−0.006 (−1.88)	0.002 (1.15)	−0.0006 (−1.72)	−0.010 (−0.79)	.9996	0.005	1.969	1.638

NOTE.—t-statistics for coefficients appear in parentheses below relevant coefficients.
* Significant at 5%.
** Significant at 1%.

testing the null hypothesis that the dependent variable is not caused
by the other variable is reported in the last column.

The F-statistic for m as the causal variable influencing Un is significant
at the 95 percent confidence level, though not at the 99 percent level.
Similarly, the F-statistic for w as a causal variable for Un is significant
at the 95 percent confidence level. None of the other causal candidates
obtains an F that would require rejecting the null hypothesis that they
do not cause unemployment. In particular, notice that the GNP deflator
does not appear to cause unemployment.

In the other direction, the F-statistics reveal that the hypothesis that
Un does not cause g or $g\$$ can be rejected at the 95 percent confidence
level. The hypothesis that Un does not cause the other four variables
cannot be rejected.

Tables 2 and 3 report summary statistics for the regressions implementing Sims's test for unemployment.[17] Two-sided distributed lags were
calculated in each direction, one with Un as the dependent variable
and the causal candidate Y as the "independent" variable, the other
with Un and Y reversed. The data were quasi-differenced by applying
the filter $(1 - .75L)^2$. Each regression included a constant and a trend,
with four lead variables and 12 lagged variables. The regressions were
first estimated by the method of least squares. Then the Fourier transform
of the distributed-lag coefficients was calculated. The amplitude of the
Fourier transform was inspected to see if peaks occurred at the seasonal
frequencies. In those cases where a peak occurred, indicating a seasonal
pattern in the coefficients, the regressions were recomputed using Theil's
mixed estimator to incorporate weak, stochastic prior information stating
that there is no seasonal pattern in the distributed lag. In particular,
suppose the regression estimated is

$$Un_t = \sum_{i=-4}^{12} \hat{b}_i Y_{t-i} + \text{residual}_t,$$

and that a seasonal pattern characterizes the b_i's. The regression was
then recalculated by adding observations on the three constraints

$$b_{-4} + b_0 + b_4 + b_8 = b_{-3} + b_1 + b_5 + b_9 + U_1,$$
$$b_{-4} + b_0 + b_4 + b_8 = b_{-2} + b_2 + b_6 + b_{10} + U_2,$$
$$b_{-4} + b_0 + b_4 + b_8 = b_{-1} + b_3 + b_7 + b_{11} + U_3,$$

where the U's are random variables obeying $EU_1 = EU_2 = EU_3 = 0$.
Theil's mixed estimator requires estimates of the standard error of the

---

[17] To save space, the graphed lag distributions and various summary statistics of the
two-sided tests have been relegated to a mimeographed appendix that is available from
the author on request. The graphs and various statistics from the Hannan efficient
regressions discussed below are also in this appendix.

TABLE 2

F-STATISTIC—TWO-SIDED TESTS

VARIABLE NAME (Y)	INDEPENDENT VARIABLE	
	Un^* (1)	$Y\dagger$ (2)
m	0.401‡	0.951§
$surp$	1.09‡	0.396§
g	0.344‖	2.854‖
$g\$$	0.374‡	1.255‡
p	0.647‖	0.479§
w	1.472‖	1.238§

NOTE.—All F's are $F(4, 50)$; significance levels are 2.56 for .95% confidence, 3.72 for .99% confidence:

Col. 1 regressions: $Y_t = \sum_{i=-4}^{12} w_i Un_{t-i}$; col. 2 regressions: $Un_t = \sum_{i=-4}^{12} w'_i Y_{t-i}$.

* F-statistic is pertinent for testing null hypothesis $w_{-4} = w_{-3} = w_{-2} = w_{-1} = 0$.
† F-statistic is pertinent for testing null hypothesis $w'_{-4} = w'_{-3} = w'_{-2} = w'_{-1} = 0$.
‡ Theil constraint used with $\sigma_u = \max w_i - \min w_i$.
§ No Theil constraint used.
‖ Theil constraint used with $\sigma_u = (\max w_i - \min w_i)/2$.

disturbances in the regression and the standard errors of U_1, U_2, and U_3. The former was taken as equal to the standard error of the residuals in the original least-squares regression. The latter standard errors were taken as equal to one another at σ_u, which was set at either $(\max_i \hat{b}_i - \min_i \hat{b}_i)$ or $(\max_i \hat{b}_i - \min_i \hat{b}_i)/2$, where the $\hat{b}_i$'s are from the original least-squares regression. The covariance of each U with all other random variables was assumed to be zero. Estimation incorporating this prior information in most cases sufficed to eliminate the seasonal in the distributed-lag coefficients.

Table 2 summarizes the F-statistics pertinent for testing the null hypothesis that the coefficients on future values of the right-side variable are zero, that is, the null hypothesis that the left-side variable does not cause the right-side variable. For no causal candidate Y does the F-statistic indicate rejecting that Y does not cause Un at the 95 percent confidence level. In particular, notice that in contrast to the results from applying the direct Granger test, it is not possible to reject the hypothesis that m or w does not cause Un. In the other direction, the F-statistic reveals that the hypothesis that g is not caused by Un must be rejected at the 95 percent confidence level. The next highest F is for $g\$$, though it is not significant at the 95 percent confidence level. Qualitatively, the overall pattern of the results is similar to that obtained by applying Granger's test, with the important exceptions of the different results rendered for whether m causes Un and for whether w causes Un.

Table 3 reports F-statistics pertinent for testing whether the coefficients on current and lagged right-hand side variables are zero in the one-sided regressions corresponding to those in table 2. Only the F-statistics

TABLE 3

F-STATISTICS FOR COEFFICIENTS ON CURRENT AND LAGGED VARIABLES:

I. $Y_t = \sum_{\alpha=0}^{12} \alpha_t Un_{t-i} + \beta_0 + B_1 t$, II. $Un_t = \sum_{\alpha=0}^{12} \gamma_i Y_{t-i} + \delta_0 + \delta_1 t$

VARIABLE NAME (Y_t)	INDEPENDENT VARIABLE	
	Un	Y_t
m	0.883^a	0.911^b
$surp$	1.685^a	$1.999*^b$
g	1.454^c	0.520^c
$g\$$	1.785^a	1.441^a
p	0.571^c	1.347^b
w	1.003^c	$2.355*^b$

NOTE.—All F's are $F(13, 54)$; all data are filtered: $(1 - .75L)^2$.
[a] Theil constraint used with $\sigma_u = \max w_i - \min w_i$.
[b] No Theil constraint used.
[c] Theil constraint used with $\sigma_u = (\max w_i - \min w_i)/2$.
* Significant at 5%.

for the regression of Un on $surp$ and Un on w are significant at the 95 percent confidence level.

Tables 4, 5, and 6 report the results of applying Granger's and Sims's tests to determine whether the long-term interest rate, as measured by the Baa yield index, is statistically exogenous as implied by our theory. Table 4 records the results of applying the direct Granger test. The F-statistic is the one pertinent for testing that the coefficients on lagged values of the causal candidate Y are all zero, so that Y does not cause or help predict the dependent variable. Where $RBaa$ is the dependent variable, w is the only causal candidate that obtains an F-statistic that is significant at the 95 percent confidence level. At that confidence level, the results are thus consistent with the implications of the theory, with the exception of the results for w, which indicate that w causes $RBaa$. In the reverse direction, the hypothesis that $RBaa$ does not cause the money supply must be rejected at the 95 percent confidence level.

For Sims's test, table 5 summarizes the F-statistics pertinent for testing the null hypothesis of no causality for the interest rate. The results are compatible with those obtained from applying Granger's test. The hypothesis that $RBaa$ is not caused by the causal candidate can be rejected at the 95 percent confidence level only for w. In the reverse direction, the hypothesis that $RBaa$ fails to cause m must be rejected at the 95 percent confidence level.

Table 6 reports the F-statistics pertinent for testing the null hypothesis that coefficients on current and lagged values of the causal candidates are zero in the one-sided regressions corresponding to those in table 5. The F's for w on $RBaa$ and $RBaa$ on w are the only ones significant at the 95 percent confidence level, though a couple of others are marginal

TABLE 4

REGRESSION OF $Y(t) = \sum_{s=1}^{4} \alpha(s)Y(t-s) + \sum_{l=1}^{6} \beta(l)X(t-l) + \delta_1 t + \delta_0$

1952II–1972III

Y	X	$\alpha(1)$	$\alpha(2)$	$\alpha(3)$	$\alpha(4)$	$\beta(1)$	$\beta(2)$	$\beta(3)$	$\beta(4)$	$\beta(5)$	$\beta(6)$	δ_1	δ_0	$\bar{R}^2$	SE of Est. Adj.	D-W	F-Statistic on All β $F(6, 60)$
RBaa	m	1.447 (11.54)	−0.734 (−3.26)	0.553 (2.41)	−0.378 (−2.87)	0.635 (0.17)	3.311 (0.50)	−2.633 (−0.39)	−4.584 (−0.68)	5.248 (0.79)	−1.016 (−0.27)	−0.0004 (−0.11)	−4.251 (−1.29)	.992	0.161	1.867	0.805
m	RBaa	1.337 (10.39)	−0.187 (−0.80)	−0.317 (−1.27)	0.194 (1.38)	−0.012 (−2.55)	0.005 (0.62)	0.017 (1.89)	−0.011 (−1.19)	−0.002 (−0.21)	0.001 (0.21)	0.00001 (0.14)	−0.129 (−1.30)	.999	0.006	1.925	2.730*
RBaa	surp	1.471 (11.45)	−0.715 (−3.16)	0.491 (2.14)	−0.290 (−2.12)	0.009 (1.48)	−0.011 (−1.15)	0.010 (1.06)	−0.007 (−0.74)	0.002 (0.19)	0.001 (0.19)	0.003 (1.61)	0.141 (1.58)	.992	0.163	1.867	0.593
surp	RBaa	1.107 (8.83)	−0.331 (−1.77)	0.156 (0.85)	−0.265 (−2.18)	0.889 (0.34)	−7.705 (−1.66)	9.335 (1.89)	−7.956 (−1.58)	5.698 (1.17)	−1.244 (−0.44)	0.053 (1.41)	2.155 (1.19)	.828	3.194	1.960	1.948
RBaa	g	1.485 (11.82)	−0.720 (−3.20)	0.423 (1.88)	−0.254 (−2.00)	−0.044 (−0.10)	0.110 (0.20)	0.421 (0.75)	−0.426 (−0.76)	−0.030 (−0.06)	0.276 (0.90)	0.002 (0.72)	−1.139 (−0.97)	.992	0.164	1.894	0.462
g	RBaa	0.918 (7.15)	−0.080 (−0.46)	0.036 (0.21)	−0.096 (−0.76)	0.060 (1.49)	−0.085 (−1.15)	0.067 (0.86)	−0.070 (−0.88)	0.047 (0.63)	−0.025 (−0.59)	0.002 (2.51)	0.990 (2.92)	.946	0.050	1.971	0.711
RBaa	g$	1.485 (11.75)	−0.758 (−3.40)	0.470 (2.11)	−0.282 (−2.25)	1.130 (0.90)	−1.303 (−0.67)	1.216 (0.64)	−1.598 (−0.84)	1.161 (0.62)	−0.145 (−0.15)	−0.002 (−0.50)	−1.640 (−1.27)	.992	0.164	1.888	0.502
g$	RBaa	1.193 (10.38)	−0.151 (−0.82)	0.218 (1.22)	−0.352 (−3.61)	−0.003 (−0.21)	0.026 (1.19)	−0.039 (−1.63)	0.024 (0.98)	−0.012 (−0.53)	0.007 (0.52)	0.001 (3.60)	0.369 (3.31)	.999	0.015	1.650	0.656
RBaa	p	1.388 (10.86)	−0.687 (−3.20)	0.375 (1.74)	−0.187 (−1.30)	5.516 (1.11)	−3.821 (−0.50)	3.812 (0.50)	6.530 (0.88)	−11.143 (−1.62)	−1.321 (−0.29)	0.007 (0.92)	2.144 (0.24)	.992	0.156	1.962	1.589
p	RBaa	1.083 (8.24)	0.003 (0.02)	0.021 (0.11)	−0.106 (−0.78)	0.003 (0.99)	−0.004 (−0.75)	0.010 (1.57)	−0.008 (−1.31)	0.0003 (0.04)	−0.0002 (−0.06)	0.00002 (0.09)	−0.004 (−0.02)	.999	0.004	2.016	1.482
RBaa	w	1.531 (11.87)	−0.770 (−3.45)	0.267 (1.21)	−0.117 (−0.92)	7.898 (2.19)	−15.196 (−2.66)	15.141 (2.48)	0.587 (0.09)	−12.076 (−2.00)	3.635 (0.93)	0.005 (0.60)	0.154 (0.36)	.993	0.146	2.017	3.199**
w	RBaa	1.148 (8.95)	−0.333 (−1.65)	0.361 (1.70)	−0.282 (−2.04)	0.004 (0.94)	0.002 (0.24)	−0.004 (−0.45)	−0.004 (−0.52)	0.005 (0.63)	0.002 (0.45)	0.001 (2.20)	0.038 (2.45)	.9996	0.005	2.065	1.704

NOTE.—t-statistics for coefficients appear in parentheses below relevant coefficients.
* Significant at 5%.
** Significant at 1%.

TABLE 5

F-STATISTICS—TWO-SIDED TESTS

VARIABLE NAME (Y)	INDEPENDENT VARIABLE	
	RBaa* (1)	Y† (2)
m	0.886‡	2.808‡
$surp$	0.708‡	1.454‡
g	0.285§	0.373‡
$g\$$	0.853§	0.661‡
p	1.339§	0.450§
w	3.251§	1.932§

NOTE.—All F's are $F(4, 50)$; significance levels are 2.56 for .95% confidence, 3.72 for .99% confidence:

Col. 1 regressions: $Y_t = \sum_{i=-4}^{12} w_i R\text{Baa}_{t-i}$; col. 2 regressions: $R\text{Baa}_t = \sum_{i=-4}^{12} w'_i Y_{t-i}$.

* F-statistic is pertinent for testing null hypothesis $w_{-4} = w_{-3} = w_{-2} = w_{-1} = 0$.
† F-statistic is pertinent for testing null hypothesis $w'_{-4} = w'_{-3} = w'_{-2} = w'_{-1} = 0$.
‡ No Theil constraint used.
§ Theil constraint used with $\sigma_u = (\max w_i - \min w_i)/2$.

TABLE 6

F-STATISTICS FOR COEFFICIENTS ON CURRENT AND LAGGED VARIABLES:

I. $Y_t = \sum_{i=0}^{12} \alpha_i R\text{Baa}_{t-i} + \beta_0 + \beta_1 t$ (SEASONAL DUMMIES INCLUDED),

II. $R\text{Baa}_t = \sum_{i=0}^{12} \gamma_i Y_{t-i} + \delta_0 + \delta_1 t$

VARIABLE NAME (Y_t)	INDEPENDENT VARIABLE	
	RBaa (1)	Y_t (2)
m	1.854[a]	0.511[a]
$surp$	1.771[a]	1.648[a]
g	0.344[b]	0.446[a]
$g\$$	0.798[b]	0.408[a]
p	1.751[b]	1.025[b]
w	2.554**[b]	2.004**[b]

NOTE.—All F's are $F(13, 54)$; all data are filtered with $(1 - .75L)^2$.
[a] No Theil constraint used.
[b] Theil constraint used with $\sigma_u = (\max w_i - \min w_i)/2$.
* Significant at 5%.
** Significant at 1%.

and may be understated because possibly too many lagged variables have been included.

Table 7 reports F-statistics pertinent for testing whether the labor force participation rate nf is exogenous with respect to various causal candidates. The model implies that n_{ft} is exogenous with respect to all variables in the model, with the possible exception of the unemployment rate. The unemployment rate can cause the labor force participation rate, say through the "discouraged-worker effect," while not destroying the

TABLE 7

F-STATISTICS—TWO-SIDED TESTS

VARIABLE NAME (Y)	INDEPENDENT VARIABLE	
	nf * (1)	Y† (2)
Un	3.060‡	0.945§
m	1.591§	0.390‡
$surp$	1.320‡	0.514§
g	1.471§‖	1.594‡
$g\$$	0.499‡	0.819§‖
p	0.901‡	1.487‡
w	0.586‡	1.498§‖

NOTE.—All F's are $F(4, 50)$; significance levels are 2.56 for .95% confidence, 3.72 for .99% confidence:

$$\text{Col. 1 regressions: } Y_t = \sum_{i=-4}^{12} w_i nf_{t-i}; \text{ col. 2 regressions: } nf_t = \sum_{i=-4}^{12} w'_i Y_{t-i}.$$

* F-statistic is pertinent for testing null hypothesis $w_{-4} = w_{-3} = w_{-2} = w_{-1} = 0$.
† F-statistic is pertinent for testing null hypothesis $w'_{-4} = w'_{-3} = w'_{-2} = w'_{-1} = 0$.
‡ No Theil constraint used.
§ Theil constraint used with $\sigma_u = (\max w_i - \min w_i)/2$.
‖ Some seasonal remains in the distributed lag weights despite the imposition of Theil smoothness prior.

"recursive" structure of the model which prevents monetary and fiscal policy variables from causing the real variables Un, nf, and y.

The F-statistics in table 7 emerge from implementing Sims's test. The only F-statistic that is significant at the 95 percent confidence level is the one pertinent for testing the null hypothesis that Un fails to cause nf. At that significance level the null hypothesis must be rejected, which is compatible with the presence of a discouraged-worker effect that is useful for predicting labor force participation. While none of the other F-statistics is significant, the regression of m_t against nf_t did obtain several large and statistically significant coefficients on leading values of nf. This indicates that one ought perhaps to be cautious about the null hypothesis that m does not cause nf, despite the insignificant F-statistic. With this possible exception, the regressions summarized in table 7 are consistent with the causal structure imposed by the model upon nf.

Table 8 reports the results of applying Granger's test to nf and various causal candidates. At the 95 percent confidence level, nf appears to cause w, p, g, and Un, while only Un appears to cause nf.[18]

[18] While the Durbin-Watson statistics from most of the two-sided regressions are close to two, there is a possibility that the presence of higher than first-order serial correlation is making inappropriate the F-statistics in the text. For this reason, the two-sided regressions were recomputed using a version of Hannan's efficient estimator, which is asymptotically equivalent to generalized least squares allowing for high-order serial correlation in the disturbances. The results are reported in the mimeographed appendix to this paper (n. 17 above). The general pattern agrees with the results in the text, though there are differences in details. For example, in the Hannan efficient results, w does not seem to cause the Baa rate or the unemployment rate. If anything, then, the Hannan efficient regressions seem more favorable to the exogeneity hypotheses imposed by the classical model than are the two-sided regressions reported in the text.

TABLE 8

$$\text{Regression of } Y(t) = \sum_{s=1}^{8} \alpha(s)Y(t-s) + \sum_{l=1}^{6} \beta(l)X(t-l) + \delta_1 t + \delta_0$$

1952II–1972III

Y	X	α(1)	α(2)	α(3)	α(4)	α(5)	α(6)	α(7)	α(8)	β(1)	β(2)
nf	Un	1.027	−0.151	−0.063	0.273	−0.227	0.101	−0.147	0.115	−0.0007	−0.0005
		(8.14)	(−0.83)	(−0.34)	(1.50)	(−1.24)	(0.60)	(−0.89)	(0.95)	(−0.52)	(−0.20)
Un	nf	1.540	−0.757	0.159	−0.390	0.430	0.017	−0.162	0.069	−21.500	22.961
		(12.02)	(−3.22)	(0.64)	(−1.57)	(1.68)	(0.07)	(−0.75)	(0.57)	(−1.75)	(1.29)
nf	m	0.919	−0.176	0.090	−0.086	0.190	−0.116	−0.101	0.028	−0.057	0.002
		(6.76)	(−0.99)	(0.50)	(−0.49)	(1.08)	(−0.67)	(−0.60)	(0.22)	(−0.64)	(0.01)
m	nf	1.441	−0.525	−0.117	0.465	−0.474	0.352	−0.228	0.121	−0.036	−0.073
		(10.29)	(−2.01)	(−0.41)	(1.62)	(−1.60)	(1.10)	(−0.71)	(0.70)	(−0.17)	(−0.25)
nf	surp	0.927	−0.086	0.028	0.114	0.022	0.013	−0.131	0.027	0.00009	0.00003
		(6.92)	(−0.48)	(0.16)	(0.64)	(0.12)	(0.08)	(−0.74)	(0.20)	(0.55)	(0.11)
surp	nf	1.089	−0.374	0.163	−0.398	0.326	−0.210	−0.102	−0.024	−22.533	−144.945
		(8.34)	(−1.93)	(0.81)	(−2.02)	(1.74)	(−1.13)	(−0.58)	(−0.20)	(−0.22)	(−1.06)
nf	g	0.943	−0.071	−0.031	0.143	0.081	−0.119	−0.155	0.105	0.013	−0.026
		(7.42)	(−0.41)	(−0.18)	(0.84)	(0.46)	(−0.64)	(−0.85)	(0.78)	(1.19)	(−1.72)
g	nf	0.931	−0.087	0.052	−0.129	0.140	−0.090	0.081	−0.147	1.917	1.033
		(7.19)	(−0.51)	(0.31)	(−0.78)	(0.92)	(−0.69)	(0.62)	(−1.57)	(1.25)	(0.50)
nf	g$	0.969	−0.128	0.014	0.037	0.022	0.046	−0.144	0.052	0.046	−0.047
		(7.27)	(−0.73)	(0.08)	(0.21)	(0.13)	(0.27)	(−0.84)	(0.41)	(1.45)	(−0.94)
g$	nf	1.082	−0.100	0.242	−0.438	0.182	−0.052	0.052	−0.098	0.440	0.553
		(8.45)	(−0.52)	(1.26)	(−2.35)	(0.93)	(−0.27)	(0.29)	(−1.04)	(0.89)	(0.80)
nf	p	0.938	−0.185	−0.011	0.039	0.050	−0.085	−0.179	0.098	0.181	−0.078
		(6.73)	(−1.02)	(−0.06)	(0.22)	(0.28)	(−0.47)	(−0.99)	(0.66)	(1.18)	(−0.37)
p	nf	0.853	0.038	0.138	0.196	−0.185	0.086	−0.145	−0.048	0.360	−0.107
		(6.61)	(0.22)	(0.79)	(1.15)	(−1.14)	(0.51)	(−0.84)	(−0.45)	(3.10)	(−0.68)
nf	w	0.920	−0.175	−0.020	0.021	0.075	−0.091	−0.173	0.081	0.207	−0.073
		(6.93)	(−0.95)	(−0.11)	(0.11)	(0.40)	(−0.50)	(−0.96)	(0.57)	(1.85)	(−0.42)
w	nf	1.049	−0.302	0.297	−0.058	0.030	−0.065	0.104	−0.143	0.553	−0.235
		(8.08)	(−1.51)	(1.47)	(−0.30)	(0.16)	(−0.34)	(0.57)	(−1.18)	(3.62)	(−1.11)

Y	X	β(3)	β(4)	β(5)	β(6)	δ₁	δ₀	$\bar{R}^2$	SE of Est Adj.	D–W	F-Statistic on All $F(6, 56)$
nf	Un	0.003	−0.007	0.009	−0.004	0.00003	−0.036	.864	0.004	2.143	2.886*
		(0.97)	(−2.62)	(3.54)	(−2.81)	(1.29)	(−0.98)				
Un	nf	−5.060	21.901	−32.547	24.041	−0.001	5.604	.916	0.351	2.097	2.223*
		(−0.29)	(1.31)	(−1.92)	(1.99)	(−0.63)	(1.76)				
nf	m	0.262	−0.384	0.312	−0.103	−0.0002	−0.288	.853	0.004	2.031	1.983
		(1.47)	(−2.12)	(1.76)	(−1.02)	(−1.74)	(−2.31)				
m	nf	0.041	0.075	−0.039	−0.137	−0.0001	−0.258	.999	0.006	2.000	0.309
		(0.13)	(0.25)	(−0.14)	(−0.69)	(−0.59)	(−1.25)				
nf	surp	−0.0001	0.0003	−0.0003	0.000001	0.00002	−0.045	.841	0.004	2.026	1.132
		(−0.51)	(1.06)	(−1.19)	(0.01)	(1.04)	(−1.18)				
surp	nf	91.625	128.847	−69.150	−53.598	−0.012	−37.639	.826	3.190	1.967	0.980
		(0.67)	(0.94)	(−0.50)	(−0.53)	(−0.66)	(−1.39)				
nf	g	−0.004	0.020	−0.016	0.016	−0.000006	−0.073	.852	0.004	2.054	1.938
		(−0.24)	(1.38)	(−1.23)	(2.09)	(−0.11)	(−1.58)				
g	nf	−0.555	−5.256	5.180	−2.354	0.002	1.066	.953	0.047	2.081	2.578*
		(−0.27)	(−2.62)	(2.44)	(−1.51)	(2.88)	(1.93)				
nf	g$	0.046	−0.105	0.073	−0.003	−0.0001	−0.113	.845	0.004	2.015	1.385
		(0.96)	(−2.16)	(1.46)	(−0.11)	(−1.23)	(−1.97)				
g$	nf	0.028	−0.746	−0.055	0.192	0.002	0.750	.999	0.015	1.692	1.343
		(0.04)	(−1.14)	(−0.09)	(0.41)	(3.86)	(3.14)				
nf	p	0.160	−0.372	0.192	−0.033	−0.0002	−0.397	.840	0.004	2.060	1.072
		(0.74)	(−1.75)	(0.97)	(−0.26)	(−1.17)	(−1.58)				
p	nf	−0.089	0.131	0.123	−0.223	0.0004	0.410	.9995	0.003	2.104	2.935*
		(−0.56)	(0.83)	(0.82)	(−1.86)	(2.38)	(2.10)				
nf	w	0.010	−0.167	0.132	−0.060	−0.0004	−0.217	.841	0.004	2.002	1.125
		(0.06)	(−0.95)	(0.78)	(−0.56)	(−1.15)	(−2.00)				
w	nf	−0.125	0.219	0.017	−0.053	0.0008	0.242	.9996	0.005	1.972	3.137**
		(−0.59)	(1.04)	(0.08)	(−0.32)	(2.25)	(2.25)				

Note.—t-statistics for coefficients appear in parentheses below relevant coefficients.
*Significant at 5%.
**Significant at 1%.

All in all, the empirical results provide some evidence that the causal structure imposed on the data by the classical model of Section I is not obscenely at variance with the data. The evidence that m seems to be caused by RBaa means that the assumption that m is exogenous, embedded in the assumed autoregression of equation (1.6), must be abandoned. But this is not essential, since for the purpose for which the model is intended (unconditional forecasting), the regression in table 4 will do just as well. Findings that contradict the model are that w seems to cause both RBaa and Un, according to both Sims's and Granger's tests. Also, according to Granger's test, m seems to cause Un, but according to Sims's test, it does not. This last discrepancy requires reconciling, as does the apparently general tendency of Granger's test to reject exogeneity more readily than does Sims's test.[19]

I do not believe that these results render a verdict on the model of Section I sufficiently negative for me to stop now before presenting estimates of the model. The causal candidate that does the most damage to the hypotheses of the model is the money wage w, which does not appear itself as a variable in the model of Section I. Causal candidates drawn from the list of variables actually appearing in the model usually do not seem to violate the hypotheses of the model, which gives some encouragement to the project of estimating the model.

IV. Estimates of the Model[20]

To estimate the model, a proxy for $E_{t-1}p_t$ was required.[21] As in a procedure previously used (Sargent 1973), the proxy for $E_{t-1}p_t$ was formed by regressing p_t against a list of variables dated $t - 1$ and earlier.[22] In

[19] In implementing Granger's test, I specified a maximal number of lagged own terms, usually four, upon which a variable was permitted to depend. If the variable in question is exogenous but follows a mixed moving-average, autoregressive process so that its autoregression is of infinite order, this misspecification could lead to erroneous rejection of the hypothesis of exogeneity. With Sims's test, premature truncation of the lag distribution will lead to too frequent rejection of the hypothesis of exogeneity when it is true. (Christopher Sims points out to me that since the autoregressive part of the direct Granger regression whitens the residuals, thereby reseasonalizing them, it is not possible for the Granger test to "ignore" the seasonal bands, as the Sims test as applied here does. This could conceivably account for some of the differences in the results of the two tests.)

[20] The estimates of the model use the data seasonally adjusted by setting their Fourier transforms equal to zero in the seasonal bands, the same data used in the tests in Section III. Estimates of the model using officially seasonally adjusted data were also made. The results, which are qualitatively similar to those summarized here, are in the mimeographed appendix (n. 17 above).

[21] For population (pop), I took the civilian population over 16 years old, while for the labor force I used the civilian labor force over 16. The labor force participation rate nf was measured as the ratio of the latter to the former. The total civilian unemployment rate was used. Notice that $nf_t + pop_t - Un_t$ approximately equals civilian employment, so my production function views GNP as a function only of civilian employment.

[22] To form the proxy for $E_{t-1}p_t$, p_t was regressed on a constant, trend, three seasonal dummies, and p, w, nf, and Un, each lagged one through four times.

each case, this list included all the predetermined variables that appear on the right side of the equation in which $E_{t-1}p_t$ appears.

Since the model is a simultaneous one, an instrumental-variables estimator was used to estimate the coefficients. Current endogenous variables that appear on the right side of an equation were replaced by the systematic part of a regression of that variable on the same variables that were used to form the proxy for $E_{t-1}p_t$ plus current values of the exogenous variables.[23]

The estimates are reported in table 9. The production function includes current and four lagged values of $n_t \equiv (n_{ft} + pop_t - Un_t)$. The estimates of the production function (item 3) are compatible with increasing returns to labor in the short run and slightly decreasing returns to labor in the long run.

The estimates reported in table 9 possess signs that agree with a priori expectations. Unexpected increases in the price level are estimated to increase the labor force participation rate and decrease the unemployment rate. Increases in the unemployment rate decrease the labor force participation rate, which is consistent with a discouraged-worker effect.

In the estimates reported in table 9, I have not included innovations in Z_t as determinants of R, so that the equation for R (the Baa rate) is simply an autoregression. Two pairs of equations for portfolio equilibrium are reported. The first pair regresses the reciprocal of the log of velocity $(m - p - y)$ against current- and lagged-interest rates, one member including and the other excluding trend. Including trend is seen to increase the coefficients on current- and lagged-interest rates and to make their sum positive. This is a common, though widely ignored, result: including a trend in postwar estimates of demand schedules for money for the United States tends to eliminate any inverse dependence of velocity on interest rates. The second pair of portfolio balance equations regresses $m - p$ on current and lagged y's and R's, again with and without trend. Including trend again has important effects on the coefficients. For my purposes, any of these four or any other reasonable demand schedule for money is suitable. Notice also that the model will work in the same "recursive" way if a demand schedule for money is dropped and replaced by a regression of $p_t + y_t$ on current and lagged m, the sort of equation estimated by Sims (1972b) and Andersen and Carlson (1970).

---

[23] The endogenous variables were replaced by the systematic part of a regression of themselves against pop_t, m_t, g_t, $surp_t$, the log of current government employment, and all of the variables reported in n. 22 above. The reader may wonder whether eqq. (1) and (2), which have lagged endogenous variables as regressors, can be consistently estimated by the technique employed. If the residuals are serially correlated, my estimates are not consistent. But it is straightforward to show that, e.g., the Un vs. p exogeneity tests of Section III can be viewed as tests for serial correlation of the disturbances in eq. (1), failure to reject exogeneity of unemployment (p's failing to cause Un) being consistent with no serial correlation. In effect, then, some testing for the null hypothesis of no serial correlation has been carried out, with results favorable to the null hypothesis.

TABLE 9

ESTIMATES OF THE MODEL (1951 I–1973 III)

Variable	Estimate

1. Un_t .... $-0.287(\hat{p}_t - E_{t-1}p_t) + 0.0043 + 0.0000007t + 1.47Un_{t-1}$
  (2.0)   (2.5)   (0.5)   (12.8)
  $- 0.59Un_{t-2} - 0.03Un_{t-3} + 0.04Un_{t-4}$*
  (2.9)   (0.1)   (0.3)

2. nf_t .... $0.149(\hat{p}_t - E_{t-1}p_t) - 0.075\hat{U}n_t - 0.038 + 0.00004t$
  (0.9)   (1.9)   (1.3)   (2.1)
  $+ 0.94nf_{t-1} - 0.11nf_{t-2} - 0.02nf_{t-3} + 0.12nf_{t-4}$†
  (8.2)   (0.7)   (0.2)   (1.0)

3. y_t .... $1.09\hat{n}_t + 0.24n_{t-1} - 0.24n_{t-2} - 0.14n_{t-3} - 0.02n_{t-4}$
  (3.5)   (1.0)   (1.0)   (0.6)   (0.1)
  $+ 0.35 + 0.0009t$‡
  (1.8)   (4.5)

4. R_t .... $1.52R_{t-1} - 0.77R_{t-2} + 0.44R_{t-3} - 0.24R_{t-4} + 0.15 + 0.0034t$§
  (13.1)   (3.7)   (2.4)   (2.1)   (1.8)   (2.0)

5a. $m_t - p_t - y_t$ .. $-0.0004\hat{R}_t - 0.0004R_{t-1} - 0.010R_{t-2} + 0.021R_{t-3}$
  (0.0)   (0.0)   (1.4)   (2.4)
  $+ 0.007R_{t-4} + 0.015R_{t-5} - 0.012R_{t-6} + 0.007R_{t-7} - 0.91$
  (0.9)   (2.1)   (1.6)   (1.0)   (212.0)
  $- 1.37 \times 10^{-3} \times t$‖
  (14.7)

5b. $m_t - p_t - y_t$ .. $-0.032\hat{R}_t - 0.006R_{t-1} - 0.027R_{t-2} + 0.014R_{t-3} - 0.007R_{t-4}$
  (2.0)   (0.7)   (3.2)   (1.6)   (0.9)
  $- 0.0003R_{t-5} - 0.018R_{t-6} - 0.004R_{t-7} - 0.22$#
  (0.0)   (2.0)   (0.5)   (59.2)

5c. $m_t - p_t$ .... $-0.0060\hat{R}_t - 0.0059R_{t-1} - 0.0091R_{t-2} + 0.0143R_{t-3}$
  (0.5)   (1.2)   (1.7)   (2.6)
  $+ 0.0080R_{t-4} + 0.0107R_{t-5} - 0.0022R_{t-6} + 0.0042R_{t-7}$
  (1.6)   (2.0)   (0.4)   (0.8)
  $+ 0.45\hat{y}_t + 0.16y_{t-1} + 0.19y_{t-2} + 0.09y_{t-3} - 0.06y_{t-4}$
  (3.3)   (1.9)   (2.3)   (1.1)   (0.9)
  $+ 0.02y_{t-5} + 0.05y_{t-6} + 0.06y_{t-7} - 0.22 - 0.0003t$**
  (0.3)   (0.8)   (1.1)   (2.6)   (2.1)

5d. $m_t - p_t$ .... $-0.0023\hat{R}_t - 0.0075R_{t-1} - 0.0089R_{t-2} + 0.0088R_{t-3}$
  (0.2)   (1.5)   (1.6)   (1.7)
  $+ 0.0045R_{t-4} + 0.0043R_{t-5} - 0.0044R_{t-6} + 0.0003R_{t-7}$
  (0.9)   (0.9)   (0.8)   (0.1)
  $+ 0.25\hat{y}_t + 0.06y_{t-1} + 0.09y_{t-2} - 0.01y_{t-3} - 0.14y_{t-4}$
  (2.5)   (0.9)   (1.3)   (0.1)   (2.2)
  $- 0.02y_{t-5} + 0.01y_{t-6} + 0.04y_{t-7} - 0.052$††
  (0.3)   (0.2)   (0.6)   (1.7)

NOTE.—t-statistics are in parentheses beneath coefficients. Hatted variables (∧) are systematic parts of regressions against instrumental variables.

* $\bar{R}^2 = .908$; SE $= .371$; D–W $= 2.07$.

† $\bar{R}^2 = .867$; SE $= .0040$; D–W $= 2.00$.

‡ $\bar{R}^2 = .95$; SE $= .00964$; D–W $= 2.03$; filter: $(1 - .6L)^2$; sum of weights on $n = +.93$; $\hat{n}_t \equiv (nf_t - U\hat{n}_t + pop_t)$; $n_t \equiv (nf_t - U\hat{n}_t + pop_t)$.

§ $\bar{R}^2 = .99$; SE $= .158$; D–W $= 1.89$; sum of weights $= .95$.

‖ $\bar{R}^2 = .93$; SE $= .00856$; D–W $= 1.97$; filter: $(1 - .6L)^2$; sum of coefficients on $R = +.024$.

$\bar{R}^2 = .28$; SE $= .01085$; D–W $= 1.91$; filter: $(1 - .8L)^2$; sum of coefficients on $R = -.080$.

** $\bar{R}^2 = .29$; SE $= .00561$; D–W $= 2.10$; filter: $(1 - .8L)^2$; sum of weights on $R = +.014$; sum of weights on $y = +.96$.

†† $\bar{R}^2 = .25$; SE $= .00576$; D–W $= 1.99$; filter: $(1 - .8L)^2$; sum of weights on $R = -.005$; sum of weights on $y = +.28$.

V. Conclusions

This paper has estimated and tested a macroeconometric model with "classical" or "monetarist" policy implications, even though it has "Keynesian" short-run properties. Some evidence for rejecting the model has been turned up, but it is far from being overwhelming and decisive. The evidence that seems most damaging to the model comes from the role that the money wage plays in apparently "causing" unemployment and the long-term interest rate. On the other hand, the tests have turned up little evidence requiring us to reject the key hypothesis of the model that government monetary and fiscal-policy variables do not cause unemployment or the interest rate. The fact that such evidence has been hard to turn up ought to be disconcerting to users of the existing macroeconometric models, since as usually manipulated those models all imply that monetary and fiscal policy *do* help cause unemployment and the interest rate.

Models of the kind presented in this paper imply that there is no scope for the government to engage in activist countercyclical policy, so that it might as well employ rules without feedback for fiscal and monetary policy, for example, Friedman's *x* percent growth rule for the money supply. In contradistinction, macroeconometric models as they are usually manipulated imply that it is optimal for the government to use rules with feedback, which may imply "leaning against the wind," contrary to Friedman's rule. If we are to have any reason to believe that rules with feedback are superior to rules without feedback, there should be empirical evidence in hand that some existing macroeconometric model can outperform models of the class studied in this paper. It is my impression that such evidence does not yet exist.

References

Andersen, Leonall C., and Carlson, Keith M. "A Monetarist Model for Economic Stabilization." Federal Reserve Bank of St. Louis *Review* (April 1970).

Bodkin, Ronald G., and Klein, Lawrence R. "Nonlinear Estimation of Aggregate Production Functions." *Rev. Econ. and Statis.* 49 (February 1967): 28–44.

Cooper, J. Phillip, and Fischer, Stanley. "Monetary and Fiscal Policy in the Fully Stochastic St. Louis Econometric Model." *J. Money, Credit, and Banking* 6 (February 1974): 1–27.

Granger, C. W. J. "Investigating Causal Relations by Econometric Models and Cross-spectral Methods." *Econometrica* 37 (July 1969): 424–38.

Lucas, Robert E., Jr. "Capacity, Overtime, and Empirical Production Functions." *A.E.R. Papers and Proc.* 60 (May 1970): 23–27.

———. "Econometric Testing of the Natural Rate Hypothesis." In *The Econometrics of Price Determination Conference*, edited by Otto Eckstein. Washington: Board of Governors, Federal Reserve System, 1972. (*a*)

———. "Expectations and the Neutrality of Money." *J. Econ. Theory* 4 (April 1972): 103–24. (*b*)

———. "Some International Evidence on Output-Inflation Trade Offs." *A.E.R.* 63 (June 1973): 326–34.

Modigliani, Franco, and Shiller, Robert. "Inflation, Rational Expectations, and the Term Structure of Interest Rates." *Economica*, n.s. 40 (February 1973): 12–43.

Poole, William. "Optimal Choice of Monetary Policy Instruments in a Simple Stochastic Macro Model." *Q.J.E.* 84 (May 1970): 197–216.

Sargent, Thomas J. "A Note on the Accelerationist Controversy." *J. Money, Credit, and Banking* 3 (August 1971): 721–25.

———. "Rational Expectations, the Real Rate of Interest, and the Natural Rate of Unemployment." In *Brookings Papers on Economic Activity*, vol. 2, edited by Arthur M. Okun and George Perry. Washington: Brookings Inst., 1973.

Sargent, Thomas J., and Wallace, Neil. "'Rational' Expectations, the Optimal Monetary Instrument, and the Optimal Money Supply Rule." *J.P.E.* 83, no. 2 (April 1975): 241–54.

Shiller, Robert. "Rational Expectations and the Structure of Interest Rates." Ph.D. dissertation, Massachusetts Inst. Tech., 1972.

Sims, Christopher A. "The Role of Approximate Prior Restrictions in Distributed Lag Estimation." *J. American Statis. Assoc.* 67 (March 1972): 169–75. (*a*)

———. "Money, Income, and Causality." *A.E.R.* 62 (September 1972): 540–52. (*b*)

———. "Seasonality in Regression." *J. American Statis. Assoc.* 69 (September 1974): 618–26.

Tobin, James. "Inflation and Unemployment." *A.E.R.* 62 (March 1972): 1–18.

Wachter, Michael. "A Labor Supply Model for Secondary Workers." *Rev. Econ. and Statis.* 54 (May 1972): 141–51.

Wallis, Kenneth S. "Seasonal Adjustment and Relations between Variables." *J. American Statis. Assoc.* 69 (March 1974): 18–31.

28

The Observational Equivalence of Natural and Unnatural Rate Theories of Macroeconomics

Thomas J. Sargent

The usual proof that Friedman's simple k-percent growth rule for the money supply is suboptimal comes from mechanically manipulating a reduced-form equation. Those manipulations, in general, show that pursuing a rule with feedback from current economic conditions to the money supply is better than following Friedman's advice. To be valid, the proof requires that, as written in one particular way, the reduced-form equation will remain unaltered when the monetary authority departs from the old "rule" used during the estimation period and follows a new one. Here I point out that there are always alternative ways of writing the reduced form, one being observationally equivalent with the other, so that each is equally valid in the estimation period. If one assumes that the first form is invariant when the policy rule is changed, the proof of the superiority of rules with feedback over Friedman's rule goes through. But if one assumes that it is the reduced form as written in the second way that remains unchanged, the proof that Friedman is wrong does not obtain—instead, the implication is that Friedman's rule does as well as any other deterministic feedback rule and better than a stochastic rule. Therefore, estimates of reduced forms alone will not permit one to settle the difference between Friedman and advocates of rules with feedback. Given any set of reduced-form estimates, there is an invariance assumption that will permit a member of either camp to make his point. In effect, then, this paper poses the question: Does the view that Friedman's k-percent feedback rule is as good as any other deterministic feedback rule place any restrictions on reduced forms? The answer is no. This is distressing since, for a given sampling interval and estimation period, the reduced-form estimates summarize everything that the data can ever tell

John Geweke, Christopher Sims, Gary Skoog, and Neil Wallace contributed valuable comments on an earlier draft of this paper. The Federal Reserve Bank of Minneapolis financed the work. The views expressed herein are solely my own and do not necessarily represent the views of the Federal Reserve Bank of Minneapolis or the Federal Reserve System.

[*Journal of Political Economy*, 1976, vol. 84, no. 3]

us. To rule on the policy issue thus requires bringing to bear theoretical considerations or doing empirical work of a kind considerably more subtle than that directed solely at estimating reduced forms. In effect, it is necessary to get some evidence on what sort of invariance assumption is the most realistic one to impose. How one does that is a delicate, though not entirely intractable, task, the discussion of which is outside the scope of this paper.

This paper is in the nature of a footnote to Lucas's (1973a) important critique of econometric policy evaluation. Lucas emphasized the critical invariance assumption behind the usual argument for rules with feedback and showed how that invariance assumption fails to hold in models with rational expectations. As extreme examples of how wrong the standard invariance assumption could be, Lucas (1972) and Sargent and Wallace (1975) have constructed particular structural models in which one deterministic rule is as good as another, so that the standard proof of the suboptimality of Friedman's rule fails spectacularly in those examples. Those examples were dependent on particular structural setups. The point of this note is that, for any estimated reduced form, there is an invariance assumption which if imposed delivers the conclusion that one deterministic rule is equivalent with any other. In effect, then, this note displays some mechanical equivalencies that force one to stumble upon Lucas's observations about the limits of the usual applications of optimal-control theory to macroeconometric models.

A casual reader of Marschak's classic paper (1953) would perhaps regard my major contention—that reduced forms alone cannot settle the policy-rules controversy—as being obvious. However, applications of optimal control to macroeconometric models do purport to extract implications about the optimal feedback rule solely from estimated reduced forms.

For simplicity, I deal with a bivariate model. I assume that during the estimation period, two variables, y_t and m_t, were described as a realization from a stationary, indeterministic stochastic process. The variable y_t measures some "goal" variable like unemployment or GNP. The variable m_t represents a potential policy instrument. I assume that during the estimation period m_t was exogenous with respect to y, and that m_t caused y_t, in Granger's sense (1969). This means that the (y, m) process can be represented in the particular (Wold) moving average form[1]

$$y_t = \alpha(L)\varepsilon_t + \beta(L)\eta_t \tag{1a}$$

$$m_t = \gamma(L)\varepsilon_t, \tag{1b}$$

[1] The paper by Sims (1972), especially his appendix, provides a useful summary of the statistical theory used here.

where

$$\alpha(L) = \sum_{j=0}^{\infty} \alpha_j L^j, \qquad \beta(L) = \sum_{j=0}^{\infty} \beta_j L^j,$$

and

$$\gamma(L) = \sum_{j=0}^{\infty} \gamma_j L^j;$$

L is the lag operator ($L^n x_t \equiv x_{t-n}$), and η_t and ε_t are mutually uncorrelated and serially uncorrelated random variables with means of zero and finite variances σ_η^2 and σ_ε^2, respectively. (I have omitted constants and any deterministic terms from representation [1], which can be included without affecting the argument.)[2]

The assumption that the Wold representation has the triangular form of (1)—that is, the assumption that m is exogenous and "causes" y—means that under one pretty general additional condition, a final-form regression of y on m can be consistently estimated by least squares. In particular, suppose that $\gamma(L)$ is invertible so that m_t has the autoregressive representation $\gamma^{-1}(L)m_t = \varepsilon_t$, where $\gamma^{-1}(L)$ is a one-sided polynomial in the lag operator L. Substituting the above equation into (1a) gives

$$y_t = \alpha(L)\gamma^{-1}(L)m_t + \beta(L)\eta_t \tag{2}$$

$$y_t = h(L)m_t + \beta(L)\eta_t,$$

where $h(L) = \alpha(L)\gamma^{-1}(L)$ is a one-sided polynomial in the lag operator L. Equation (2) is a "final form" for y in terms of m and is consistently estimated by least squares, since the η_t process is orthogonal to the m_t process. Assuming that $\beta(L)$ has a one-sided inverse, the "reduced form" for y_t can be obtained as[3] $\beta(L)^{-1}y_t = \beta(L)^{-1}h(L)m_t + \eta_t$, or

$$y_t = \sum_{i=0}^{\infty} a_i m_{t-i} + \sum_{i=0}^{\infty} b_i y_{t-i-1} + \eta_t, \tag{3}$$

where

$$a(L) = \sum_{i=0}^{\infty} a_i L^i = \beta(L)^{-1}h(L)$$

and

$$[1 - Lb(L)] = \left(1 - \sum_{i=0}^{\infty} b_i L^{i+1}\right) = \beta(L)^{-1}.$$

[2] I will also assume that ε and η are mutually and serially independent, which facilitates the computations below but is not essential. Abandoning that assumption would require replacing mathematical expectations with linear least-squares forecasts at several points below. With that replacement, my argument would go through.

[3] I am assuming that $\beta(L)$ and σ_η^2 are so normalized that $\beta_0 = 1$, which implies that the zero-order coefficient of $\beta(L)^{-1}$ is also unity.

The reduced form (3) expresses y in terms of current and lagged m's and lagged y's with a disturbance that is serially uncorrelated and orthogonal to the variables on the right-hand side of the equation. Thus the reduced form (3) can be consistently estimated by least squares.

Write (3) as

$$y_t = a(L)m_t + b(L)y_{t-1} + \eta_t. \tag{4}$$

It is now easy to illustrate the elements of the usual argument that it is optimal for the policy authority to set m via a rule with feedback from lagged y's to current m. Suppose that the authority's goal is to set m in order to minimize the variance of y. Suppose that the parameters of the reduced form (4) will remain unaltered when the authority abandons (1b), which described policy during the estimation period, and implements a new feedback rule. (Suppose also that $a(L)$ has a one-sided inverse under convolution, which is not really necessary but rules out unseemly "instrument instability" problems.) Then it is straightforward to show that the authority would minimize the variance of y by using the feedback rule

$$a(L)m_t = -b(L)y_{t-1}, \tag{5}$$

which is a rule for setting m_t as a function of lagged m's and lagged y's. In general, some of the b_j's are not zero, so that it is optimal for the authority to incorporate feedback from lagged y's to m, presumably to "lean against the wind." So a rule without feedback is suboptimal.

As Lucas (1973b) has emphasized, a key assumption in the above argument for rules with feedback is that the parameters of the reduced form (4) remain unchanged when the authority abandons the rule used during the estimation period and uses a new one. Lucas argued that if the reduced form incorporates the influence of people's expectations, and if expectations are formed in a well-informed or "rational" way, that assumption is not appropriate. Here I point out that there always seems to be an interpretation of the reduced form (4) which completely vitiates the preceding demonstration of the superiority of rules with feedback.

I begin by noting that from (1b) $\gamma_0\varepsilon_t = m_t - E_{t-1}m_t$, where $E_{t-1}m_t$ is the mathematical expectation of m_t conditioned on past m's and past y's. In this case, since m is exogenous in the estimation period, lagged y's don't help explain m once lagged m's are taken into account, so that in the estimation period $E_{t-1}m_t \equiv E(m_t \mid m_{t-1}, m_{t-2}, \ldots, y_{t-1}, y_{t-2}, \ldots) = E(m_t \mid m_{t-1}, m_{t-2}, \ldots)$. The random variable $\gamma_0\varepsilon_t$ is the "innovation" of m_t—the part that can't be predicted on the basis of past m's (or past y's). Now substituting $\varepsilon_t = (1/\gamma_0)(m_t - E_{t-1}m_t)$ into (1a) and rearranging gives $\beta(L)^{-1}y_t = (1/\gamma_0)\beta(L)^{-1}\alpha(L)(m_t - E_{t-1}m_t) + \eta_t$, or

$$y_t = c(L)(m_t - E_{t-1}m_t) + b(L)y_{t-1} + \eta_t, \tag{6}$$

where

$$\frac{1}{\gamma_0}\, \beta(L)^{-1}\alpha(L) \;=\; c(L) \;=\; \sum_{i=0}^{\infty} c_i L^i,$$

and where $b(L)$ is as defined under (3).[4] Equation (6) is an alternative version of the reduced form that is equivalent with the version (3) or (4) from the point of view of representing things during the estimation period. Notice that (4) and (6) have identical residuals and so fit equally well.

If we assume that the reduced form (6) remains unaltered when the authority abandons (1b) and adopts a deterministic feedback rule giving m as an exact function of past m's and past y's, a strong sort of "neutrality" result emerges. For under any deterministic feedback rule, say one of the form

$$m_t = s_1 m_{t-1} + s_2 m_{t-2} + \cdots + r_1 y_{t-1} + r_2 y_{t-2} + \cdots, \qquad (7)$$

it is true that

$$E_{t-1} m_t = m_t, \qquad (8)$$

identically in t. Substituting (8) into (6) gives $y_t = b(L)\, y_{t-1} + \eta_t$, which is an autoregressive representation for y that holds regardless of the values of the particular parameters $s_1, s_2, \ldots r_1, r_2, \ldots$ of the feedback rule (7) selected by the authority. The assumption that it is the reduced-form representation (6) that remains unchanged as the policy rule is altered leads to the conclusion that one deterministic feedback rule is as good as any other. There is thus no reason to expect that the authority can do better than it can by implementing the x-percent growth rule recommended by Friedman.

The preceding "neutrality" demonstration rests on the arbitrary assumption that it is the reduced-form representation (6) that remains unaltered when the authority institutes a new policy rule outside the estimation period. Of course, the earlier demonstration of the superiority of a rule with feedback depended on the equally arbitrary but different assumption that it was the reduced-form representation (4) that remained unchanged from the estimation period even once the new policy rule was instituted. From the viewpoint of extracting policy implications, assuming invariance for the reduced-form representation (4) or (6) thus gives drastically different implications. Yet, from the point of view of representing the reduced form during the estimation period, (4) and (6) are exactly equivalent. This is what leads me to the conclusion that the empirical evidence from a single estimation period alone, which can be

---

[4] Notice that $c(L)(m_t - E_{t-1}m_t) = c_0(m_t - E_{t-1}m_t) + c_1(m_{t-1} - E_{t-2}m_{t-1}) + c_2(m_{t-2} - E_{t-3}m_{t-2}) + \cdots$.

completely summarized by (4) or (6) and an autoregression for m, can never settle things between advocates of rules with feedback and advocates of rules without feedback.

Perhaps this could be dismissed as a mere curiosity if macroeconomists agreed that as between (4) and (6) one of these ways of writing the reduced form is much more likely to remain unchanged when policy changes. The problem is that there is no such agreement. While in the past most macroeconomists have regarded (4) as invariant under changes in the policy rule, that assumption depends critically on the assumption that peoples' expectations are formed using fixed-weight, autoregressive schemes that in general are not "rational." Lucas (1973b) has argued forcefully against that assumption, but it remains true that the assumption still underlies most macroeconometric policy evaluation and is an essential element of most applications of control theory to macroeconometric models. On the other hand, reduced-form representations resembling (6) are supposed to be invariant under changes in the policy rule according to some structural macroeconomic models incorporating rational expectations and Lucas's (1973a) formulation of the aggregate supply function.[5] In such models, current and maybe lagged innovations in the money supply are what agents respond to.

The upshot is that the invariance of neither (4) nor (6) to changes in the policy rule would now command a concensus among macroeconomists. The current state of macroeconomic theory seems to me to be very far from supplying a reliable basis for ruling out one of these invariance assumptions in favor of the other. For that reason, I believe that the observational equivalence of (4) and (6) provides some cause to be circumspect about economists' ability to be sure that rules with feedback clearly dominate rules without feedback (or vice versa).

The reader may wonder whether my assumptions that m is exogenous with respect to y and that m causes y in effect rig things in the preceding argument. They don't. Those assumptions were made to guarantee that a y-on-m reduced form was identifiable and estimable. The estimability of such a reduced form is a sine qua non for the usual argument that rules with feedback dominate rules without feedback. One alternative set of assumptions would have been that y and m caused each other, so that there was mutual feedback between y and m. Only under special circumstances, an instance of which is analyzed in Appendix B, is a y-on-m reduced form identified in a system with mutual feedback. As Appendix B illustrates, for systems with mutual feedback that are identifiable through a priori restrictions, there obtains the same observational equivalence as analyzed in the text. Another alternative assumption would have been that y was exogenous with respect to m in

---

[5] For example, see Sargent and Wallace (1975).

the estimation period. I have elsewhere advanced the notion that the hypothesis of exogeneity of certain goal variables y (e.g., unemployment) with respect to certain policy instruments m (e.g., the money supply) is a naive, model-free way of stating the natural-rate hypothesis.[6] Exogeneity of y with respect to m can readily be shown to be compatible with the notion that one deterministic rule is as good as any other on a certain invariance assumption. On the other hand, it is straightforward to show that an alternative invariance assumption could be imposed that would imply that Friedman's rule is suboptimal. This is shown in Appendix A.

The present argument only shows how reduced forms estimated for a given sampling interval (i.e., quarterly or monthly) over a given estimation period cannot settle the policy-rules controversy. That does not mean that there is no way that empirical evidence can be brought to bear on the question. Presumbly, by estimating reduced forms for various subperiods or countries across which policy rules differed systematically, light can be shed on what way of writing the reduced form remains invariant.[7] Alternatively, by studying data more and less finely aggregated over time, different implications of our two invariance assumptions might be extracted and tested. Both of these paths involve considerable subtleties. Very little satisfactory evidence has yet been assembled along either path.

Appendix A

How "Classical" Models Can Be Interpreted in "Keynesian" Ways

This Appendix illustrates how, for classical models in which real variables are econometrically exogenous with respect to policy variables, there is a way of writing the reduced form which, if invariant under rules changes, implies that rules with feedback are optimal. Therefore, evidence that real variables are econometrically exogenous with respect to policy variables, which I have argued (Sargent 1976) is a strong, model-free way of stating the natural-rate hypothesis, has "classical" policy implications on one kind of invariance assumption but does not on another. The argument in this Appendix is thus the other half of the observational equivalence dilemma, since here I start with a model originally thought to be very "neutral" or classical and produce an invariance assumption that rationalizes rules with feedback.

Consider a "structural" model of the form

$$\lambda(L) y_t = \gamma(m_t - E_{t-1} m_t) + u_t, \gamma > 0 \tag{A1}$$

$$m_t = d(L)\varepsilon_t, \tag{A2}$$

---

[6] See Sargent (1976).

[7] Lucas's (1973a) international comparisons provide an excellent example of this approach.

where

$$\lambda(L) = \sum_{i=0}^{\infty} \lambda_i L^i, \, d(L) = \sum_{i=0}^{\infty} d_i L^i;$$

$\lambda(L)$ and $d(L)$ both have one-sided inverses under convolution, and u_t and ε_t are mutually and serially independent random variables with means of zero and finite variances. The model (A1)-(A2) is a two-variable example of the "classical" model described by Sargent (1976). Here innovations in m (money) produce sympathetic movements in y. In this model, y is exogenous with respect to m, and m is exogenous with respect to y. Though y and m are correlated, neither one helps predict the other. To see that m is exogenous with respect to y, notice that (A1) and (A2) can be rearranged in the triangular Wold representation,

$$y_t = \lambda^{-1}(L)\gamma d_o \varepsilon_t + \lambda^{-1}(L)u_t \tag{A3}$$

$$m_t = d(L)\varepsilon_t, \tag{A4}$$

the existence of which shows that m is exogenous with respect to y by virtue of Sims's theorem 1. To see that y is exogenous with respect to m, observe directly from (A1) that

$$E_{t-1}y_t = -\sum_{i=1}^{\infty} \lambda_i y_{t-1},$$

which shows that m does not help predict y once lagged y's are accounted for. Alternatively, rewrite (A1)-(A2) as

$$y_t = \lambda^{-1}(L)w_t \tag{A5}$$

$$m_t = d(L)\phi w_t + d(L)\xi_t, \tag{A6}$$

where $w_t \equiv \gamma d_0 \varepsilon_t + u_t$, and ξ_t and ϕ obey $\varepsilon_t = \phi w_t + \xi_t$, $E(\xi_t | w_t) = 0$ (ϕ is the regression coefficient of ε_t against w_t, ξ_t being the residual). Since ξ_t is orthogonal to w_t and since both are serially uncorrelated by construction, it follows that (A5)-(A6) is a Wold representation for the $(y_t - m_t)$ process. The existence of such a triangular Wold representation establishes that y is exogenous with respect to m, again by virtue of Sims's theorem 1.

Inverting (A4) and substituting it into (A3) delivers $\lambda(L)y_t = \gamma d_o d(L)^{-1}m_t + u_t$, which is a $y - on - m$ reduced form which is consistently estimated by least squares, since u_t is orthogonal to lagged y's and current and lagged m's. This is exactly the form of reduced form manipulated and assumed invariant under alternative policy rules in the proof that Friedman's rule is suboptimal.

If the reduced form (A1) is invariant under rules changes, then one deterministic rule is as good as any other. Thus, there are alternative ways of deriving policy implications from empirical evidence generated by a "classical" model like (A1)-(A2). Depending on what sort of invariance assumption is imposed, drastically different inferences follow about the implications of different feedback rules.

Appendix B

Observational Equivalence in the Presence of Feedback from y to m

Suppose that during the estimation period the $y - m$ process possessed the vector autoregressive representation

$$y_t = a(L)y_{t-1} + b(L)m_{t-1} + \varepsilon_t \tag{B1}$$

$$m_t = c(L)y_{t-1} + d(L)m_{t-1} + u_t, \tag{B2}$$

where

$$a(L) = \sum_{j=0}^{\infty} a_j L^j,$$

etc., and ε_t and u_t are serially independent random variables with means zero and finite variance. In general, $E(\varepsilon_t u_t) \neq 0$, although it is easy to prove that $E(\varepsilon_t u_s) = 0$ for $t \neq s$. The last equality follows because, for example, u is the residual in a projection of m on lagged m's and y's and so is orthogonal to them. Since lagged u's and ε's are linear combinations of lagged y's and m's, it follows that current u is orthogonal to lagged u's and ε's. Here ε_t and u_t are the one-step-ahead prediction errors for y_t and m_t, respectively, both predictions being conditional on lagged m's and lagged y's. Consistent with usual usage, by a $y-$on$-m$ reduced form I mean a regression of y on past y's and current and past m's. Analogously, by a $m-$on$-y$ reduced form I mean a regression of m on past m's and current and past y's. For a system with probability distribution characterized by (B1)-(B2), the implied pair of $y-$on$-m$, $m-$on$-y$ reduced forms is identifiable only if sufficient a priori information is imposed on the covariance between the disturbances in the two reduced forms and on the contemporaneous coefficient in either the $y-$on$-m$ reduced form or the $m-$on$-y$ reduced form. Here I will impose the restrictions that there is no contemporaneous feedback from y to m and that the reduced-form disturbances are contemporaneously orthogonal. These restrictions serve to identify the y-m feedback structure. In particular, (B2) gives the "feedback rule" that governs m in the sample period. To find the y-on-m reduced form in terms of the parameters of (B1)-(B2), first project ε_t on u_t to get the decomposition $\varepsilon_t = \rho u_t + \xi_t$, $E(\xi_t \cdot u_t) = 0$, $\rho = Eu_t\varepsilon_t/Eu_t{}^2$. Then subtract ρm_t from (B1) and rearrange to obtain

$$y_t = [a(L) - \rho c(L)]y_{t-1} + \rho m_t + [b(L) - \rho d(L)]m_{t-1} + \xi_t. \quad (B3)$$

Equation (B3) is a y-on-m reduced form with a disturbance ξ_t that is orthogonal to the regressors and also serially uncorrelated. Hence, the parameters of (B3) will be consistently estimated by least squares. Notice that (B2) is also consistently estimated by least squares.

Write (B3) more compactly as

$$y_t = h(L)y_{t-1} + g(L)m_t + \xi_t, \quad (B3')$$

where $h(L) = a(L) - \rho c(L)$, $g(L) = \{\rho + L[b(L) - \rho d(L)]\}$.

Then solve (B2) for m_t in terms of lagged y's and current and lagged u's: $m_t = [1 - Ld(L)]^{-1}c(L)y_{t-1} + [1 - Ld(L)]^{-1}u_t$. Substituting this for m_t in (B3') gives $y_t = \{h(L) + g(L)[1 - Ld(L)]^{-1}c(L)\}y_{t-1} + g(L)[1 - Ld(L)]^{-1}u_t + \xi_t$ or

$$y_t = i(L)y_{t-1} + j(L)(m_t - E_{t-1}m_t) + \xi_t, \quad (B4)$$

where $i(L) = \{h(L) + g(L)[1 - dL(L)]^{-1}c(L)\}$, $j(L) = g(L)[1 - Ld(L)]^{-1}$, and ξ_t is orthogonal to lagged y's and current and lagged u's (i.e., $[m_t - E_{t-1}m_t]$'s). So (B4) is consistently estimated by least squares.

Now (B3') and (B4) have identical residuals and thus are observationally equivalent. The argument in the text thus goes through for this system.

References

Granger, C. W. J. "Investigating Causal Relations by Econometric Models and Cross-spectral Methods." *Econometrica* 37 (July 1969): 424–38.

Lucas, Robert E., Jr. "Expectations and the Neutrality of Money." *J. Econ. Theory* 4 (April 1972): 103–24.

———. "Some International Evidence on Output-Inflation Tradeoffs." *A.E.R.* 63 (June 1973): 326–34. (*a*)

———. "Econometric Policy Evaluation: A Critique." Working Paper, Carnegie-Mellon Univ., 1973. (*b*)

Marschak, Jacob. "Economic Measurements for Policy and Prediction." In *Studies in Econometric Method,* edited by William C. Hood and T. C. Koopmans. Cowles Foundation Monograph no. 14. New Haven, Conn.: Yale Univ. Press, 1953.

Sargent, Thomas J. "A Classical Macroeconometric Model for the United States." *J.P.E.* 84, no. 2 (April 1976): 207–37.

Sargent, Thomas J., and Wallace, Neil. "Rational Expectations, the Optimal Monetary Instrument, and the Optimal Money Supply Rule." *J.P.E.* 83, no. 2 (April 1975): 241–54.

Sims, Christopher A. "Money, Income, and Causality." *A.E.R.* 62 (September 1972): 540–52.

29

Unanticipated Money Growth and Unemployment in the United States

Robert J. Barro

The hypothesis that forms the basis of this empirical study is that only unanticipated movements in money affect real economic variables like the unemployment rate or the level of output. This hypothesis is explicit in "rational expectation" monetary models, such as those of Robert Lucas (1972, 1973), Thomas Sargent and Neil Wallace, and the author (1976a). However, the proposition that only the unanticipated part of money movements has real effects is clearly more general than the specific setting of these models.

In order to implement and test the hypothesis empirically, it is necessary to quantify the notions of anticipated and unanticipated money movements. Accordingly, the first part of the analysis specifies a simple model of the money growth process. The variables that turn out empirically to have a systematic effect on U.S. money growth, using annual observations from 1941 to 1973, are a measure of federal government expenditure relative to "normal," a lagged unemployment rate, and two lagged values of money growth. Anticipated money growth is then viewed as the prediction that could have been obtained by exploiting the systematic relation between money growth and this set of independent variables.

The measure of unanticipated money growth—actual growth less the anticipated portion—that is obtained in Section I is used in Section II as an explanatory variable for the unemployment rate—the real economic variable that is focused on in the present study. Over the 1946–73 period, the contemporaneous and two annual lag values of unanticipated money growth turn out to have effects that are significantly negative on unemployment. Further, the hypothesis that only the unanticipated part of

The National Science Foundation has supported this research. I have benefited from comments on earlier drafts by Jack Carr, Bob Hodrick, Pieter Korteweg, Bob Lucas, Michael Parkin, and Chris Sims.
[*American Economic Review*, 1977, vol. 67, no. 2]

money expansion influences unemployment receives strong support from
some empirical tests.

The final sections discuss unemployment predictions, implications for
policy, and some possibilities for extension of the research.

I. Analysis of Money Growth

A. *Setup of the Equation*

The money growth rate equation used in this study applies to annual
observations for the 1941–73 period. The equation includes the following
variables: a measure of federal government expenditure relative to normal, the lagged unemployment rate, and two lagged values of money
growth. The government expenditure variable captures an aspect of the
revenue motive for money creation. In my 1976*b* paper I describe a theoretical model in which an exogenous level of government expenditure is
financed by a combination of taxes and money issue. (Extensions to include public debt and nongovernment money do not alter the main conclusions.) Each method of finance involves administrative and other dead-
weight costs that increase, ceteris paribus, at an increasing rate with the
amount of revenue raised by that method. However, the costs of raising a
given amount of revenue by either method are assumed to decline with an
increase in national income. In addition, the costs associated with taxation
are assumed to depend negatively on the amount of fixed "capital" that
has been accumulated in tax-raising capacity. For example, the setting up
of an income tax and of an institutional apparatus for administering this
tax are viewed as increases in tax-raising capital that reduce the collection
costs imputed by the government to any particular amount of revenue
raised by taxes. The amount of capital invested in the tax-raising "industry" is, itself, endogenous to the model, but adjustment-type costs associated with changes in taxing capacity imply that the current amount of
capital will depend on "long-run" values of such variables as government
expenditure and national income, rather than simply on the current
values.

The breakdown of the total government budget between the two revenue components—and therefore the rate of money growth—is determined
to minimize the total costs associated with raising revenue.[1] With a fixed
amount of tax-raising capital—which depends, among other things, on the
long-run level of government expenditure—an increase in the current government budget leads to increases in both types of revenue and, hence, to
an increase in the growth rate of money. This type of response would
apply especially to periods of wartime during which there are sharp, tem-

---

[1] Edmund Phelps (1973) has a theoretical discussion of inflation within a public finance
context.

porary increases in the size of the government budget. The long-run response of money to an increase in the government budget—for example, to the secular growth of federal government spending relative to GNP that occurred from the 1930s to the 1960s—would be different, because it would lead also to an increase in tax-raising capital. Since "permanent" expansions in the share of GNP that is absorbed by government lead to an expansion of taxing capacity, it is possible—depending on the form of the "production function" that generates tax revenues—that no change in the money growth rate would occur. In this situation it is only increases in government expenditure relative to normal that would induce monetary expansion.

Specifically, my equation for money growth uses the variable

$$FEDV \equiv \log{(FED)} - [\log{(FED)}]^*$$

where *FED* is real expenditure of the federal government and $[\log{(FED)}]^*$ refers to the normal value of this expenditure. Empirically, $[\log{(FED)}]^*$ was generated from the adaptive formula[2]

$$[\log{(FED)}]^*_t = \beta[\log{(FED)}]_t + (1 - \beta)[\log{(FED)}]^*_{t-1}$$

that is, $[\log{(FED)}]^*$ is an exponentially declining distributed lag of $\log{(FED)}$. The equation reported below uses the value of the adaptation coefficient, $\beta = 0.2$ per year (see n. 5). Values of *FEDV* corresponding to this value of β are tabulated from 1941 to 1975 in table 1.

In the empirical analysis I test the hypothesis that it is only the difference between $\log{(FED)}$ and $[\log{(FED)}]^*$ that influences money expansion, with no separate effect of the level of federal expenditure. This hypothesis is supported by the empirical evidence over 1941 to 1973, so that the main analysis includes only the *FEDV* variable.

The money growth equation also includes a measure of lagged unemployment. A positive response of money growth to this variable could reflect two elements. First, there could be a countercyclical policy response of money to the level of economic activity. (The subsequent analysis has important implications for the efficacy of this type of policy.) Second, a decline in real income lowers holdings of real balances, which would reduce the amount of government revenue from money issue for a given value of the money growth rate. As shown by the author (1976*b*), the optimal response to a decline in income below its normal level would be an increase in the money growth rate. My empirical analysis does not separate out these two possible sources of countercyclical money response.

---

[2]It would be preferable to generate $[log\ (FED)]^*$ from a prediction relation based on the time-series properties of *log (FED)*. Costs of adjustment in taxing capacity would then also have to be taken into account in specifying the reaction of money growth to optimal predictions of future values of *log (FED)*. I have not yet proceeded along these lines.

TABLE 1

VALUES OF THE FEDERAL EXPENDITURE, MILITARY PERSONNEL, AND MINIMUM WAGE VARIABLES

	$FEDV(\beta = .2)$	MIL		MINW
1941	.803	...		...
1942	1.356	...		...
1943	1.369	...		...
1944	1.161	...		...
1945	.812	...		...
1946	−.131	.105		.228
1947	−.338	.012	(.048)	.203
1948	−.196	.022	(.044)	.191
1949	−.016	.048		.180
1950	−.033	.049		.323
1951	.199	.092		.301
1952	.307	.106		.284
1953	.303	.105		.269
1954	.151	.099		.258
1955	.090	.090		.248
1956	.089	.083		.307
1957	.123	.081		.298
1958	.167	.075		.283
1959	.139	.073		.273
1960	.116	.071		.262
1961	.157	.071		.283
1962	.179	.077		.328
1963	.157	.073		.325
1964	.143	.072		.334
1965	.136	.071		.325
1966	.204	.079		.315
1967	.245	.086		.392
1968	.248	.087		.426
1969	.195	.085		.421
1970	.173	0	(.075)	.402
1971	.165	0	(.065)	.367
1972	.188	0	(.056)	.344
1973	.172	0	(.052)	.322
1974	.154	0	(.048)	.408
1975	.195	0	(.046)	.426
1976	(.18)	(0)		(.42)
1977	(.18)	(0)		(.39)
1978	(.18)	(0)		(.36)

NOTE.—$FEDV(\beta = .2)$, MIL, and $MINW$ are the federal expenditure, military personnel, and minimum wage variables, as defined in the text. The military values shown in parentheses for certain years are the actual ratios of military personnel to the male population aged 15–44, ignoring the absence of a selective draft for all or part of those years. The $FEDV$ value of .18, shown in parentheses for 1976–78, corresponds to the average value over 1960–75. The $MINW$ value shown in parentheses for 1976 is an estimated value that takes account of the rise in the nominal minimum wage on January 1, 1976. The 1978 value of .36 is the sample average over 1960–75. For purposes of predicting unemployment for 1977 and beyond, it is assumed that the $MINW$ variable will fall over a 2-year period from its 1976 value to the average value of .36.

Finally, the money growth equation includes two lagged values of money growth as "explanatory" variables. Presumably, these lagged dependent variables pick up any elements of serial dependence or lagged adjustment that have not been captured by the other independent variables.

The form of the systematic part of the money growth equation is

$$DM_t = \alpha_0 + \alpha_1 DM_{t-1} + \alpha_2 DM_{t-2} + \alpha_3 FEDV_t + \alpha_4 UN_{t-1}$$

where M_t is an annual average of M_1 (see n. 18 below on the money definition), $DM_t \equiv \log(M)_t - \log(M)_{t-1}$ measures the annual average money growth rate, $FEDV_t \equiv \log(FED)_t - [\log(FED)]_t^*$, as defined above,[3] and $UN_{t-1} \equiv \log(U/(1-U))_{t-1}$, where U is the annual average unemployment rate in the total labor force (which includes military personnel). The form in which the unemployment rate enters corresponds to the form of the unemployment equation given below.

B. Estimated Equation

The estimated money growth equation for the 1941–73 period is, with standard errors in parentheses,[4]

$$DM_t = \underset{(.031)}{.087} + \underset{(.15)}{0.24 DM_{t-1}} + \underset{(.13)}{0.35 DM_{t-2}}$$
$$+ \underset{(.015)}{.082 \cdot FEDV_t} + \underset{(.010)}{.027 \cdot UN_{t-1}}, \tag{2}$$

where $R^2 = .90$, $\hat{\sigma} = .020$, $DW = 2.39$, (sample average of $DM = .057$), and $\hat{\sigma}$ is the standard error of estimate.

Consider, first, the coefficient on the federal expenditure variable, $FEDV$.[5] The estimated value of .08 implies that a 10 percent increase in real federal expenditure—holding fixed the normal expenditure and lagged values of DM—would raise DM_t by .8 of a percentage point per year. Historically, the extreme values of $FEDV$ have occurred during and just after wartime periods. For example, the 1943 value of $FEDV = 1.37$ implies (with DM_{t-1} and DM_{t-2} held fixed, so that .08 is the applicable coefficient) that DM_t would be 11 percentage points per year higher than when $FEDV$ is zero, while the 1947 value of $FEDV = -.34$ implies that DM_t would be 3 percentage points per year less than otherwise.[6]

---

[3]Data on federal government expenditures are from the *Economic Report of the President*, various issues. The figures on the nominal federal budget were divided by the *GNP* deflator (1958 = 1.0).

[4]A measure of the contemporaneous or lagged value of the federal government deficit relative to *GNP* is insignificant when added to equation (2). A lagged value of the inflation rate (based on the *GNP* deflator) or of the interest rate on prime commercial paper is also insignificant.

[5]Based on the fit of the money growth equation, the maximum likelihood estimate of the adaptation coefficient β is in the interval between 0.15 and 0.20, with an asymptotic 95 percent confidence interval of (0.1, 0.4). Since the unemployment results showed little sensitivity to variations in β over the interval from 0.15 to 0.30, I have limited the reported results to the case of $\beta = 0.20$.

[6]Note, however, that $FEDV$ has not been normalized to make the long-run average value equal to zero. Since the normal value of government expenditure is generated by a distributed lag of actual values, secular growth of the public sector implies that the typical measured value of $FEDV$ will be positive. It turns out that constant growth of real expenditures at rate g would generate a $FEDV$ value of $g(1-\beta)/\beta$, which equals $4g$ at $\beta = 0.2$. From 1949 to 1973 the average annual growth rate g is .050, so that the corresponding "long-run average" value of $FEDV$ is .20. However, growth of the public sector at 5 percent per year would not seem to be permanently sustainable.

The hypothesis that government expenditure enters into the determination of money growth only as the difference $FEDV \equiv \log{(FED)} - [\log{(FED)}]^*$ has been tested by entering $FEDV$ and $\log{(FED)}$ separately into the DM equation. The estimated coefficient of $\log{(FED)}$ (.010, standard error = .010) differs insignificantly from zero, and there is little change in the estimated coefficients on the other variables. (The results are similar if FED is measured as a ratio to a trend value of real GNP.) Accordingly, the results are consistent with the view that only temporary movements in federal expenditure stimulate monetary expansion.

Consider next the coefficient on the lagged unemployment variable. The estimated value of .03 implies that a 10 percent increase in U—that is, an increase by .5 percentage point starting from $U = 5$ percent—would imply a reaction of next year's money growth by about .3 of a percentage point per year. Hence, an increase by 1 percentage point in the unemployment rate induces an increase in next year's money growth rate by about .6 of a percentage point per year.[7]

Finally, the regression results indicate persistence effects with an estimated DM_{t-1} coefficient of 0.24 and an estimated DM_{t-2} coefficient of 0.35. If the error term in equation (2) is assumed to follow a first-order Markov process $u_t = \rho u_{t-1} + \varepsilon_t$, the maximum likelihood estimate of ρ is $-.35$ (the estimated coefficient on DM_{t-1} is then 0.45 and that on DM_{t-2} is 0.21). However, the estimated value of ρ differs insignificantly from zero at the 5 percent level—the asymptotic chi-square value is 2.6 with a critical value of 3.8. Since the inclusion of a nonzero value for ρ also has a negligible impact on the subsequent analysis of unemployment, I have limited the main analysis to the case where $\rho = 0$.

A notable aspect of the estimated DM equation is that it implies a normal, or long-run average, money growth rate. For a given value of the constant term and the federal expenditure and unemployment variables, the equation specifies the mean value of DM (both in a short-run sense conditioned on given values of DM_{t-1} and DM_{t-2}, and also in a long-run unconditional sense). For example, if the unemployment rate is 4.3 percent, the average estimated "natural rate" during the 1960s (as discussed below), and if the $FEDV$ variable takes on an "average" value of .20 (see n. 6), the implied long-run mean value of DM is 4.4 percent per year.

If the DM equation had contained a distributed lag of past DM values with the lag coefficients summing to one, as is true in the adaptive expectations formula developed by Cagan (1956), then the model would not have the property of possessing a natural or long-run mean value of the money growth rate. Presumably, the formulation with lag weights summing to

---

[7]From either the countercyclical policy or optimal revenue-raising viewpoints, it would seem preferable to enter the unemployment variable relative to its perceived long-run average value. The results on unemployment over 1946 to 1973, below, suggest that the principal movement in this long-run average value may have occurred since 1970. However, I have not yet attempted to adjust the unemployment variable along these lines.

unity would provide a satisfactory framework for predicting DM only if money growth were, in fact, generated by a nonstationary process (e.g., a random walk, or a random walk observed with error as in Muth [1960]) for which a long-run mean did not exist. If the money growth process is stationary, it would not be expected that the sum of the lag weights in money growth predictions would equal one. It follows that any implicit tests of expectation formation concerning money growth that are based on lag weights summing to one would not generally be meaningful—a point that was made in a general context by Sargent (1971).

C. Prior Predictions of Money Growth

For the present analysis, the purpose of fitting a money growth equation is to obtain a division of money growth into anticipated and unanticipated components. The theoretical proposition is then that only the unanticipated part of money growth will influence unemployment. There is a basic problem to consider in using an estimated money growth equation to specify the concept of anticipated money growth. Consider the formulation of this anticipation for date t, $\widehat{DM}_t$. This anticipation could be based on information that was available up to date $t - 1$, and might also include partial information applicable to date t. However, $\widehat{DM}_t$ should not be based on any information that becomes available only after date t. For example, if the estimated values from the DM regression for the 1941–73 period were used to obtain $\widehat{DM}$ for 1950, then information subsequent to 1950 would be used to "predict" that year's money growth. Specifically, later observations on $(DM, FEDV, UN)$ would be used to estimate the coefficients of the DM relation, and these coefficients would then be applied to the 1950 values of the independent variables to obtain $\widehat{DM}$ for 1950. However, it should be noted that the manner in which later observations affect earlier values of $\widehat{DM}$ is solely through pinning down the estimates of the coefficients in the DM equation. If individuals have information about the money growth structure beyond that conveyed in prior observations (e.g., from the experiences of other countries or on theoretical grounds), then the use of the overall sample period, 1941–73, may be reasonable even for the earlier dates.

A procedure that avoids the use of later observations to generate earlier predictions involves obtaining $\widehat{DM}_t$ from a regression in which the coefficients are estimated from data only up to date $t - 1$. In this approach there would be as many DM equations (each incorporating data up to $t - 1$) as there were predicted values, $\widehat{DM}_t$. In this context it would also be natural to consider the possibility of weighting the observations so that more recent information was counted more heavily in forming predictions.[8]

---

[8]Heavier weighting of recent observations can be rationalized along the lines of the adaptive regression model, as discussed in Cooley and Prescott (1973).

In my earlier study (1975), which is available on request, I devoted a good deal of space to estimations that based money growth predictions solely on prior observations. Since it turned out that the implications for the analysis of unemployment was minor, I have not included this discussion. For the present analysis I use the estimated values of DM from the

TABLE 2

VALUES OF MONEY GROWTH AND UNEMPLOYMENT

	DM	$\widehat{DM}$	DMR	U	$\hat{U}$	$U\text{-}\hat{U}$	$UNAT$
1939	.114	...	...	...	...	...	...
1940	.151	...	...	.095	...	...	...
1941	.160	.166	−.007	.058	...	...	...
1942	.180	.212	−.032	.029	...	...	...
1943	.265	.201	.064	.015	...	...	...
1944	.162	.192	−.031	.010	...	...	...
1945	.150	.158	−.008	.016	...	...	...
1946	.068	.055	.013	.037	.039	−.002	.034
1947	.047	.038	.009	.038	.043	−.005	.051
1948	.004	.017	−.012	.037	.044	−.007	.048
1949	−.010	.013	−.023	.057	.053	.004	.042
1950	.026	.006	.019	.052	.059	−.007	.048
1951	.044	.026	.018	.031	.031	.000	.039
1952	.049	.037	.012	.028	.025	.003	.036
1953	.024	.041	−.017	.027	.032	−.005	.035
1954	.015	.024	−.008	.052	.044	.008	.036
1955	.031	.027	.004	.042	.043	−.001	.037
1956	.012	.021	−.009	.039	.042	−.003	.040
1957	.005	.023	−.018	.041	.049	−.008	.041
1958	.012	.020	−.007	.065	.054	.011	.041
1959	.037	.030	.007	.053	.046	.007	.041
1960	−.001	.030	−.031	.053	.046	.007	.041
1961	.021	.033	−.013	.065	.062	.003	.042
1962	.022	.033	−.012	.053	.059	−.006	.042
1963	.029	.033	−.004	.055	.053	.002	.043
1964	.039	.035	.004	.050	.047	.003	.044
1965	.042	.037	.005	.043	.041	.002	.043
1966	.044	.042	.002	.037	.038	−.001	.042
1967	.039	.043	−.004	.036	.042	−.006	.043
1968	.068	.042	.026	.034	.040	−.006	.044
1969	.061	.041	.020	.034	.030	.004	.044
1970	.044	.047	−.004	.047	.046	.001	.064
1971	.067	.049	.018	.057	.054	.003	.062
1972	.063	.056	.006	.054	.048	.006	.060
1973	.071	.061	.010	.048	.049	−.001	.059
1974	.055	.056	−.001	.055	.056	−.001	.064
1975	.042	.062	−.020	.083	.071	.012	.065
1976	...	.065	...	...	.081	...	.065
1977	...	.065	...	...	.068	...	.063
1978	...	.069	...	...	.061	...	.061

NOTE.—$DM_t \equiv log\,(M_t) - log\,(M_{t-1})$, where M is an annual average of M_1 from the *Federal Reserve Bulletin*; $\widehat{DM}$ is the estimated value from equation (2); $DMR \equiv DM - \widehat{DM}$; U is the annual average unemployment rate (data are given in the *Economic Report of the President*), based on the total labor force, which includes military personnel. Data for 1940–43 were adjusted for treatment of government "emergency workers," as discussed in Michael Darby (1976); $\hat{U}$ is an estimated value from equation (4); $UNAT$ is derived from equation (4) with all DMR values set equal to zero. Values of DM for 1976–78 are based on the value $FEDV = .18$. The 1977–78 values of DM use the value of $\hat{U}$ from the preceding year. The values of $\hat{U}$ (and $UNAT$) subsequent to 1975 are based on $DMR = 0$ for 1976 and beyond, $MIL = 0$, and the $MINW$ values indicated in table 2.

1941–73 regression, equation (2), to form a time-series of anticipated money growth $\widehat{DM}$. Unanticipated money growth, $DMR \equiv DM\text{-}\widehat{DM}$, then corresponds to the residuals from this equation. The values of $\widehat{DM}$ and DMR from equation (2) are indicated in table 2.[9]

II. Analysis of Unemployment

A. Setup of the Equation

The effects of monetary expansion on unemployment are measured by the impact of current and lagged values of unanticipated money growth, $DMR \equiv DM\text{-}\widehat{DM}$. The number of lags to introduce was not established from a priori reasoning, although Lucas (1975) presents a theoretical rationale for persistence effects of monetary shocks in this type of model. Empirically, it turned out that the current and two annual lag values of DMR had significant effects on unemployment.

Aside from monetary variables, the unemployment equation includes two "real" variables. The first is a measure of military conscription. The specific variable is[10]

$$MIL \equiv \frac{\text{Military personnel}}{\text{Male population aged 15–44}}$$

for years in which a "selective" military draft law was in effect (all years since 1946 except for April 1947 to June 1948 and 1970–73).[11] The value $MIL = 0$ was entered for the nonselective draft law years. Values of MIL are tabulated from 1946 to 1975 in table 2. Aside from the possible direct employment effect of conscription on draftees, a selective draft would provide incentives for eligible civilians to enter a low draft-probability status. One effect would involve the choice of remaining in school rather than entering the labor force—an effect that would reduce the measured unemployment rate if the affected individuals had an above-average tendency toward unemployment. A second effect involves the choice between working and unemployment for labor market participants. On this count, con-

---

[9]Note that $\widehat{DM}_t$ is calculated from the contemporaneous value of $FEDV$, rather than from a lagged value. The rationale is that the principal movements in $FEDV$, which are dominated by changes in wartime activity, would be perceived sufficiently rapidly to influence $\widehat{DM}$ without a lag. For example, in 1946 the value of $\widehat{DM}$ is much lower than in 1945 because of the contemporaneous downward movement in $FEDV$.

[10]Data sources are *Historical Statistics of the United States* (1960, pp. 736, 8, and 10); and *Statistical Abstract of the United States*, various issues.

[11]A discussion of the draft law in the United States up to 1970 is contained in Rafuse (1970). The lottery draft period from 1970 to June 1973 (during which there were draft calls for 1970–71) was taken out since the lottery draft does not provide the same incentives to avoid unemployment as appear to operate during a selective draft. See the discussion below. Periods with zero draft calls, but with a selective draft law in effect (February 1949 to June 1950) were included with the draft period.

scription would work toward reducing the unemployment rate if draft probabilities were highest, ceteris paribus, for unemployed persons.

The second real variable measures the impact of the minimum wage rate. This variable, tabulated under the heading *MINW* from 1946 to 1975 in table 2, is defined as the ratio of the applicable minimum wage to private, nonfarm average hourly earnings, multiplied by the proportion of covered nonsupervisory employment.[12] The *MINW* variable would have a positive effect on the unemployment rate if the negative impact of the minimum wage on employment dominates the probable negative effect on labor force participation.[13]

The form for the systematic part of the unemployment equation,[14] used for annual observations over 1946–73, is[15]

$$\log \left(U/(1 - U) \right)_t = a_1 DMR_t + a_2 DMR_{t-1} + a_3 DMR_{t-2}$$
$$+ a_4 MIL_t + a_5 MINW_t. \tag{3}$$

Since the sample period begins in 1946, the values for *DMR* start in 1944. It may be worth noting that, since the dependent variable in equation (3) depends on a distributed lag of *DMR* values, the unemployment rate can be serially correlated even if the *DMR* (and the *MIL* and *MINW* variables) were not. (The *DMR* values would not be serially correlated if $\widehat{DM}_t$ were an efficient predictor of DM_t, based on information that included an observation of DM_{t-1}.)

---

[12]From 1947 to 1968 this variable was calculated by the Bureau of Labor Statistics and reported in Mincer (1976, table 1.6). For 1946 and 1969 to 1975 the variable is estimated from data contained in Weiss (1975, tables 1–3).

[13]I also considered an unemployment compensation variable, which was defined as average benefits per recipient relative to average hourly earnings multiplied by the fraction of covered employment. In my initial investigations this variable was insignificant in the unemployment equation. However, I have recently recalculated the unemployment compensation variable to take account of taxes on earnings and to incorporate a fuller measure of unemployment compensation coverage. This revised variable does turn out to have a significantly positive effect on the unemployment rate. The other coefficients in the estimated unemployment equation are insensitive to the inclusion of this variable, except that the minimum wage variable becomes less important. I plan to report on these results more fully at a later time.

[14]The form confines the unemployment rate to the interval (0, 1).

[15]Since *DMR* is based on estimated coefficients of the *DM* relation, equation (2), there would be small-sample problems of errors in the independent variables in equation (3). The main impact would seem to be a bias toward zero in the estimated *DMR* coefficients. In obtaining estimates of the *a*-coefficients in equation (3) and the α-coefficient in equation (1), it would be preferable to carry out a joint maximum likelihood estimation. In contrast with my two-stage procedure, the choice of the α-estimates in the money growth equation would then give some weight to the effect on the fit of the unemployment equation, through the selection of the *DMR* values that enter into equation (3). In my procedure the α-estimates are chosen solely to obtain a least-squares fit in equation (1). For the case of normally distributed error terms, the *a*-estimates would be chosen in both cases to obtain a least-squares fit in equation (3), conditional on the *DMR* values. Since my procedure yields consistent estimates (assuming serially independent error terms) and the alternative, nonlinear procedure requires a large amount of numerical calculation, I have not carried out the joint maximum likelihood estimation.

B. *Estimated Equation Based on Unanticipated Money Growth Rates*

With *DMR* measured as the residuals from equation (2), the estimated unemployment equation is, with standard errors in parentheses,[16]

$$\log\left(U/(1-U)\right)_t = -3.07 - 5.8DMR_t - 12.1DMR_{t-1}$$
$$(.15) \quad (2.1) \qquad (1.9)$$
$$- 4.2DMR_{t-2} - 4.7MIL_t + 0.95MINW_t, \tag{4}$$
$$(1.9) \qquad (0.8) \qquad (.46)$$

where $R^2 = .78$, $\hat{\sigma} = .13$, $DW = 1.96$, average of $|U - \hat{U}| = .0043$.

Equation (4) includes a contemporaneous and two annual lag values of *DMR*. Additional lag terms were insignificant. The implied lag pattern (the form of which was not constrained ex ante) for unemployment behind unanticipated money growth has a triangular shape, with the strongest effect appearing after a one-year lag. The contemporaneous and two-year lag effects are of about equal size.[17] The t-values associated with a null hypothesis of a zero coefficient are 6.4 for DMR_{t-1}, 2.8 for DMR_t, and 2.2 for DMR_{t-2}. The F-value for the three *DMR* coefficients jointly is $F_{22}^3 = 21.0$ (5 percent critical value $= 3.1$). More detailed aspects of the estimated *DMR* coefficients and of the estimated coefficients for the *MIL* and *MINW* variables will be discussed below.

In evaluating the fit of equation (4), a useful measure is the average absolute residual for implied estimates of the unemployment rate (generated from a straightforward, though not quite statistically valid, transformation of the dependent variable, $\log[U/1-U]$). This average value is .0043—that is, the average error in estimated unemployment rates is somewhat more than .4 of a percentage point.[18]

The Durbin-Watson statistic from equation (4) of 1.96 indicates absence of first-order serial correlation in the residuals. This result is surprising, given the autocorrelated nature of the U-series,[19] since a lagged dependent

[16]I have carried out a similar analysis (1975) using the *log* of output (real *GNP*) instead of the unemployment rate as a dependent variable (with a time trend included as an additional explanatory variable). The results correspond in major respects to those discussed below for unemployment.

[17]The estimated coefficient of DMR_t could be biased toward zero if there is a contemporaneous policy feedback from U_t (current period unemployment) to $\hat{DM}_t$. The response of money growth to lagged unemployment was already taken into account in forming the anticipated money growth rate $\hat{DM}_t$. Presumably, this problem of within-period policy response would be lessened if the length of the observation period were reduced by moving to quarterly data. I plan to carry out that extension at a later time.

[18]I have redone the unemployment analysis with two alternative definitions of the money stock, M_2 and high-powered money (see the author [1975] for details). It turns out that the M_1 definition is superior in terms of the fit for unemployment. In a form parallel to equation (4), the M_2 definition yields an R^2 of .31 with an average absolute error for U of .0076—about twice that of the M_1 form. For high-powered money the R^2 is .49 with an average absolute error for U of .0066.

[19]An autoregression of UN_t on UN_{t-1} yields the estimated coefficient .40, standard error $= .14$.

variable was not included to soak up the serial correlation.[20] In fact, if $\log{(U/1 - U)}_{t-1}$ is added to equation (4), its estimated coefficient is .09, standard error $= .10$, which differs insignificantly from zero.

C. Results with Total Money Growth Rates

Unemployment regressions have also been run based on total money growth rates DM, rather than on the unanticipated part of growth DMR. For a regression that includes a contemporaneous and two lagged values of DM along with the military and minimum wage variables, none of the estimated DM coefficients turns out to be individually significantly different from zero, and an F-test for joint significance yields the statistic $F_{22}^3 = 2.6$, which is below the 5 percent critical value of 3.1. The fit of the regression is indicated by $R^2 = .38$—half that of the DMR equation. The inclusion of a third lag of DM into the unemployment equation has a negligible impact. When DM_{t-4} is included the fit improves noticeably, although the estimated coefficients on DM_{t-2} and DM_{t-3} are positive. The estimated equation with four lags is

$$
\begin{aligned}
\log{[U/(1 - U)]}_t = &-2.46 - 1.2DM_t - 5.7DM_{t-1} + 0.7DM_{t-2} \\
&\;\;(.34)\quad(2.9)\qquad(2.7)\qquad\quad(2.5) \\
&+ 3.5DM_{t-3} - 3.2DM_{t-4} - 4.5MIL_t - 0.3MINW_t, \\
&\;\;\;(1.8)\qquad\quad(1.5)\qquad\quad(1.4)\qquad\quad(1.0)
\end{aligned}
\tag{5}
$$

where $R^2 = .52$, $\hat{\sigma} = .20$, $DW = 1.68$, and average of $|U - \hat{U}| = .0059$. The F-value for the joint hypothesis that all five DM coefficients are zero is $F_{20}^5 = 3.0$, which is above the 5 percent critical value of 2.7. The fit of the equation with four lagged values of DM is indicated by $R^2 = .52$, average absolute error for $U = .0059$. Hence, the fit is still considerably poorer than that obtained in equation (4) with two lagged values of the DMR variable.

D. Tests that Only Unanticipated Money Growth Affects Unemployment

A key hypothesis of this study is that only the unanticipated part of money growth influences unemployment. This hypothesis can be tested by running a regression that includes simultaneously sets of DMR and DM variables, and then seeing whether the deletion of the DM variables, which amounts to a set of linear restrictions on the coefficients, produces a significant worsening of the fit. The resulting test statistic is $F_{19}^3 = 1.4$ (5 percent critical value $= 3.1$) when two lagged values of DMR and DM are included, and $F_{15}^5 = 2.0$ (5 percent critical value $= 2.9$) when four lagged values of each are included. Hence, the hypothesis that only the unanticipated part of money growth is relevant to unemployment is accepted by these tests.

[20]Except for the indirect effect of lagged U on $D\widehat{M}$. However, that effect was estimated from a separate equation, so that the usual problem of correlation between a lagged dependent variable and a serially correlated error term would not arise here.

The procedure can also be carried out in reverse by deleting the DMR values while retaining the DM values. When two lagged values of DMR and DM are included, the test statistic is $F_{19}^3 = 15.7$. In the four-lag case the result is $F_{15}^5 = 8.2$. Therefore, the reverse hypothesis that the DMR values are irrelevant to unemployment, given the DM values, can easily be rejected.

A point to stress about these tests is that they can be carried out at all only because predictors of DM_t other than its own history—DM_{t-1}, DM_{t-2}, etc.—have been included in the money growth equation. For example, suppose that $\widehat{DM}_t$ were generated solely as a function of DM_{t-1}, say, $\widehat{DM}_t = \alpha_0 + \alpha_1 DM_{t-1}$. In this case a regression of unemployment on a series of $DMR \ (\equiv DM - \widehat{DM})$ values could not possibly fit better than a regression of the same form on a series of DM values that included one additional lagged term. The use of the DMR values would amount, in this situation, solely to imposing a restriction on the coefficients that describe the effect of the DM variables on unemployment, so that (if no adjustment is made for the difference in degrees of freedom) the DMR regression would necessarily show a poorer fit. Hence, the superior fit of the DMR form of the unemployment equation reflects the impact of the additional predictors—namely, the federal expenditure and lagged unemployment variables—that were included in the money growth equation.

To make this point directly I have obtained DMR values from money growth equations that involve solely the history of DM. An illustrative case, which includes 3 lagged values of DM over the 1941–73 period, is the following:

$$DM_t = .011 + .76DM_{t-1} + .30DM_{t-2} - .30DM_{t-3},$$
$$(.008) \quad (.17) \qquad (.21) \qquad (.14)$$

where $R^2 = .77$, $\widehat{\sigma} = .031$, $DW = 2.16$. Calculating DMR values as the residuals from the above equation leads to the estimated unemployment equation for 1946–73,

$$\log (U/1 - U)_t = -3.00 + 1.2DMR_t - 4.9DMR_{t-1}$$
$$(.31) \quad (2.9) \qquad (2.7)$$
$$- 1.9DMR_{t-2} - 2.6MIL_t + 0.2MINW_t,$$
$$(2.4) \qquad (1.3) \qquad (0.9)$$

where $R^2 = .31$, $\widehat{\sigma} = .23$, $DW = 0.95$, which shows a substantially poorer fit than that obtained with the alternative DMR values from equation (2). Hence, a "naive" model that bases $\widehat{DM}_t$ solely on the history of money growth would be inadequate for explaining unemployment.[21]

Further perspective on the distinction between actual and unantici-

---

[21]If lagged values up to DM_{t-10} are included, the R^2 of the DM equation rises to .89 and that of the unemployment equation rises to .35. Allowing for first-order serial correlation of the error term in the DM equation does not materially affect any of these results.

pated money growth can be obtained by substituting into the estimated unemployment relation, equation (4), from the condition $DMR_t \equiv DM_t - \widehat{DM}_t$, where $\widehat{DM}_t$ is generated from the estimated money growth relation, equation (2). The resulting "reduced form" expresses unemployment as a function of $(DM_t, \ldots, DM_{t-4})$; $(FEDV_t, \ldots, FEDV_{t-2})$; $(UN_{t-1}, \ldots, UN_{t-3})$; MIL_t; and $MINW_t$. Specifically, the coefficients that derive from this substitution are indicated as hypothesized values in the first column of table 3. It is also possible to estimate the reduced form for unemployment in a direct, unconstrained manner—a process that yields the estimated coefficients and standard errors that are also shown in table 3.

The use of the DMR form of the unemployment relation, equation (3), corresponds to a set of constraints on the manner in which the reduced form independent variables influence unemployment. Specifically, the use of equation (3) with DMR values generated from equation (2) amounts to reducing the number of independent coefficients to be estimated in the unemployment relation from (14) in the unconstrained reduced form to (6) in the DMR form.[22] If the DMR specification in equation (3) is appropriate, then these 8 coefficient constraints should not significantly worsen the fit of the unemployment equation—heuristically, the hypothesized coefficients in table 3 should not differ "too much" from the estimated ones (taking account of standard errors). An overall test of the hypothesis is based on a comparison of restricted and unrestricted sums of squared

---

[22]There are also 5 coefficients to be estimated in the DM equation, but this estimation was carried out separately from the fitting of the unemployment relation.

TABLE 3

HYPOTHESIZED AND ESTIMATED COEFFICIENTS OF REDUCED FORM
FOR UNEMPLOYMENT

	Hypothesized	Estimated	Standard Error
C	−1.2	−1.1	(0.5)
DM_t	−5.8	−2.5	(2.6)
DM_{t-1}	−10.7	−12.5	(2.9)
DM_{t-2}	0.8	−5.8	(4.6)
DM_{t-3}	5.2	4.4	(1.8)
DM_{t-4}	1.5	2.3	(1.6)
$FEDV_t$	0.5	0.3	(0.7)
$FEDV_{t-1}$	1.0	1.3	(0.4)
$FEDV_{t-2}$	0.3	0.8	(0.5)
UN_{t-1}	0.2	−0.3	(0.4)
UN_{t-2}	0.3	0.5	(0.2)
UN_{t-3}	0.1	0.2	(0.2)
MIL_t	−4.7	−8.8	(2.2)
$MINW_t$	0.9	−0.6	(0.7)

residuals which leads to the statistic $F^8_{14} = 1.4$, which is less than the 5 percent critical value of 2.7. Hence, this test also supports the use of the DMR form of the unemployment equation.

The listing of the reduced form coefficients in table 3 brings out another point, which relates to the discussion of observational equivalence in Sargent (1976). Namely, the DMR form of the unemployment equation is equivalent to a form that contains DM values (in this case up to DM_{t-4}), along with the FEDV and lagged UN variables (up to $FEDV_{t-2}$ and UN_{t-3}, respectively) that were included in the DM relation. The exclusion of the FEDV and lagged UN variables from the form of the unemployment relation, equation (3), constitutes a set of identifying restrictions that permits an observational separation between the DMR and DM forms of the unemployment equation. The above tests of the distinction between these two forms then amount to tests of the joint hypothesis that (a) $\widehat{DM}$ is generated in accordance with equation (2); (b) DM influences unemployment only in the form, $DMR \equiv DM - \widehat{DM}$; and (c) the FEDV and lagged UN variables that appear in equation (2) do not enter directly in equation (3). Of course, the acceptance of the joint null hypothesis by the above statistical tests provides support for each element of the hypothesis, namely for (a) and (b), which were the main objects of interest.

It would be possible, nevertheless, to interpret the estimated reduced form for unemployment (table 3, col. 2) as indicating the influence of actual money growth DM, along with direct influences of the FEDV, lagged UN, MIL, and MINW variables (with the coefficients of the DM, FEDV, and lagged UN variables satisfying the restrictions implied by the DMR form out of pure coincidence). However, this interpretation leaves a number of results that require a theoretical explanation: (1) the *positive* effect of the FEDV variables on unemployment, in contrast with the negative effect that would be predicted along Keynesian lines; (2) the presence of positive coefficients on DM_{t-3} and DM_{t-4}; and (3) the stronger (positive) contribution of UN_{t-2} than of UN_{t-1}. These three sets of results are readily explained by the theory that relates unemployment to DMR values.

E. Properties of the Estimated Unemployment Equation

I will now discuss some detailed properties of the estimated DMR form of the unemployment relation, which is rewritten here for convenience,

$$\log (U/1 - U)_t = -3.07 - 5.8 DMR_t - 12.1 DMR_{t-1}$$
$$(.15) \quad (2.1) \qquad\quad (1.9)$$
$$- 4.2 DMR_{t-2} - 4.7 MIL_t + 0.95 MINW_t. \tag{4}$$
$$(1.9) \qquad\quad (0.8) \qquad\quad (.46)$$

Consider the magnitudes of the estimated DMR coefficients. The coefficient of -12 on DMR_{t-1} implies that an increase by 1 percentage point per year in the unanticipated money growth rate would reduce next year's unemployment rate by a proportion of about 12 percent, or by about .6 of a percentage point at an initial unemployment rate of 5 percent. However, the contemporaneous impact of this DMR shift would be only about half as large. If the increase in DMR by 1 percentage point per year were sustained over a 3-year period (which would be an unusual event), then the full effect would be a reduction of the unemployment rate by about 1 percentage point.

It should be stressed that the lag pattern for money growth that is described in equation (4) refers to unanticipated rather than actual money growth. The implied lag pattern in terms of actual money growth—given the money growth relation as estimated in equation (2)—is shown as the hypothesized coefficients in table 3. Because of the positive effects of DM_{t-1} and DM_{t-2} on the current value of anticipated money growth, the lag pattern for unemployment in terms of DM differs markedly from that in terms of DMR. Two important differences are, first, the "mean" lag effect from DM to unemployment is shorter than that associated with DMR; and, second, there are positive coefficients in the DM form even when the DMR form is restricted to negative coefficients. Quantitatively, the lag pattern for DM that is shown in column 1 of table 3 accords with the well-known 6- to 18-month lag between (actual) money growth and economic activity that has been reported by Friedman (1969, p. 180). A lack of distinction between actual and unanticipated money growth can also account for some of the apparent variability of the lag in Friedman's results (pp. 180–81).

Equation (4) also indicates the importance of the military variable (t-value of 5.9). The magnitude of the effect implied by the coefficient of -4.7 is that an increase by 1 percentage point in the ratio of military personnel to the male population aged 15–44 would reduce the unemployment rate by a proportion of about 4.7 percent; that is, by about .2 of a percentage point at $U = 5$ percent. Expressed alternatively, if changes in the labor force are neglected, an increase by an amount X in the number of military personnel would reduce the number of unemployed by about $0.5X$ (assuming that $U = .05$) and that the ratio of the labor force to the male population aged 15–44 takes on its 1973 value of 2.0).[23]

---

[23]If the distinction between selective draft and nonselective draft years is dropped (which affects 1947–48 and 1970–73), the estimated unemployment rate equation becomes

$$\log\left(U/1 - U\right)_t = -2.88 - 4.5DMR_t - 10.1DMR_{t-1}$$
$$\qquad\quad (.20) \quad (2.5) \qquad\quad (2.3)$$
$$\qquad - 1.5DMR_{t-2} - 7.1MIL_t + 1.11MINW_t, R^2 = .68,$$
$$\qquad\quad (2.2) \qquad\quad (1.6) \qquad\quad (.56)$$

$\hat{\sigma} = .16$, $DW = 1.38$, average of $|U - \hat{U}| = .0049$.

The fit of the equation is poorer than that of equation (4), but the general implications are not altered.

The estimated minimum wage coefficient in equation (4) is positive and has a t-value of 2.1. Using the 1973 values of average hourly earnings ($3.92) and fraction covered (.79), and starting from $U = .05$, the implication is that an increase by $1 in the minimum wage would raise the unemployment rate by about 1 percentage point. Viewed alternatively, if the minimum wage ($1.60 in 1973) were set to zero, the estimated fall in the unemployment rate would be by about 1.33 percentage points.

Given the estimated relation from equation (4), it is possible to calculate values of unemployment associated with $DMR = 0$ for all t—that is, with fully anticipated current and past monetary expansion. I will refer to these unemployment rates as natural values ($UNAT$).[24] In the present setup, the natural unemployment rate depends on the values of the military and minimum wage variables and on the constant term. Values of $UNAT$ derived from equation (4), and the values of MIL and $MINW$ shown in table 1, are indicated from 1946 to 1975 in table 2. This table also contains actual unemployment rates and the estimated values and residuals from equation (4). The pattern of results in this table is as follows.

With the end of World War II and the associated drop in military personnel, the estimated natural unemployment rate rose from about 1.5 percent to about 3.5 percent in 1946 and 5 percent in 1947–48 (partially non-draft law years). Although there was a large cutback in money growth, from rates above 15 percent per year during World War II to 6.8 percent in 1946 and 4.7 percent in 1947, the money growth equation implies that this cutback was anticipated because of the sharp decline in federal expenditure. In fact, the estimated values, $D\widehat{M} = 5.5$ percent in 1946 and 3.8 percent in 1947, imply that these two years were characterized by unanticipated monetary expansion. Accordingly, the unemployment rates for 1946–48 remained at about 4 percent—below the natural rate for 1947–48. The unanticipated monetary contraction of 1948–49 ($DMR = -.012$ and $-.023$, respectively) implied increases in the unemployment rates for 1949 and 1950.

For the Korean War years of 1951–53, an expansionary element was an increase in the military variable that lowered the natural unemployment rate to 3.5–4 percent. This factor, combined with unanticipated monetary expansion from 1950 to 1952 (DMR values of .019, .018, and .012, respectively), led to unemployment rates in the neighborhood of 3 percent for 1951–53. From the end of the Korean War through 1969, the maintenance of a selective draft law with high levels of military personnel implied small variations in the natural unemployment rate. In particular, with $UNAT$ confined to a range of 4.0 to 4.4 percent from 1956 to 1969, movements in

[24]Because of nonlinearities, these values differ from expected unemployment rates derived from equation (4) with an additive, constant variance error term. The (positive) gap between the expected unemployment rate and the natural rate, as defined, increases with the variance of the error term and with the variance of DMR.

the natural rate have a minor effect on estimated unemployment rates during this period.

In 1954 the unanticipated monetary contraction of 1953 ($-.017$) was the main contributor to the rise in unemployment (though my U-estimate of .044 is below the actual value of .052). For 1954–55, the unanticipated parts of money growth were small, implying values of U near the natural rate of 4 percent for 1955–56. The unanticipated monetary contraction in 1956 ($-.009$) led to an estimated U-value for 1957 of 4.9 percent, although the actual value was only 4.1 percent. On the other hand, my estimate for U in 1958 is 5.4 percent (reflecting the additional monetary contraction of $-.018$ in 1957), which substantially underestimates the actual value of 6.5 percent. For 1959–60, the estimates are about .5 percentage point below the actual values, which were themselves about 1 percentage point above the natural rates.

Perhaps the most interesting monetary behavior of the post-World War II period is the absolute contraction of money that occurred during 1960. This behavior represented the first absolute decline in money since 1949, but more significantly, the estimate for anticipated money growth in 1960 is 3.0 percent, as contrasted with 1.3 percent for 1949. Hence, the unanticipated monetary contraction for 1960 was -3.1 percent—the largest absolute value of DMR for the entire post-World War II period. According to the estimated equation, this large negative value of DMR for 1960 accounted for the sharp rise in the unemployment rate in 1961 to over 6 percent—about 2 percentage points above the natural rate.

From 1963 to 1967 there was a period of monetary stability, in the sense of small deviations between actual and anticipated values of DM. The response in U was a gradual downward movement, first to the natural rate in 1965, and then slightly below in 1966–67. There was then a sharp monetary expansion in 1968 ($DMR = .026$), which ended the brief period of "constant growth rate rule" for money.[25] In 1968–69 the unemployment rate of 3.4 percent was about 1 percentage point below the natural rate.

The explanation of behavior in 1970 is complicated since it hinges on the treatment of the switch to the lottery draft as equivalent, in terms of unemployment effects, to a removal of conscription (see n. 23). The assumption that the military variable was zero from 1970 on implies a natural rate since 1970 of 6 to 6.5 percent (depending on the value of the $MINW$ variable)—an increase of 1.5 to 2 percentage points from the 4.4 percent value for 1969. Given the rise in the natural rate, the maintenance of 1970 unemployment at only 4.7 percent of the labor force reflected the continuing impact of the strong monetary expansion that occurred in 1968–69. The monetary behavior from 1971 to 1973 was expansionary,

---

[25]I use this expression to signify predictability of DM, rather than constancy per se.

and the unemployment rate remained .5 to 1 percentage point below the natural rate during this period.

F. Unemployment Predictions

The unemployment and money growth rate relations, estimated from data up to 1973, can be used to form projections for 1974 and beyond. For 1974, the predicted value of DM is 5.6 percent per year, as compared to an actual value of 5.5 percent. Hence, the DMR value for 1974 is close to zero.The prediction from equation (4) for the 1974 unemployment rate is 5.6 percent, which almost coincides with the actual value of 5.5 percent.

For 1975, the predicted value of DM (conditioned on the value $DM_{t-1} = .055$ for 1974) is 6.2 percent per year. Since the actual value of DM for 1975 is 4.2 percent, the monetary contraction during this year is measured by $DMR = -2.0$ percent. Using the ex post values, $DMR = -.001$ for 1974 and $-.020$ for 1975, the "predicted" value for 1975 unemployment turns out to be 7.1 percent. Since the actual average of unemployment rates during 1975 is 8.3 percent, there is an underprediction of unemployment by about the same magnitude as for the 1958 contraction.

For 1976 and 1977 (using the value, $FEDV = .18$, which is the average over the 1960–75 period), the predicted value for DM is 6.5 percent per year.[26] Using values of $DMR = 0$ for 1976 and beyond (which is appropriate ex ante), assuming a zero value for MIL, and using the values of $MINW$ that are shown in table 1, the predicted unemployment rates are 8.1 percent for 1976, 6.8 percent for 1977, and 6.1 percent (the natural rate) for 1978 and beyond. Based on observations for the first few months, it appears that the model will overpredict 1976 unemployment.

III. Some Policy Implications

Acceptance of the hypothesis that only the unanticipated part of money growth affects unemployment has some important policy implications. One result is that the systematic feedback from unemployment to money growth that appears in equation (2) has no implications for the time path of unemployment itself—a result that accords with the theoretical propositions in Sargent and Wallace (1975) and the author (1976a). Only movements in money that depart from the usual countercyclical response affect subsequent unemployment rates.[27] This observation raises questions con-

[26]This high value of $\widehat{DM}$ reflects the high value of lagged unemployment. It may be preferable to measure unemployment relative to its perceived long-run value, which has apparently increased since 1970 (see 7). This modification would lower the values of $\widehat{DM}$ for the 1970s, but a quantitative adjustment would require a measure of the perceived long-run value of unemployment.

[27]However, the present analysis has not dealt with the possible temporary impact of structural shifts in the money growth process, as discussed theoretically in Taylor (1975). Such shifts did not appear to be important over the 1941–73 period (see the author, 1975).

cerning the rationality of the countercyclical policy response that appears in equation (2). One possibility is that the reaction of money to lagged unemployment reflects optimal public finance considerations (see Section I and the author [1976b]), rather than an attempt at economic stabilization.

Similar conclusions apply to the response of money to the federal budget variable, *FEDV*. Increases in federal expenditure above its normal level (with the military variable held fixed) reduce unemployment only if the accompanying increase in money is larger than the usual amount.[28] In fact, if actual money growth is held constant, an increase in *FEDV* raises unemployment because of the associated increase in anticipated money growth. (Some preliminary results indicate that this effect is important during the middle 1930s.)

IV. Conclusions and Extensions

The starting point for this study was the hypothesis that only unanticipated movements in money would affect economic activity. That hypothesis was quantified by interpreting anticipated money growth as the amount that could have been predicted based on the historical relation between money growth and a specified set of explanatory variables. For the United States from 1941 to 1973 these variables included a measure of federal expenditure relative to normal, a lagged unemployment rate, and two annual lag values of money growth. Unanticipated money growth was then measured as actual growth less the amount obtained from this predictive relationship. The current and two annual lag values of unanticipated money growth were shown to have considerable explanatory value for unemployment. Further, some statistical tests confirmed the underlying hypothesis that actual money growth was irrelevant for unemployment, given the values of unanticipated money growth.

The results reported in this paper would be more reliable if they could be replicated for other experiences. For the United States I am currently working on the unemployment and output experiences back to 1890. Since the structure of the money growth process prior to World War II appears different from that estimated for the 1941–73 period, the long-period evidence will permit a much more powerful test of the hypothesis that only unanticipated money growth affects unemployment. Further, it will be possible to test the hypothesis advanced by Lucas (1973) that shifts in the

---

[28]I attempted to find a direct fiscal effect on unemployment by entering the full-employment federal government deficit (measured as a ratio to the outstanding stock of privately held public debt) into the unemployment equation. This variable was insignificant (estimated coefficient of -0.7, standard error $= 1.0$), as were lagged values of the deficit and measures of the deficit relative to its "anticipated" value.

prediction variance of money would alter the response of unemployment to monetary shocks.

Finally, although the present analysis was directed toward the effects of money on unemployment (with related implications for output), the division of money growth into anticipated and unanticipated parts also has important implications for inflation. I plan to deal with this topic in a subsequent paper.

References

Barro, R. J. "Unanticipated Money Growth and Unemployment in the United States." Working paper., Univ. Rochester, July 1975.
———. "Rational Expectations and the Role of Monetary Policy." *J. Monet. Econ.* 2 (January 1976): 1–32. (a)
———. "Optimal Revenue Collection and the Money Growth Rate." Manuscript, 1976. (b)
Cagan, P. "The Monetary Dynamics of Hyperinflation." In *Studies in the Quantity Theory of Money,* edited by Milton Friedman. Chicago: Univ. Chicago Press, 1956.
Cooley, T. F., and Prescott, E. "Varying Parameter Regression: A Theory and Some Applications." *Ann. Econ. Soc. Measurement* 2 (1973): 463–74.
Darby, M. R. "Three-and-a-Half Million U.S. Employees Have Been Mislaid; or, an Explanation of Unemployment, 1934–1941." *J.P.E.* 84 (February 1976): 1–17.
Friedman, M. "The Supply of Money and Changes in Prices and Output." In *The Optimum Quantity of Money and Other Essays.* Chicago: Aldine, 1969.
Lucas, R. E. "Expectations and the Neutrality of Money." *J. Econ. Theory* 4 (April 1972): 103–24.
———. "Some International Evidence on Output-Inflation Tradeoffs." *A.E.R.* 63 (June 1973): 326–34.
———. "An Equilibrium Model of the Business Cycle." *J.P.E.* 83 (December 1975): 1113–44.
Mincer, J. "Unemployment Effects of Minimum Wages." *J.P.E.* 84, pt. 2 (August 1976): S87–S104.
Muth, J. F. "Optimal Properties of Exponentially Weighted Forecasts." *J. Amer. Statis. Assoc.* 55 (June 1960): 299–306.
Phelps, E. S. "Inflation in the Theory of Public Finance." *Swedish J. Econ.* 75 (March 1973): 67–82.
Rafuse, J. L. "United States' Experience with Volunteer and Conscript Forces." *Studies Prepared for the President's Commission on an All-Volunteer Armed Force,* vol. 2. Washington, 1970.
Sargent, T. J. "A Note on the 'Accelerationist' Controversy." *J. Money, Credit, Banking* 3 (August 1971): 721–25.
———. "The Observational Equivalence of Natural and Unnatural Rate Theories of Macroeconomics." *J.P.E.* 84 (June 1976): 631–40.
Sargent, T. J., and Wallace, N. " 'Rational' Expectations, the Optimal Monetary Instrument, and the Optimal Money Supply Rule." *J.P.E.* 83 (April 1975): 241–54.
Taylor, J. B. "Monetary Policy during a Transition to Rational Expectations." *J.P.E.* 83 (October 1975): 1009–21.

Weiss, A. Statement before the Subcommittee on Labor Standards of the House
   Education and Labor Committee. Washington, November 1975.
U.S. Bureau of the Census. *Historical Statistics of the United States, Colonial Times to
   1957*. Washington, 1960.
————. *Statistical Abstract of the United States*. Washington, various issues.
U.S. Council of Economic Advisers. *Economic Report of the President*. Washington,
   various years.

30

Unanticipated Money, Output, and the Price Level in the United States

Robert J. Barro

Earlier analysis of unanticipated money growth is extended to output (GNP) and the price level (GNP deflator) for recent U.S. experience. Price level determination is more complicated than output determination, because both anticipated and unanticipated money movements are involved. Empirical results accord well with the model—notably, they support the key hypothesis of a one-to-one, contemporaneous link between anticipated money and the price level. Precise estimates are obtained for the lagged responses of output and prices to unanticipated money movements. Cross-equation comparisons indicate that the price response to unanticipated money movements has a longer lag than the output response. A form of lagged adjustment in money demand can account for this difference. The forecasts for inflation average 5.5 percent per year for 1977–80.

In an earlier empirical study (Barro 1977*a*), I discussed the concept of unanticipated money growth and the hypothesis that only this component of monetary change would influence real variables like the unemployment rate. The present study applies the analysis to output and extends the framework to a consideration of the price level and hence to the rate of inflation. The nature of the monetary influence on the price level is more complicated than that for output or the unemployment rate, because both anticipated and unanticipated movements in money must be taken into

This work is part of a project on money, expectations, and economic activity that is being supported by the National Science Foundation. The present research was completed while I was a national fellow at the Hoover Institution. Portions of this paper will be included in a study of inflation by the U.S. Treasury. I have benefited from comments by Takeshi Amemiya, Paul Evans, Herschel Grossman, Bob Hall, Bronwyn Hall, Leonardo Leiderman, Bob Lucas, Ben McCallum, Franco Modigliani, and Hal White.

[*Journal of Political Economy*, 1978, vol. 86. no. 4]

account. In fact a key hypothesis to be tested is that anticipated movements in the money stock (with expected rate of inflation-type effects held
fixed) would be reflected in one-to-one, contemporaneous movements of
the price level.

This paper reports empirical results on the relation of money to output
(real GNP) and the price level (the GNP deflator) for the post–World War
II period in the United States. The results for output are basically satisfactory and resemble the earlier findings for unemployment. The results
for the price level also accord well with the underlying model—in particular, the hypothesis of a one-to-one, contemporaneous link between anticipated money and the price level is supported by the empirical evidence.
The results also provide precise estimates of the lagged response of the
price level and the rate of inflation to unanticipated money movements.
Substantial space is devoted to a cross-equation comparison of the output
and price level responses to monetary movements. The price level response
appears to be drawn out relative to the output response. However, the two
patterns can be reconciled by a form of lagged adjustment in the money-
demand function.

The first part of the paper deals with the money-growth process, the
second part with output, and the third part with the price level. Part IV
discusses predictions for 1977 onward, while Part V combines the various
pieces of the analysis to simulate a dynamic "Phillips curve." The last part
discusses some promising extensions of the research.

I. Money-Growth Equation

The money-growth equation, which is used to divide observed money
growth into anticipated and unanticipated components, corresponds in
form to the expression that was used in my earlier analysis (Barro 1977a,
pp. 101–5). In this formulation the money-growth rate is related to a
measure of federal government expenditure relative to normal (which
captures an aspect of the revenue motive for money creation), a lagged
measure of the unemployment rate (which reflects countercyclical response
of money growth), and two annual lagged values of money growth (which
pick up persistence effects not captured by the other explanatory variables). Aside from an extension of the sample to 1976, the only change from
the previous setup is that the estimation now weighs the World War II
observations less heavily than the postwar values. This differential weighting is appropriate because of the larger error variance that apparently
prevailed during the war. Each variable observation from 1941 to 1945 is
multiplied by 0.36—a value that was determined iteratively along with the
estimation of the money-growth equation from a maximum likelihood
criterion. Each observation from 1946 to 1976 receives a unit weight in the
estimation.

Using annual observations from 1941 to 1976, the estimated money-growth equation is, with standard errors in parentheses,

$$DM_t =$$

$$0.082 + 0.41DM_{t-1} + 0.21DM_{t-2} + 0.072FEDV_t + 0.026UN_{t-1},$$
$$(0.027) \quad (0.14) \qquad (0.12) \qquad (0.016) \qquad (0.009) \qquad (1)$$
$$R^2 \text{ (weighted)} = 0.77, \text{ D-W} = 1.9, \hat{\sigma} = 0.015,$$

where D-W is the Durbin-Watson statistic,[1] $\hat{\sigma}$ is the standard error of estimate (applying to the error term for the post–World War II period), M is an annual average of the $M1$ definition of the money stock, and $DM_t \equiv \log (M_t) - \log (M_{t-1})$ is the annual average growth rate of money. The variable $FEDV_t \equiv \log (FED_t) - [\log (FED)]_t^*$ measures federal expenditure relative to "normal," where FED_t is current real expenditure and $[\log (FED)]_t^*$ is an exponentially declining distributed lag of current and past values of log (FED), using an adaptation coefficient of 0.2 per year (as discussed in Barro 1977a, p. 103). The variable $UN \equiv \log (U/1 - U)$ is a cyclical variable, where U is the unemployment rate in the total labor force.

The main difference between the present estimates and the earlier ones appears in the estimated coefficients of the lagged money-growth variables, DM_{t-1} and DM_{t-2}, which are now 0.41, 0.21, as compared with the previous estimates, 0.24, 0.35. The suggestion of negative serial correlation of the residuals in the earlier equation, for which the estimate of the first-order serial correlation coefficient was $-.35$, is absent in the present results (see n. 1). These differences stem from the lower weight that is now attached to the World War II observations.

The estimated values from equation (1), $\widehat{DM}_t$, and the residuals, $DMR_t \equiv DM_t - \widehat{DM}_t$, are used to measure, respectively, the anticipated and unanticipated components of money growth. This concept of anticipated money growth is discussed in the earlier study (pp. 105–6). The estimated values, $\widehat{DM}$ and DMR, are indicated along with values of actual money growth in table 1, columns 1–3.

II. Output Equation

The form of the equation for output (real GNP) is similar to that specified for the unemployment rate in my earlier work. The hypothesis that money growth influences output only when this growth is unanticipated implies that current and lagged values of DMR enter the output equation, but current and lagged values of actual money growth, DM, are excluded.

---

[1] The value of the Durbin h-statistic, which is more appropriate in a model with a lagged dependent variable (see, e.g., Maddala 1977, p. 372), is 0.6, which differs insignificantly from zero.

TABLE 1
Values of Money Growth and Output

	DM	$\widehat{DM}$	DMR	$\widehat{\log(y)}$	$\widehat{\widehat{\log(y)}}$	$\widehat{\log(y)} - \widehat{\widehat{\log(y)}}$
	(1)	(2)	(3)	(4)	(5)	(6)
1941	.160	.171	−.011	...	...	...
1942	.179	.207	−.028	...	...	...
1943	.265	.202	.063	...	...	...
1944	.162	.207	−.045	...	...	...
1945	.150	.148	.003	...	...	...
1946	.068	.066	.002	.033	.027	.006
1947	.047	.036	.011	−.022	−.022	.001
1948	.004	.017	−.013	−.016	−.018	.002
1949	−.010	.007	−.017	−.046	−.033	−.012
1950	.026	.003	.023	.003	−.005	.007
1951	.044	.029	.015	.045	.050	−.006
1952	.049	.038	.012	.047	.062	−.015
1953	.024	.041	−.016	.049	.035	.014
1954	.015	.020	−.004	.001	.008	−.007
1955	.031	.024	.007	.030	.016	.015
1956	.012	.023	−.011	.016	.005	.012
1957	.005	.018	−.013	−.001	−.013	.011
1958	.012	.016	−.004	−.039	−.014	−.025
1959	.037	.028	.008	−.016	.004	−.019
1960	−.001	.033	−.033	−.029	−.023	−.006
1961	.021	.025	−.005	−.039	−.036	−.004
1962	.022	.034	−.012	−.018	−.020	.002
1963	.029	.031	−.002	−.015	−.019	.005
1964	.039	.034	.005	.001	.004	−.003
1965	.042	.037	.004	.023	.013	.009
1966	.044	.041	.003	.045	.022	.024
1967	.039	.041	−.003	.037	.019	.017
1968	.068	.039	.029	.044	.045	−.001
1969	.061	.044	.017	.034	.066	−.032
1970	.038	.046	−.008	−.005	−.009	.004
1971	.065	.044	.021	−.010	−.006	−.005
1972	.068	.057	.012	.010	.006	.004
1973	.072	.061	.011	.028	.000	.028
1974	.053	.059	−.006	−.025	−.015	−.010
1975	.042	.059	−.017	−.079	−.050	−.029
1976	.049	.061	−.012	−.054	−.065	.011
				A	B	
1977		.058		−.056	−.061	
1978		.067		−.042	−.046	
1979		.068		−.035	−.037	
1980		.068		−.032	−.034	
∞		.070		−.032	−.034	

Note.—$DM_t \equiv \log(M_t) - \log(M_{t-1})$, where M is an annual average of M_1 from recent issues of the *Federal Reserve Bulletin*, incorporating the revision of data from the February 1976 issues. $\widehat{DM}$ is the estimated value from eq. (1). Predicted values for 1977 and later years use the 1976 value of *FEDV* (0.18). $DMR \equiv DM - \widehat{DM}$. y is real GNP in 1972 dollars (U.S. Council of Economic Advisers 1977, p. 188). For 1946–76, $\log(y_t) \equiv \log(y_t) - 2.985 - 0.0354 \cdot t$ is output relative to trend based on the estimated constant (2.953 + 0.549($\overline{MIL}$), where $\overline{MIL} = 0.0585$ is the mean value of the military variable over the 1946–76 period) and time trend in eq. (3). $\widehat{\log(y)}$ from 1946 to 76 is the estimated value based on eq. (3). From 1977 on, predicted values labeled A are based on the estimated output eq. (3). Values labeled B are based on the jointly estimated coefficients shown in eq. (13). Output predictions assume that $MIL = DMR = 0$ from 1977 on.

Empirically, the contemporaneous and three annual lag values of *DMR* turn out to be important for explaining output. The persisting output effect of monetary shocks implied by the inclusion of lagged values of the *DMR* variable can be rationalized from the impact of shocks on stock variables, such as stocks of productive capital (Lucas 1975), which are carried forward into future periods. An analogous argument, based on adjustment costs for changes in labor input, is developed in Sargent (1977).

In addition to monetary influences, the output equation includes a time-trend variable—intended to capture the secular movement of "normal" output—and the military-personnel (draft-pressure) variable, *MIL* (tabulated in table 2), that was included in my previous study of unemployment.[2] In that study (pp. 106–7) the military variable was viewed as measuring the incentive, operating through differential probabilities of being conscripted into the military, for avoiding the status "unemployed." For example, the incentive to stay in school or to take a job rather than be unemployed was viewed as a response to the military draft—partly reflected in reduced labor-force participation rates and partly in higher employment rates of labor-market participants—that would show up as a corresponding reduction in unemployment rates. Subsequent analysis that I have carried out on unemployment rates stratified by sex and age (to be reported) indicates that the response to the military variable is concentrated in younger males, which supports the interpretation of this variable as a draft-pressure effect on labor supply rather than an aggregate demand effect. With respect to output, the military variable would be expected to operate positively only through the induced employment response, since the effects that involve a disincentive to labor-force participation would operate inversely on output.[3] Hence the argument for including the military variable as an expansionary element is less persuasive in the case of output than in the case of the unemployment rate.

The form of the output equation is

$$\log (y_t) = a_0 + a_1 DMR_t + a_2 DMR_{t-1} + a_3 DMR_{t-2} + a_4 DMR_{t-3}$$
$$+ a_5 MIL_t + a_6 t + u_t, \quad (2)$$

where y is real GNP in 1972 dollars and u_t is a stochastic term with the usual properties.

[2] A contemporaneous or lagged value of a terms-of-trade variable is insignificant when added to the output equation. The *MIL* variable is defined as the ratio of military personnel to the male population aged 15–44 for years in which a selective draft was in operation. The variable takes on a zero value at other times (parts of 1947–48 and 1970–76). See n. 4 below on the effect of removing the distinction between years that do and do not have a selective draft. A minimum-wage-rate variable, which appeared in my previous analysis of unemployment, is insignificant when added to the output equation.

[3] To the extent that draftees receive lower wages than they would in alternative civilian occupations, there would be an additional negative effect of the military variable on measured GNP.

TABLE 2

Values of the Price Level, Inflation Rate, and Other Variables

	log (P) (1)	$\widehat{\log (P)}$ (2)	log (P) − $\widehat{\log (P)}$ (3)	DP (4)	$\widehat{DP}$ (5)	r (6)	G/y (7)	MIL (8)
1945...	−.968	−.545	−.422	.024	...	.026	.416	.350
1946...	−.823	−.636	−.189	.145	...	.025	.122	.105
1947...	−.699	−.626	−.073	.125	...	.026	.077	.012 (.048)
1948...	−.633	−.632	−.001	.066	.068	.028	.087	.022 (.044)
1949...	−.642	−.626	−.016	−.010	.007	.027	.100	.048
1950...	−.624	−.627	.003	.019	.016	.026	.088	.049
1951...	−.557	−.573	.016	.066	.050	.029	.141	.092
1952...	−.545	−.546	.001	.012	.011	.030	.179	.106
1953...	−.529	−.523	−.006	.015	.022	.032	.184	.105
1954...	−.516	−.524	.009	.013	.005	.029	.155	.099
1955...	−.494	−.491	−.004	.022	.025	.031	.133	.090
1956...	−.464	−.463	.000	.031	.031	.034	.128	.083
1957...	−.431	−.434	.003	.033	.030	.039	.132	.081
1958...	−.414	−.419	.005	.017	.012	.038	.137	.075
1959...	−.393	−.383	−.010	.021	.031	.044	.127	.073
1960...	−.375	−.387	.012	.017	.006	.044	.123	.071
1961...	−.367	−.364	−.003	.009	.012	.044	.127	.071
1962...	−.348	−.337	−.011	.018	.030	.043	.129	.077
1963...	−.334	−.328	−.006	.014	.020	.043	.123	.073
1964...	−.319	−.318	.000	.015	.016	.044	.115	.072
1965...	−.297	−.312	.015	.022	.007	.045	.109	.071
1966...	−.264	−.279	.015	.033	.018	.051	.115	.079
1967...	−.236	−.238	.002	.028	.026	.055	.124	.086
1968...	−.191	−.176	−.015	.044	.059	.062	.122	.087
1969...	−.143	−.127	−.016	.049	.064	.070	.113	.085
1970...	−.090	−.077	−.012	.053	.065	.080	.103	0 (.075)
1971...	−.041	−.054	.013	.050	.036	.074	.094	0 (.065)
1972...	.000	−.003	.003	.041	.038	.072	.087	0 (.056)
1973...	.056	.057	.000	.056	.057	.074	.078	0 (.052)
1974...	.152	.154	−.003	.095	.098	.086	.079	0 (.048)
1975...	.241	.231	.009	.089	.079	.088	.080	0 (.046)
1976...	.291	.293	−.002	.050	.052	.084	.076	0 (.045)

	A	B			A	B		
1977...	.364	.354			.073	.063		
1978...	.420	.410			.056	.056		
1979...	.463	.460			.043	.050		
1980...	.504	.507			.041	.047		
1981...	.552	.557			.048	.050		
1982...	.607	.612			.055	.055		
∞.....	...	...			.059	.061		

Note.—P is the GNP deflator (1972 = 1.0) (U.S. Council of Economic Advisers 1977, p. 190). $\widehat{\text{Log } (P)}_t$ from 1945–76 is the estimated value from eq. (9). Predicted values from 1977 on use the predicted values of M implied by the money-growth-rate predictions in table 1. The predictions also use the 1976 values of G/y and r. Values of DMR from 1977 on are assumed to be zero. Projection A uses the coefficients from eq. (9), while projection B utilizes the coefficients from the joint estimation shown in eq. (13) (with lagged values up to DMR_{t-5} included). $DP_t \equiv \log (P_t) - \log (P_{t-1})$. $\widehat{DP_t} \equiv \widehat{\log (P_t)} - \log (P_{t-1})$ (based on the actual previous value, $\log [P_{t-1}]$, up to 1977). r is Moody's Aaa index of corporate bond rates (U.S. Council of Economic Advisers 1977, p. 260). G is real federal government purchases of goods and services in 1972 dollars (ibid., p. 187). y is defined in the note to table 1. MIL is the ratio of military personnel (U.S. Council of Economic Advisers 1977, p. 218) to the male population aged 15–44 (estimated from data in U.S. Department of Commerce [1975, pp. 10, 15] and from *Statistical Abstract of the U.S.*, various issues) for years in which a selective draft was in effect. Figures shown in parentheses are the actual values of the military personnel ratio, ignoring the absence of a selective draft for all or part of those years.

The estimated output equation, based on annual observations from 1946 to 1976 and using the residuals from equation (1) to measure DMR, is

$$\log (y_t) = 2.95 + 1.04DMR_t + 1.21DMR_{t-1} + 0.44DMR_{t-2}$$
$$\quad\;\; (0.04) \quad (0.21) \qquad\quad (0.22) \qquad\qquad (0.21)$$

$$+ 0.26DMR_{t-3} + 0.55MIL_t + 0.0354 \cdot t, \quad (3)$$
$$(0.16) \qquad\qquad (0.09) \qquad\quad (0.0004)$$

$R^2 = .9980$, R^2 with y measured relative to trend $= .82$, D-W $= 1.8$,
$$\hat{\sigma} = 0.016,$$

where $\hat{\sigma}$ again denotes the standard error of estimate. Additional lagged values of the DMR variable are insignificant when added to equation (3). The results indicate absence of serial correlation in the residuals. Further, if a lagged value of the dependent variable, $\log (y_{t-1})$, is added to the equation, its estimated coefficient, 0.06, standard error $= 0.09$, differs insignificantly from zero.

As in the earlier case for unemployment, the output equation indicates a strong expansionary effect of current and lagged values of unanticipated money growth. The main difference from the unemployment results (Barro 1977a, p. 108—an updated version of the unemployment-rate equation is similar in this respect) is that the pattern of lagged output response to DMR shows a relatively greater weight on the contemporaneous value. (Also, the DMR_{t-3} variable, which was insignificant in the case of the unemployment rate, seems to have a weak positive effect on output.) As before, the most important expansionary effect of unanticipated money growth appears in the 1-year lag value, DMR_{t-1}.

The sum of the four DMR coefficients for output, 3.0, implies that a money shock of $DMR = 1$ percent per year that persisted over a 4-year period (which would be a very unusual pattern of persistence, because the anticipated value, $\widehat{DM}_t$, makes use of lagged observations on actual money growth) would raise output by about 3.0 percent. Since the corresponding estimated effect on the unemployment rate (starting from a value for U of 5 percent) was a reduction by somewhat more than 1 percentage point, there is an implicit Okun's Law type of relation in which money-induced percentage increases in output and reductions in percentage points of the unemployment rate occur on about a three-to-one basis.

The estimated output effect of the military variable is surprisingly strong and significant, considering the discussion above of the role of this variable. In fact the estimated coefficient in equation (3) implies that military-induced percentage increases in output and reductions in percentage points of the unemployment rate occur on an almost three-to-one basis— that is, along about the same estimated Okun's Law relation that applies to unanticipated money movements. It is possible that the military-personnel variable is proxying for effects other than the influence of draft pressure on labor supply. However, the variable does not seem to be merely a proxy for government expenditure, since real government purchases of goods and services (total government or federal alone) or of defense items are insignificant when added to equation (3), with the *MIL* variable remaining significant.[4]

Equation (3) also indicates an estimated trend rate of growth of real GNP of about 3.5 percent per year.

Table 1 contains actual and estimated values of output relative to trend, $\log \widetilde{(y)}$, as calculated by subtracting from $\log (y)$ the estimated time trend and constant from equation (3)—see the note to table 1 for details. The estimated values of $\log \widetilde{(y)}$ trace out the major patterns of boom and recession that are shown by the actual values. (See Barro [1977a, pp. 112–13] for a discussion of the business-cycle pattern in terms of the unemployment rate in relation to the movements in the *DMR* series.) The equation underestimates the contraction of 1958–59, the boom in 1966–67, and the sharp cutback of output in 1975. However, the model accounts well for the immediate post–World War II behavior of output, 1946–49; for the Korean and post-Korean experience, 1951–54; and for the recession and recovery period after 1960, 1961–65. A discussion of predictions from the output equation will be deferred until Part IV below.

Following the form of my previous analysis of unemployment, I have tested the hypothesis that only the unanticipated part of monetary change, *DMR*, influences output. An estimated-output equation that substitutes current and lagged values of actual money growth, *DM*, for the *DMR* values is

$$\log (y_t) = 3.13 + 0.95DM_t + 0.53DM_{t-1} - 0.20DM_{t-2}$$
$$\quad (0.08) \quad (0.26) \quad\quad (0.26) \quad\quad (0.23)$$

$$- 0.27DM_{t-3} + 0.31MIL_t + 0.0335 \cdot t, \quad (4)$$
$$(0.16) \quad\quad (0.15) \quad\quad (0.0007)$$

$R^2 = .997$, R^2 with y measured relative to trend $= .70$, D-W $= 1.1$,
$$\hat{\sigma} = 0.021.$$

---

[4] The estimated coefficient of the *MIL* variable also does not depend on the inclusion of the 1970–76, nonselective draft years, for which the *MIL* variable was set to zero (n. 2 above). If the sample is limited to the 1946–69 period, the coefficient estimates are very close to those reported in eq. (3), and a test for including the 1970–76 observations with the earlier ones yields the statistic $F_{17}^7 = 1.2$, which is well below the 5 percent critical value of 2.6. If the military variable is not set to zero for the nonselective draft years, the estimated output equation over the 1946–76 period becomes

$$\log (y_t) = 2.95 + 0.96DMR_t + 0.94DMR_{t-1} + 0.16DMR_{t-2} + 0.04DMR_{t-3}$$
$$(0.05) \quad (0.23) \quad\quad (0.24) \quad\quad (0.22) \quad\quad (0.17)$$
$$+ 0.97 MIL_t + 0.0351 \cdot t,$$
$$(0.18) \quad\quad (0.0004)$$
$$R^2 = .9977, \text{ D-W} = 1.5, \hat{\sigma} = 0.017.$$

The standard error of estimate rises only slightly with this change in specification—from 0.016 to 0.017—but the estimated coefficients on the DMR_{t-2} and DMR_{t-3} variables become insignificant, and the point estimate of the *MIL* coefficient increases substantially.

The relative statistical performance of equations (4) and (3) is indicated by the standard errors of estimate (0.021 vs. 0.016) and by the D-W statistics (1.1 vs. 1.8). It is also worth noting that the estimated coefficients on DM_{t-2} and DM_{t-3} in equation (4) are negative (see below), although individually insignificantly different from zero.

In order to test for the irrelevance of the DM variables for output determination, given the values of the DMR variables, I estimated an output equation that included simultaneously the variables $DM_t, \ldots, DM_{t-3}$ and $DMR_t, \ldots, DMR_{t-3}$. The test statistic associated with the deletion of the four DM variables from the joint equation turns out to be $F_{20}^4 = 0.2$, so that the hypothesis that actual money growth is irrelevant for output, given the inclusion of unanticipated money growth, is accepted. (Note that a test for irrelevance of a set of anticipated money-growth variables, $\widehat{DM_t}, \ldots, \widehat{DM_{t-3}}$, given the inclusion of the DMR variables, would yield the identical test statistic.) The reverse test associated with the deletion of the four DMR variables, while retaining the set of DM values, yields the statistic $F_{20}^4 = 3.6$, which exceeds the 5 percent critical value of 2.9. Hence these tests reinforce the earlier results for the unemployment rate concerning the importance of the DMR variables and the irrelevance of the DM variables.

It should be stressed that the lag pattern of monetary effects on output shown in equation (3) refers to unanticipated money growth rather than to money growth per se. The response of output to actual values of money growth can be derived—assuming a given structure of the money-growth process, as estimated in equation (1)—by substituting into equation (3) from the condition $DMR \equiv DM - \widehat{DM}$, where $\widehat{DM}$ is given from equation (1). The resulting "reduced form" expresses output as a function of $DM_t, \ldots, DM_{t-5}$; $FEDV_t, \ldots, FEDV_{t-3}$; $UN_{t-1}, \ldots, UN_{t-4}$; MIL_t; and t. With respect to monetary effects on output, the point estimates of the lag pattern turn out to be $1.04DM_t + 0.78DM_{t-1} - 0.27DM_{t-2} - 0.17DM_{t-3} - 0.20DM_{t-4} - 0.05DM_{t-5}$. The positive predictive role of lagged values of DM in the money-growth equation (1) implies that lagged values of DM in the reduced form have a net output effect that is less expansionary than the direct effect of the corresponding lagged DMR value in equation (3) (because values of $\widehat{DM}$ are positively related to earlier values of DM). Accordingly, the lag of output behind actual money growth in the reduced form is shorter than that expressed in terms of unanticipated money growth in equation (3). Further, negative coefficients can appear on lagged values of DM in the reduced form (in the present case from date $t - 2$ onward) although the output effect of the DMR values is expansionary throughout. It should also be recalled that—as pointed out in a general context by Lucas (1972)—the reduced-form expression for output as a function of DM values does not have immediate implications for monetary "stabilization" policy, because any (perceived) change in "policy"—that is, in the structure of the money-growth process, such as a change in the reaction of DM_t to lagged unemployment—would alter the coefficients of the reduced form. This point is already evident from the form of equation (3), which indicates that only unanticipated movements of money affect output.[5]

III. Price Level Equation

A. Setup of the Price Equation

In order to derive the form of the price equation, I begin with an expression for the demand for money,

$$\log (M_t) - \log (P_t) = b_0 + b_1 \log (X_t) - b_2 r_t + b_3 t + \varepsilon_t, \quad (5)$$

where M is the nominal money stock, P is the price level (GNP deflator), X is a measure of real expenditure pertinent to money demand, r is a nominal interest rate (measured empirically by the Aaa corporate bond rate; see below), t is a time trend, and ε is a random term that is not necessarily independent of the stochastic term, u, in the output equation (2). The coefficients satisfy the conditions $b_1 > 0$, $b_2 > 0$, $b_3 \gtreqless 0$, with the last coefficient reflecting any trend elements in money demand associated with the development of financial institutions, etc. The formulation in equation (5) neglects any lags in the adjustment of money demand to changes in X, r, etc. Although this representation is convenient, the subsequent empirical results suggest that it may be too restrictive. Hence some possibilities for lagged adjustment of money demand are considered in a later section.

The real expenditure determinant of money demand, X, is assumed to be linearly related to real GNP (denoted again by y) for a given value of real federal purchases of goods and services, G. For a given value of total GNP, an increase in G reduces the volume of expenditure pertinent to money demand (especially since federal government holdings of money are excluded from the money-stock definition), so that X is inversely related to G. I use the specification

$$X = c(y - \gamma G), \quad (6)$$

where $c > 0$ and $0 \leq \gamma \leq 1$. The value $\gamma = 1$ would apply if federal purchases of goods and services were entirely irrelevant to the quantity of real money demanded by the nonfederal sector. Since government purchases involve sales of equal magnitude from the nonfederal sector and since money demand would depend on the volume of both sales and purchases in this sector (with the components of GNP other than federal purchases implying both a final sale and a final purchase in the nonfederal

---

[5] However, eq. (3) is itself a partial reduced form—e.g., shifts in the variance of the money-growth process would be expected to alter the coefficients of the DMR variables along the lines discussed in Lucas (1973) and Barro (1976).

sector),[6] the value $\gamma \approx \frac{1}{2}$ may be reasonable. The exclusion of state and local government purchases from the G variable amounts to treating the state and local sector as comparable to the private sector in terms of money-demand behavior. (Empirically, for the period considered, it is not possible to distinguish the definition of G exclusive of state and local government purchases from that inclusive of these purchases.) The present formulation also neglects any effect of government transfer activities on money demand. (Empirically, the inclusion of federal or total government transfers in the G variable does not have a significant effect on the results.)

Using equations (5) and (6) and the approximation $\log (y - \gamma G) \approx \log (y) - \gamma G/y$, which is satisfactory over the sample period since $\gamma G/y \ll 1$ applies, leads to the price level equation $\log (P_t) = $ constant $+ \log (M_t) - b_1 \log (y_t) + b_1 \gamma (G/y)_t + b_2 r_t - b_3 t - \varepsilon_t$. Substituting for $\log (y_t)$ from equation (2) then implies

$$\begin{aligned} \log (P_t) = {} & \text{constant} + \log (M_t) - b_1(a_1 DMR_t + a_2 DMR_{t-1} \\ & + a_3 DMR_{t-2} + a_4 DMR_{t-3}) - b_1 a_5 MIL_t + b_1 \gamma (G/y)_t \quad (7) \\ & + b_2 r_t - (b_1 a_6 + b_3)t - (\varepsilon_t + b_1 u_t). \end{aligned}$$

Abstracting for the moment from possible endogeneity of some of the right-hand variables (notably G/y and r), equation (7) implies the following hypotheses concerning monetary effects on the price level:[7]

1. Given current and lagged DMR values (and the nominal interest rate, r_t, which would reflect anticipated inflation rates), there is a one-to-one effect of $\log (M_t)$ on $\log (P_t)$. Fully perceived movements in the money stock—which correspond to changes in M_t while holding fixed current and lagged DMR values (weighted in accordance with their effects on current output)—have equiproportionate, contemporaneous effects on the price level.

2. Current and lagged values of DMR have negative effects on the price level (for given values of M_t, r_t, etc.). The pattern of lagged DMR effects corresponds, with the opposite sign, to the pattern in the output equation. If real money demand is unit elastic in real expenditure ($b_1 = 1$), then the DMR pattern in the price level equation corresponds in magnitude

---

[6] This statement does not hold for international transactions components of GNP, which may be worth further examination in the context of demand for money. A more general discussion of the transactions measure in money-demand functions is contained in Enzler, Johnson, and Paulus (1976).

[7] My initial inclination was to specify an equation in terms of the inflation rate, $DP_t \equiv \log (P_t) - \log (P_{t-1})$, rather than the price level. From the perspective of eq. (7), it is clear that the inflation rate would depend on the current money-growth rate, DM_t, and on *changes* in the DMR and other variables that appear on the right-hand side of the price level equation. If the error term in eq. (7) is serially independent (or does not show strong positive serial correlation), then the error in the first-difference rate of inflation form would show strong negative serial correlation.

and shape to the pattern in the output equation.[8] More generally, the *DMR* patterns would correspond in shape but not necessarily in magnitude.

3. Given M_t and the *DMR* values (and r_t, etc.), lagged values of the money stock—$M_{t-1}, M_{t-2}, \ldots$ —or, equivalently, current and lagged values of actual money growth—$DM_t, DM_{t-1}, \ldots$ —are irrelevant to the determination of the price level.

4. In the present formulation, changes in expected inflation rates that correspond to changes in expected growth rates of money or other variables are reflected in the nominal interest rate, r_t. The relation between monetary movements and r_t has not yet been explored. However, an increase in r_t, for given values of the *DMR*s, etc., has a positive effect on P_t.

B. Estimated-Price Equation

Two problems with estimation of equation (7) are the endogeneity of $(G/y)_t$, through its dependence on y_t, and the likely endogeneity of r_t.[9] With respect to the G/y variable, I have made two modifications that yield essentially equivalent results. First, I have used $G/\hat{y}$ as an instrument for G/y, where $\hat{y}$ is the value exp $[\overline{\log (y)}]$ and $\overline{\log (y)}$ is calculated from the estimated-output equation (3). Second, I have changed the specification of equation (7) by replacing G/y with log (G). This procedure and the previous one yield essentially the same statistical fit for the price equation and also yield similar estimates for the coefficients of the other variables. Since the estimated coefficient on the G/y variable in the first approach is readily interpreted in terms of the underlying model, I report only results in this form.

With respect to the interest-rate variable (the Aaa corporate bond rate), the estimation problem would derive from correlation with the error term of equation (7). (It can be noted that this estimation problem is equivalent to the familiar one of estimating the coefficient of a nominal interest rate as one of the right-hand variables in a money-demand function.) Since I have not yet developed an analysis that relates the interest rate to exogenous variables such as money shocks, expected growth rates of money,

[8] Equivalently, nominal income would be invariant with the *DMR*s (for given values of M_t and r_t) in this case. I treat nominal income throughout as a derivative concept, implied by the underlying values of output and the price level, rather than using the (odd, but popular) approach of determining nominal income first and then considering its breakdown between output and the price level.

[9] The error terms of eqq. (7) and (2) would not generally be independent, although the correlation between ε_t (shifts in money demand) and u_t (shifts in output) would also have to be taken into account. Surprisingly, it turns out that the estimated residuals from the two equations are not significantly correlated: the correlation is $+0.15$ for the residuals from eqq. (3) and (9). In general, a joint estimation of eqq. (7) and (2) could exploit any relation among the error terms, but the impact of this extension turns out to be negligible in the present case.

and other factors, I have carried out estimation of the price equation with a lagged interest rate variable, r_{t-1}, used as an instrument for r_t.[10] The use of r_{t-1} as an instrument would eliminate correlation between the interest-rate variable and the error term of equation (7) (thereby leading to consistent estimation at the expense of some lost efficiency) if the error term is itself serially uncorrelated. The estimation of the price equation might be improved by the development of an empirical model of interest-rate determination (which I plan to work on). However, the main short-coming of the present procedure may not be with estimation of the co-efficients in equation (7) but, rather, with the lack of a full reduced-form description of the influence of money, etc., on the price level. The channels of monetary effects on prices that involve variations in the nominal interest rate are not observed when the interest-rate variable is held fixed sepa-rately, as in the present analysis.

Another possible problem with estimation of equation (7) would be correlation of the error in the money-growth equation—that is, DMR—with the errors in the money-demand or output equations. The first corre-lation could arise if the monetary authority is willing and able to "offset" shifts in money demand. The second correlation would appear if counter-cyclical monetary response operates with a shorter lag than that assumed in equation (1).[11] (The correlation with the contemporaneous output shock would also affect the estimate of the DMR_t coefficient in the output equation [3].) Although the present analysis does not deal with these problems, it seems that the most serious questions would arise about the estimate of the DMR_t coefficient in equation (7). It also seems that corre-lation of the DMR variables with the error term in equation (7) would not prejudice the results toward acceptance of the null hypotheses that were set out above.

From some preliminary work, it became clear that the immediate post–World War II observations on the price level were heavily influenced by a residual effect of the extensive wartime controls (see below for a formal analysis of this period). Accordingly, I concentrate the empirical analysis on price equations that are estimated over the 1948–76 period. It also turned out that two additional lagged values of the DMR variable, DMR_{t-4} and DMR_{t-5}, were significant when added to equation (7), so that the reported results include the values $DMR_t, \ldots, DMR_{t-5}$. The MIL variable, which was important in the output equation, turns out to

---

[10] An OLS regression of r_t on r_{t-1} alone from 1948 to 1976 yields

$$r_t = 0.001 + 1.01r_{t-1}, \quad R^2 = .96, \quad \text{D-W} = 1.7, \quad \hat{\sigma} = 0.004.$$
$$(0.002) \quad (0.04)$$

[11] However, preliminary results with quarterly data suggest that biases from this source may not be serious.

be insignificant in the price equation, and I report results separately with this variable excluded.

Table 3 contains the basic empirical results for the price equation. The results apply to annual observations for the 1948–76 period and measure P by the GNP deflator (1972 base) and r by the Aaa corporate bond rate.[12] Results are given with the MIL variable excluded or included and with the coefficient of $\log (M_t)$ unrestricted or constrained to equal unity, in which case $\log (P_t) - \log (M_t)$ becomes the effective dependent variable. For convenience, I write out the estimated equation (from table 3, line 1) that excludes the MIL variable and leaves the coefficient on $\log (M_t)$ unrestricted:

$$
\begin{aligned}
\log (P_t) = &-4.60 + 1.02 \log (M_t) - 0.74 DMR_t - 1.48 DMR_{t-1} \\
&(0.26)\quad (0.07)\qquad\qquad\quad (0.17)\qquad\quad (0.21) \\
&- 1.79 DMR_{t-2} - 1.36 DMR_{t-3} - 0.72 DMR_{t-4} \\
&(0.25)\qquad\qquad (0.23)\qquad\qquad (0.20) \\
&- 0.34 DMR_{t-5} + 0.59 (G/y)_t + 3.7 r_t - 0.0108 \cdot t, \\
&(0.16)\qquad\qquad (0.14)\qquad\quad (1.1)\quad\ (0.0020)
\end{aligned}
\tag{8}
$$

$$
R^2 = .9987, \text{D-W} = 1.8, \hat{\sigma} = 0.012.
$$

The addition of the insignificant MIL variable has a negligible effect on the estimates (table 3, line 2). The results indicate absence of serial correlation in the residuals. Further, if a lagged dependent variable is added to equation (8), its estimated coefficient, 0.07, SE = 0.27, differs insignificantly from zero. It also turns out that ordinary-least-squares (OLS) estimates are close to those shown in equation (8), in which $G/\hat{y}$ and r_{t-1} were used as instruments. The main difference in the OLS results is a reduction in the estimated coefficients of the G/y and r variables, which become 0.52, SE = 0.11, and 2.7, SE = 0.6, respectively.

Test of a unit coefficient on $\log(M_t)$.—The estimated coefficient of the $\log (M_t)$ variable in equation (8), 1.02, SE = 0.07, conforms with the null hypothesis of a unit coefficient. With lagged values of the money stock excluded from equations (7) and (8) (tests of this proposition are carried out below), the hypothesis of a unit coefficient on $\log (M_t)$ can be viewed as a test for the absence of money illusion. In this sense this hypothesis may be regarded as being on a different level (less specific to the particular theory under test but essential for confidence in the other results) from the other propositions to be considered. Accordingly, table 3 provides estimates of price level equations in which the coefficient of $\log (M_t)$ is constrained to be exactly unity (which amounts to using the negative of the

---

[12] The interest rate on prime commercial paper and the rate on savings and loan shares are insignificant when added to eqq. (8) or (9) below.

TABLE 3

ESTIMATED PRICE LEVEL EQUATIONS; 1948–76 SAMPLE

	Const.	Log (M_t)	DMR_t	DMR_{t-1}	DMR_{t-2}	DMR_{t-3}	DMR_{t-4}	DMR_{t-5}	G/y	r	t	MIL	R^2	D-W	$\hat{\sigma}$	SSE
			DM_t	DM_{t-1}	DM_{t-2}	DM_{t-3}	DM_{t-4}	DM_{t-5}								
1.	−4.60 (.26)	1.02 (.07)	−.74 (.17)	−1.48 (.21)	−1.79 (.25)	−1.36 (.23)	−.72 (.20)	−.34 (.16)	.59 (.14)	3.7 (1.1)	−.0108 (.0020)	...	.9987	1.78	.0116	.00241
2.	−4.63 (.26)	1.02 (.07)	−.73 (.18)	−1.46 (.21)	−1.79 (.24)	−1.35 (.23)	−.72 (.20)	−.34 (.16)	.62 (.19)	3.4 (1.1)	−.0105 (.0021)	−.06 (.18)	.9988	1.85	.0116	.00227
3.	−4.55 (.13)	1.0	−.74 (.17)	−1.48 (.20)	−1.78 (.24)	−1.34 (.22)	−.69 (.17)	−.32 (.14)	.59 (.14)	3.8 (0.9)	−.0106 (.0018)	...	.9987	1.72	.0115	.00250
4.	−4.58 (.15)	1.0	−.74 (.17)	−1.46 (.21)	−1.78 (.24)	−1.33 (.22)	−.69 (.17)	−.32 (.14)	.63 (.19)	3.6 (1.0)	−.0102 (.0019)	−.06 (.18)	.9987	1.78	.0114	.00235
5.	−5.61 (.57)	1.06 (.10)	−1.40 (.28)	−.72 (.29)	−.82 (.29)	−.05 (.23)	−.18 (.22)	.39 (.22)	.73 (.44)	0.4 (1.7)	−.0012 (.0031)	...	.9968	1.54	.0184	.00612
6.	−5.61 (.63)	1.06 (.11)	−1.40 (.29)	−.72 (.30)	−.82 (.30)	−.05 (.23)	−.18 (.23)	.38 (.23)	.72 (.57)	0.4 (2.0)	−.0012 (.0039)	.00 (.31)	.9968	1.54	.0190	.00613
7.	−5.36 (.33)	1.0	−1.32 (.25)	−.72 (.29)	−.81 (.29)	−.02 (.22)	−.16 (.22)	.34 (.21)	.70 (.43)	1.1 (1.1)	−.0009 (.0031)	...	.9965	1.34	.0185	.00651
8.	−5.37 (.40)	1.0	−1.32 (.26)	−.72 (.30)	−.81 (.30)	−.02 (.23)	−.16 (.23)	.35 (.22)	.71 (.57)	1.0 (1.5)	−.0007 (.0040)	−.02 (.31)	.9965	1.35	.0190	.00647

NOTE.—Log (M_t) coefficient set = 1.0 for lines 3 and 4, 7 and 8. All data are annual. The dependent variable is log (P_t). G/y and r_{t-1} are used as instrumental variables in the estimations. t is a time-trend variable. Other variables are defined and tabulated in tables 1 and 2. D-W is the Durbin-Watson statistic, $\hat{\sigma}$ is the standard error of estimate, and SSE is the error sum of squares.

log of real money balances as a dependent variable). The estimated equation with this constraint that corresponds in form to equation (8) is, from table 3, line 3,

$$\log (P_t) = -4.55 + \log (M_t) - 0.74 DMR_t - 1.48 DMR_{t-1}$$
$$\quad\quad\quad (0.13) \quad\quad\quad\quad\quad (0.17) \quad\quad\quad (0.20)$$

$$\quad - 1.78 DMR_{t-2} - 1.34 DMR_{t-3} - 0.69 DMR_{t-4}$$
$$\quad\quad (0.24) \quad\quad\quad\quad (0.22) \quad\quad\quad\quad (0.17) \quad\quad\quad\quad\quad (9)$$

$$\quad - 0.32 DMR_{t-5} + 0.59(G/y)_t + 3.8 r_t - 0.0106 \cdot t,$$
$$\quad\quad (0.14) \quad\quad\quad\quad (0.14) \quad\quad\quad (0.9) \quad\quad (0.0018)$$

$$R^2 = .9987, \text{ D-W} = 1.7, \hat{\sigma} = 0.012.$$

Again, the estimates are not materially affected by including the insignificant *MIL* variable (table 3, line 4), and there is no indication of serial correlation in the residuals. If the lagged variable, $\log (P/M)_{t-1}$, is added to equation (9), its estimated coefficient, 0.10, SE = 0.21, differs insignificantly from zero. Ordinary-least-squares estimates are again close to the instrumental estimates, except for some reduction in the estimated coefficients of the G/y and r variables. The OLS estimates of these coefficients are 0.50, SE = 0.11, and 2.9, SE = 0.5, respectively.

Estimates of DMR *coefficients.*—All six of the estimated *DMR* coefficients in equation (9) are negative—that is, conforming in sign to the underlying theory—and all are individually significantly different from zero. The precision with which the lagged response of the price level to unanticipated money growth is estimated and the smooth triangular shape of the lag pattern are striking features of the results.

In terms of quantitative correspondence to the *DMR* lag pattern estimated in the output equation (3), it can be seen that the DMR_t and DMR_{t-1} coefficients correspond reasonably well, but the coefficients on the other lag values are much larger in magnitude in the price equation than in the output equation. The significance of the DMR_{t-4} and DMR_{t-5} variables in the price equation, as contrasted with their insignificance in the output equation, is one aspect of this cross-equation discrepancy. A formal comparison of the *DMR* coefficients from the price and output equations is carried out below.

Test for irrelevance of actual money-growth variables.—The price level equation can also be estimated with the *DMR* values replaced by corresponding values of actual money growth, *DM*. Since $\log (M_t)$ is included separately as an explanatory variable, this form of the price equation amounts to regressing $\log (P_t)$ on $\log (M_t)$, $\log (M_{t-1})$, . . . , $\log (M_{t-6})$, and the other explanatory variables. Table 3, lines 5–8, reports results based on the *DM* variables. The estimated equation that uses *DM* values but otherwise corresponds in form to equation (9) is, from line 7 of the table,

$$\log (P_t) = -5.36 + \log (M_t) - 1.32 DM_t - 0.72 DM_{t-1}$$
$$\quad\quad (0.33) \quad\quad\quad\quad (0.25) \quad\quad (0.29)$$

$$\quad - 0.81 DM_{t-2} - 0.02 DM_{t-3} - 0.16 DM_{t-4} + 0.34 DM_{t-5}$$
$$\quad\quad (0.29) \quad\quad\quad (0.22) \quad\quad\quad (0.22) \quad\quad\quad (0.21)$$

$$\quad + 0.70(G/y)_t + 1.1 r_t - 0.0009 \cdot t, \quad\quad\quad\quad\quad\quad (10)$$
$$\quad\quad (0.34) \quad\quad (1.1) \quad (0.0031)$$

$$R^2 = .9965, \text{ D-W} = 1.3, \hat{\sigma} = 0.019.$$

Two observations on the estimates are, first, that the DM variables provide a much poorer fit to the price level than that obtained with the use of the DMR values ($\hat{\sigma} = 0.012$ from eq. [9] vs. $\hat{\sigma} = 0.019$ from eq. [10]) and, second, that the estimated pattern of coefficients in the DM form is difficult to interpret.

The test for irrelevance of lagged DM values in the price level equation —given the values of log (M_t) and the DMR variables—can be carried out by running a regression of log (P_t) on an array of explanatory variables that includes simultaneously the two sets $DMR_t, \ldots, DMR_{t-5}$ and $DM_t, \ldots, DM_{t-5}$ and then examining the impact on the sum of squared residuals of deleting the set of DM values. This procedure, for the case where the MIL variable is excluded and the log (M_t) coefficient is con- strained to equal unity, yields the test statistic $F^6_{13} = 1.7$, 5 percent critical value $= 2.9$.[13] Therefore the hypothesis that current and lagged values of DM [and hence the values of log $(M_{t-1}), \ldots, \log (M_{t-6})$] are irrelevant to the determination of P_t—given the values of M_t and the DMRs—is accepted. A reverse test for the deletion of the six DMR variables, while retaining the set of DM values, yields the statistic $F^6_{13} = 7.9$, so that the importance of the DMRs (and the empirical distinction between the DMR and DM concepts) is confirmed by this test. The same conclusions obtain if the MIL variable is included and if the log (M_t) coefficient is unrestricted. A simultaneous test that the coefficient of the log (M_t) variable is unity *and* that the set of DM variables is irrelevant, which involves a test of seven coefficient restrictions, yields the statistic (with the MIL variable excluded) $F^7_{12} = 1.7$, which is below the 5 percent critical value of 2.9. (A simul- taneous test that the log $[M_t]$ coefficient is unity and that the DMR vari- ables are irrelevant yields $F^7_{12} = 7.2$.) The acceptance of the joint hy- pothesis that the log (M_t) coefficient is equal to unity and that the set of DM variables is irrelevant is important, because it implies acceptance of the basic hypothesis that perceived movements in the money stock—that is,

[13] In the context of instrumental estimates, this critical value is only an approximation.

changes in M_t with the DMR values and r_t held constant—imply equi-proportionate, contemporaneous movements in the price level.

Estimates of other coefficients in the price equation.—The estimated coefficient of the G/y variable in equation (9), 0.59, SE = 0.14, is positive, significantly different from zero, and in the vicinity of the plausible value of $\frac{1}{2}$ (assuming a unit income elasticity of money demand, b_1: see below). The tabulation of this variable in table 2 indicates that the movement of G/y (which is based on federal purchases of goods and services—a concept that is dominated by defense expenditure) has been downward since 1968. The drop in G/y from 0.12 in 1968 to 0.08 in 1976 implies, according to the estimated coefficient from equation (9), that the 1976 price level is about 2.5 percent lower than it would have been if G/y had remained at its 1968 level. The other important movement of G/y during the sample period is the sharp increase with the start of the Korean War in 1951, followed by a strong decrease from 1953 to 1955. The 1951 movement of federal expenditure implies, on this count, an estimated price level increase from 1950 of about 3 percent (although the estimated price level for 1951 is still about 1.5 percent below the actual value). The expenditure decline from 1953 to 1955 implies, on this count, a price level decrease by about 3 percent.

The point estimate of the interest-rate coefficient in equation (9) implies a money-demand elasticity of -0.19 at the sample mean of r over the 1948–76 period and an elasticity of -0.32 at the 1976 value of r. It should be noted that the interest-rate variable is important for "explaining" some of the recent movements in the price level. For example, the rise in the interest rate from 0.074 in 1973 to 0.086 in 1974 "accounts for" 0.046 out of the total price level increase of 0.095 for 1974. It is likely that the interest-rate movements reflect changes in anticipated inflation, but the present analysis does not make that connection explicit.

The estimated time trend, -0.011, SE = 0.002, is significantly negative, but only 1.1 percent per year in magnitude. Since the estimated time-trend coefficient in the output equation (3) is 0.035, it follows from the forms of equations (5) and (7) that the estimates imply a negative trend in the demand for money over the 1948–76 period of about 2.4 percent per year (assuming a unit income elasticity of money demand, b_1: see below). It would be preferable to relate this trend to movements in variables that explicitly measure changes in financial structure or other forces, especially since the stability of the relation between money demand and time per se is doubtful. However, I have not made any progress along these lines.

As mentioned above, the estimated coefficient of the MIL variable is insignificant throughout (table 3, lines 2, 4, 6, 8), although the standard error of about 0.2 in the DMR equations is substantial. This result contrasts with the significant, positive coefficient on the MIL variable that was obtained in the output equation (3) (0.55, SE = 0.09). In light of the discussion of the military variable in Part II above, the insignificant effect on the price level does more to provide further doubt about the meaning of the estimated effect on output rather than to question the price level results.

Cross-equation tests of coefficients in the price and output equations.—As noted above, the pattern of estimated *DMR* coefficients in the price equation appears to differ from that in the output equation. A formal test of correspondence of these two sets of coefficients involves, first, a joint estimation of the output and price equations subject to the constraint that the *DMR* coefficients be of opposite sign and equal magnitude aside from multiplication by the income elasticity of money demand, b_1, in equation (7) and, second, a comparison by means of a likelihood ratio test of the residuals in the constrained calculation with those from the unconstrained case. The constrained estimates are determined from a nonlinear three-stage least-squares routine (from the TSP regression package), which also provides estimates of the variances and contemporaneous covariance of the error terms across the output and price equations. In the present circumstance this covariance turns out to be negligible (n. 9 above). For purposes of carrying out a likelihood ratio test, the estimates that omit constraints on the coefficients have also been obtained from the joint procedure that includes estimates of the variances and contemporaneous covariance of the error terms. In the present context, the output and price level equations are both estimated over the 1948–76 period with $DMR_t, \ldots, DMR_{t-5}$ used as explanatory variables. The military variable has also been included in both equations. In one set of calculations, a separate military coefficient was estimated for the price and output equations in both unconstrained and constrained forms, while in another set the two military coefficients were restricted in the constrained form, along with the *DMR* variables, to have coefficients in the two equations that were of opposite sign and of equal magnitude except for multiplication by b_1 in equation (7). Since the size of the estimated *MIL* coefficient is much higher in the output equation than in the price equation, it would be anticipated that the null hypothesis of corresponding coefficients across the two equations is less likely to be accepted when the restriction on the *MIL* coefficients is included as part of the null hypothesis.

The basic outcome of the cross-equation test is that the null hypothesis of consistent *DMR* coefficients in the output and price level equations is rejected at the 5 percent level. For example, for the case where the coefficient of $\log (M_t)$ in the price equation is restricted to equal unity (results are similar if this coefficient is unrestricted) and the coefficients of the two *MIL* variables are left unrestricted throughout, the likelihood ratio implies the test statistic, which is distributed asymptotically as a χ^2 variable with degrees of freedom equal to the number of coefficient restrictions (in this case 5), of 19.1, which exceeds the 5 percent critical value of 11.1.[14] For the case where the two MIL coefficients are also constrained as a part of the null hypothesis, the test statistic is 41.1, which is well above the 5 percent critical value with 6 degrees of freedom of 12.6.

Lagged adjustment of money demand.—The statistical tests above support the impression from equations (3) and (9) that the pattern of price level response to the DMR variables is drawn out relative to the output response. From the perspective of the underlying model, an obvious possibility for "explaining" this behavior would be to modify the form of the money-demand function, as expressed in equations (5) and (6), to allow for some dependence of log $(M/P)_t$ on lagged values of the explanatory variables— log (y), G/y, and r. However, the most common form of partial adjustment, which would amount to introducing log $(M/P)_{t-1}$ as an additional deter-minant of current money demand, would not account for the results. This form would rationalize the inclusion of the lagged variable, log $(P/M)_{t-1}$, in the price equation (7). However, as noted above, the estimated coeffi-cient of this variable differs insignificantly from zero. Put another way, this form of partial adjustment implies that log (P_t), relative to log (M_t), would depend on a distributed lag of log (y), G/y, and r, which implies not only an elongated response of the price level to the DMR variables but also a dependence of the current price level on lagged values of G/y and r (and MIL). In fact lagged values of G/y and r (and MIL) are insignificant when added to equation (7) (in an OLS regression), which is consistent with the insignificant effect of the log $(P/M)_{t-1}$ variable that was referred to above.

A form of partial adjustment that can account for the cross-equation results involves a special response of money demand to temporary move-ments in income, as stressed by Darby (1972). Consider the division of $\log(y_t)$ from equation (2) into a "temporary" component, $\log(y_t^\tau) = a_1 DMR_t + a_2 DMR_{t-1} + a_3 DMR_{t-2} + a_4 DMR_{t-3} + u_t$, and a "perma-nent" component, $\log(y_t^P) = a_0 + a_5 MIL_t + a_6 t$. Suppose that tempo-rary income has a strong effect on current money demand that dissipates only gradually in accordance with an adjustment parameter, λ. In this case a modified form of the money-demand function would be[15]

---

[14] The constrained coefficient estimates and asymptotic standard errors for this case are, for the income elasticity of money demand, $b_1 = 1.42$ (0.23); for the DMR co-efficients, $a_1 = 0.72$ (0.15), $a_2 = 0.94$ (0.15), $a_3 = 0.87$ (0.15), $a_4 = 0.60$ (0.13), $a_5 = 0.29$ (0.10), $a_6 = 0.19$ (0.08); and for the other coefficients,

$$\log (y_t) = 2.930 + 0.70 MIL_t + 0.0355 \cdot t,$$
$$\qquad\quad (0.053) \quad (0.11) \qquad (0.0005)$$

$$\log (P_t) = -4.765 + \log (M_t) + 0.37(G/y)_t + 2.0r_t - 0.0074 \cdot t + 0.04 MIL_t.$$
$$\qquad\quad (0.131) \qquad\qquad\quad (0.17) \qquad (0.9) \quad (0.0017) \qquad (0.17)$$

[15] The G/y and MIL variables are treated as "permanent" elements in this specification.

$$\log (M_t) - \log (P_t) = b_0 + b_1[\log (y_t^P) - \gamma(G/y)_t] - b_2 r_t + b_3 t$$
$$+ b_4[\log (y_t^\tau) + (1 - \lambda) \log (y_{t-1}^\tau) + (1 - \lambda)^2 \log (y_{t-2}^\tau) + \ldots]$$
$$+ \varepsilon_t, \quad (11)$$

where $0 \le \lambda < 1$, b_1 is the elasticity of money demand with respect to permanent income, and b_4 is the elasticity with respect to current temporary income.[16]

From the definitions above of $\log (y_t^P)$ and $\log (y_t^\tau)$, equation (11) can be used to obtain a price equation that generalizes equation (7),

$$\log (P_t) = \text{constant} + \log (M_t) - b_4\{a_1[DMR_t + (1 - \lambda)DMR_{t-1}$$
$$+ \ldots] + a_2[DMR_{t-1} + (1 - \lambda)DMR_{t-2} + \ldots] + a_3(DMR_{t-2}$$
$$+ \ldots) + a_4(DMR_{t-3} + \ldots)\} - b_1 a_5 MIL_t + b_1 \gamma(G/y)_t + b_2 r_t$$
$$- (b_1 a_6 + b_3)t - \varepsilon_t - b_1[u_t + (1 - \lambda)u_{t-1} + \ldots]. \quad (12)$$

Accordingly, each variable DMR_{t-i} is now replaced by a distributed lag, $DMR_{t-i} + (1 - \lambda)DMR_{t-i-1} + \ldots$. It is also apparent from equation (12) that values of λ below one will generate, at least qualitatively, the observed pattern of behavior in which the price level response to DMR values is elongated relative to the output response. Moreover, in this formulation it is only the contemporaneous values of G/y, r, and MIL that would affect the current price level.[17]

The output and price level estimates can now be examined for cross-equation consistency from the standpoint of the output equation (2) and the modified price equation (12). Since b_4 and λ have to be estimated (by means of the nonlinear three-stage least-squares procedure), there are now only two restrictions corresponding to the imposition of a common set of coefficients, $a_1, \ldots, a_4$, across the two equations. However, the form of equation (12) for the price level implies two additional restrictions relative to the form in equation (9), which permitted unrestricted coefficient estimates on $DMR_t, \ldots, DMR_{t-5}$. (Lagged values only up to DMR_{t-5} are also used in the restricted form.) The basic finding is that the results

[16] The log-linear form is solely for algebraic convenience. Darby's (1972, pp. 929–30) discussion suggests that a different functional form may be more appropriate for relating "transitory money demand" to "transitory income." However, the log-linear representation seems adequate to account for the present empirical results.

[17] The error term in eq. (12) would show positive serial correlation if $0 \le \lambda < 1$ and ε_t and u_t are serially independent. In fact the estimated residuals from the price equation (9) do not exhibit serial correlation. One possible explanation is that the u_t part of "transitory income" does not have the distributed lag effect on money demand that is postulated in eq. (11). It is also necessary to reconcile the lack of correlation between the residuals of eqq. (3) and (9) (n. 9 above) and the lower value of σ from the price equation (9) than that in the output equation (3). In the context of the forms of the error terms in eqq. (2) and (12), these results require strong negative correlation between the output shift (u_t) and the money-demand shift (ε_t).

are in accord with these restrictions. For the case of a unit coefficient on
log (M_t) (and where no cross-equation restriction is imposed on the *MIL*
coefficients),[18] the likelihood ratio implies a test statistic of 5.1, which is
below the 5 percent critical value for the χ^2 distribution with 4 degrees of
freedom of 9.5. Hence the generalization of the money-demand function
does reconcile the apparent conflict between the output and price level
responses to the *DMR* values. The full set of constrained estimates and
asymptotic standard errors is

Current temporary income elasticity of money demand:

$$b_4 = 0.85, \text{ SE} = 0.13,$$

adjustment parameter: $\lambda = 0.40$, SE $= 0.07$,

common *DMR* coefficients: $a_1 = 0.98$, $a_2 = 1.15$, $a_3 = 0.68$, $a_4 = 0.24$,
$\qquad\qquad\qquad\qquad\quad$ (0.17) $\qquad$ (0.17) $\qquad$ (0.16) $\qquad$ (0.17)

$$\log (y_t) = 2.942 + 0.58 MIL_t + 0.0355 \cdot t \ (R^2 = .9975, \text{D-W} = 1.9),$$
$\qquad\qquad$ (0.047) $\quad$ (0.10) $\qquad\quad$ (0.0004)

$$\log (P_t) = -4.641 + \log (M_t) + 0.47(G/y)_t + 3.0r_t \qquad\qquad (13)$$
$\qquad\qquad$ (0.115) $\qquad\qquad\qquad$ (0.15) $\qquad$ (0.8)

$$\qquad - 0.0092 \cdot t + 0.01 MIL_t \ (R^2 = .9986, \text{D-W} = 1.8).$$
$\qquad\quad$ (0.0015) $\qquad$ (0.15)

The estimates for $a_1, \ldots, a_4$, together with the values for b_4 and λ and
the form of equation (12), imply that the estimates for the $DMR_t, \ldots,$
DMR_{t-5} variables in the unrestricted form of the price equation (9)
should be -0.83, -1.48, -1.46, -1.08, -0.65, and -0.39.[19] As suggested by the likelihood ratio test statistic above, these figures accord well
with the unrestricted estimates shown in equation (9).

In one sense these results indicate conformity between the output and
price level coefficient estimates in the context of a perhaps plausible money-
demand representation that allows for gradually dissipating effects of temporary income (with an adjustment coefficient, λ, on the order of 0.4 per
year). On the other hand, the admission of partial adjustment in the
money-demand function—while possibly theoretically and empirically
warranted—substantially weakens the discriminatory power of the cross-
equation tests. Since the utilized form of adjustment is only one of many
possible specifications and since the chosen form was dictated more by
prior empirical results than from ex ante theorizing, it seems clear that
these results do not provide strong support for the underlying model.

---

[18] A cross-equation restriction would arise here only if the value of b_1 or γ were specified
ex ante. For plausible values of b_1 or γ, it still seems that the output effect of the *MIL*
variable is unduly large relative to the price level effect.

[19] The DMR_{t-6} coefficient would be -0.23. If this variable is added to eq. (9), its
estimated coefficient is -0.15, SE $= 0.16$.

Rather, the results have a more modest interpretation—that cross-equation inconsistency would not be a basis for rejecting the model.

Lagged response of the price level to money movements.—As in the case of the output equation, the effects of lagged money growth on the price level have been expressed in terms of DMR values rather than DM values. The response of log (P_t) to current and lagged values of money can be derived—again assuming the stability of the money-growth process, as estimated in equation (1)—by using the condition $DMR \equiv DM - \widehat{DM}$, where $\widehat{DM}$ is determined from equation (1). (This procedure holds fixed the nominal interest rate, r_t, and therefore misses any monetary effects on the price level that operate through interest-rate variations. The G/y variable is also held fixed in this analysis.) Substituting for the DMR values in equation (12) and using the joint coefficient estimates listed in equation (13) leads to the following point estimates of the reduced-form lag effects from the money stock to the price level (which is equivalent to the lag effects from actual money growth, DM, to the inflation rate):[20] 0.17 log (M_t) − 0.31 log (M_{t-1}) + 0.46 log (M_{t-2}) + 0.51 log (M_{t-3}) + 0.27 log (M_{t-4}) + 0.00 log (M_{t-5}) − 0.03 log (M_{t-6}) − 0.03 log (M_{t-7}) + 0.01 log (M_{t-8}). Two important observations about this lag pattern are, first, that there is at most a weak near-term positive link between the money stock and the price level and, second, that there is a long lag—in the 2- to 4-year range—in the main positive effect of money on the price level.[21] With regard to the first observation, a point to stress is that this weak near-term link between money and prices is consistent with the property that anticipated money movements are reflected in one-to-one, contemporaneous movements of the price level. This basic hypothesis—associated with a unit coefficient on log (M_t) and with the irrelevance of the DM variables in the price equation—has already been accepted for the equation that yielded the pattern above of reduced-form lag effects from money to prices.[22] The long lag in the response of the price level to money movements can be "explained" from two elements—first, the dependence of output on lagged values of the DMR variable, which would itself produce about a 2-year lag of prices behind money, and, second, the dependence of money demand on lagged values of temporary income, which lengthens the lag to the 2- to 4-year range.

[20] This calculation does not terminate with the DMR_{t-5} value but, rather, includes the full distributed lag implied by the form of eq. (12).

[21] Similarly long lags in the impact of (actual) money movements on the price level have been noted by Selden (1976, p. 5) and Gordon (1975, p. 647).

[22] Hence Gordon's criterion (1975, p. 615), "Is the effect of money on prices instantaneous, as required by the rational-expectations literature, or does it operate with a long lag?" does not make sense. The effect of anticipated money movements on the price level can be virtually instantaneous at the same time that unanticipated movements (and hence actual movements of money in a reduced form that holds fixed the predictors of money growth) affect the price level only with a long lag.

ROBERT J. BARRO

Pre-1948 observations and the residual effect of wartime price controls.—The hypothesis that price level observations from the immediate post–World War II period are generated from the same model that generated the observations from 1948 to 1976 can be decisively rejected. For example, for the case where the coefficient of $\log(M_t)$ is constrained to equal one and the *MIL* variable is excluded (changes in these features are unimportant in the present context), the test statistic for including the 1946–47 observations in equation (9) is $F^2_{19} = 55.5$, 5 percent critical value $= 3.5$; while that for the 1945–47 observations is $F^3_{19} = 83.2$, 5 percent critical value $= 3.1$. An extrapolation of the price level estimates from equation (9) to the 1945–47 years (table 2, cols. 2, 3) shows that the equation overestimates the reported price level by about 7.5 percent in 1947, 19 percent in 1946, and 42 percent in 1945.

On the other hand, an output equation of the form of equation (2) can satisfactorily encompass the 1945–47 observations. The test statistics are $F^2_{22} = 0.2$, 5 percent critical value $= 3.4$, for the inclusion of the 1946–47 observations; and $F^3_{22} = 0.9$, 5 percent critical value $= 3.0$, for the 1945–47 observations.[23]

A possible interpretation of the price level and output results for 1945–47 is that the controls, which were gradually eased from 1946 on, principally affected the reported price level without having real effects on output, the economically relevant price level, etc. Under this interpretation, the extrapolation of the post-1948 estimated price equation to the 1945–47 period (table 2, col. 2) may provide better estimates than the reported price indices of the economically relevant price level for these years. According to this approach, the reported price increase by 14.5 percent from 1945 to 1946 would be converted to a price *decrease* of 9 percent, the reported price increase by 12.5 percent from 1946 to 1947 would be converted to an increase of 1 percent, and the reported price increase by 6.5 percent from 1947 to 1948 would be converted to a decrease of 0.5 percent.

Price controls in the post-1948 period.—The two instances of general price-control programs since 1948 are the Korean War controls for 1951–52 and the more recent experiment from August 1971 through roughly 1973. (I exclude the wage-price guideposts episode from 1962 to roughly 1966 as being a priori nonserious, although the within-sample residuals from equation [9] are -1.1 percent for 1962 and -0.6 percent for 1963.) The within-sample residuals from equation (9) (table 2, col. 3) for the five "control years"[24] are $+1.6$ percent for 1951, $+0.1$ percent for 1952,

---

[23] Using extrapolations of the money-growth equation back to 1937 to form the required *DMR* values, it appears that the output equation is stable at least back to 1941. The price level equation, which substantially overestimates the reported price level for 1943–44, appears to be roughly back on track in 1942. The unemployment rate equation is stable back to 1942 but substantially underestimates the actual value in 1941.

[24] I have included the 1971 observation with this group, although it could be argued that this observation is affected by expectations of controls prior to August, which might raise the reported average price level for the year.

+1.3 percent for 1971, +0.3 percent for 1972, and 0.0 percent for 1973. More interestingly for the present purpose, if an extrapolation to the 5 control years is made from a relation of the form of equation (9) that is estimated only over the "noncontrol years," 1948–50, 1953–70, and 1974–76, the residuals are +3.9 percent for 1951, +1.9 percent for 1952, +1.2 percent for 1971, −0.3 percent for 1972, and −1.3 percent for 1973. A similar pattern of residuals obtains if the extrapolation is from the 1948–50, 1953–70 sample. An extrapolation from the 1948–70 sample yields the residuals: +2.8 percent for 1971, +0.7 percent for 1972, and 0.0 percent for 1973. Hence there is no indication from these calculations of a downward effect of controls on the price level.

Considering the pattern of residuals above, it seems unnecessary to carry out a formal F-test of the hypothesis that controls lower the reported price level. (Such a test is carried out in an earlier version of this paper: Barro 1977b.) However, it is worth noting two difficulties with price-control analyses that are based either on extrapolated residuals or on an F-test for a shift in the parameters of a price equation. (See Oi 1976 for some additional issues in this context.) First, the extent and probability of controls is unlikely to be exogenous with respect to shifts in the price equation. (This interconnection might explain the apparently strong, perverse effect of controls during the Korean War, although the large wartime increase in the G/y variable is already held constant in the price equation.) If controls are an indicator of a positive shift in the price equation, then the tests would be biased toward rejecting the hypothesis that controls lower the price level. Second, the present type of test neglects the possible impact of controls on the right-hand variables of the price equation. The present analysis would reveal only the effects of controls for given values of the explanatory variables. In particular, it would be worth examining the possible effect of controls on the interest rate, although that investigation will require an extension of the analysis to interest-rate determination. Despite these caveats, it is difficult to see how the post-1948 experience can be used to argue that controls significantly depress the price level,[25] even if one abstracts from the distinction between the reported and actual price levels during a controls period.

Post-1974 behavior of money demand.—It is worth examining whether the estimated-price equation shows any indication of the post-1974 breakdown in the money-demand function that has been noted by Enzler et al. (1976), Goldfeld (1976), and others. The within-sample residuals from equation (9) (table 3, col. 2) for 1974–76 are −0.3, +0.9, and −0.2 percent, respectively. If a relation of the form of equation (9) is fitted only

---

[25] This conclusion seems to agree with that reached by Feige and Pearce (1976, p. 295) and to conflict with results obtained by Gordon (1975, p. 640). However, it is difficult to make a satisfactory comparison with Gordon's results, because his measurement of the price level by the private deflator exclusive of food and energy components involves a mixing up of absolute and relative price movements.

through 1973, the extrapolated residuals for 1974–76 are 0.0, +1.5, and +0.3 percent, respectively. A test for unchanged structure for 1974–76 yields the statistic $F_{16}^3 = 0.8$, which is well below the 5 percent critical value of 3.2. Hence the results do not support the hypothesis of a structural break in money demand after 1974. This conclusion is in accord with recent money-demand estimates reported by Hamburger (1977). The difference in Hamburger's and my results from those in the studies above may derive from the use of a long-term rather than a short-term interest rate. At a theoretical level, the long-term interest rate could be more pertinent than the short-term rate to money demand even if short-term assets were the closer substitute for money. Since the long rate would represent a weighted average of anticipated future short rates, it would affect current money demand if there were lump-sum, investment-type costs associated with changing average holdings of cash through changes in the timing of transactions, shifts to new types of assets, etc.

IV. Predictions

Predictions for 1977 onward of money growth, output, and the price level (and the rate of inflation) are contained in tables 1 and 2. The money-growth-rate predictions assume that federal expenditure relative to normal, *FEDV*, remains at its 1976 level[26] and that unemployment rates from 1977 on correspond to the predictions from an updating of my earlier study (Barro 1977*a*, p. 102). The predicted values for money growth (table 1, col. 2) are 5.8 percent for 1977 and 6.7 percent for 1978, rising from there to a long-run predicted value of 7.0 percent per year. This high long-run prediction for the money-growth rate reflects the response of *DM* to the lagged unemployment rate (eq. [1] above), combined with an estimate of the current and future "natural" unemployment rate in the vicinity of 6.5 percent. Even if this unemployment-rate estimate is correct, the response of money growth in the circumstance of a permanently high level of the unemployment rate may not conform to the countercyclical response that was estimated in equation (1) over a sample period where the natural rate was, in the main, much lower than 6.5 percent. Although presently I do not have a better procedure for forecasting money growth, it is important to recognize that inflation-rate forecasts are sensitive to these forecasts for money growth. (However, the output predictions, which are based on *DMR* values, are not sensitive in the same way to the money-growth projections.)

With respect to output predictions (table 1, col. 5), note first that the

[26] Since the *FEDV* variable has not been normalized to make its average value equal to zero in the context of secular growth of the public sector, this value for *FEDV* (0.18) is positive. Normalization of the *FEDV* variable would affect none of the substantive results.

1976 value of actual output relative to trend, $\widetilde{\log (y)}$, is -5.4 percent, as compared with an estimated value of -6.5 percent. For the forecast period (assuming that the values of the *MIL* variable and all future *DMR*s are equal to zero), the predictions for output relative to trend implied by the estimated equation (3), which are labeled A in table 1, are -5.6 percent for 1977, -4.2 percent for 1978, -3.5 percent for 1979, and -3.2 percent for 1980 onward. (The negative estimate of the long-run value for $\widetilde{\log [y]}$ is implied by the assumed zero value for the military variable, in contrast to the positive value of this variable that prevailed over most of the sample period.) Predictions based on the jointly estimated coefficients that are shown in equation (13), which are labeled B in table 1, are basically similar. The prediction pattern reflects the gradual decay in influence of the contractionary monetary behavior (negative values of *DMR*) from 1974–76. In terms of forecasts for growth rates of real GNP, the implied values based on equation (3) are 3.4 percent for 1977 (using the actual value of 1976 output as a base)—which is just under the trend rate of growth—4.9 percent for 1978, 4.3 percent for 1979, 3.8 percent for 1980, and 3.5 percent—the estimated trend rate of growth—for 1981 and beyond.

Two sets of price level and inflation-rate predictions are shown in table 2. Projection A uses the coefficients from the estimated price equation (9), while projection B utilizes the jointly estimated coefficients that are shown in equation (13). Both projections assume that the G/y and r variables remain at their 1976 levels and that values of *DMR* from 1977 on are equal to zero. The largest difference in the two projections occurs for the 1977 forecast—projection A implies a 7.3 percent inflation rate, while projection B yields only a 6.3 percent rate. Both projections show some tapering off of inflation to 1980—to just above 4 percent per year in the first case and just below 5 percent per year in the second. Finally, both projections imply some increase in the inflation rate after 1980—to a long-run value of 5.9 percent per year in the first case and 6.1 percent per year in the second. These long-run values are implied by the long-run prediction for money growth of 7.0 percent per year, together with an estimated time trend in the price equation of -1.1 and -0.9 percent per year, respectively.

V. A Simulated "Phillips Curve"

The present results on money growth, output, and the price level and the earlier results on the unemployment rate can be combined to describe some aspects of the dynamics of economic response to monetary disturbances. This description amounts to tracing out a dynamic Phillips curve in which temporary movements of output and the unemployment rate relative to "normal" values are associated with departures of the price level and inflation rate from their normal values. The main features of this analysis can be illustrated from an exercise in which there is an initial "steady state" (produced, say, by a long series of zero DMR values) that is disturbed in year 0 by a positive money shock, say, $DMR = 0.01$. Subsequent money shocks are assumed to be absent (i.e., $DMR = 0$ for year 1 onward) and changes in other "exogenous" variables such as r,[27] MIL, and G/y are also not considered.

The behavior of money growth is assumed to be described by equation (1) and that of output and the price level by the jointly estimated coefficients shown in equation (13). The unemployment rate (which enters in the determination of anticipated values of DM in eq. [1]) is based on an updated form of the equation from my earlier study (Barro 1977a, p. 108).[28] Table 4 indicates the resulting time pattern of estimated values for DM, log (M), U, log (y), Dy (the growth rate of output), log (P), DP (the inflation rate), log (y) + log (P) (nominal GNP), and $Dy + DP$ (the growth rate of nominal GNP)—all expressed as deviations from normal or trend values.

The positive money shock in year 0 produces an expansion that is concentrated in years 0–2 in terms of a higher level of output and a lower rate of unemployment and in year 0 in terms of a higher growth rate of output. The level of output is most of the way back toward normal by year 3 and completely back by year 4. By implication, the growth rate of output is below normal in years 2–4. The unemployment rate is back to its natural value by year 3.

The price level, which is raised slightly above its normal trend in year 0, actually falls below this trend for years 1 and 2. The price level moves above trend in year 3 and strongly above trend in years 4–6. Correspondingly, the inflation rate is above normal in year 0, well below normal in year 1, about normal in year 2, and well above normal in years 3–5. In the present example, the price level remains permanently above trend (corresponding to the permanent shift above trend in the money stock), but the inflation rate returns asymptotically to its normal value.

The last two columns of table 4 indicate the implications of the output and price level paths for the level and growth rate of nominal GNP. Nominal GNP rises strongly along with real GNP in year 0 but declines in years 1–3. Nominal GNP grows from year 4 on along with the increases in the price level.

The simulation illustrates the sense in which a temporary economic high

---

[27] Clearly, endogenous movements of the nominal interest rate could be occurring, although the use of a long-term (Aaa corporate bond) rate makes the assumed constancy of r more plausible in the present example.

[28] The pattern of DMR coefficients in this equation is $-6.5DMR_t - 11.7DMR_{t-1} - 5.5DMR_{t-2}$. The estimated natural unemployment rate for 1976 from this equation is 6.7 percent.

TABLE 4

A Simulated "Phillips Curve"

Year	DMR	DM	Log (M)	U	Log (y)	Dy	Log (P)	DP	Log (y) + Log (P)	Dy + DP
0........	.010	.0100	.0100	−.004	.0102	.0102	.0018	.0018	.0120	.0120
1........	0	.0024	.0124	−.007	.0118	.0016	−.0019	−.0037	.0099	−.0021
2........	0	.0001	.0125	−.003	.0068	−.0050	−.0015	.0004	.0053	−.0046
3........	0	−.0009	.0116	.000	.0025	−.0043	.0012	.0027	.0037	−.0016
4........	0	−.0004	.0112	.000	.000	−.0025	.0049	.0037	.0049	.0012
5........	0	−.0003	.0109	.000	.000	.000	.0071	.0022	.0071	.0022
6........	0	−.0002	.0106	.000	.000	.000	.0083	.0012	.0083	.0012
7........	0	−.0002	.0105	.000	.000	.000	.0091	.0008	.0091	.0008
8........	0	−.0001	.0104	.000	.000	.000	.0096	.0005	.0096	.0005
9........	0	−.0001	.0103	.000	.000	.000	.0098	.0002	.0098	.0002
10........	0	−.0001	.0102	.000	.000	.000	.0099	.0001	.0099	.0001

NOTE.—The table indicates values for each variable relative to normal or trend values for the simulation discussed in Part V of the text. The output and price level responses are based on the jointly estimated coefficients shown in eq. (13). In the case of the price level, the influence of the lagged DMR variables is allowed to extend beyond the DMR_{t-5} value that was included in the empirical estimation.

(principally in years 0–2) produced by an *unanticipated* monetary expansion is associated with a delayed (from year 3 on) temporary increase in the inflation rate and a somewhat further delayed (especially from year 4 on) but permanent increase above trend in the price level.

It is not appropriate to view the type of dynamic interplay between output and prices that is described in table 4 as a menu for a policy trade-off. Some fallacies in this view have been pointed out in Lucas (1972), Sargent and Wallace (1975), Barro (1976), et al. At the risk of repetition, a principal point is that the monetary stimulus assumed in table 4 must be unanticipated, so that perceived changes in systematic policy—for example, shifts in the extent of feedback from the unemployment rate or other variables to the money-growth rate—would not produce the output and unemployment-rate responses that are shown in the simulation.

A different viewpoint, exemplified by Taylor (1975), is that unanticipated monetary changes can be engineered by the monetary authority in a systematic, presumably countercyclical manner.[29] This approach assumes, first, that individuals do not appreciate that the monetary authority is pursuing a policy of systematic deception (which could produce an unstable situation) and, second, that the private sector is in a reactive position vis-à-vis an activist, independent policymaker. Under these two conditions, the private sector is naturally viewed as adapting its expectations gradually (perhaps along Bayesian lines) to shifts in policy. An alternative perspective on policy is that it reflects the views of the private sector, as channeled through the political process, with respect to such basic issues as being on or off the gold standard, whether or not to establish a central monetary authority like the Federal Reserve, whether to pursue a "Full Employment Act" economic policy or a steady money-growth policy, etc. In this view the basic structure of monetary determination is likely to be stable over long periods (as I believe is true as a good approximation in the United States for the post–World War II period and is probably also true for the gold standard period from 1880 to 1914), although the process would be subject to infrequent, discrete changes. Examples of such changes for the United States would seem to be the return to gold in 1879, the establishment of the Federal Reserve in 1914, the changes in the role of gold during World War I and in 1933, and the passage of the Full Employment Act in 1946. It remains to be seen whether the recent heightening of attention to the amount and stability of the money-growth rate will pro-

---

[29] If unanticipated monetary changes can in fact be generated systematically through deceptive policy, it is unclear how such a policy could improve the performance of a well-functioning private economy. Clearly, some type of externality or transaction-cost argument would have to be invoked. The more likely outcome of unpredictable monetary policy is that it would exacerbate the information problems faced by private agents, as discussed in Barro (1976, sec. 3). In any case, a convincing normative theory of deceptive (countercyclical) monetary policy has not yet been developed.

duce another change in basic policy. In any event, if these types of policy changes themselves reflect the workings of the political process or developments in the domestic or international economy, there is no reason to believe that the (average) expectation of changes in policy structure would lag behind the actual changes. Although a period surrounding a discrete change in policy structure might be marked by substantial uncertainty and difference of opinion, it seems just as likely that the average expectation would lead, rather than lag, the actual changes in policy.

VI. Extensions of the Research

The extension of the anticipated/unanticipated money concept to the determination of the price level fills an important gap in my earlier empirical analysis. Although the results on price level determination seem basically favorable to the approach, there are numerous issues that warrant further attention.

The analysis brings out the role of the nominal interest rate in the determination of the price level. The research could be usefully extended to an explanation of the relation of interest rates to monetary and other variables. I am currently working on a theoretical investigation that relates the anticipated/unanticipated money viewpoint to interest-rate determination. This theoretical work will eventually be implemented empirically.

It would be important to extend the results obtained from recent observations in the United States to the longer time-series experience. This extension is both difficult and potentially fruitful, because it requires an explicit treatment of the types of substantial structural shifts in the money growth process (movements on or off the gold standard, establishment of the Federal Reserve, etc.) that were discussed in Part V above. The performance of the approach in this environment will be a major test of the usefulness of the anticipated/unanticipated money concept.

Finally, the present analysis does not detail the mechanism by which unanticipated movements in money affect real variables like output and unemployment. The precise channels are likely to involve unanticipated movements in the price level, which are the focus of theoretical models developed by Lucas (1973), Barro (1976), et al. However, the contemporaneous response of the GNP deflator to monetary shocks that has been isolated in the present empirical study may be too weak to provide the principal link between money and output. An extension of the analysis to additional "price" variables like the nominal wage and the wholesale price index and a consideration of producers' inventories may be important in clarifying the process by which monetary shocks translate into output responses. The analysis of interest rates, as discussed above, may also be important in this context.

References

Barro, Robert J. "Rational Expectations and the Role of Monetary Policy." *J. Monetary Econ.* 2 (January 1976): 1–32.
————. "Unanticipated Money Growth and Unemployment in the United States." *A.E.R.* 67 (March 1977): 101–15. (*a*)
————. "Unanticipated Money, Output, and the Price Level in the United States." Univ. Rochester, July 1977. (*b*)
Darby, Michael R. "The Allocation of Transitory Income among Consumers' Assets." *A.E.R.* 62 (December 1972): 928–41.
Enzler, J.; Johnson, L.; and Paulus, J. "Some Problems of Money Demand." *Brookings Papers Econ. Activity*, no. 1 (1976), pp. 261–80.
Federal Reserve Bulletin. (February 1976 and other issues.)
Feige, Edgar L., and Pearce, Douglas K. "Inflation and Incomes Policy: An Application of Time Series Models." *J. Monetary Econ.* 2 (suppl., *The Economics of Price and Wage Controls*; 1976): 273–302.
Goldfeld, Stephen M. "The Case of the Missing Money." *Brookings Papers Econ. Activity*, no. 3 (1976), pp. 683–730.
Gordon, Robert J. "The Impact of Aggregate Demand on Prices." *Brookings Papers Econ. Activity*, no. 3 (1975), pp. 613–70.
Hamburger, Michael J. "Behavior of the Money Stock: Is There a Puzzle?" *J. Monetary Econ.* 3 (July 1977): 266–88.
Lucas, Robert E., Jr. "Econometric Testing of the Natural Rate Hypothesis." In *The Econometrics of Price Determination Conference, October 30–31, 1972, Washington, D.C.*, edited by O. Eckstein. Washington: Board of Governors of the Federal Reserve System and Soc. Sci. Res. Council, 1972.
————. "Some International Evidence on Output-Inflation Tradeoffs." *A.E.R.* 63 (June 1973): 326–34.
————. "An Equilibrium Model of the Business Cycle." *J.P.E.* 83, no. 6 (December 1975): 1113–44.
Maddala, G. S. *Econometrics.* New York: McGraw-Hill, 1977.
Oi, Walter. "On Measuring the Impact of Wage-Price Controls: A Critical Appraisal." *J. Monetary Econ.* 2 (suppl., *The Economics of Price and Wage Controls*; 1976): 7–64.
Sargent, Thomas J. "The Persistence of Aggregate Employment and the Neutrality of Money." Unpublished manuscript, 1977.
Sargent, Thomas J., and Wallace, Neil. " 'Rational' Expectations, the Optimal Monetary Instrument, and the Optimal Money Supply Rule." *J.P.E.* 83, no. 2 (April 1975): 241–54.
Selden, Richard T. "Money and Inflation: Some International Comparisons." Unpublished manuscript, November 1976.
Taylor, John. "Monetary Policy during a Transition to Rational Expectations." *J.P.E.* 83, no. 5 (October 1975): 1009–21.
U.S. Council of Economic Advisers. *Economic Report of the President.* Washington: Government Printing Office, 1977.
U.S. Department of Commerce, U.S. Bureau of the Census. *Historical Statistics of the United States, Colonial Times to 1970.* Washington: Government Printing Office, 1975.
————. *Statistical Abstract of the U.S.* Washington: Government Printing Office, various issues.

31

Rules Rather than Discretion:
The Inconsistency of Optimal Plans

Finn E. Kydland
Edward C. Prescott

Even if there is an agreed-upon, fixed social objective function and policymakers know the timing and magnitude of the effects of their actions, discretionary policy, namely, the selection of that decision which is best, given the current situation and a correct evaluation of the end-of-period position, does not result in the social objective function being maximized. The reason for this apparent paradox is that economic planning is not a game against nature but, rather, a game against rational economic agents. We conclude that there is *no* way control theory can be made applicable to economic planning when expectations are rational.

I. Introduction

Optimal control theory is a powerful and useful technique for analyzing dynamic systems. At each point in time, the decision selected is best, given the current situation and given that decisions will be similarly selected in the future. Many have proposed its application to dynamic economic planning. The thesis of this essay is that it is not the appropriate tool for economic planning even when there is a well-defined and agreed-upon, fixed social objective function.

We find that a discretionary policy for which policymakers select the

We would like to thank Walter Dolde, Leif Johansen, Robert E. Lucas, Jr., Christopher A. Sims, and Neil Wallace, who all provided comments on an earlier draft. We also would like to acknowledge the support of the Guggenheim Foundation, National Science Foundation, and the Bank of Norway.
[*Journal of Political Economy*, 1977, vol. 85, no. 3]

best action, given the current situation, will not typically result in the social objective function being maximized. Rather, by relying on some policy rules, economic performance can be improved. In effect this is an argument for rules rather than discretion, but, unlike Friedman's (1948) argument, it does not depend upon ignorance of the timing and magnitude of the effects of policy.

The reasons for this nonintuitive result are as follows: optimal control theory is an appropriate planning device for situations in which current outcomes and the movement of the system's state depend only upon current and past policy decisions and upon the current state. But, we argue, this is unlikely to be the case for dynamic economic systems. Current decisions of economic agents depend in part upon their expectations of future policy actions. Only if these expectations were invariant to the future policy plan selected would optimal control theory be appropriate. In situations in which the structure is well understood, agents will surely surmise the way policy will be selected in the future. Changes in the social objective function reflected in, say, a change of administration do have an immediate effect upon agents' expectations of future policies and affect their current decisions. This is inconsistent with the assumptions of optimal control theory. This is not to say that agents can forecast future policies perfectly. All that is needed for our argument is that agents have *some* knowledge of how policymakers' decisions will change as a result of changing economic conditions. For example, agents may expect tax rates to be lowered in recessions and increased in booms.

The paradox also arises in situations in which the underlying economic structure is not well understood, which is surely now the case for aggregate economic analyses. Standard practice is to estimate an econometric model and then, at least informally, to use optimal-control-theory techniques to determine policy. But as Lucas (1976) has argued, since optimal decision rules vary systematically with changes in the structure of series relevant to the decision maker, any change in policy will alter the structure of these rules. Thus changes in policy induce changes in structure, which in turn necessitate reestimation and future changes in policy, and so on. We found for some not implausible structures that this iterative procedure does not converge, and, instead, stabilization efforts have the perverse effect of contributing to economic instability. For most examples, however, it did converge, and the resulting policy was consistent but suboptimal. It was consistent in the sense that at each point in time the policy selected was best, given the current situation. In effect the policymaker is failing to take into account the effect of his policy rule upon the optimal decison rules of the economic agents.

In this paper, we first define consistent policy and explain for the two-period problem why the consistent policy is suboptimal. The implications of the analysis are then considered for patent policy and flood-control problems for which consistent policy procedures are not seriously considered. Then, for the aggregate demand management problem, it is shown that the application of optimal control theory is equally absurd, at least if expectations are rational. Doing what is best, given the current situation, results in an excessive level of inflation, but unemployment is no lower than it would be if inflation (possibly deflation or price stability) were at the socially optimal rate. Consistency for infinite-period recursive economic structures is then considered. In equilibrium, optimizing agents follow rules which specify current decisions as a function of the current state.[1] Methods are developed for computing these equilibrium decision rules for certain specialized structures. The methods are used to evaluate alternative investment-tax-credit policies designed both to stabilize and to yield optimal taxation. Among the policies evaluated is the suboptimal consistent policy. Within the class of feedback policy rules, we found that the optimal one depended upon the initial conditions. Thus it was not optimal to continue with the initial policy in subsequent periods; that is, the optimal policy was inconsistent.

II. Consistent Policy

Let $\pi = (\pi_1, \pi_2, \ldots, \pi_T)$ be a sequence of policies for periods 1 to T (which may be infinite) and $x = (x_1, x_2, \ldots, x_T)$ be the corresponding sequence for economic agents' decisions. An agreed-upon social objective function

$$S(x_1, \ldots, x_T, \pi_1, \ldots, \pi_T) \tag{1}$$

is assumed to exist.[2] Further, agents' decisions in period t depend upon all policy decisions and their past decisions as follows:

$$x_t = X_t(x_1, \ldots, x_{t-1}, \pi_1, \ldots, \pi_T), \qquad t = 1, \ldots, T. \tag{2}$$

In such a framework an optimal policy, if it exists, is that feasible π which maximizes (1) subject to constraints (2). The concept of consistency is less obvious and is defined as follows:

> *Definition:* A policy π is *consistent* if, for each time period t, π_t maximizes (1), taking as given previous decisions, $x_1, \ldots, x_{t-1}$, and that future policy decisions (π_s for $s > t$) are similarly selected.

---

[1] The original objective of this research was to demonstrate the applicability of optimal control methods in a rational-expectations world. We recognized the nonoptimality of the consistent solution obtained by using control-theory techniques, but initially considered this a minor problem. Further thought, in large part motivated by C. A. Sims's criticism of our initial analyses, led us to the radical conclusions of this essay.

[2] Uncertainty is not the central issue of this essay. As with Arrow-Debreu state-preference theory, one need only define the decision elements to be functions contingent upon observables to incorporate uncertainty as is done for the stabilization example in Sec. V.

The inconsistency of the optimal plan is easily demonstrated by a two-period example. For $T = 2$, π_2 is selected so as to maximize

$$S(x_1, x_2, \pi_1, \pi_2), \tag{3}$$

subject to

$$x_1 = X_1(\pi_1, \pi_2)$$

and

$$x_2 = X_2(x_1, \pi_1, \pi_2). \tag{4}$$

For a plan to be consistent, π_2 must maximize (3), given the past decisions π_1, x_1, and constraint (4). Assuming differentiability and an interior solution, then necessarily

$$\frac{\partial S}{\partial x_2} \frac{\partial X_2}{\partial \pi_2} + \frac{\partial S}{\partial \pi_2} = 0.$$

The consistent policy ignores the effects of π_2 upon x_1. For the optimal decision rule, the first-order condition is

$$\frac{\partial S}{\partial x_2} \frac{\partial X_2}{\partial \pi_2} + \frac{\partial S}{\partial \pi_2} + \frac{\partial X_1}{\partial \pi_2} \left[\frac{\partial S}{\partial x_1} + \frac{\partial S}{\partial x_2} \frac{\partial X_2}{\partial x_1} \right] = 0.$$

Only if either the effect of π_2 upon x_1 is zero (i.e., $\partial X_1/\partial \pi_2 = 0$) or the effect of changes in x_1 upon S both directly and indirectly through x_2 is zero (i.e., $[\partial S/\partial x_1 + \partial S/\partial x_2 \, \partial X_2/\partial x_1] = 0$) would the consistent policy be optimal.

Pollak (1968) resolved a planning inconsistency which arose because different generations had different preference orderings by assuming at each stage that the policy selected was best (relative to that generation's preferences), given the policies which will be followed in the future. For the T-period problem, the π_T is determined which, conditional upon previous decisions π_t and x_t, is best:

$$\pi_T = \Pi_T(\pi_1, \ldots, \pi_{T-1}, x_1, \ldots, x_{T-1}).$$

Once the functional relationship Π_T is known, the determination of the best policy rule $\pi_{T-1} = \Pi_{T-1}(\pi_1, \ldots, \pi_{T-2}, x_1, \ldots, x_{T-2})$ can be determined, and in general the consistent policy

$$\pi_t = \Pi_t(\pi_1, \ldots, \pi_{t-1}, x_1, \ldots, x_{t-1})$$

can be determined once future policy rules are known. With such a procedure, the policy decision at each stage is optimal, given the rules for future policy selection.[3] But as the simple example illustrated, this procedure is suboptimal.

Two examples follow:

The issues are obvious in many well-known problems of public policy. For example, suppose the socially desirable outcome is not to have houses built in a particular flood plain but, given that they are there, to take certain costly flood-control measures. If the government's policy were not to build the dams and levees needed for flood protection and agents knew this was the case, even if houses were built there, rational agents would not live in the flood plains. But the rational agent knows that, if he and others build houses there, the government will take the necessary flood-control measures. Consequently, in the absence of a law prohibiting the construction of houses in the flood plain, houses are built there, and the army corps of engineers subsequently builds the dams and levees.

A second example is patent policy. Given that resources have been allocated to inventive activity which resulted in a new product or process, the efficient policy is not to permit patent protection. For this example, few would seriously consider this optimal-control-theory solution as being reasonable. Rather, the question would be posed in terms of the optimal patent life (see, e.g., Nordhaus 1969), which takes into consideration both the incentive for inventive activity provided by patent protection and the loss in consumer surplus that results when someone realizes monopoly rents. In other words, economic theory is used to predict the effects of alternative policy rules, and one with good operating characteristics is selected.

III. The Inflation-Unemployment Example

The suboptimality of the consistent policy is not generally recognized for the aggregate demand management problem. The standard policy prescription is to select that policy which is best, given the current situation. This may seem reasonable, but for the structure considered, which we argue is a plausible abstraction of reality, such policy results in excessive rates of inflation without any reduction in unemployment. The policy of maintaining price stability is preferable.

---

[3] There are some subtle game-theoretic issues which have not been addressed here. Peleg and Yaari (1973) criticized Pollak's solution because sometimes it did not exist and proposed an alternative solution to the noncooperative intergeneration game. As explained by Kydland (1975b), in the language of dynamic games, Pollak used the feedback solution and Peleg and Yaari the open-loop solution. For policy selection, the policymaker is dominant, and for dominant-player games, the open-loop solution is inconsistent (see Kydland 1975a, 1975b for further details). That is why Peleg and Yaari's solution was not considered here.

The attempts of economists to rationalize the apparent trade-off between unemployment and inflation in modern theoretical terms have resulted in models with the following structure: unemployment (employment) is a decreasing (increasing) function of the discrepancy between actual and expected inflation rates. This example assumes such a relationship and that it is linear:

$$u_t = \lambda(x_t^e - x_t) + u^*, \tag{5}$$

where u_t is unemployment in period t, λ a positive constant, x_t the inflation rate, x_t^e the forecasted or expected inflation rate, and u^* the natural rate implied by these theories. As has been recently shown by Phelps and Taylor (1975), one need not rely upon imperfect information across firms about the "generality" of shock or imperfect foresight about the persistence of shock over time to obtain a similar relationship. They obtained one by assuming price rigidities, namely, that prices and wages are set prior to the realization of demand.

The crucial issue is what assumption to make concerning price expectations. The conventional approach is to assume that expectations depend in some mechanical ad hoc way upon past prices. If so, control theory would be an appropriate tool to determine the optimal path of unemployment and inflation. The policy decision in each period would consider both current outcomes and a proper evaluation of the terminal price expectations state variable. Such a treatment of expectations is difficult to justify either on a priori or empirical grounds. A change in administration which reflects a change in the relative costs society assigns to unemployment and inflation will have an immediate effect upon expectations—contrary to the implicit assumption of the proponents of control theory. Moreover, private agents or their agents have as much information about the economic structure as does the policymaker and some information concerning the implicit objective function which rationalizes policy selections. Therefore their forecasts of future policy behavior will be related to actual policy selection. This does not imply that policy is perfectly predicted, but then neither is the behavior of private agents. Just partial predictability of policy is sufficient to invalidate the use of optimal control theory.

For this example, we shall assume that the expectations are rational, so that the mathematical expectation of inflation equals the expected rate:

$$x_t^e = Ex_t.$$

Whether forecasts are rational is still open to debate. In Sargent (1973) the rational-expectations hypothesis is tested and accepted. He also explains why many other tests that rejected the hypothesis are invalid. He does not, however, comment on the Hirsch and Lovell (1969) test

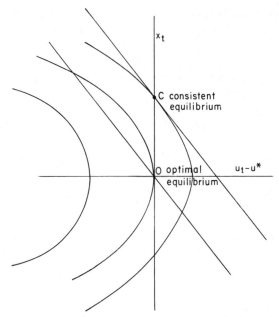

Fig. 1.—Consistent and optimal equilibrium

which used direct measures of expectations and found that forecast errors were systematically related to lagged sales, so we will do so. Responses to this finding are that there may be biases in their measurement of expectations, and these biases are related to lagged sales. This is not implausible, given the subtleness of the expectations concept and the imprecision of survey instruments. Further, even if there were a systematic forecast error in the *past*, now that the Hirsch and Lovell results are part of agents' information sets, future forecast errors should not be subject to such biases.

To complete the model, a theory of policy selection is needed. Here it is assumed that there is some social objective function which rationalizes policy choice:

$$S(x_t, u_t).$$

If the rationalization is not perfect, a random term must be introduced into the function. The consistent policy maximizes this function subject to the Phillips curve constraint (5).

Figure 1 depicts some Phillips curves and indifference curves. From (5) the Phillips curves are straight lines having slope $-\lambda^{-1}$ and intersecting the vertical axis at x_t^e. For a consistent equilibrium, the indifference curve must be tangent to a Phillips curve at a point along the vertical axis— as at point C. Only then are expectations rational and the policy selected best, given the current situation. The indifference curves imply that the socially preferred inflation rate is zero, which seems consistent with the public's preferences. We of course recognize that inflation is a tax on reserves and currency, and a more informed public might prefer some positive or negative inflation rate. If so, x_t need only be interpreted as deviation from the optimal rate. The outcome of a consistent policy selection clearly is not optimal. If the policymakers were compelled to maintain price stability and did not have discretionary powers, the resulting equilibrium would have no higher unemployment than the consistent policy. The optimal equilibrium is point O, which lies on a higher indifference curve than the consistent-equilibrium point C.

It is perhaps worthwhile to relate our analysis to that of Taylor's (1975), in which he found that the optimal monetary policy was random in a rational-expectations world. Similar results would hold for our problem if uncertainty in the social objective function had been introduced. Both for his structure and for ours, the optimal policy is inconsistent, and consequently it is not optimal for the policymaker to continue with his original policy rules.

IV. Consistent Planning for the Infinite Horizon

The method of backward induction cannot be applied to infinite-period problems to determine a consistent policy because, unlike the finite-period problem, there is no final period with which to begin the induction. For recursive structures, however, the concept of consistency can be defined in terms of policy *rules*. Suppose that the economy at time t can be described by a vector of state variables y_t, a vector of policy variables π_t, a vector of decision variables x_t for the economic agents, and a vector of random shocks ε_t which are temporally independent. The movement over time of these variables is given by the system of equations

$$y_{t+1} = F(y_t, \pi_t, x_t, \varepsilon_t).$$

Let the feedback policy rule for future periods be

$$\pi_s = \Pi^f(y_s), \qquad s > t. \tag{6}$$

For certain structures, rational economic agents will in the future follow a rule of the form

$$x_s = d^f(y_s; \Pi^f). \tag{7}$$

It is important to note that changes in policy rule Π^f change the functional form of d^f, a point convincingly made by Lucas (1976) in his critique of current econometric policy-evaluation procedures. The decisions of agents in the current period will have the form

$$x_t = d^c(y_t, \pi_t; \Pi^f).$$

Again, it is important to note that expectations of future policy affect current decisions. For example, the effect of an increase in the investment tax credit will depend upon the expected future levels of the investment tax credit.

If, in addition, the social objective function is of the form

$$\sum_{s=t}^{\infty} \beta_\pi^s q(x_s, y_s, \pi_s), \qquad 0 < \beta_\pi < 1,$$

and the objective is to minimize its expected value, the optimal value for π_t will depend upon both y_t and Π^f, the policy rule which will be used in the future. In other words, the best policy rule for the current period $\Pi^c(y)$ is functionally related to the policy rule used in the future $\Pi^f(y)$, say

$$\Pi^c = g(\Pi^f).$$

A stationary policy rule Π is consistent if it is a fixed point of mapping g, for then it is best to use the same policy rule as the one expected to be used in the future.[4]

Suppose policymakers and agents do not have a clear understanding of the dynamic structure of the economy. Over time, agents will grope for and most likely converge to the equilibrium rules of forms (6) and (7). Policymakers taking the decision rules of agents as given, when evaluating alternative decisions, typically would consider the trade-off of current outcomes relative to the desirability or value of the end-of-period state. Assuming that their valuation of the terminal state is approximately correct, they will be selecting the approximately consistent policy, assuming also that agents have approximately rational expectations. Thus it seems likely that the current practice of selecting that policy which is best, given the current situation, is likely to converge to the consistent but *suboptimal* policy.[5]

It is hard to fault a policymaker acting consistently. The reason that such policies are suboptimal is not due to myopia. The effect of this decision upon the entire future is taken into consideration. Rather, the suboptimality arises because there is no mechanism to induce *future* policymakers to take into consideration the effect of their policy, via the expectations mechanism, upon *current* decisions of agents.

---

[4] This is the solution concept used by Phelps and Pollak (1968) for an infinite-period second-best growth problem when different generations had inconsistent preferences.

[5] Optimal policy refers to the best policy, assuming it exists, within a certain class of policies. Within the class of linear feedback rules $\Pi(y_t)$, we found that the best policy rule depended upon the initial condition. The most general class of decision policies are characterized by a sequence of probability measures indexed by the history $\{\Pi_t(x^t, \pi^t, y^t)\}$, with the superscripted variables denoting all previously observed values of the variables. It was necessary to consider probability distributions because for some games a randomized strategy will be optimal and not dominated by a deterministic one. For games against nature, only deterministic strategies need be considered.

V. The Investment-Tax-Credit Example

In this section an equilibrium framework is developed for evaluating a class of investment-tax-credit policies. The assumed technological structure is similar to the one used by Jorgenson (1963), though increasing costs associated with rapid adjustment in capacity are assumed. A firm uses k_t units of capital and n_t units of labor to produce an output $Ak_t^\alpha n_t^{(1-\alpha)}$. Output price is p_t, and the real wage is assumed to be a constant, say 1. Investment planned in period t and carried out that period and the next, x_t, does not become productive until period $t+2$. The relationship between current productive capital, planned investment, and future productive capital is

$$k_{t+2} = x_t + (1 - \delta)k_{t+1},$$

where δ is the constant physical rate of depreciation. Investment costs associated with x_t, the new investment plans in period t, occur in both period t and period $t+1$. This reflects the fact that time is required to expand capacity, and investment expenditures occur over the entire time interval. The fraction of the investment effort induced by plan x_t in the current period is ϕ, and the fraction induced in the subsequent period is $1 - \phi$. The investment rate in period t is then

$$z_t = \phi x_t + (1 - \phi)x_{t-1}.$$

Following Haavelmo (1960), Eisner and Strotz (1963), Lucas (1967), Gould (1968), and Treadway (1969), we assume that the investment expenditures are an increasing convex function of the rate of capital expansion z_t. In order to insure constant returns to scale in the long run, the function is assumed to have slope equal to the price q of capital goods at $z_t = \delta k_t$. Making the quadratic approximation, the investment expenditures in period t are then

$$i_t = qz_t + \gamma(z_t - \delta k_t)^2,$$

where γ is positive. Observe that i_t depends upon investment plans in both the current and previous periods and that, if x_t is constant over time and sufficient to maintain the capital stock, $i_t = qx_t$.

The gross cash inflow during period t is

$$p_t Ak_t^\alpha n_t^{(1-\alpha)} - p_t n_t - i_t. \tag{8}$$

In period t a tax rate θ is applied to sales less labor costs and depreciation. Letting Ψ be the fraction of the "true" depreciation being tax deductible, the tax bill is then

$$\theta(p_t Ak_t^\alpha n_t^{(1-\alpha)} - p_t n_t - \Psi\delta k_t). \tag{9}$$

Finally, an investment tax credit is offered at the value π_t, so there will be a tax offset of

$$\pi_t z_t. \tag{10}$$

The view is that the adjustment cost term reflects costs internal to the firm and therefore not eligible for the investment tax credit.[6]

The net cash inflow in period t is (8) less (9) plus (10). The objective of the firm is to maximize the expected present value of this net cash inflow stream. Maximizing each period's cash flow over the period's n_t, the objective function to be maximized becomes

$$E \sum_{t=0}^{\infty} \beta^t [(1 - \theta)p_t \alpha \lambda k_t + \theta \Psi \delta k_t - (q - \pi_t)z_t - \gamma(z_t - \delta k_t)^2],$$

where $\lambda = [1/(1 - \alpha)][A(1 - \alpha)]^{1/\alpha}$ is output per unit of capital and β is the discount factor.

The inverse aggregate demand function is assumed to be linear. Letting capital letters denote the aggregates of the corresponding variables for the individual firms, the inverse demand function is of the form

$$p_t = a_t - b\lambda K_t,$$

where b is a positive constant, a_t is a stochastic demand shift parameter, and K_t is the aggregate capital stock for the firms. We assume that a_t is subject to the first-order autoregressive process

$$a_{t+1} = \rho a_t + \varepsilon_t, \qquad -1 < \rho < 1, \tag{11}$$

where the ε_t are positive independent random variables with mean μ and variance σ_ε^2.

For the economy to be in equilibrium, the expected and actual distribution of the random elements must be equal. Here we are assuming rational expectations of Muth (1961) and of Lucas and Prescott (1971). Brock (1972) has characterized such expectations schemes as being self-fulfilling. We are implicitly assuming that the economy is Hicksian in the sense that a single consumer could have the implicit excess demand function. For such economies wealth effects net out, and our equilibrium yields the same allocation as the Arrow-Debreu state preference equilibrium upon extension of their analysis to infinite-dimensional space.

In the Appendix we develop direct methods for computing the competitive equilibrium, given the policy rule.[7] Also discussed in the Appendix is the stability of the equilibrium.

---

[6] We are also implicitly assuming a per unit rather than a percentage tax credit.

[7] If policy does not depend upon agents' decisions, the competitive equilibrium is efficient and therefore maximizes the utility of the economy-wide consumer, a fact exploited in Lucas and Prescott (1971) to characterize the competitive equilibrium. For these examples, policy rules are of the feedback variety and depend upon past decisions of private economic agents. In effect this introduces an externality. Suppose, e.g., that future investment tax credits depend positively upon the magnitude of future capital stocks. If all agents invest less now, future capital stocks will be smaller and, consequently, future investment tax credits larger. Because of this externality, the competitive equilibrium will not in general maximize the utility of the economy-wide consumer, given the policy rule. This is why it was necessary to devise direct methods.

The policymakers are choosing values for π in each time period so as to minimize the value of some social preference function. We use a quadratic approximation of a function which includes the terms likely to carry any weight. The assumed form is

$$E \sum_{t=0}^{\infty} \beta_{\pi}^t [\omega_1(\lambda K_t - g_1)^2 + \omega_2(Z_t - g_2)^2 + \omega_3(\lambda K_t + Z_t - g_3)^2$$
$$+ \omega_4(p_t - p_{t-1})^2 + \omega_5 \pi_t Z_t + \omega_6 \pi_t^2],$$

where each ω_i, $i = 1, \ldots, 6$, indicates the relative weight on each of the components. The terms g_1, g_2, and g_3 are targets for real output of the industry, for real investments, and for the total of the two, respectively. Reasons for including the tax credit in the loss function are that the amount paid may have to be collected elsewhere in the form of taxes and inefficiencies generally caused by such measures.

Our examples assume that a passive investment-tax-credit stabilization policy had been pursued in the past and that the function describing investment behavior was equilibrium, given this passive policy. They also assume that econometricians have estimated the investment relationship [8] and that the policymaker uses control theory to determine which policy rule is optimal under the incorrect assumption that the equilibrium investment function is invariant to the policy rule used. Subsequent to the implementation of this policy rule, the economy moves to the new equilibrium investment function. Econometricians revise their estimate of the investment function, arguing that there has been structural change, and the policymaker uses optimal control to determine a new policy rule. The change in policy induces still another change in the investment function, which in turn induces a change in the policy rule, once the shift in the investment function is recognized. This iterative process, we think, captures the essence of what is actually happening. We observe that econometricians are continually revising their estimates of the structure on the basis of which new policies are devised and are continually surprised to find that the structure has changed.

Our results can be summarized as follows:

Factor shares, the capital output ratio, tax rates, and capital consumption allowances were used to deduce not unreasonable values for parameters of technology and preferences with the exception of ϕ, the distributed lag coefficient of investment, and ρ, the autoregressive parameter of the

---

[8] We recognize that there may be problems involved in estimating the investment function because of perfect multicollinearity between π_t and the other independent variables. However, the model could be modified to permit random fluctuations in the price of capital. For estimation purposes, one would then, instead of using the investment tax credit, use the price of capital which is affected by the tax credit in a predictable way.

aggregate demand relation.[9] Only these parameters and the parameters of the objective function were subject to variation. Space constraints preclude more than a brief summary of the results.[10]

Typically the iterative process of the policy rule change inducing investment function change inducing policy rule change, etc., did converge. Given that it converges, the limiting policy rule is consistent in the sense described in Sections II and IV. In all cases for which it did converge, we searched for and found linear feedback policy rules which were superior to this consistent rule, typically by a substantial amount.

For one example ($\omega_1 = 2$, $\omega_2 = 4$, $\omega_3 = 1$, $\omega_4 = 10$, $\omega_5 = 20$, $\omega_6 = 10$, and $\rho = 0.6$), the application of optimal control initially improved the performance of the economy relative to the assumed objective function. For the first two iterations, the economy was subject to less fluctuation and fluctuated about a preferred point. After the third iteration, however, performance deteriorated, and the consistent policy to which the process converged was decidedly inferior to the passive policy for which the investment tax credit was not varied. The difference in performance corresponded roughly to the variables being 10 percent on average away from their targets.

For another example ($\omega_1 = 1$, $\omega_2 = 2$, $\omega_3 = 1$, $\omega_4 = 10$, $\omega_5 = 3$, $\omega_6 = 20$, and $\rho = -0.6$), the iterative process did not converge. Changes in the policy rule induced ever larger changes in the investment function. The variables fluctuated about their targeted values but fluctuated with increased amplitude with each iteration. This is a very disturbing result, for it indicates that current practice, if continued, could conceivably result in even greater fluctuations than are now being experienced.

There are two lessons we learned from the examples. First, the use of optimal control theory is hazardous and could very well increase economic fluctuations or even make a stable economy unstable. Second, even when it does work reasonably well, it can be improved upon by following some other simple feedback rule.

This is not an argument that economic fluctuations are either desirable or unavoidable. That our economy has experienced periods of reasonable stability is evidence that much of the fluctuation is avoidable. Rather, it is a plea for the use of economic theory to evaluate correctly the performance of a policy rule before it is implemented. We emphasize that

[9] The values used for the fixed parameters were $\delta = 0.1$, $\theta = 0.5$, $A = 1.15$, $\gamma = 0.03$, $\alpha = 0.28$, $b = 0.4$, $\lambda = 0.7$, $q = 1$, $\beta = \beta_\pi = 0.9$, $\phi = 0.3$, and $\sigma_\varepsilon = 0.03$. Given ρ, the parameter μ was chosen so as to give a mean of 2.5 for a_t. For instance, if $\rho = 0.6$, as in the first example, we get $\mu = 1$. In the examples discussed, we used $g_1 = 2.008$, $g_2 = 0.2837$, and $g_3 = 2.292$, which are the stationary levels of the corresponding target variables when the passive policy of $\pi_t = 0$ is used in every period.

[10] More details of the results of the numerical examples can be found in our original working paper, which is available upon request.

optimal control theory can *not* be made applicable to economic planning by taking into consideration the way changes in the policy rule change the behavioral equation of the model when expectations are rational.

VI. Discussion

The analysis has implications in other situations as well. Kydland (1975*a*) has explored the implications for a dynamic oligopoly problem with a dominant firm. Like the policymaker, the dominant firm takes into consideration the reaction of the other agents in selecting its decision. Precisely the same paradox arises.

The analysis also has implications for constitutional law. A majority group, say, the workers, who control the policy might rationally choose to have a constitution which limits their power, say, to expropriate the wealth of the capitalist class. Those with lower discount rates will save more if they know their wealth will not be expropriated in the future, thereby increasing the marginal product and therefore wage and lowering the rental price of capital, at least for most reasonable technological structures.

Still another area is the current energy situation. We suspect that rational agents are not making investments in new sources of oil in the anticipation that price controls will be instituted in the future. Currently there are those who propose to tax away "excessive" profits of the oil companies with the correct argument that this will not affect past decisions. But rational agents anticipate that such expropriations may be made in the future, and this expectation affects their current investment decisions, thereby reducing future supplies.

VII. Summary and Conclusions

We have argued that control theory is not the appropriate tool for dynamic economic planning. It is not the appropriate tool because current decisions of economic agents depend upon expected future policy, and these expectations are not invariant to the plans selected. We have shown that, if in each period the policy decision selected is the one which maximizes the sum of the value of current outcomes and the discounted valuation of the end-of-period state, the policy selected will be consistent but not optimal. This point is demonstrated for an investment-tax-credit policy example, using a rational-expectations equilibrium theory with costs of adjustment and distributed lags for expenditures. In fact, active stabilization effects did, for some distributed lag expenditure schedules, contribute to economic instability and even make a stable economy unstable.

The structures considered are far from a tested theory of economic fluctuations, something which is needed before policy evaluation is undertaken. The implication of this analysis is that, until we have such a theory, active stabilization may very well be dangerous and it is best that it not be attempted. Reliance on policies such as a constant growth in the money supply and constant tax rates constitute a safer course of action.

When we do have the prerequisite understanding of the business cycle, the implication of our analysis is that policymakers should follow rules rather than have discretion. The reason that they should not have discretion is not that they are stupid or evil but, rather, that discretion implies selecting the decision which is best, given the current situation. Such behavior either results in consistent but suboptimal planning or in economic instability.

If we are not to attempt to select policy optimally, how should it be selected? Our answer is, as Lucas (1976) proposed, that economic theory be used to evaluate alternative policy rules and that one with good operating characteristics be selected. In a democratic society, it is probably preferable that selected rules be simple and easily understood, so it is obvious when a policymaker deviates from the policy. There could be institutional arrangements which make it a difficult and time-consuming process to change the policy rules in all but emergency situations. One possible institutional arrangement is for Congress to legislate monetary and fiscal policy rules and these rules to become effective only after a 2-year delay. This would make discretionary policy all but impossible.

Appendix

Let y be the state variables and x the decision variables for the firm. There is a linear relationship between the next period's state variables, y_{t+1}, and the current x_t and y_t:

$$y_{t+1} = f(x_t, y_t). \tag{A1}$$

The movement of economy-wide state variables Y and aggregate (or per firm) decision variables X are described by the same linear function:

$$Y_{t+1} = F(X_t, Y_t). \tag{A2}$$

We also include a vector of autonomous shocks, W, which are subject to a first-order autoregressive process,

$$W_{t+1} = \Omega W_t + \eta_t, \tag{A3}$$

where Ω is a matrix of fixed coefficients and η a random vector with finite variances. In the vector W we may also include other variables on which decisions can depend and which may be common to the firm and the economy as a whole. An example would be the lagged price level of output.

The firm's objective is to maximize

$$E\left[\sum_{t=0}^{T} \beta^t R(x_t, y_t, X_t, Y_t, W_t, \pi_t)\right], \quad 0 < \beta < 1,$$

where π_t is a vector of policy variables assumed to be given by a sequence of linear policy rules,

$$\pi_t = \Pi_t(Y_t, W_t), \quad t = 0, \ldots, T, \tag{A4}$$

which in equilibrium are correctly anticipated by the firm.

The cash-flow function R is quadratic. The decisions x_t are selected sequentially conditional on y_t, X_t, Y_t, and W_t. Let $v_t(y_t, Y_t, W_t)$ be the value of the firm at time t. The v_t functions satisfy the recursive relationship

$$v_t(y_t, Y_t, W_t) = R(x_t, y_t, X_t, Y_t, W_t, \pi_t) + \beta E[v_{t+1}(y_{t+1}, Y_{t+1}, W_{t+1})] \tag{A5}$$

subject to constraints (A1)–(A4) and one additional constraint. To explain this last constraint, note that, since x_t is chosen so as to maximize the valuation at time t, if v_t is quadratic and the right-hand side of (A5) concave in x_t, the x_t which maximizes the right-hand side of (A5), taking as given X_t, Y_t, W_t, and the motion of the economy-wide state variables, will be linearly related to y_t, X_t, Y_t, W_t, and π_t:

$$x_t = d_t(y_t, X_t, Y_t, W_t, \pi_t). \tag{A6}$$

In order for the economy to be in equilibrium, we have to impose the constraint that, when firms behave according to (A6), the aggregate or per firm X_t is indeed X_t. Therefore[11]

$$X_t = d_t(Y_t, X_t, Y_t, W_t, \pi_t),$$

which can be rewritten as

$$X_t = D_t(Y_t, W_t, \pi_t). \tag{A7}$$

As the constraints are all linear and the right-hand side of (A5) quadratic, the function v_t is quadratic, given that v_{t+1} is quadratic. The function v_{T+1} is the null function and therefore trivially quadratic, so by induction all the v_t are quadratic. The equilibrium per firm decision function for each time period t is given by (A7).

If the social objective function is quadratic of the form

$$E\left[\sum_{t=0}^{T} \beta_\pi^t S(X_t, Y_t, W_t, \pi_t)\right], \quad 0 < \beta_\pi < 1,$$

the determination of the consistent policy is straightforward. Let

$$u_t(Y_t, W_t) = E\left[\sum_{i=t}^{T} \beta_\pi^{i-t} S(X_i, Y_i, W_i, \pi_i)\right],$$

given that policy is selected consistently and that the economy is competitive. Thus the function u_t gives the total expected value of the social objective function from period t throughout the rest of the horizon for the consistent policy. By backward induction

$$u_t(Y_t, W_t) = \min_{\pi_t} \{S(X_t, Y_t, W_t, \pi_t) + \beta_\pi E[u_{t+1}(Y_{t+1}, W_{t+1})]\},$$

---

[11] We think of a large corporation as being the aggregate of several small firms. Therefore the effect of an investment-tax-credit policy is proportional to size.

subject to (A2), (A3), and (A7). If u_{t+1} is quadratic, a quadratic function is being minimized subject to linear constraints. Therefore u_t must be quadratic if u_{t+1} is quadratic. As $u_{T+1} = 0$ and is thus trivially quadratic, all the u_t are quadratic by backward induction, and the consistent policy is a linear function of Y and W:

$$\pi_t = \Pi_t(Y_t, W_t).$$

It is perhaps worthwhile to make the connection between the structure just analyzed and the one described in Section V. The state vector is

$$y_t = (k_t, x_{t-1})',$$

and the linear equations governing its movement over time are

$$y_{t+1} = \begin{pmatrix} 1 - \delta & 1 \\ 0 & 0 \end{pmatrix} y_t + \begin{pmatrix} 0 \\ 1 \end{pmatrix} x_t.$$

The equations governing the economy-wide variables are the same. Furthermore,

$$W_{t+1} \equiv a_{t+1} = \rho a_t + \varepsilon_t \equiv \Omega W_t + \eta_t.$$

The revenue function R for the firm is

$$(1 - \theta)\alpha\lambda p_t k_t + \theta\Psi\delta k_t - (q - \pi_t)z_t - \gamma(z_t - \delta k_t)^2,$$

which has the assumed form, given that

$$p_t = a_t - b\lambda K_t$$

and

$$z_t = \phi x_t + (1 - \phi)x_{t-1}.$$

Finally, the social objective function S given by

$$\omega_1(\lambda K_t - g_1) + \omega_2(Z_t - g_2) + \omega_3(\lambda K_t + Z_t - g_3) \\ + \omega_4(p_t - p_{t-1})^2 + \omega_5\pi_t Z_t + \omega_6\pi_t^2$$

also has the quadratic form, given the assumed definitions of the variables.

Computations for the Infinite-Period Problem

Equilibrium decision rules for agents were determined as the limit of first-period decision rules as the life of the economy went to infinity. There is an interesting and as yet unsolved problem as to the uniqueness of the equilibrium.[12] For these examples the equilibrium associated with a stationary policy rule did appear to be unique, for when we used the method of successive approximation in the value space (i.e., the v function in [A5]) the value function and therefore decision rules converged to the same limit for a number of initial approximations. For some unreasonable policy rules and finite T, there were no competitive equilibria.

Consistent solutions were computed in two different ways. The first determined the first-period consistent policy for T-period problems and the limit determined as T went to infinity. The second determined the nth approximation to the consistent-equilibrium investment function X^n, given the nth approximation to the consistent policy rule Π^n, using the methods described above. Optimal control theory was then used to determine the policy Π^{n+1} which would be

---

[12] Standard dynamic programming arguments such as those of Denardo (1967) could not be applied because there was not monotonicity of the mapping in the value space.

optimal if X^n were not to change as a result of the change in Π^n. Given initial linear feedback rule Π^0, sequences of linear rules $\{\Pi^n, X^n\}$ were obtained. When such sequences existed and converged, the limits constituted a consistent policy rule and the corresponding equilibrium investment function. In no case did we ever obtain two different consistent policies for the same structure, though both methods of successive approximations were used and a number of different starting values tried.

Stability of the Competitive Equilibrium

We also checked whether the computed competitive equilibria were stable, as follows: given the expected aggregate investment function (which implies expectations) at stage n,

$$X = G_n(y, W, \pi),$$

and given structural relations (A2) and (A3), one finds the optimal firm investment function

$$x = d_n(y, X, Y, W, \pi),$$

which in the aggregate becomes

$$X = D_n(Y, W, \pi).$$

Now let

$$G_{n+1}(Y, W, \pi) = G_n(Y, W, \pi) + \xi[D_n(Y, W, \pi) - G_n(Y, W, \pi)].$$

For the numerical examples in Section V for which we found competitive equilibria, this process converged for various initial aggregate investment functions G_0 for $\xi = 1$ and of course for smaller positive values of ξ as well.

References

Brock, W. A. "On Models of Expectations That Arise from Maximizing Behavior of Economic Agents over Time." *J. Econ. Theory* 5 (December 1972): 348–76.

Denardo, E. "Contraction Mappings in the Theory Underlying Dynamic Programming." *SIAM Review* 9 (April 1967): 165–77.

Eisner, R., and Strotz, R. "Determinants of Business Investment." In Commission on Money and Credit, *Impacts of Monetary Policy.* Englewood Cliffs, N.J.: Prentice-Hall, 1963.

Friedman, M. "A Monetary and Fiscal Framework for Economic Stabilization." *A.E.R.* 38 (June 1948): 245–64.

Gould, J. P. "Adjustment Costs in the Theory of Investment of the Firm." *Rev. Econ. Studies* 35 (January 1968): 47–55.

Haavelmo, T. *A Study of the Theory of Investment.* Chicago: Univ. Chicago Press, 1960.

Hirsch, A. A., and Lovell, M. C. *Sales Anticipations and Inventory Behavior.* New York: Wiley, 1969.

Jorgenson, D. W. "Capital Theory and Investment Behavior." *A.E.R.* (Proc.) 53 (May 1963): 247–59.

Kydland, F. "Equilibrium Solutions in Dynamic Dominant Player Models." Discussion Paper, Norwegian School of Economics and Business Administration, 1975. (*a*)

——. "Noncooperative and Dominant Player Solutions in Discrete Dynamic Games." *Internat. Econ. Rev.* 16 (June 1975): 321–35. (*b*)

Lucas, R. E., Jr. "Adjustment Costs and the Theory of Supply." *J.P.E.* 75, no. 4, pt. 1 (August 1967): 321–34.

————. "Econometric Policy Evaluation: A Critique." In *The Phillips Curve and Labor Markets*, edited by K. Brunner and A. H. Meltzer. Amsterdam: North-Holland, 1976.

Lucas, R. E., Jr., and Prescott, E. C. "Investment under Uncertainty." *Econometrica* 39 (September 1971): 659–81.

Muth, J. F. "Rational Expectations and the Theory of Price Movements." *Econometrica* 29 (July 1961): 315–35.

Nordhaus, W. D. *Invention Growth and Welfare: A Theoretical Treatment of Technological Change*. Cambridge, Mass.: M.I.T. Press, 1969.

Peleg, B., and Yaari, M. E. "On the Existence of a Consistent Course of Action When Tastes Are Changing." *Rev. Econ. Studies* 40 (July 1973): 391–401.

Phelps, E. S., and Pollak, R. A. "On Second-best National Saving and Game-Equilibrium Growth." *Rev. Econ. Studies* 35 (April 1968): 185–99.

Phelps, E. S., and Taylor, J. B. "Stabilizing Properties of Monetary Policies under Rational Price Expectations." Department of Economics Working Paper no. 75-7607, Columbia Univ., 1975.

Pollak, R. A. "Consistent Planning." *Rev. Econ. Studies* 35 (April 1968): 201–8.

Sargent, T. J. "Rational Expectations, the Real Rate of Interest, and the 'Natural' Rate of Unemployment." *Brookings Papers on Economic Activity*, no. 2 (1973), pp. 429–72.

Taylor, J. B. "Monetary Policy during a Transition to Rational Expectations." *J.P.E.* 83, no. 5 (October 1975): 1009–22.

Treadway, A. B. "On Rational Entrepreneurial Behavior and the Demand for Investment." *Rev. Econ. Studies* 36 (April 1969): 227–39.

32

On the Time Consistency of Optimal Policy in a Monetary Economy

Guillermo A. Calvo

We study the time consistency of optimal monetary policy in a framework akin to the one in Friedman (1969, chap. 1) but we assume away lump sum taxation—all taxes are distortionary. Our major result is that under perfect foresight (as defined in Calvo [1977a] and Sargent and Wallace [1973]) optimal monetary policy is bound to be time inconsistent. The paper is closely related to the previous works of Auernheimer (1974), and Kydland and Prescott (1977).

The central objective of this paper is to discuss the time consistency of Ramsey-Friedman optimal policy (i.e., one that maximizes a sum of instantaneous utilities, where the latter depend on consumption and real monetary balances). The main ingredients of the model are that individuals are *rational*, as defined in Calvo (1977a) and Sargent and Wallace (1973), and that the issuance or absorption of money is socially costly. The last element distinguishes the present analysis from that in Friedman (1969), where it is assumed that the quantity of money can be costlessly controlled by resorting to lump-sum taxation, but it makes our model similar in spirit to the one analyzed in Phelps (1973).

The time-consistency issue is by no means a new one in economics. Strotz (1955–56) appears to be the first one to have raised it in relation to an individual consumer in a paper that inspired several other contributions (see, e.g., Hammond 1976). Loosely speaking, inconsistency arises in those papers because the individual's taste changes over time. More re-

This paper has greatly benefited from comments by Jacob A. Frenkel, Robert E. Lucas, Jr., Edmund S. Phelps, Edward C. Prescott, and a lively discussion of an earlier version of the paper in the Money and Banking Workshop at the University of Chicago. I am especially grateful to Bob Lucas for studying a discrete-time version of the model that helped me better understand the issues. This work was supported by a grant from the National Science Foundation.

[*Econometrica*, 1978, vol. 46, no. 6]

cently, however, Kydland and Prescott (1977) (see also Prescott [1977] for
more examples and a survey of the literature) have discovered a family of
models exhibiting time inconsistency where the source of the problem lies
in the technology (particularly the government's fiscal technology) and
in the assumption that people hold rational expectations. Although they
briefly touch upon a monetary economy, the central results of their remarkable paper are given in a context where money plays no essential role.

In the monetary literature, Auernheimer (1974) appears to be the first
one to have noticed that time inconsistency could arise if the government
attempts to maximize the revenue from money creation.[1] However, the
main thrust of his highly perceptive paper has to do with the determination of optimal policy under constraints (like "honest government" rules)
that precluded the existence of time inconsistency. The latter was further
examined in Calvo (1976, esp. sec. 3) in terms of a slight variation of
Auernheimer's model. Utilizing the new concepts of rationality (perfect
foresight there) that had been recently expounded by Sargent and Wallace
(1973), I was able to show that the policy that maximizes discounted
revenue of money creation was bound to be time inconsistent. However,
two important questions were left unanswered there, namely, (i) does
there exist an optimal policy (time consistent or not), and (ii) is time
inconsistency a direct consequence of a disharmony between the government's and individuals' objectives (as could be the case in Auernheimer
[1974], and it certainly is in Calvo [1976])?

The first question is a rather important one because it could possibly
happen that the very nature of monetary models with rational expectations prevented the existence of an optimal policy, a fact that would obviously make the time inconsistency results devoid of any meaning. The
second question is also of some interest because the results would cease to
be so worrisome and surprising if they simply sprang from the government's attempt to "cheat" the private sector.

In this paper we will give a positive answer to the first question and a
negative one to the second. Existence will be discussed in terms of a
Cagan–Sargent–Wallace (Auernheimer 1974; Cagan 1956; Sargent and
Wallace 1973) monetary model. The latter and the time-inconsistency re-
sults are presented in Section I, while the proof of existence is relegated to
Appendix 1.

On the other hand, the issue pertaining to the second question above is
analyzed in terms of a Sidrauski-type economy, recently studied in a per-
fect-foresight context by Brock (1974) and Calvo (1975). We will show that
time inconsistency of optimal policy is bound to arise even when the government attempts to maximize the welfare of the "representative" individ-

---

[1]In a sense, then, Auernheimer's paper is a forerunner of the literature surveyed by Prescott (1977).

ual (or family). Since the basic difference between this model and that considered by Friedman (1969, chap. 1) is our assumption that lump-sum taxation is not a feasible policy tool, our result also shows that the time consistency of Friedman's optimum quantity of money (OQM) rule is strongly dependent on the availability of that kind of policy. Due to the cumbersome technicalities inherent to this case the proofs are sketched out in Appendix 2.

Section II is devoted to a verbal discussion of the time-inconsistency issue and to a brief elaboration on some possible solutions.

The paper is closed in Section III with a discussion of possible extensions.

I. Model and Results

We will now postulate a very simple model of a monetary economy with perfect foresight which incorporates the central ingredients necessary for generating time inconsistency.

We will assume that the economy produces a homogeneous output c which is entirely consumed. Output is a (twice-continuously differentiable) function of net (real) taxes x satisfying

$$c = f(x), \quad f''(x) < 0 \text{ for all } x, \quad f(0) > 0 \quad \text{and} \quad f'(0) = 0. \quad (1)$$

Thus, output attains its maximum level when taxes are zero, and there exist $\underline{x} < 0$ and $\bar{x} > 0$ such that

$$
\begin{aligned}
f(\underline{x}) &= f(\bar{x}) = 0, \\
f(x) &> 0 \quad \text{for} \quad \underline{x} < x < \bar{x};
\end{aligned}
\quad (2)
$$

hence the relevant domain of f is the closed interval $[\underline{x}, \bar{x}]$. Equation (1) is our (admittedly extremely simplified) way of assuming that the types of taxation policies open to the government are all distortionary—the first crucial ingredient of our story.[2]

The demand for real monetary balances, m^d, is given by

$$\ln m^d = -a\pi^*, \quad a > 0, \quad (3)$$

where π^* denotes the expected rate of inflation. This is, of course, the functional form utilized by Cagan (1956). The more complicated and

---

[2]The assumption that q depends on *net* taxes may be a bit disturbing to the reader. More plausible would be to set $c = \tilde{f}(x_1, x_2)$ where $x_{1,2}$ are gross taxes and subsidies, respectively, and assume $\tilde{f}_i < 0, i = 1,2$. In this model it would be inefficient to have $x_i > 0$ for $i = 1, 2$. Thus if the government is efficient we have, recalling $x \equiv x_1 - x_2$,

$$
\begin{aligned}
c &= \tilde{f}(x, 0) \quad \text{if } x \geq 0, \\
&= \tilde{f}(0, -x) \quad \text{if } x \leq 0,
\end{aligned}
$$

which is essentially what we asserted in (1).

certainly economically more satisfactory case where the demand for money is derived from utility maximization is considered in Appendix 2.

An important concept for our discussion is that of a *perfect foresight path*. Here we will follow the approach pioneered by Sargent and Wallace (1973) (see also Calvo [1977a], according to which a perfect foresight path originated at $t = t_0$ is one along which all markets are cleared, expectations are fulfilled, and, furthermore, the price level is expected to be a positive, continuous,[3] and right-differentiable function of time, from the present to the indefinite future.[4] (In what follows t_0 will sometimes be referred to as the "present time.") Again following Sargent and Wallace (1973), the fulfillment-of-expectations conditions is taken to mean

$$\pi_t^* = \pi_t \quad \text{for all} \quad t \geqslant t_0, \tag{4}$$

where $t = t_0$ is the present time and π_t is the proportional right-hand derivative of p_t (the price level at t), i.e., $\pi_t \equiv \dot{p}_t^+/p_t$, where $\dot{p}_t^+$ is the right-hand derivative of p at t.

The market-clearing condition implies

$$m_t^d = \frac{M_t}{p_t} \equiv m_t, \quad \text{for all} \quad t \geqslant t_0 \tag{5}$$

where M_t is the nominal stock of money at t.[5]

An important characteristic of the above definition of perfect foresight—and one that the reader must firmly keep in mind to avoid being mystified by the ensuing developments—is that it puts no constraint on the *present* price level, i.e., on p_{t_0}, in relation to its past values, i.e., in relation to p_t for $t < t_0$. Thus although we constrained p to be continuous and right-differentiable for all $t \geqslant t_0$, we have imposed no regularity conditions like left-continuity or differentiability at t_0. Consequently, p could "take a jump" at t_0 with respect to its past values. Thus, under perfect foresight, the past behavior of the price level imposes no constraint on its

---

[3]Continuity of the expected price level path can easily be justified when there is an asset like neoclassical capital as an alternative to money, because an anticipated jump in the price level would lead individuals to try to shift away from money into capital or vice versa, a situation that would be inconsistent with market clearing (see Calvo 1977a). In the present context, where there is no capital accumulation, the continuity condition is less compelling. However, if we assume that output is storable, a reasoning like the one given above (and in Calvo 1977a) could again be used to argue that expected price jumps would not be consistent with market clearing. See also note 6.

[4]There is another condition on convergence to a steady state which will be introduced later on in connection with the uniqueness issue (see App. 1).

[5]The money market is the only one for which equilibrium will be required in the present section because it is the only one market for which supply and demand functions are going to be modelled (this is also the case in Calvo [1976] and Sargent and Wallace [1973]). In Appendix 2, however, the equilibrium condition will be imposed on both the money and the output market.

equilibrium future values. See Sargent and Wallace (1973) for a clear and convincing exposition of this principle.

We assume that government debt consists entirely of money, and we will examine paths where government consumption is identically equal to zero (see Sec. III where the implications of relaxing this assumption are briefly discussed). Under these assumptions we must have

$$M_t = M_{t_0} - \int_{t_0}^{t} p_v x_v \, dv, \quad t \geqslant t_0 \quad \text{(government's budget constraint)}.$$

(6)

By (2) it is natural to constrain x_v (all $v \geqslant t_0$) to be in the interval $[\underline{x}, \overline{x}]$. For analytical convenience we will also constrain x_v to be right-continuous and piece-wise continuous on the interval $[t_0, \infty]$. Therefore, since by definition, in a perfect foresight path, p_v is continuous for all $v \geqslant t_0$, it follows from (6) that *in a perfect foresight path originated at $t = t_0$, M_t is continuous and piece-wise differentiable for $t \geqslant t_0$.* The latter coupled with (3)–(5) implies that π_t is continuous for all $t \geqslant t_0$ and, hence, that *in a perfect foresight path originated at $t = t_0$, p_t is continuously differentiable for all $t \geqslant t_0$.*

Since

$$\frac{\dot{M}_t}{p_t} \equiv \dot{m}_t + \pi_t m_t$$

(7)

and, by (3)–(6),

$$\pi_t = -\frac{\ln m_t}{a} \quad \text{(implied by clearing of the money market and self-fulfilling expectations)},$$

(8a)

$$\frac{\dot{M}_t}{p_t} = -x_t \quad \text{(implied by government's budget constraint)},$$

(8b)

we have that in a perfect foresight path originated at $t = t_0$

$$x_t = \frac{m_t \ln m_t}{a} - \dot{m}_t$$

(9)

at all points $t \geqslant t_0$ such that x_t is continuous; thus (9) holds piece-wisely on the interval (t_0, ∞). This, and the previous assumption on x_t, also shows that *along a perfect foresight path originated at $t = t_0$, $\dot{m}_t$ is right-continuous and piece-wise continuous on the interval (t_0, ∞).*

Suppose now that the government's objective function is given by

$$\int_{t_0}^{\infty} [u(c_t) + v(m_t)] e^{-\delta(t - t_0)} \, dt$$

(10)

(if the integral fails to converge, paths are ordered by Weiszäcker's overtaking principle [1965]). This is the type of objective function studied by Friedman (1969, chap. 1) and more recently by Phelps (1973). Separability is assumed in order to simplify the mathematical derivations but it is in no way essential for the central results. We also assume

> $u(c)$ and $v(m)$ are defined on $(0, \infty)$ and twice continuously (11a)
> differentiable and strictly concave;

$$\lim_{c \to 0} u(c) = \lim_{m \to 0} v(m) = -\infty; \tag{11b}$$

$u' > 0$ for all $c > 0$, and there exists $m = m^F$ such that $v'(m^F) = 0.$ (11c)

Assumption (11a) is just a "regularity" condition that will simplify the mathematics; (11b) will serve the purpose of ruling out "corners" (i.e., $c = 0$ or $m = 0$) along intervals of the optimal plan (as defined below). The assumption on u in (11c) is perfectly standard; the assumption on the existence of m^F, on the other hand, could be dispensed with but at the cost of not being able to define an optimum quantity of money (OQM). I decided to keep it given the importance that such a concept has in related issues of monetary theory (see Friedman 1969).

Let us define

$$h(x) = u[f(x)]. \tag{12}$$

By (1), (2), and (11) we have

> $h(x)$ is defined on $(\underline{x}, \overline{x})$, it is twice-continuously differentiable and (13a)
> strictly concave;

$$\lim_{x \to \underline{x}} h(x) = \lim_{x \to \overline{x}} h(x) = -\infty; \tag{13b}$$

$$h'(x) \gtreqless 0 \quad \text{as} \quad x \lesseqgtr 0. \tag{13c}$$

We are now prepared to analyze the problem of maximizing (10) along perfect foresight paths. In view of our previous discussion the latter is equivalent to maximizing (10) subject to (9) and $\underline{x} < x_t < \overline{x}$ for all t. Furthermore, m_{t_0} is free to take any value in the interval $(0, \infty)$—because p_{t_0} is free to take any positive value; m_t, as shown before, is constrained to be continuous on (t_0, ∞), and $\dot{m}_t$ to be piece-wise continuous over the same interval. Taking (9) and (12) into account, the government's problem can therefore be stated as follows:

$$\max_{\{m\}} \int_{t_0}^{\infty} \left[h\left(\frac{m_t \ln m_t}{a} - \dot{m}_t \right) + v(m_t) \right] e^{-\delta(t-t_0)} \, dt \tag{14}$$

subject to

$$0 < m_{t_0},$$ (15a)

m_t *continuous and* $\dot{m}_t$ *right-continuous and piece-wise continuous*
on $[t_0, \infty)$, (15b)

$$\underline{x} < \frac{m_t \ln m_t}{a} - \dot{m}_t < \bar{x} \text{ at all points where } \dot{m} \text{ is defined.}$$ (15c)

Sufficient conditions for existence and uniqueness of a solution are given in the Appendix. In what follows we will take existence and, to simplify the exposition, also uniqueness for granted; the optimal m-path when calculated at t_0 is indicated $m^*(t; t_0)$, $t > t_0$.

The first question that we have to solve is whether the government has enough tools to generate the optimal m-path. Remember that in this model we are letting the price level be determined by "market forces," so the government cannot directly choose the values of m; it can only do so indirectly by operating through people's expectations. We will show in Appendix 1 that $m^*(t; t_0)$ could be generated by announcing the path of M which is *associated* with the optimal plan; the latter is easily calculated because along the optimal plan we should have

$$p_t = \frac{M_t}{m^*(t; t_0)};$$ (16)

thus, recalling (6)

$$M_t = M_{t_0} - \int_{t_0}^{t} \frac{M_v}{m^*(v; t_0)} x_v \, dv.$$ (17)

This formula can be used to calculate the associated M-path given the optimal x-path since, recalling (9), we have

$$x_t = \frac{m^*(t; t_0) \ln m^*(t; t_0)}{a} - \dot{m}^*(t; t_0),$$ (18)

for all t where $\dot{m}^*$ is defined.

We will now turn to the time-inconsistency issue. Formally we will say that there is time inconsistency if for some $\theta > 0$ we have

$$m^*(t; t_0) \neq m^*(t; t_0 + \theta)$$ (19)

for some $t \geqslant t_0 + \theta$. In other words, there is time inconsistency if the optimal value of m at $t > t_0$ when calculated at time t_0 is not optimal from the vantage point of some future time (before t). The implications of time inconsistency for optimal monetary policy will be discussed in the next section.

Since the optimum problem at t_0 is identical to the one faced at $t_0 + \theta$ it is quite clear from (19) that in order to rule out time inconsistency we must have

$$m^*(t; t_0) = \text{some constant};\qquad (20)$$

we will now argue that it is very unlikely that (20) is satisfied. Without loss of generality, we will carry the discussion for the case $t_0 = 0$.

Clearly, an optimal *stationary* policy is equivalent to the Golden Rule for this model and, recalling (14), should therefore maximize

$$h\left(\frac{m \ln m}{a}\right) + v(m).\qquad (21)$$

By (11) and (13) there is an interior solution (i.e., with $0 < m$), the first order condition being

$$h'\left(\frac{m \ln m}{a}\right)\frac{1 + \ln m}{a} + v'(m) = 0.\qquad (22)$$

In order to rule out time inconsistency we must have $m^*(t; 0) \equiv \bar{m}$ where $\bar{m}$ is some m maximizing (21). For if the latter does not hold it is clear that $m^*(t; 0)$ would not be constant as required by (20).

We show in the Appendix that a necessary condition for an optimal policy at $t = 0$ is

$$h'(x_0) = 0\qquad (23)$$

or, by (13c), $x_0 = 0$ (i.e., zero taxes at time zero). For our present discussion it will be enough to prove (23) for m constant optimal policies since, as argued above, those are the only candidates if time consistency is going to prevail.

By (18), if $m_t \equiv \bar{m}$ then

$$x_t = \frac{\bar{m} \ln \bar{m}}{a} = \bar{x} \text{ for all } t.\qquad (24)$$

Suppose, contradicting (23), $h'(\bar{x}) \neq 0$. Consider a new path where

$$m_t = \bar{m} + A\left(1 - \frac{t}{t_1}\right)^2, \quad 0 \leqslant t < t_1,$$
$$= \bar{m}, \; t \geqslant t_1,\qquad (25)$$

for some constant A and time $t_1 > 0$. Thus, for $A > 0$, for example, the new path looks like the one in figure 1.

Furthermore, by (9), its associated x_t satisfies

$$x_t = \frac{m_t \ln m_t}{a} + 2A\frac{t_1 - t}{t_1^2}, \quad 0 \leq t < t_1,$$
$$= \bar{x}, \quad t \geq t_1.\qquad (26)$$

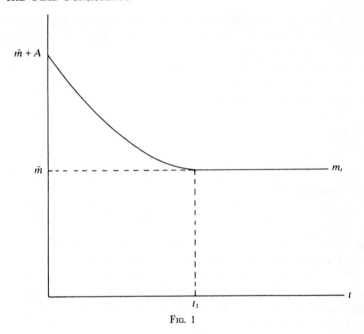

FIG. 1

Hence, recalling (10), the difference between the government's utility at $t = 0$ derived from the new path and the one having $m_t = \bar{m}$ for all t is

$$\int_0^{t_1} \left\{ h\left(\frac{m_t \ln m_t}{a} + 2A\frac{t_1 - t}{t_1^2}\right) + v(m_t) - h(\bar{x}) - v(\bar{m}) \right\} e^{-\delta t}\, dt. \tag{27}$$

Differentiating (27) with respect to A at $A = 0$ we get, recalling (25),

$$\int_0^{t_1} \left\{ \left[h'(\bar{x})\frac{1 + \ln \bar{m}}{a} + v'(\bar{m}) \right]\left(1 - \frac{t}{t_1}\right)^2 + h'(\bar{x})2\frac{t_1 - t}{t_1^2} \right\} e^{-\delta t}\, dt. \tag{28}$$

As t_1 goes to zero the integral of the first term inside the curly brackets in (28) times $e^{-\delta t}$ converges to zero because $[1 - (t/t_1)]$ is a number between zero and one. On the other hand

$$2\frac{h'(\bar{x})}{t_1^2} \int_0^{t_1} (t_1 - t)e^{-\delta t}\, dt \tag{29}$$

is seen to converge to $h'(\bar{x})$ as t_1 tends to zero by twice applying L'Hôpital rule. Hence, for sufficiently small t_1, (29) has the sign of $h'(\bar{x})$ implying, therefore, that (27) can be made positive by setting A sufficiently close to zero and

$$A \gtrless 0 \quad \text{as} \quad h'(\bar{x}) \gtrless 0. \tag{30}$$

In words, we have found that if $h'(\bar{x}) \neq 0$ it *is possible to increase the government's utility by increasing (decreasing) m_0 over m if $h'(\bar{x}) > 0\ (>0)$*, i.e., recalling (13c) if $\bar{x} < 0$ (>0). Consequently, if a Golden Rule path were to be optimal we should have $h'(\bar{x}) = 0$ or, equivalently, $\bar{x} = 0$. This proves (23) for optimal stationary paths.

In view of the above discussion and combining (22) and (23), we can then conclude that a necessary condition for an optimal policy to be time consistent is that $m_t = \bar{m}$ for all t and

$$\bar{x} = 0, \tag{31a}$$

$$v'(\bar{m}) = 0. \tag{31b}$$

But, by (9), (31a) requires $\ln \bar{m} = 0$ and hence $\bar{m} = 1$. Then the fulfillment of (31) is dependent upon

$$v'(1) = 0 \quad \text{(or, recalling [11c], } m^F = 1), \tag{32}$$

a condition that cannot be derived from the assumptions of the model. We can then assert that optimal policies will not generally be time consistent—the exception possibly being when $v'(1) = 0$, i.e., $m^F = 1$.

Equation (31b) has a strong resemblance to the OQM full-liquidity condition, except that in the standard analysis (see Friedman 1969, chap. 1) the government maximizes the utility of the representative individual and here we have made no reference to the latter. With that caveat in mind, however, the value of m satisfying (31b) may still be called the OQM because it gives the satiation level of real monetary balances *as seen by the government*. In these terms, our results can be stated in the following suggestive manner: *A time-consistent optimal policy should generate the OQM and be associated with zero distortionary taxes and/or subsidies at every point in time*. The problem in the present economy arises because the two conditions cannot in general be simultaneously fulfilled: the OQM requires in general imposition of distortionary taxes or subsidies.

To summarize, we have argued (a complete proof is in Appendix 1) that it is optimal to set taxes equal to zero at the beginning of the plan given that taxes (or subsidies) reduce output, and that one is free to choose the initial condition for real monetary balances. The latter is a direct consequence of the important fact that in perfect foresight paths, as here defined, the "present" price level is free to take a jump with respect to its past values, and that this can only happen at the beginning of the plan because the future expected path of prices is constrained to be continuous, or to put it in an economically more meaningful way, because after the future economic policy is announced today our rational individuals will realize that future price jumps will be inconsistent with market clearing (recall note 3) and would, therefore, not expect them. Thus at the start of a plan, the government has, so to say, one degree of freedom that is lost for future points in time (when seen from the present time) due to the nature of perfect foresight expectations. When the future arrives, however, expectations of the (then) present held in the (then) past lose all their relevance. The government can therefore recover the lost degree of freedom when replanning in the future. As a consequence if future plans are going to be consistent with that in the present, optimal taxes should be zero at all points in time, and thus, by (6) nominal money supply should also remain constant over time; but, as shown by (31) and (32), such a plan would be "dominated" by another where taxes are constant over time and different from zero except, perhaps, in the special case where the OQM is attained at a specific value ($= 1$ in our model).[6]

On the other hand, if, contrary to our assumptions, it is possible to resort to lump sum (nondistortionary) taxation (as in Friedman 1969, chap. 1), the optimal policy at t_0 would clearly be to generate the OQM for all $t \geqslant t_0$ because fiscal policy could be arranged in such a way that c is always at its maximum level; hence inconsistency would not arise.

II. Discussion of the Results and of Some Solutions to the Time Inconsistency Dilemma

With perfect foresight—or more generally with rational expectations— expectations are formed on the basis of the structure of the economy and information about the government's intended policy. Thus, at any time t an opportunistic planner could try to deceive people so as to induce them to, for instance, hold the OQM and produce the maximum output at t. But such a strategy is probably worthless after individuals learn the trick because it would not be rational for them to trust what the government says. The time inconsistency of optimal policy disclosed in the previous section also implies that the planner will change the announced policy in the future and, hence, run into the same kind of difficulties indicated above. The reasons, however, are more subtle. The concept of optimality at time t_0 that is defined in Section I requires that the optimal policy at t_0 maximize government's utility under the assumption that *there is no cheating whatsoever*. In fact, from a formal point of view this optimality concept is identical to the one discussed by, for example, Arrow and Kurz (1970, chaps. 5–8), who did not encounter any case of time inconsistency.

Time inconsistency is in our model due to (a) the nature of the demand for money and (b) the fact that its creation implies in general the use of distortionary taxation. The first element enters the picture because the amount of *real* monetary balances that people are willing to hold today, say, depends on the rate of inflation between today and tomorrow, but the balances held tomorrow are not; they are only a function of the rate of

---

[6]Lucas (unpublished notes) has proven essentially the same result in the context of a discrete-time finite-horizon version of this model, which indicates that one could considerably relax the continuity condition discussed in note 3 and still be able to show time inconsistency. Another discrete-time example is given in Calvo (1976).

inflation between tomorrow and the ensuing day. Notice that this would not be so if we were talking of capital instead of money because its (real) quantity at t_0, say, would be determined by decisions taken in the past.[7]

Consequently, continuing with the discrete-time story, from the vantage point of today changes in the expected price level of tomorrow in relation to today's will affect the real stock of money today and will, therefore, have to be taken into account by an optimizing government; when tomorrow arrives, however, those changes are irrelevant. This opens the door for time inconsistency. But it is not sufficient for it, because we have also shown that no time inconsistency would arise (in our model) if it is possible to lump-sum tax or subsidize (this highlights the essentiality of point b above).

Readers familiar with Bellman's *Optimality Principle* (see Arrow and Kurz 1970, chap. 2) would probably not be entirely convinced by the above remarks.[8] For if a planner with unchanging tastes and full information has any reason to depart at time $t_0 + h$, $h > 0$, from a plan that looked optimal at t_0, then it would seem to follow that the plan could not have been optimal at time t_0 either, given that maximizing a sum from t_0 to $+\infty$ requires that the plan also maximizes the sum from $t_0 + h$ to $+\infty$. This is, of course, impeccable reasoning *if the constraints facing the planner at time t_0 are the same as those at time $t_0 + h$*; but such is not the case, because in a world of rational expectations the planner at t_0 who discloses the nature of his plan can only consider surprise-free paths on the interval (t_0, ∞); the same planner at $t_0 + h$ is again constrained to surprise-free plans on $(t_0 + h, \infty)$ but he is in no way bound to choose only among those plans that would be considered surprise-free (or fully anticipated) when coupled with the history from t_0 to $t_0 + h$, and seen from the standpoint of time t_0. Time inconsistency arises because it is optimal to exploit that element of surprise, and the latter, by the very nature of the rationality hypothesis, cannot be planned in advance.

Time inconsistency of optimal policy in a rational world has devastating implications: it devoids the optimum problem studied in Section I of any meaning whatsoever because rational individuals realize that it will be optimal for the government in the future to modify the policies which are optimal from the standpoint of today. As a consequence, any proposal for solving that problem must entail a revision of the government's objectives or a constraint on the set of feasible policies. Here we will discuss the second type of alternative. The former alternative is explored in the next section. However, before getting into that we wish to clarify a question related to point (*ii*) mentioned in the introduction—namely, does time

---

[7]This argument carries over to the case of heterogeneous capital as long as the planner's utility depends on the stock of each one of them, and not on some arbitrary aggregate.

[8]I am very thankful to my friend and colleague Ronald Findlay for extremely helpful discussions on this topic.

inconsistency arise because the government does not maximize the utility of the representative individual?

A negative answer to the question will be given in Appendix 2 where we show that time inconsistency is also generally true in a world of identical and infinitely lived individuals or families with utility function

$$\int_{t_0}^{\infty} [u(c_t) + v(m_t)]e^{-\delta(t-t_0)} \, dt \tag{33}$$

and where the demand for money and consumption at every point in time are derived from utility maximization under perfect foresight. This will leave no doubt, we hope, that time inconsistency is not necessarily a consequence of a disharmony between public and private interests or of the Samuelson-Diamond imperfections that may arise when individuals have a finite life (see Diamond 1965; Samuelson 1958).

Let us now turn to consider some possible solutions to the time-inconsistency dilemma. It is clear that no inconsistency arises if the government optimizes at t_0, say, and abides by the dictates of that policy for all $t \geqslant t_0$; so one possible proposal could be constraining the government to do just that for a given t_0. The determination of t_0, however, does not appear to be a trivial matter. Notice that all planners after t_0 would be forced to non-optimize even when it is, in principle, feasible for them to revise the value of t_0. In a realistic situation, of course, such revisions will breed distrust on the part of the private sector and might, hence, be counterproductive. But since that can only be determined after more is known about the individuals' response to those policy changes, the expedient of setting a fixed date for optimization appears at best to be incomplete.

Auernheimer (1974) suggested setting up a rule by which money supply is adjusted so as to prevent the present price level from jumping with respect to its past values, which obviously solves the time-inconsistency problem. However, although in Auernheimer's model such a rule could possibly be argued to be the one "an honest government" (his words) would like to pursue, its moral appeal is greatly diminished in the present context because, as pointed out above, we encounter time inconsistency even when the government attempts to maximize the welfare of the representative individual, that is to say, in a context where there is not a shade of malevolence or dishonesty at play. Consequently, this suggestion is subject to the same criticisms of the previous criterion since, in the absence of a moral argument, Auernheimer's solution is essentially the same as the latter.

Another solution which is consistent with much of the literature on the maximization of revenue from money creation (see Friedman 1971; Marty 1967) is the Golden Rule—i.e., the maximization of steady-state utility. This solution will certainly work in the simple model of the previous section but it is meaningless in more realistic settings where due to the presence of "state variables" (e.g., different types of durable capital) the economy is simply not at a steady state.

Finally there is the Phelps-Pollak solution to time inconsistency (Phelps and Pollak 1968; Phelps 1975) in which, roughly speaking, the present government maximizes discounted utility taking as given the policies of future governments. However, although time inconsistency is avoided by construction it has the serious drawback that solutions are in general Pareto inefficient, uniqueness cannot be easily ensured,[9] and, rather disturbingly, there may be two solutions where one is strictly Pareto superior to the other (i.e., every government would be better off in one of them compared to the other; see Phelps [1975]).

III. Closing Remarks

1. The model studied in this paper can be enriched and modified in several directions without changing the central time-inconsistency results. This is so, in particular, if we allow for positive government consumption. As a matter of fact, one can show that if the latter enters into the government's objective function, and income affects the demand for money, time inconsistency could arise even when money supply is constrained to be constant over time.

2. In the model of Section I, time consistency would prevail, however, if instead of (10) we postulated the government's utility to be

$$\inf_{t \geqslant t_0} \{u(c_t) + v(m_t)\}. \tag{34}$$

One can easily show that the Golden Rule of the model in Section I maximizes (34) (but also that many other paths do). The objective function given by (34) bears a strong resemblance with the *maximin principle* (see Calvo 1977*b*; Phelps and Pollack 1968; Phelps and Riley 1978; Rawls 1971) and it would be consistent with it if, for instance, $u(c_t) + v(m_t)$ could be thought of as the utility of generation t (or of government t). It remains to be investigated, however, whether an objective function like (34) or, more generally, the maximin principle leads to time consistent optimal policies in more realistic cases.

3. Although our discussion has centered around economies where individuals are rational, the reader should not be led to conclude that these types of difficulties are inherent in only those cases. To be sure, any econ-

---

[9]In the model of Section I, e.g., one can show that every steady state is a Phelps-Pollak solution. However, see Calvo (1976) and Kydland and Prescott (1977) for an example where the solutions are unique. In order to realize how inefficient this type of solution could be, the reader is referred to Calvo (1976) where it is shown that in a context where the government's objective is to maximize the revenue from money creation, Phelps-Pollak solution calls for setting the rate of expansion of the money supply at its maximum *feasible* level.

omy where individuals are sensitive to the announcement of future policies has, in principle, the seeds of time inconsistency. As an example, consider the case where the demand for money is a function of money supply at $t + 1$ ($\equiv \mu_{t+1}$). Assuming, as in Section I, that money issuance (absorption) is distortionary, it is clear that if a monetary policy maximizes (10) it will have $\mu_t = 0$ for $t_0 \leqslant t < t_0 + 1$ since the latter maximizes output in that interval and has no effect on the demand for money (given that the demand for money is a function of μ_{t_0+1}). At $t_0 + 1$ the optimal policy would again call for setting $\mu_t = 0$, for $t_0 + 1 \leqslant t < t_0 + 2$, and so on. Thus, if there is a time-consistent policy it should have $\mu_t \equiv 0$ for all t. But, in the same fashion of Section I, one can show that, except in one exceptional case, the $\mu_t \equiv 0$ policy will be dominated by another one where $\mu_t \equiv$ a nonzero constant.

Appendix 1

By (14), the Hamiltonian of the maximum problem stated in Section I when $t_0 = 0$ is

$$H = h\left(\frac{m_t \ln m_t}{a} - \dot{m}_t\right) + v(m_t) + \lambda_t \dot{m}_t, \quad t \geqslant 0, \tag{A1}$$

where λ is the costate variable of m. (From here on time subscripts will be deleted unless they are strictly necessary.) Maximization of H with respect to $\dot{m}$ yields

$$h'(x) = \lambda; \tag{A2}$$

thus, given (13), (A2) has a unique solution and we can set

$$x = \tilde{x}(\lambda), \quad \tilde{x}'(\lambda) < 0, \quad \tilde{x}(0) = 0. \tag{A3}$$

Let us define

$$\bar{H} = \max\{H : \dot{m} \text{ any number}\}; \tag{A4}$$

then

$$\bar{H} = h[\tilde{x}(\lambda)] + v(m) + \lambda\left[\frac{m \ln m}{a} - \tilde{x}(\lambda)\right] \tag{A5}$$

and hence

$$\frac{\partial^2 \bar{H}}{\partial m^2} = v''(m) + \lambda\frac{1}{am} \tag{A6}$$

which is negative if $\lambda \leqslant 0$. This fact will be instrumental below for proving existence and uniqueness.

Applying the techniques of optimal control (see, e.g., Arrow and Kurz 1970) we get

$$\dot{\lambda} = -v'(m) - \lambda\left[\frac{1 + \ln m}{a} - \delta\right]. \tag{A7}$$

Also, by (9) and (A3),

$$\dot{m} = \frac{m \ln m}{a} - \tilde{x}(\lambda). \tag{A8}$$

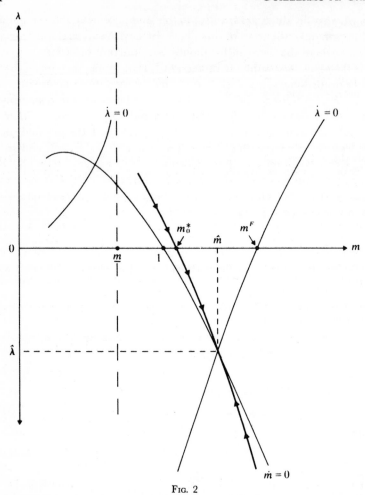

FIG. 2

(A7 and A8) must be satisfied in an optimal solution; their phase diagram is depicted in figure 2 under the assumption that $(1/a) > \delta > 0$ and the OQM m (indicated by m^F) is larger than one. By (8a), the latter is equivalent to saying that the rate of inflation associated with the OQM is negative. Furthermore, we have assumed that there is a steady state like $(\widehat{\lambda}, \widehat{m})$ in the diagram. A sufficient condition for the latter—given all previous assumptions—can be shown to be

$$f\left(\frac{m^F \ln m^F}{a}\right) > 0, \tag{A9}$$

which simply says that it is feasible to generate the OQM.[10] Since m_0 is free to take any nonnegative value and by (11b) $m_0 = 0$ could not be optimal, the follow-

[10]The point m in figure 2 indicates the value of m such that $1 + \ln m = a\delta$; since we made the realistic assumption that $a\delta < 1$ it follows that $m < 1$.

ing transversality condition at the origin must hold:

$$\lambda_0 = 0. \tag{A10}$$

Thus (23) follows immediately from (A2) and (A10).

The path starting at m_0^* in figure 2 and converging to $(\hat{\lambda}, \hat{m})$ satisfies all the above necessary conditions and also

$$\lim_{t \to \infty} m_t \lambda_t e^{-\delta t} = 0. \tag{A11}$$

Hence, since on that path $\lambda_t \leqslant 0$ for all t, then (A6) holds for all t which allows us to apply the sufficiency theorem for optimal controls (see Kamien and Schwartz 1971) for proving that such a path is in fact optimal at $t = 0$. The strict concavity of H with respect to m for $\lambda \leqslant 0$ ensures uniqueness.

Notice that by (A3), (A10), and figure 2, optimal x starts at zero and monotonically approaches $x(\hat{\lambda}) > 0$. Thus along the optimal plan both m and x are monotonically increasing functions of time. Also, by (8a), optimal π starts at $(-\ln m_0^*/a) < 0$ and monotonically decreases toward $(-\ln \hat{m}/a)$. Time inconsistency arises because at any future time the government faces the same maximization problem and will therefore set initial m at the level indicated by m_0^* in figure 2—implying that the plan which is optimal from the standpoint of time zero will cease to be so in the future.

Now suppose that at time 0 the government announces M according to formula (17) employing the optimal path of m and x to generate it. Clearly

$$\frac{\dot{M}_t}{M_t} = -\frac{\ln m^*(t; 0)}{a} + \frac{\dot{m}^*(t; 0)}{m^*(t; 0)}.$$

Hence

$$\frac{1}{a} \int_t^\infty e^{-(s-t)/a} \left\{ \ln M_0 + \int_0^s \left[-\frac{\ln m^*(v; 0)}{a} + \frac{\dot{m}^*(v; 0)}{m^*(v; 0)} \right] dv \right\} ds$$

$$= \frac{1}{a} \int_t^\infty e^{-(s-t)/a} \ln M_s \, ds$$

exists for all $t \geqslant 0$ because m^* converges to $\hat{m}$ (see fig. 2). But the last expression is the natural log of the only perfect foresight path of p generated by the associated M path if all of Sargent and Wallace (1973) and Calvo (1977a) characterizations of perfect foresight paths are adopted (see Sargent and Wallace 1973, eq. 5). Thus the perfect foresight path of p is uniquely determined by announcing the M path associated with the optimal plan. It is now an easy matter to check that given that path of prices, equilibrium m follows the m^* path.

In other words, we have given conditions under which there exists a money supply path such that if it is announced at time zero it maximizes the government's utility (at time zero) in an environment where economic agents hold rational expectations. This policy has the characteristic that taxes are zero at the beginning of the plan and monotonically increase toward $\hat{x} > 0$. Thus distortions are minimized at time zero and increase with time. (The fact that taxes are zero at the beginning of the plan does not follow from the assumption that $\delta > 0$, as one might inadvertently tend to think—it follows instead from the fact that p_0 and thus m_0, is free to jump.) Given that government expenditures are kept equal to zero, the positivity of future taxes implies that money supply is a decreasing function of time.

Appendix 2

Here we will present a sketch of the proof that time inconsistency is bound to arise in a world of identical families with a utility function like (33) and a government whose aim is to maximize the welfare of the representative individual.

A family takes x_t—and hence net output $f(x_t)$—and π_t as exogenously given and maximizes (33) with respect to $m(\cdot)$ and $c(\cdot)$ subject to the budget constraint

$$\dot{m}_t = f(x_t) - c_t - \pi_t m_t, \quad t \geq t_0,$$

an initial stock of real monetary balances. This is a control problem for which the associated Hamiltonian is

$$H = u(c) + v(m) + \gamma[f(x) - c - \pi m]. \tag{A12}$$

Hence, maximization with respect to c yields

$$u'(c) = \gamma \tag{A13}$$

and we must have

$$\dot{\gamma} = -v'(m) + \gamma[\pi + \delta]. \tag{A14}$$

In a perfect foresight path (5) holds and there is equilibrium in the output market. Hence assuming that output cannot be accumulated and making the number of families equal to one, we have,

$$c_t = f(x_t) \quad \text{for all } t, \tag{A15}$$

which, in view of (A13) and (A14) implies (defining $\mu = \dot{M}/M$)

$$u''[f(x)]f'(x)\dot{x}_t = -v'(m) + u'[f(x)]\left[\mu - \frac{\dot{m}}{m} + \delta\right] \tag{A16}$$

or

$$\dot{m} = \frac{m}{u'[f(x)]}\{-v'(m) + u'[f(x)](\mu + \delta) - u''[f(x)]f'(x)\dot{x}\}. \tag{A16}'$$

On the other hand, it is clear that (8b) is equivalent to $x_t = -\mu_t m_t$; thus

$$\dot{x} = -\dot{\mu}m + \mu\dot{m}. \tag{A17}$$

Combining (A16)$'$ and (A17) we then get

$$\dot{m} = \frac{m}{u'[f(x)] - \mu m u''[f(x)]f'(x)}\{-v'(m) + u'[f(x)](\mu + \delta) + u''[f(x)]f'(x)\dot{\mu}m\}; \tag{A18}$$

hence, recalling that $x = -\mu m$, in perfect foresight equilibrium

$$\dot{m} = \Psi(m, \mu, \dot{\mu}) \tag{A19}$$

where Ψ is defined for all $m > 0$, μ and $\dot{\mu}$ except at (m, μ) such that the denominator of the right-hand side of (A18) vanishes; but, since by (8b) the latter is only a function of μm we could constrain functions f and u such that the denominator of (A18) never vanishes and, hence, Ψ is defined for all $m > 0$, μ and $\dot{\mu}$. We assume such is the case in what follows.

The government maximizes (33) subject to (A15) and (A19). In order to apply the techniques of optimal control we will think of m and μ as "state variables" and $\dot{\mu}$ as the "control"; furthermore we are free to choose m_0 and μ_0. The Hamiltonian becomes

$$H = u[f(-\mu m)] + v(m) + \gamma_1 \psi(m, \mu, \dot{\mu}) + \gamma_2 \dot{\mu} \tag{A20}$$

where γ_1 and γ_2 are the costate variables of m and μ, respectively.

For basically the same reasons given in the text, if there is a time-consistent optimal policy at $t = 0$, then there must be one with a constant m. Since the transversality conditions at the origin are

$$\gamma_i(t_0) = 0, \quad i = 1, 2, \tag{A21}$$

one can also argue that there must be a choice of "supporting" costate variables such that

$$\gamma_i(t) = 0 \quad \text{for all } t \text{ and } i = 1, 2. \tag{A22}$$

But the γ_i's must satisfy

$$\dot{\gamma}_1 = u'f'\mu - v' - \gamma_1\psi_m + \gamma_1\delta, \tag{A23a}$$

$$\dot{\gamma}_2 = u'f'm - \gamma_1\psi_\mu + \gamma_2\delta. \tag{A23b}$$

Thus (A22) and (A23) imply $f' = 0$ and $v'(m) = 0$. Hence, as in the example discussed in the text, time consistency requires $x = 0$ (no taxes) and the OQM. But, as before, those two conditions will not hold at the same time in general. So also here optimal policies are time inconsistent in general.

References

Arrow, K. J., and Kurz, M. *Public Investment, the Rate of Return, and Optimal Policy.* Baltimore: Johns Hopkins, 1970.

Auernheimer, L. "The Honest Government Guide to the Revenue from the Creation of Money." *J.P.E.* 82 (1974): 598–606.

Black, F. "Uniqueness of the Price Level in Monetary Growth Models with Rational Expectations." *J. Econ. Theory* 7 (1974): 53–65.

Brock, W. A. "Money and Growth: The Case of Long-Run Perfect Foresight." *Internat. Econ. Rev.* 15 (1974): 750–77.

Cagan, P. "The Monetary Dynamics of Hyperinflation," in *Studies in the Quantity Theory of Money,* edited by M. Friedman. Chicago: Univ. Chicago Press, 1956.

Calvo, G. A. "On Models of Money and Perfect Foresight." Discussion Paper 74-7520, Columbia Univ., November 1975, forthcoming in *Internat. Econ. Rev.*

———. "Optimal Seigniorage from Money Creation: An Analysis in Terms of the Optimum Balance of Payments Deficit Problem." Discussion Paper 75-7618, Columbia Univ., February 1976, forthcoming in *J. Monetary Econ.*

———. "The Stability of Models of Money and Perfect Foresight: A Comment." *Econometrica* 45 (1977): 1737–40. (a)

———. "Optimal Maximin Accumulation with Uncertain Future Technology." *Econometrica* 45 (1977): 317–27. (b)

Diamond, P. A. "National Debt in a Neoclassical Growth Model." *A.E.R.* 55 (1965): 1126–50.

Friedman, M. "Government Revenue from Inflation." *J.P.E.* 79 (1971): 846–56.

———. *The Optimum Quantity of Money and Other Essays.* Chicago: Aldine, 1969.

Hammond, P. J. "Changing Tastes and Coherent Dynamic Choice." *Rev. Econ. Studies* 43 (1976): 159–74.

Kamien, M. I., and Schwartz, N. L. "Sufficient Conditions in Optimal Control Theory." *J. Econ. Theory* 1 (1971): 207–14.

Kydland, F. E., and Prescott, E. C. "Rules Rather than Discretion: The Inconsistency of Optimal Plans." *J.P.E.* 85 (1977): 473–93.

Marty, A. L. "Growth and the Welfare Cost of Inflationary Finance." *J.P.E.* 75 (1967): 71–76.

Phelps, E. S. "Inflation in the Theory of Public Finance." *Swedish J. Econ.* 75 (1973): 67–82.

————. "The Indeterminacy of Game-Equilibrium Growth in the Absence of an Ethic." In *Altruism, Morality and Economic Theory,* edited by E. S. Phelps. New York: Russell Sage Found. 1975.

Phelps, E. S., and Pollak, R. A. "On Second-Best National Saving and Game-Equilibrium Growth." *Rev. Econ. Studies* 35 (1968): 185–99.

Phelps, E. S., and Riley, J. G. "Rawlsian Growth: Dynamic Programming of Capital and Wealth for Intergenerational Justice." *Rev. Econ. Studies* 45 (1978): 103–20.

Prescott, E. C. "Should Control Theory Be Used for Economic Stabilization?" Carnegie-Rochester Conference Series on Public Policy, supplement to the *J. Monetary Econ.* 7 (1977): 13–38.

Rawls, J. *A Theory of Justice.* Cambridge: Harvard Univ. Press, 1971.

Sargent, T. J., and Wallace, N. "The Stability of Models of Money and Perfect Foresight." *Econometrica* 41 (1973): 1043–48.

Samuelson, P. A. "An Exact Consumption-Loan Model in Interest with or without the Social Contrivance of Money." *J.P.E.* 66 (1958): 467–82.

Strotz, R. H. "Myopia and Inconsistency in Dynamic Utility Maximization." *Rev. Econ. Studies* 23 (1955–56): 165–80.

Weizsäcker, C. C. "Existence of Optimal Programs of Capital Accumulation for an Infinite Time Horizon." *Rev. Econ. Studies* 32 (1965): 85–104.

33

Estimation and Control of a Macroeconomic Model with Rational Expectations

John B. Taylor

The paper investigates an econometric method for selecting macroeconomic policy rules when expectations are formed rationally. A simple
econometric model of the U.S. is estimated subject to a set of rational
expectations restrictions using a minimum distance estimation technique. The estimated model is then used to calculate optimal monetary
policy rules to stabilize fluctuations in output and inflation, and to derive a long-run tradeoff between price stability and output stability
which incorporates the rationally formed expectations. The optimal
tradeoff curve is compared with actual U.S. price and output stability
and with the results of a monetary policy rule with a constant growth
rate of the money supply.

A troublesome shortcoming with contemporary methods of quantitative
macroeconomic policy is the failure to take full account of business and
consumer reactions to the policies formulated. This problem is characteristic of both policy simulation and formal optimal control techniques, each
of which is based on reduced form econometric models in which output
and price expectations are formed by fixed coefficient distributed lag
structures. Since these lag structures show no direct relationship to government policy, the mechanisms generating expectations are in general incon-

I am grateful to Phillip Cagan, Guillermo Calvo, Phoebus Dhrymes, Robert Lucas, Ben-
nett McCallum, Edmund Phelps, Edward Prescott, and Kenneth Wallis for useful comments, and to Sung-Hwi Lee for valuable research assistance. An earlier version of this paper,
dated August 1976, was presented at the summer meeting of the Econometric Society in
Ottawa. Note that the empirical results in this version are based on U.S. quarterly data,
while those in the earlier version are based on monthly data. This research has been supported by grants from the Social Science Research Council and the National Science Foundation.

[*Econometrica*, 1979, vol. 47, no. 5]
© 1979 by The Econometric Society

sistent with the expectations of firms and consumers who are aware of this policy.[1]

Finding empirical methods to deal with this problem is potentially important for a number of reasons. The social welfare gains expected from plans which rely on unresponsive expectations are likely to be significantly cut short, and perhaps made perversely negative, as people learn about policy through observation. Proper policy formulation therefore requires either the difficult task of modelling how people learn about unannounced plans,[2] or the apparently easier task of publicly announcing plans, assuming that these will be incorporated in peoples' information sets. Announcement of policy plans may also have a direct stabilization effect by creating an atmosphere in which business and labor can avoid inflationary wage and price decisions: the removal of some uncertainty regarding inflation may reduce the incentives for inflationary bias in wage and price settlements. A number of central banks have already begun to announce their near-term monetary growth plans, and other central banks may soon follow suit. If quantitative macroeconomic policy methods are to be useful in such an environment, they must be able to incorporate the effects of this public announcement. Despite this apparent importance, however, there has been little empirical work on the problem.

The object of this paper is to investigate an empirical method to take account of these expectation effects. The method involves estimating an econometric model in which expectations are rational, and subsequently using this estimated model to calculate optimal monetary control rules. The rational expectations approach constrains the expectation variables to be consistent with the announced policies, and therefore is a way to avoid the problem mentioned above. The model estimated here is highly aggregated, but has the advantage of permitting concentration on the technical problems of estimation and control with rational expectations. Section 1 introduces the basic assumptions of the model and shows how it can be reduced to a policy-invariant form suitable for estimation and control. In Section 2 the model is estimated using U.S. quarterly data from 1953 through 1975, employing a minimum distance estimation technique which takes account of the restrictions imposed by the rational expectations. In Section 3 the estimated model is used to calculate an optimal monetary control rule which incorporates the rational expectations restrictions. The main result of this policy calculation is an empirical efficiency

---

[1]This problem was emphasized in the important critique by Lucas (1976) based on a rational expectations analysis. One reason for the lack of attempts to revise the methodology along the lines suggested by Lucas might be the related (though quite different) critique emphasized by Sargent and Wallace (1975) that monetary policy does not affect output at all with rational expectations. The methodological approach suggested in this paper is relevant because the Sargent-Wallace proposition does not hold in our model.

[2]One approach to modelling how people learn about policy is examined in Taylor (1975).

locus representing the best long-term tradeoff between output stability and inflation stability. This efficiency locus is measured in terms of the fluctuations of output and inflation about target values, and is compared with the actual performance of the U.S. economy during the 1953–75 period and with the performance of a fixed monetary growth rule.

1. The Structure of the Model

The model we shall work with is a very small one in which all consumption and investment demands have been reduced to a single aggregate demand equation, and all wage and price decisions have been reduced to a single aggregate price determination equation. For the purpose of finding policy rules to stabilize output and inflation, such an aggregated model is sufficient if its parameters are policy-invariant; that is, if the model is *structural* in the sense that the parameters can be treated as fixed over the relevant range of potential changes in the policy rule.[3]

Some of the parameters of the model are made structural through the use of rational expectations. For example, the parameters in the expected inflation and expected output equations are structural because these equations are consistent with the overall model and hence with the behavior of policy. If adaptive expectations were used, then the coefficients of expectation would not be policy-invariant. Other parameters of the model are made structural by assumption. For example, the accelerator coefficient in the investment function is assumed to be unaffected by changes in policy over a certain range. Hence, this paper deals explicitly with one common type of parameter variation problem—that caused by ad hoc treatment of expectations—assuming that other types of potential parameter variations are relatively small.[4]

The model is assumed to take the following form:

$$y_t = \beta_1 y_{t-1} + \beta_2 y_{t-2} + \beta_3(m_t - p_t) + \beta_4(m_{t-1} - p_{t-1}) \\ + \beta_5 \widehat{\pi}_t + \beta_6 t + \beta_0 + u_t, \tag{1}$$

$$\pi_t = \pi_{t-1} + \gamma_1 \widehat{y}_t + \gamma_0 + v_t, \tag{2}$$

$$u_t = \eta_t - \theta_1 \varepsilon_{t-1}, \tag{3}$$

$$v_t = \varepsilon_t - \theta_2 \varepsilon_{t-1}, \tag{4}$$

where y_t is the log of real expenditures measured as a deviation from trend, m_t is the log of money balances during period t, p_t is the log of aggregate price level prevailing during period t, π_t is the rate of inflation defined as

[3]Sims (1980) defines structure this way.

[4]It should be emphasized that, without some assumptions, it is impossible to prove whether this model, or another, is structural in the sense used here. See Sargent (1976).

$p_{t+1} - p_t$, $\widehat{\pi}_t$ is the conditional expectation of π_t given information through period $t - 1$, $\widehat{y}_t$ is the conditional expectation of y_t given information through period $t - 1$, and η_t and ε_t are random shocks to the output and inflation equations. The random vector (η_t, ε_t) is assumed to be serially uncorrelated with mean 0 and variance-covariance matrix Ω.

Equation (1) is the aggregate demand equation. As with more elaborate econometric models, it can be derived from conventional IS-LM relationships. Aggregate demand consists of consumption, investment, government, and net foreign demand. Each of these in turn may depend on such variables as current and lagged values of income and money balances, nominal interest rates, and the expected rate of inflation. These equations can be reduced to an IS relationship by aggregating and solving for total aggregate demand as a function of the nominal interest rate, the expected inflation rate, and other variables including lags. On the LM side, the demand for real money balances depends, with a distributed lag, on the nominal interest rate and the level of aggregate demand. Solving this LM equation for the interest rate and substituting into the IS equation results in the aggregate demand function considered here.

For simplicity we assume that all these relationships can be approximated by functions which are log-linear in real balances and aggregate output and linear in the expected rate of inflation. Because the focus of this paper is on stabilization policy we abstract from long-run growth considerations by measuring output as a deviation from trend. The time trend is included in the IS equation to allow for long-run secular trends in the money demand function and in the components of aggregate demand.

The two lagged values of output are sufficient to capture multiplier-accelerator effects, but may also represent other sources of persistence. One theoretical reason for the lagged value of real money balances is the partial adjustment of these balances to changes in interest rates and income. Since this partial adjustment can be represented by a lagged value of real balances in the money demand equation, we would expect that β_4 should be opposite in sign to β_3 and less in absolute value. Alternatively, real balances may have a direct impact on expenditures which operates with a lag. We will assume throughout the analysis which follows that the β coefficients in equation (1) are invariant to changes in the process generating the policy variable.

Equation (2) is the price determination equation. Note that with π_t defined as $p_{t+1} - p_t$, equation (2) implicitly describes how p_{t+1} is set. Since π_t is a function of v_t (as well as predetermined variables), p_{t+1} is a function of variables with subscripts no greater than t. Likewise p_t is a function of variables before t, and is therefore predetermined at time t. This predeterminacy of p_t is important for what follows.

The rationale for equation (2) is that prices and wages (with a markup to prices) are set in advance of the periods during which they apply (as was assumed by Phelps and Taylor [1977]). Moreover these prices and wages are not set by all firms simultaneously, and in addition are maintained (on the basis of long-term profit considerations) for more than one period. Hence, price and wage decisions are staggered and the multiperiod contracts overlap each other. Equation (2) is meant to approximate such an economy. At any point in time some (but not all) firms will be adjusting their wages and prices and must therefore take into account not only the expected tightness in their market (represented by $\widehat{y}_t$ in the aggregate) but also the most recent price and wage decisions of other firms (represented by π_{t-1}). In particular prices will increase more rapidly than π_{t-1} if markets are expected to be tighter than average ($\widehat{y}_t > 0$). A more explicit derivation of such an equation based on a simple two period model of staggered pricing is given in Appendix A, but the important aspect of the equation is that the purpose of the lagged inflation rate is not to represent an expectation of π_t, as it might in an expectations augmented Phillips curve. Rather π_{t-1} represents the fact that price and wage decisions of some firms are given at the time that other firms are setting prices and wages, and consequently the current decisions must be made relative to those predetermined values. In fact, the expectation of π_t involves all variables in the model—not just π_{t-1}.

Equation (2) has an important characteristic which is common to most rational expectations models whether based on sticky or flexible prices: it is perfectly accelerationist. In other words there is no way that output can be raised *permanently* above its secular trend growth rate without *accelerating* rates of inflation. In the long run the Phillips curve is vertical, though in the short run (with π_{t-1} predetermined) it is not. Note that by entering a constant term in equation (2) we allow for the fact that the zero change inflation point ($\Delta\pi_i = 0$) may not occur where output equals its estimated secular trend.

Equations (3) and (4) describe the stochastic structure of the random shocks. The shock to the inflation equation has a first-order moving average form. This specification allows a fraction θ_2 of a given shock to the inflation rate to be transitory with only $1 - \theta_2$ of the shock persisting into the subsequent period. In terms of the staggered pricing model, one economic interpretation of this error structure is that firms realize that there are some nonrecurrent errors or mistakes in the index of other firms' prices; these should not be fully incorporated into their own prices.

The inclusion of two lagged dependent variables in equation (1) leaves very little identifiable serial correlation in the error term u_t. However, the presence of *real* money balances in this equation suggests that the lagged shock from the price equation should be included in the error structure of u_t. A nonrecurrent shock to the price level will change real balances in equation (1) as much as a recurrent shock. But the first type of shock will have a much smaller effect on aggregate demand. Adding the lagged price shock to the equation will allow for this differential effect. Hence, the rationale for equation (3).

For estimation and control this model must be written in a form which does not depend on the unobservable expectations variables $\widehat{\pi}_t$ and $\widehat{y}_t$. Such a form can be obtained by solving for $\widehat{\pi}_t$ and $\widehat{y}_t$ in terms of the predetermined variables at time $t - 1$ (expectations are conditional on period $t - 1$ information), and substituting these solutions into (1) and (2). That the model does not contain expectations of π_{t+i} and y_{t+i} for $i > 0$, is a useful simplification. If these multiperiod expectations did appear in the model, then certain complications involving stability or non-uniqueness questions could arise (see Taylor 1977a, e.g.). Nevertheless, the estimation and control procedures discussed below could be implemented—with suitable modifications—if multiperiod expectations appeared.[5] It should also be emphasized that $\widehat{\pi}_t$ and $\widehat{y}_t$ are expectations of "future variables" since the conditioning date is $t - 1$. The simplification arises from the omission of forward difference equations in the expectations, rather than from the omission of forward expectations.

In order to solve for $\widehat{\pi}_t$ and $\widehat{y}_t$ recall that p_t is predetermined at time t. We will assume that the money supply m_t is also predetermined so that the conditional expectation of m_t given information through period $t - 1$ is equal to m_t itself. This would be the case, for example, if the policy procedure for determining m_t as a function of past observable information was fairly accurately known during the estimation period. (This does not necessarily imply that policy was determined by a constant parameter feedback rule.) We will not directly estimate a policy function for m_t because we can obtain consistent estimates of the structural parameters of (1) and (2) without such estimation. If the policy function is not misspecified, then joint estimation of an m_t equation may increase the efficiency of the estimates. However a misspecified policy function could seriously bias the structural estimates of (1) and (2). In this case a robust estimator seems preferable despite a possible loss in efficiency.

With m_t and p_t predetermined, both these variables can be treated as part of the information set at period $t - 1$. Therefore, taking conditional

[5]The main modification for *estimation* when multiperiod forecasts appear would involve some procedure to generate conditions for solving the forward difference equation in the conditional forecasts. For example, since near-term expectations would depend on longer term expectations of future policy variables, a policy function for the money supply should be specified and estimated. See Sargent (1977). The assumption used in this paper is convenient because it avoids the problem of specifying and estimating a policy function, but similar nonlinear estimation techniques could be used once a policy function was specified. The required modifications for *control* calculations when multiperiod forecasts appear are outlined in note 12 below.

expectations in (1) and (2) using (3) and (4), we have

$$\widehat{y}_t = \beta_1 y_{t-1} + \beta_2 y_{t-2} + \beta_3(m_t - p_t) + \beta_4(m_{t-1} + p_{t-1})$$
$$+ \beta_5\widehat{\pi}_t + \beta_6 t + \beta_0 - \theta_1\varepsilon_{t-1}, \tag{5}$$

$$\widehat{\pi}_t = \pi_{t-1} + \gamma_1\widehat{y}_t + \gamma_0 - \theta_2\varepsilon_{t-1}. \tag{6}$$

Solving these for $\widehat{\pi}_t$ and $\widehat{y}_t$ and substituting these solution values into (1) and (2) gives

$$y_t = a[\beta_1 y_{t-1} + \beta_2 y_{t-2} + \beta_3(m_t - p_t) + \beta_4(m_{t-1} - p_{t-1}) + \beta_5\pi_{t-1}$$
$$+ \beta_6 t + \beta_5\gamma_0 + \beta_0 - (\beta_5\theta_2 + \theta_1)\varepsilon_{t-1}] + \eta_t, \tag{7}$$

$$\pi_t = a[\gamma_1(\beta_1 y_{t-1} + \beta_2 y_{t-2} + \beta_3(m_t - p_t) + \beta_4(m_{t-1} - p_{t-1})) + \pi_{t-1}$$
$$+ \gamma_1\beta_6 t + \gamma_1\beta_0 + \gamma_0 - (\gamma_1\theta_1 + \theta_2)\varepsilon_{t-1}] + \varepsilon_t, \tag{8}$$

where $a = (1 - \beta_5\gamma_1)^{-1}$.

(It should be noted that this solution procedure can be performed using matrix notation by defining the vector $z_t = (y_t, \pi_t)'$ as in Section 3 below and solving for $\widehat{z}_t$. Hence the derivation of the form (7) and (8) can easily be generalized to higher order systems.)

The reduced form equations (7) and (8) are suitable for estimation and optimal policy calculation. The rational expectations assumption has placed restrictions on the coefficients of these two equations: the 16 coefficients of the predetermined variables (including the lagged disturbance) depend on the 11 unknown parameters in the structural model. Hence, the coefficients of this reduced form are policy-invariant since the parameters of the structural model are. This policy-invariance would not hold if $\widehat{\pi}_t$ and $\widehat{y}_t$ were assumed to be generated by adaptive expectations, for then the coefficients of expectation in the adaptive formulas would change when the policy rule changed. This in turn would alter the coefficients of the reduced form for $\widehat{\pi}_t$ and $\widehat{y}_t$.

2. Estimation

Equations (7) and (8) form a vector autoregressive moving-average model with restrictions on the parameters. These restrictions must be satisfied if expectations are to be consistent with the model and with the effects of economic policy. Hence, if the model is to be used for policy purposes— which is our intention here—its parameters should be estimated using a technique which takes account of these restrictions. Constraining the model should also improve the statistical efficiency of the estimators but the more important reason is to insure that expectations will be consistent with economic policy.

In order to estimate (7) and (8) subject to the stated restrictions we use a minimum distance estimator discussed by Malinvaud (1970). Writing the model in vector form we have

$$z_t = A(\alpha)x_t + w_t, \qquad w_t = e_t - \theta e_{t-1}, \tag{9}$$

where

$$z_t = (y_t, \pi_t)',$$

$$x_t = (y_{t-1}, y_{t-2}, m_t - p_t, m_{t-1} - p_{t-1}, \pi_{t-1}, t, 1)',$$

$$e_t = (\eta_t, \varepsilon_t)',$$

$$\alpha = (\beta_0, \beta_1, \beta_2, \beta_3, \beta_4, \beta_5, \beta_6, \gamma_0, \gamma_1),$$

$$A(\alpha) = a \begin{bmatrix} \beta_1 & \beta_2 & \beta_3 & \beta_4 & \beta_5 & \beta_6 & (\beta_5\gamma_0 + \beta_0) \\ \gamma_1\beta_1 & \gamma_1\beta_2 & \gamma_1\beta_3 & \gamma_1\beta_4 & 1 & \gamma_1\beta_6 & (\gamma_1\beta_0 + \gamma_0) \end{bmatrix},$$

$$\theta = a \begin{bmatrix} 0 & \beta_5\theta_2 + \theta_1 \\ 0 & \gamma_1\theta_1 + \theta_2 \end{bmatrix},$$

and where $Ee_t e_t' = \Omega$ and $Ee_t e_s' = 0$ for $t \neq s$. From equations (7) and (8), $a = (1 - \beta_5\gamma_1)^{-1}$.

The minimum distance estimator (MDE) for this model is obtained by minimizing

$$\sum_{t=1}^{T} e_t' S e_t \tag{10}$$

for some positive definite matrix S. As described in more detail in Appendix B, we iterate the MDE by setting S equal to $(\Sigma_{t=1}^{T} \hat{e}_t \hat{e}_t')^{-1}$ where the $\hat{e}_t$ are the estimated residuals from the previous iteration. Briefly, given values of the serial correlation parameters θ_1 and θ_2, a minimum distance gradient algorithm is used to obtain the minimum with respect to the elements of α. A grid search technique is then used to calculate the smallest of these minima with respect to θ_1 and θ_2.

In a recent paper on the econometric implications of rational expectations Wallis (1980) considers the estimation of a reduced form system of equations similar to (9) but without serial correlation, and suggests an algorithm to compute the maximum likelihood estimate subject to the rational expectations constraints. Wallis also investigates another estimation problem: that of estimating the parameters of equations which contain more than one current endogenous variable. This problem would correspond to estimating, for example, the marginal propensity to consume out of current income in our model—a parameter which is implicit in the β-coefficients of equation (1). We do not consider such estimation here because our main concern is with calculating optimal control rules, and the reduced form equations (7) and (8) are suitable for this purpose since the parameters are policy-invariant.

The model was estimated using aggregate U.S. quarterly data over the period from 1953:I through 1975:IV. The particular series used for y_t, m_t, and p_t are the deviations of the log of real GNP from the log of potential GNP, the log of M_1 and the log of the GNP deflator, respectively (all seasonally adjusted). The potential GNP series is the recently revised estimate of the Council of Economic Advisers and the other series are taken from the NBER data base. They incorporate the 1976 NIPA revisions.

The parameter estimates and an estimate of the variance-covariance matrix[6] of these estimates are reported in table 1. The estimates of β_1 and

TABLE 1

MINIMUM DISTANCE ESTIMATES OF THE MODEL 1953I–1975IV

Output Equation:
$$y_t = 1.167 y_{t-1} - .324 y_{t-2} + .578(m_t - p_t) - .484(m_{t-1} - p_{t-1}) - .447\widehat{\pi}_t + .0000843t + .0720 + u_t,$$
$$(13.3) \quad\quad (3.6) \quad\quad (3.3) \quad\quad\quad (2.5) \quad\quad\quad\quad (1.4) \quad\quad (1.1) \quad\quad\quad (2.1)$$
$$u_t = \eta_t + .38\varepsilon_{t-1}, \quad \widehat{\omega}_\eta = .007916.$$

Price Equation:
$$\pi_t = \pi_{t-1} + .0180\widehat{y}_t + .000515 + v_t,$$
$$(3.1) \quad\quad\quad (3.0)$$
$$v_t = \varepsilon_t - .67\varepsilon_{t-1}, \quad \widehat{\omega}_\varepsilon = .003661.$$

Autocorrelations and Cross Correlations of Estimated Residuals: *

s	0	1	2	3	4	5	6	7	8
$\rho(\varepsilon_t, \varepsilon_{t-s})$	1.000	−.020	−.023	.077	.038	−.025	.100	.145	−.136
$\rho(\varepsilon_t, \eta_{t-s})$	0.012	−.025	−.016	−.009	.050	.071	−.061	.055	.101
$\rho(\eta_t, \varepsilon_{t-s})$	0.012	−.139	−.070	−.147	−.125	−.054	−.082	.016	−.139
$\rho(\eta_t, \eta_{t-s})$	1.000	−.002	.034	.115	−.031	−.127	−.031	−.125	−.075

Variance-Covariance Matrix of Estimated Coefficients:†

β_1	β_2	β_3	β_4	β_5	β_6	β_0	γ_1	γ_0
.77(2)	−.68(2)	−.39(2)	.31(2)	−.10(2)	.16(5)	.59(3)	.41(5)	.15(6)
	.81(2)	.54(2)	−.61(2)	.42(2)	.38(6)	.51(3)	.43(4)	.71(6)
		.31(1)	−.33(1)	.39(1)	−.19(5)	.20(2)	.17(4)	.31(6)
			.38(1)	−.47(1)	−.58(6)	−.36(2)	−.11(4)	−.25(6)
				.96(1)	−.32(5)	−.56(2)	.31(4)	.76(6)
					.61(8)	.18(5)	−.10(7)	−.26(10)
						.12(2)	−.39(5)	−.58(8)
							.34(4)	.65(6)
								.29(7)

NOTE.—The symbols are defined in the text. Absolute asymptotic t-ratios are printed below the estimated coefficients. The estimated standard errors of the equations are denoted by $\widehat{\omega}_\eta$ and $\widehat{\omega}_\varepsilon$.
*The correlations involving lags of s periods are calculated from the estimated residuals over the sample period 1953III + s through 1975IV.
†The numbers in parentheses represent the negative power of 10. Also see note 5 in the text concerning the interpretation of this variance-covariance matrix.

β_2 indicate that the aggregate output function is stable for fixed values of the other explanatory variables. Writing the terms $1.17y_{t-1} - .32y_{t-2}$ as $.85y_{t-1} + .32(y_{t-1} - y_{t-2})$ shows the magnitude of the "acceleration com-

[6] The estimated variance-covariance matrix of $\widehat{\alpha}$ is computed from the derivatives of (10) with respect to the elements of $\underline{\alpha}$. A better estimate of the variance-covariance matrix would take into account the possible correlation between these estimates and the estimates of θ_1 and θ_2, but such an estimate is not easily obtainable with the estimation routines used here. The estimated variance-covariance matrix reported here is conditional on $(\widehat{\theta}_1, \widehat{\theta}_2)$ and is likely to understate the standard errors.

ponent" which is added to the first-order autoregression. The estimated coefficients of each of the real balance terms are significantly different from zero, as is their sum $\beta_3 + \beta_4$. The coefficient of β_4 is negative with absolute value less than β_3, which is consistent with a partial adjustment hypothesis on the money demand equation as discussed in Section 1. The coefficient of the expected inflation rate is negative but not very significant. This sign is opposite to what one would expect on intertemporal substitution grounds—a higher price of future goods relative to current goods should stimulate expenditures. One explanation for the negative sign is that the income effect of a higher expected future price level dominates the substitution effect. Another is that higher expected inflation creates uncertainty which depresses expenditures.[7]

The coefficient of the excess aggregate demand variable in the inflation equation has a positive sign which is in accord with the basic assumption of the model: excess aggregate demand increases inflation. The intercept term in the equation is positive and significantly different from zero which indicates that inflation will be increasing when the economy is operating at the current estimate of potential GNP. The nonaccelerating inflation point occurs at a GNP gap of about 2.9 percent (i.e., $\Delta \pi_t = 0$ when $y_t = -.029$).

The estimated coefficient of .0180 in the price equation indicates that inflation will be reduced by .29 percentage points (at annual rates) for each year that GNP is 1 percent below the nonaccelerating inflation point (.018 $\times$ 4 $\times$ 4 = .288). Using an Okun's law multiplier of 3, this translates into a .9 percentage point drop in inflation for each year that the unemployment rate is 1 percentage point above the nonaccelerating inflation rate. For example, in 1975 the GNP gap averaged about 8.7 percent, or 5.8 percent above the nonaccelerating inflation value. According to the estimate in table 1, this had the effect of reducing the rate of inflation by about 1.7 percentage points during the year.[8]

[7]The optimal control rules reported below do not appear to attempt to "exploit" the presence of the expected inflation rate in the IS equation, unless social preferences place only a very small weight on inflation fluctuations. In other words the estimated policy rules are likely to be robust to errors in estimating β_5. On the other hand, the policy rules are very sensitive to γ_1, and the policy problem would have little meaning if $\hat{\gamma}_1$ were the wrong sign. Such robustness considerations are useful for determining how appropriate optimal control techniques are when parameters are subject to estimation errors.

[8]As a general test of the specification of the model and the constraints imposed by the rational expectations, we also estimated the reduced form equation (9) over the same sample period without constraints. An approximate test of the model can then be obtained from the constrained and unconstrained estimates of the variance-covariance matrix Ω of the residuals ϵ_t. Under the assumption that our iterated estimate of Ω (that is, the iteration of S described in the text) converges to the maximum likelihood estimate under normality (conditional on the initial value of the disturbances) the statistic $T[\log |\hat{\Omega}| - \log |\hat{\Omega}_u|]$ has an asymptotic χ^2 distribution with degrees of freedom equal to the number of constraints (5 in this case), where $\hat{\Omega}_u$ is the unconstrained estimate and $\hat{\Omega}$ is the estimate reported in table 1. The value of this statistic is 12.8 which has a marginal significance level of 2.5 percent. Hence, if one takes the specification of the model as a maintained hypothesis, then the constraints imposed by the rational expectations are not strongly rejected by the data.

With regard to the error structure reported in table 1, the first-order moving average parameter θ_2 indicates that on average 67 percent of any shock to the inflation equation is temporary, disappearing in the following period. Further, the negative sign of θ_1 implies that nominal balances do not fully adjust to every shock in the price level. This vector moving average error formulation leaves little serial correlation, as is indicated by the estimates of the autocorrelation and cross-correlation functions reported in table 1. (Note, however, that the standard errors of these correlations are likely to be somewhat less under the null hypothesis of no correlation, than they would be if calculated from the unobservable ε_t and η_t rather than from the estimated $\hat{\varepsilon}_t$ and $\hat{\eta}_t$.) Finally, there is very little contemporaneous correlation between ε_t and η_t.

3. Determination of the Optimal Policy Rules

Because the parameters of equations (7) and (8) are invariant to the mechanism generating the money supply and because the level of money balances appears explicitly, these equations are suitable for calculating monetary feedback rules using optimal control techniques. In order to obtain empirical specifications for such feedback rules we will treat the estimated values of the parameters of (7) and (8) as equal to their true values. This certainty equivalence approach does not deal explicitly with the joint aspects of estimation and control, but has been found to give good results, at least for large sample sizes,[9] and is frequently used in econometric applications of optimal control theory.

The role of monetary policy in this model is to reduce the fluctuations of real output and inflation about average target levels. A logical target for output is the nonaccelerating inflation level of output given by the estimated values of equation (2). Attempts to achieve an average output level higher than this value ($y_t = -.029$) will result in constantly accelerating rates of inflation and would not therefore be consistent with any reasonable objective for inflation. Determining a target level for inflation is more troublesome, however, and would involve a welfare analysis which considers the benefits and costs of alternative average levels of inflation. In order to focus on the stabilization problem we will assume that such an analysis has been completed and that the optimal target rate of inflation is therefore given.

Let y^* and π^* represent these target levels for output and inflation. A loss function which measures the weighted cost of fluctuation about these target levels is given at any point in time by

$$\lambda(y_t - y^*)^2 + (1 - \lambda)(\pi_t - \pi^*)^2 \tag{11}$$

[9] See Taylor (1974) for an analysis of the large sample results in a simple regression model. In using such an argument for the model considered here, we are implicitly assuming that these results can be generalized, though no formal proof is yet available.

where $0 \leqslant \lambda \leqslant 1$. We will focus primarily on finding monetary feedback rules to minimize the expected value of this loss function for the steady state distribution of y_t and π_t. This is equivalent to finding a feedback rule to minimize the expected value of an undiscounted sum of such losses over an infinite time horizon.[10]

In order to describe the optimization procedure we introduce a matrix notation which summarizes the autoregressive and the moving average dynamics as well as the impact of the money supply on these dynamics.[11] Let d_t be the deviation of the log of real money balances from some trend; that is

$$d_t = m_t - p_t - \delta_1 t - \delta_0. \tag{12}$$

Then, by replacing $m_t - p_t$ with d_t in (7) and (8), these equations can be centered on y^* and π^*, and the constant and time trends can be omitted. That is, (7) and (8) can be written as

$$Y_t = BY_{t-1} + cd_t + r_t \tag{13}$$

where

$$Y_t = (y_t, y_{t-1}, d_t, \pi_t, \varepsilon_t)',$$

$$r_t = (\eta_t, 0, 0, \varepsilon_t, \varepsilon_t)',$$

$$c = a(\beta_3, 0, a^{-1}, \gamma_1\beta_3, 0)',$$

$$B = a \begin{bmatrix} \beta_1 & \beta_2 & \beta_4 & \beta_5 & (\beta_5\theta_2 + \theta_1) \\ a^{-1} & 0 & 0 & 0 & 0 \\ 0 & 0 & 0 & 0 & 0 \\ \gamma_1\beta_1 & \gamma_1\beta_2 & \gamma_1\beta_2 & 1 & (\gamma_1\theta_1 + \theta_2) \\ 0 & 0 & 0 & 0 & 0 \end{bmatrix},$$

and where y_t and π_t now represent *deviations* from y^* and π^*. In terms of this notation the loss function can be written as

$$Y_t' \Lambda Y_t \tag{14}$$

where Λ is a square weighting matrix with the first diagonal element equal to λ, the fourth diagonal element equal to $(1 - \lambda)$, and the remaining elements equal to zero.

With the price level p_t predetermined, the real money balance term d_t can be set at any desired level by the monetary authorities. Consequently d_t can serve as a control variable, and the optimal control problem is to find a feedback rule for d_t to minimize the expected value of the loss

---

[10]Such an undiscounted sum can be normalized so that it converges using a stochastic version of the Ramsey deviation from bliss approach.

[11]The procedure used here for dealing with moving average disturbances in control problems by adding these disturbances to the state vector was suggested by Pagan (1975).

function (14) subject to the stochastic dynamics in (13). Hence, the model is now in a form to which existing optimal control procedures can be applied directly (see Chow 1975). We will consider feedback rules of the form

$$d_t = g_1 y_{t-1} + g_2 y_{t-2} + g_3 d_{t-1} + g_4 \pi_{t-1} + g_5 \varepsilon_{t-1}$$
$$= g Y_{t-1}. \tag{15}$$

Thus, real balances are set according to the most recent observation on the state vector Y_{t-1}. Note that although real balances are predetermined, they are clearly not exogenous. The actual stochastic behavior of real balances will depend on the interaction of the policy rule with the structural distributions of output and prices.

Using optimal control techniques (see Chow 1975, p. 170), the value of the vector g which minimizes the expected value of (14) in the steady state is given by

$$g = -(c'Hc)^{-1}c'HB \tag{16}$$

where the matrix H is the solution of the equations

$$H = \Lambda + (B + cg)'H(B + cg). \tag{17}$$

Given the estimated values of the parameters in B and c, we can determine the matrix H and the feedback vector g for any value of λ. The matrix H can be calculated iteratively by computing successive approximations $H_{i+1} = \Lambda + D'H_i D$ where $D = (B + cg)$, starting from some initial approximation H_0 (see Anderson 1971, p. 182). The matrix Λ is a good initial value for this iterative procedure.[12]

Before reporting the results of the optimal control calculation, some discussion of recent research by Calvo (1978), Kydland and Prescott (1977), and Prescott (1977) on the problem of time inconsistency is in order. This research has shown that if expectations are rational, then conventional optimal control techniques may be inappropriate because policymakers will have incentive to change their original plan at a later date, when desired economic behavior—partially motivated by anticipations of the original plan—has been achieved. Given this potential inconsistency of optimal policies, an alternative approach would be to forgo optimal poli-

---

[12] A modification of this procedure to deal with a model in which $\widehat{y}_{t+i}$ and $\widehat{\pi}_{t+i}$ for $i > 0$ appear can be briefly described as follows: By definition, the policy problem described here minimizes $E \operatorname{tr} \Lambda \Sigma$ subject to the steady state constraint $\Sigma = V + G'\Sigma G$ where $G \equiv (B + cg)$ is the matrix of lag coefficients in $Y_t = GY_{t-1} + r_t$. Note that the matrix G is a linear function of g; hence (16) is analogous to "generalized linear least squares." If $\widehat{y}_{t+i}$ and $\widehat{\pi}_{t+i}$ for $i > 0$ appeared in (1) and (2), then, given a policy rule of the form (15) and certain terminal conditions, the reduced form of the system can be shown to be of the same form $Y_t = GY_{t-1} + r_t$ but with the matrix G a *nonlinear* function of the elements of g. Hence, the computation of steady state policy involves the same type of minimization problem as that posed above. However, the nonlinearity of G would involve a more complex computation problem analogous to "generalized nonlinear least squares."

cies, and design policies which are consistent. Such consistent policies are analogous to noncooperative solutions in game theory, and in general are suboptimal. In this paper only optimal policies are considered, the hypothesis being that policymakers—with concern about the long-run system effects of policy—will not change plans in midstream. In other words we assume that the cooperative solution will be maintained, either because policymakers operate under an incentive system which generates such behavior or because such behavior is legally enforced.[13] Our use of an infinite time horizon with no discounting is in keeping with such an assumption. In any case if such an assumption is made, then the optimal control techniques used here are appropriate.

The values of the feedback coefficients for the optimal monetary rules corresponding to several values of λ are given in table 2. The optimal

TABLE 2

OPTIMAL POLICY REACTION FUNCTIONS AND RESULTING OUTPUT-INFLATION VARIATION

Weight on Output Fluctuations (λ)	Reaction Coefficients		Optimal Standard Deviation of Output (σ_y) (%)	Optimal Standard Deviation of Inflation (σ_π) (%)
	π_{t-1}	ε_{t-1}		
.01	−15.11	9.49	2.14	1.64
.10	−4.32	2.24	1.35	2.04
.20	−2.65	1.11	1.19	2.28
.50	−0.86	−0.09	1.01	2.88
.70	−0.17	−0.55	0.93	3.32
.90	0.29	−0.86	0.85	3.96

NOTE.—Reaction of monetary policy to y_{t-1}, y_{t-2}, and d_{t-1} is identical for all values of λ when there is no cost of control. The coefficients of these variables are −2.02, .56, and .84, respectively. Standard deviation of inflation is given at an annual rate. The reaction coefficients and the standard deviation pairs are computed using the estimated coefficients in table 1 and employing an optimal control technique described in the text.

reactions of monetary policy to the lagged values of output and the lagged value of real balances are identical for all values of λ. In particular $g_1 = -2.02$, $g_2 = .56$, and $g_3 = .84$ for all λ. Hence, the only difference between feedback rules which are inflation-regarding (small λ) and those which are output-regarding (large λ), is in their reaction to lagged inflation and to the previous price shock (g_4 and g_5). Several optimal values for

[13]For a further discussion of these issues, see the comments by Taylor (1977b) on the paper by Prescott (1977). An important practical issue is whether such incentives do exist as part of the political system. It is illustrative to examine the potential for a policy shift in the model of this paper. According to equation (2) the rate of inflation will be reduced if output is *expected* to be below "full employment" output. According to (5) and (6) such a planned recession will be expected by the public if the monetary authorities announce a sufficiently low value of m_t in their plan. Having achieved an expected recession and a corresponding moderation of inflation, the authorities could then fool the public by changing their plan and setting a higher value of m_t to guarantee full employment according to (1). Note that actual m_t appears in (1), while expected m_t appears in (2). The optimization techniques presented in this paper assume that such intentional policy shifts do not occur.

g_4 and g_5 are listed in the second and third columns of table 2 for values of λ ranging from .01 to .90.

When λ is small the optimal policy reacts to increases in inflation above the target level by sharply reducing the growth rate of real balances. However, this deflationary response is softened to the extent that the rise in inflation is expected to be nonrecurrent, as represented by the offsetting positive coefficient of ε_{t-1}. As λ is increased, indicating less concern about fluctuations in inflation, these reaction coefficients move toward zero; in other words monetary policy is more accommodating to changes in the inflation rate. (When λ gets very large the coefficient of π_{t-1} becomes positive, but remains small; policy then attempts to offset the influence of the expected inflation rate in equation (1) in order to stabilize output. Choice of a policy in this range would be very unlikely, however, because of the extraordinarily large fluctuations in inflation; when $\lambda = 1$ the variance of inflation is infinite.)

That the optimal response of policy to lagged values of output and real balances is identical, regardless of the relative concerns about inflation and output, is an important characteristic of the model. The economic reason for the result is that fluctuations in output directly increase fluctuations in inflation through the influence of aggregate demand on prices. In other words policy will reduce the variability of *both* output and inflation by reducing the "own-persistence" of business cycle fluctuations; that is, by offsetting the influence of y_{t-1} and y_{t-2} on y_t. For example, if the inflation rate is currently on target and the economy begins to fall into a recession, then the optimal policy is to stimulate the economy back to full employment as quickly as possible. But, if the inflation rate is above target, then the optimal policy (assuming that the weight on inflation fluctuations is positive) calls for a slower return to full employment. These implications of the optimal control calculation are not inconsistent with many current theories of macroeconomic policy, though these are not usually stated in terms of the variability of output and inflation.

It should be noted that these policy rules do not display instrument instability. Including the policy instrument in the loss function reduces the reaction coefficients, but also detracts from economic performance.

4. The Output-Inflation Variance Tradeoff

There is no long-run tradeoff between the level of output and the level of inflation in this model—the Phillips curve is vertical in the long run. However, there is a long-run tradeoff between fluctuations in output and fluctuations in inflation. In other words there is a "second-order" Phillips curve which is not vertical in the long run. In order to determine this long-run tradeoff, we need the steady state values of $\sigma_y^2 = E(y_t - y^*)^2$ and

$\sigma_\pi^2 = E(\pi_t - \pi^*)^2$ corresponding to various values of λ. The graph of σ_y versus σ_π then traces out a minimum variability efficiency locus between output and inflation. This efficiency locus is the tradeoff curve.[14]

For a particular feedback vector g (which is a function of λ), the stochastic behavior of the vector Y_t is described by (13) with $d_t = gY_{t-1}$. Hence the steady-state variance-covariance matrix of Y_t is given by the matrix Σ which satisfies the equations

$$\Sigma = V + (B + cg)'\Sigma(B + cg) \tag{18}$$

where V is the variance-covariance matrix of r_t. Equation (18) is analogous to equation (17) and can be solved by the same iterative procedures described in Section 3. Since Y_t is measured in deviation form, the required values of σ_y^2 and σ_π^2 can be obtained from the first and fourth diagonal elements of the variance-covariance matrix Σ.

The fourth and fifth columns of table 2 give several values of σ_y and σ_π calculated according to the above procedure (σ_π has been multiplied by 4 to give annual rates and both standard deviations are stated as percents). These same values are plotted to trace out an efficiency locus in figure 1. As one would expect, the tradeoff curve is downward sloping with small values of λ giving points on the upper part of the curve. The minimum value of σ_y is .8 percent but is not reached for finite σ_π; the minimum value of σ_π is 1.44 percent and is reached when σ_y is 6.37 percent. Hence the tradeoff becomes vertical when output fluctuations reach a standard deviation of slightly over 6 percent.

A striking characteristic of the tradeoff curve is its sharp curvature: its slope increases from about $-1/4$ to -4 as σ_y increases from 1 to 2 percent. Hence, only extremely uneven concerns about inflation or unemployment (i.e., only very steep or very flat indifference curves) would lead policymakers to choose a monetary rule which generates output variability outside this 1 to 2 percent range.

5. Efficient Rules Versus Actual U.S. Performance and Constant Money Growth

It is informative to compare this estimated tradeoff curve with actual U.S. economic performance over the sample period and with the simulations of a constant growth rate rule (CGRR) for the money supply. To determine the actual values of σ_y and σ_π we need target levels for the output gap ($-y^*$) and the rate of inflation (π^*). For output we use the nonaccelerating inflation point $y^* = -.029$, which is consistent with the model considered here, and not much different from the sample mean ($-.019$) of y. For the

---

[14] The tradeoff between output and price stability is most easily characterized in terms of the standard derivations of output and inflation in this model. Other characterizations may be more convenient in other models.

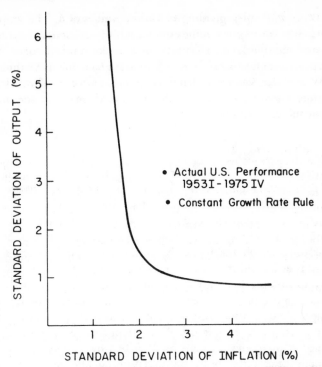

FIG. 1.—Output-Inflation Variation Tradeoff. (Source: see table 2. The points on this tradeoff curve represent the optimal standard deviations of quarterly output and inflation rates stated at annual rates in percentages. Output is measured as a deviation from a "full-employment" output.)

inflation target, we use the sample mean inflation rate of 3.5 percent, although this probably overstates π^* and hence gives an underestimate of σ_π. The resulting estimated values are $\sigma_y = 3.13$ percent and $\sigma_\pi = 2.59$ percent over the 1953I–1975IV period; this pair is shown in figure 1. It is evident that the actual U.S. economic performance was inefficient during this period according to these criteria, but perhaps not as inefficient as one would have expected. Note that in percentage terms there is more room for reduction in output fluctuations than in inflation fluctuations, if the 3.5 percent target inflation is reasonable. (Recall that lowering π^* would move the actual performance point to the right, and indicate more potential improvement on the inflation front).

The performance of the rational expectations economy under a CGRR can be determined by substituting the implied real balance feedback coefficients g into equation (18). For a CGRR real balances have an elasticity of -1 with respect to the inflation rate, and an elasticity of 1 with respect to lagged real money balances. Hence, the vector g is equal to $(0, 0, 1, -1, 0)$ when the growth rate of the nominal money supply is constant.[15] This value of g gives $\sigma_y = 2.54$ percent and $\sigma_\pi = 2.66$ percent, which is inefficient relative to the estimated tradeoff curve. It is interesting that this simple rule gives an output variance considerably below the actual U.S. performance. It does not quite dominate this performance because the inflation variance is slightly higher. However, if we evaluated U.S. performance at a 3 percent rather than a 3.5 percent target inflation rate, then the CGRR would clearly dominate.

6. Concluding Remarks

The central purpose of this paper has been to present an econometric method for selecting macroeconomic policy when expectations are formed rationally. The method consists of two steps: First, a structural econometric model with rational expectations is estimated using a minimum distance estimation technique. The estimation technique insures that the restrictions imposed on the model by rational expectations are satisfied. Second, this estimated model is used to calculate optimal monetary control rules to stabilize fluctuations in output and inflation. Since the estimated parameters of the model satisfy the rational expectations restrictions, peoples' expectations will be consistent with the policy rule selected. Hence, the method takes account of the reaction of people to expectations of changes in the policy variable as described by the policy rule.

Although the emphasis of the paper is on issues of econometric methodology, a number of results with potential economic policy implications have been derived: (i) Although there is no long-run tradeoff between the level of inflation and the level of output, there does exist a second-order Phillips curve tradeoff between fluctuations in output and fluctuations in inflation which is not vertical in the long run. This tradeoff was estimated for the U.S. economy over the 1953–75 period and is downward sloping: over the relevant range of this curve business cycle fluctuations can be reduced only by increasing the variability of inflation. (ii) As one would expect the optimal monetary policy accommodates increases in inflation when there is great concern with stabilizing output and little concern with fluctuations in inflation. On the other hand, the optimal policy is extremely nonaccommodative when fluctuations in inflation are viewed as very harmful. Even in this latter case, however, the optimal policy accommodates nonrecurrent shocks to the inflation rate. Reacting too strongly to such temporary shocks is inefficient and leads to an unnecessarily high variability of inflation. (iii) The partial elasticity of the optimal policy rule with respect to deviations of the economy from its potential growth path, is identical regardless of the slope of the output-inflation variance indifference curve. Reducing the "own-persistence" of output is desirable for reducing variability of inflation as well as output. (iv) The actual performance of the U.S. economy of the 1953–75 period was ineffi-

---

[15] The constant rate of money growth can be absorbed in the δ_1 coefficient of equation (12).

cient relative to the estimated tradeoff. Given the shocks to the economy during this period the standard deviation of output could have been about two percentage points lower for the same variability of inflation. (v) Simulation of a constant growth rate rule (CGRR) for the money supply in the rational expectations model gives a variability of output which is less than the actual U.S. performance over the sample period. If one evaluated U.S. inflation performance using a target inflation rate of 3 percent, then the CGRR would also give a smaller variability of inflation, and would consequently dominate actual U.S. performance. However, the CGRR is still inefficient relative to the combinations of output and inflation fluctuations that the model indicates are feasible.

Appendix A: Lagged Price Effect due to Staggered Overlapping Contracts

In Section 1 it was argued that the lagged inflation rate on the right-hand side of the price determination equation (2) can be explained by staggered overlapping price and wage contracts at fixed predetermined levels. While some firms are setting prices and wages, other firms will have already made their pricing decisions and these old prices and wages will be maintained at fixed levels during part of the new contract period. Hence, the firms setting prices and wages now will do so relative to the given price and wage decisions of other firms and according to expected demands in their markets.

To illustrate how such pricing behavior can lead to aggregate price equations like (2) we consider in this appendix a very simple model with two types of firms and two period contracts. The model is meant to be suggestive rather than a rigorous derivation of equation (2). Suppose that type 1 firms set prices to take effect at the beginning of odd-numbered time periods, and type 2 firms set prices to take effect at the beginning of even-numbered periods. For each type of firm the price remains in effect for two periods.[16] Thus, if q_t represents the log of prices set to begin in period t (by type 1 firms if t is odd, and by type 2 if t is even) then the log of the geometric aggregate price during period t is

$$p_t = .5(q_{t-1} + q_t). \tag{A1}$$

Consider a representative type 1 firm deciding what price to set for periods t and $t + 1$. The firm knows that for the duration of period t the price of type 1 firms is fixed at q_{t-1} and will change at the end of period t to q_{t+1} which is currently unknown. A reasonable pricing assumption—which is analogous to that proposed by Phelps (1970) in a nonstaggered model—is that the representative firm sets its price higher than the average price it expects other firms to set, when markets are tight, and conversely sets a relatively low price in slack markets. That is,

$$q_t = .5(q_{t-1} + \widehat{q}_{t+1}) + \alpha(\delta_t + \widehat{\delta}_{t+1}), \tag{A2}$$

where the first term on the right-hand side represents the expected average price of the type 2 firms during periods t and $t + 1$, and where δ_t is a measure of market excess demand. As in Section 1 the "hat" notation represents conditional expectations given information at time $t - 1$.

---

[16]This assumption distinguishes this model from that of Fischer [5] where two different wage levels are set for the following two periods. Hence in Fischer's model the wage can be set so as to equate expected supply and demand in both periods. Akerlof [1] considers an overlapping model similar to the one discussed here.

As an example of the type of aggregate price behavior which is implied by (A2) suppose that δ_t is a serially uncorrelated random variable with zero mean. Then a stochastic process for q_t which satisfies (A2) under the rational expectations assumption can be found by substituting the trial solution $q_t = \pi_1 q_{t-1} + \pi_2 q_{t-2} + \alpha \delta_t$ into (A2) and solving for π_1 and π_2. A solution is $\pi_1 = 2$ and $\pi_2 = -1$, so that[17]

$$q_t = 2q_{t-1} - q_{t-2} + \alpha \delta_t. \tag{A3}$$

Therefore from (A1) the aggregate price level p_t follows the second-order autoregressive—first-order moving average process,

$$p_{t+1} = 2p_t - p_{t-1} + .5\alpha(\delta_{t+1} + \delta_t). \tag{A4}$$

Or, in terms of the inflation rate,

$$\pi_t = \pi_{t-1} + \alpha \overline{\delta}_t, \tag{A5}$$

where δ_t is a measure of average excess demand in period t and $t + 1$. Equation (A5) is similar to traditional disequilibrium price adjustment assumptions except that the rate of change in the inflation rate, rather than the rate of change in price, depends on the level of excess demand. But the important result is that lagged prices appear on the right-hand side of the equation. In more elaborate models the dynamics will generally be of higher order and will depend on economic policy.[18] Since actual pricing is certainly more elaborate than in this simple model, the aggregate price equation (2) in the text can only serve as an approximation. Note also that the δ_{t+1} term is not explicitly treated in equation (2).

Appendix B: Use of the Minimum Distance Estimator for Rational Expectations Models

According to the notation of Section 3, the reduced form model we estimate is of the form

$$z_t = A(\alpha)x_t + w_t, \quad w_t = e_t - \theta e_{t-1}, \tag{B1}$$

where e_t is a serially uncorrelated random vector with mean zero and variance-covariance matrix Ω. Because expectations are assumed to be formed rationally, the 14 elements of the matrix A are restricted in the sense that they are functions of the 9 unknown elements in the parameter vector α. Similar restrictions will be imposed on the reduced form parameter matrix A in other types of rational expectations models. Hence, the notation $A(\alpha)$ is quite general and the following estimation technique is not confined to the rational expectations model considered in this paper.

If w_t were uncorrelated ($\theta = 0$), then the minimum distance estimator (MDE) of α could be obtained by minimizing

$$\sum_{t=1}^{T} [z_t - A(\alpha)x_t]'S[z_t - A(\alpha)x_t] \tag{B2}$$

with respect to α, for some positive definite matrix S. Malinvaud (1970) proposed that the MDE be iterated by setting S to $(\Sigma_{t=1}^{T} \widehat{e}_t \widehat{e}_t')^{-1}$ at each iteration where the $\widehat{e}_t$ are the residuals from the previous iteration, and derived the asymptotic distribution of the estimates; he also suggested that this iterated MDE would converge

---

[17]Some important nonuniqueness problems arise in this type of model and are explored in Phelps (1978).

[18]Incorporating the dependence of these dynamics on policy is a potentially important extension of the model examined in this paper and is the subject of my own current research.

to the maximum likelihood estimator, calculated as if w_t were normally distributed. Phillips (1976) proved that under certain conditions the iterated MDE does converge to this maximum likelihood estimator at least for large sample sizes. Computer routines for calculating the iterated MDE and the asymptotic variance covariance matrix are now widely available. For example TSP (Time Series Processor version 2.7) has such a minimum distance estimator routine which appears to work well in many applications. At least in the case of serially uncorrelated disturbances such routines are therefore readily applicable for estimating reduced forms of rational expectations models.

If θ is not equal to the zero matrix, but the elements of θ are known, then this iterated MDE can be modified to deal with the implied serial correlation. From (B1) we have that

$$e_t = \sum_{i=1}^{t} \theta^{t-i} w_i + \theta^t e_0$$

$$= \sum_{i=1}^{t} \theta^{t-i} z_i - \sum_{i=1}^{t} \theta^{t-i} A(\alpha) x_i + \theta^t e_0. \tag{B3}$$

Given e_0, (B3) can be used to calculate e_t and the MDE is then obtained by minimizing

$$\sum_{t=1}^{T} e_t' S e_t \tag{B4}$$

with respect to α. When θ is not known and when there are no restrictions placed on the elements of θ a simple procedure is feasible: for each value of θ in a given region, (B4) is minimized with respect to α as above. The MDE is then given by the value of θ which gives the smallest value for the minimum of (B4).

A simple recursive relationship can be used to calculate e_t as a function of the elements of θ. Write $\Sigma_{i=1}^{t} \theta^{t-i} A(\alpha) x_i$ as

$$\sum_{i=1}^{t} (x_i' \otimes \theta^{t-i}) \operatorname{vec} A(\alpha) = X_t^* \operatorname{vec} A(\alpha) \tag{B5}$$

where $X_t^* = \Sigma_{i=1}^{t} (x_i' \otimes \theta^{t-i})$, and let $z_t^* = \Sigma_{i=1}^{t} \theta^{t-i} z_i$. Then, for $e_0 = 0$,

$$e_t = z_t^* - X_t^* \operatorname{vec} A(\alpha). \tag{B6}$$

The variables z_t^* and X_t^* are functions of the elements of θ and can be calculated from the relations

$$z_t^* = z_t + \theta z_{t-1}^*, \tag{B7}$$

$$X_t^* = (x_t' \otimes I) + X_{t-1}^* (I \otimes \theta). \tag{B8}$$

Hence, using (B6) and these recursive relations the MDE can be calculated for a given θ with the same algorithms designed for the serially uncorrelated case. In the applications considered here, the lower off-diagonal element of θ is zero; hence the first equation of the transformed model contains all the elements of $A(\alpha)$, while the second contains only the elements in the second row of $A(\alpha)$.

In applying this estimation technique to the model of this paper we took the initial condition $e_0 = 0$. Hence the estimates are conditional at this value, though with 88 observations we would expect that the final estimates are not sensitive to this condition. With only two elements of θ unknown, a two-dimensional grid search was used to determine the MDE estimate of θ. (Note that in this model the rational expectations assumption does not put any restrictions on θ. Although β_5 and γ_1 enter into the elements of θ, these are not restrictive, since there are exactly two unknown elements in θ and two free parameters θ_1 and θ_2 which do not appear elsewhere in the model.)

References

Akerlof, G. A. "Relative Wages and the Rate of Inflation." *Q.J.E.* 83 (1969): 353–74.

Anderson, T. W. *The Statistical Analysis of Time Series.* New York: Wiley, 1971.

Calvo, G. A. "On the Time Consistency of Optimal Policy in a Monetary Economy." *Econometrica* 46 (1978): 1411–28.

Chow, G. C. *Analysis and Control of Dynamic Economic Systems.* New York: Wiley, 1975.

Fischer, S. "Long-Term Contracts, Rational Expectations, and the Optimal Money Supply Rule." *J.P.E.* 85 (1977): 191–205.

Kydland, F. E., and Prescott, E. C. "Rules Rather Than Discretion: The Inconsistency of Optimal Plans." *J.P.E.* 85 (1977): 473–93.

Lucas, R. E. "Econometric Policy Evaluation: A Critique." In *The Phillips Curve and Labor Markets,* edited by K. Brunner and A. H. Meltzer. Amsterdam: North-Holland, 1976.

Malinvaud, E. *Statistical Methods of Econometrics.* Amsterdam: North-Holland, 1970.

Pagan, A. "Optimal Control of Econometric Models with Autocorrelated Disturbance Terms." *Internat. Econ. Rev.* 16 (1975): 258–63.

Phelps, E. S. "Money Wage Dynamics and Labor Market Equilibrium." In *Microeconomic Foundations of Employment and Inflation Theory,* edited by E. S. Phelps et al. New York: Norton, 1970.

———. "Disinflation without Recession: Adaptive Guideposts and Monetary Policy." *Weltwirtschaftliches Archiv* 114 (1978): 783–809.

Phelps, E. S., and Taylor, J. B. "Stabilizing Powers of Monetary Policy under Rational Expectations." *J.P.E.* 85 (1977): 163–90.

Phillips, P. C. B. "The Iterated Minimum Distance Estimator and the Quasi-Maximum Likelihood Estimator." *Econometrica* 44 (1976): 449–60.

Prescott, E. C. "Should Control Theory Be Used for Economic Stabilization?" In *Optimal Policies, Control Theory and Technology Exports,* edited by K. Brunner and A. H. Meltzer. Amsterdam: North-Holland, 1977.

Sargent, T. J. "The Observational Equivalence of Natural and Unnatural Rate Theories of Unemployment." *J.P.E.* 84 (1976): 631–40.

———. "The Demand for Money during Hyperinflations under Rational Expectations: I." *Internat. Econ. Rev.* 18 (1977): 59–82.

Sargent, T. J., and Wallace, N. " 'Rational' Expectations, the Optimal Monetary Instrument and the Optimal Money Supply Rule." *J.P.E.* 83 (1975): 241–54.

Sims, C. A. "Macroeconomics and Reality." *Econometrica* 48 (1980): 1–48.

Taylor, J. B. "Asymptotic Properties of Multiperiod Control Rules in the Linear Regression Model." *Internat. Econ. Rev.* 15 (1974): 472–84.

———. "Monetary Policy during a Transition to Rational Expectations." *J.P.E.* 83 (1975): 1009–1021.

———. "Conditions for Unique Solutions in Stochastic Macroeconomic Models with Rational Expectations." *Econometrica* 45 (1977): 1377–85. (a)

———. "Control Theory and Economic Stabilization: A Comment." In *Optimal Policies, Control Theory and Technology Exports,* edited by K. Brunner and A. H. Meltzer. Amsterdam: North-Holland, 1977. (b)

Wallis, K. F. "Econometric Implications of the Rational Expectations Hypothesis." *Econometrica* 48 (1980): 49–74.

34

Estimation and Optimal Control of Dynamic Game Models under Rational Expectations

Gregory C. Chow

This paper extends the author's recent (1979) paper on the estimation of rational expectations models in two directions. First, two players are introduced instead of only one, and the estimation of a model of dynamic games is studied under the assumption of a dominant player or a noncooperative Nash equilibrium. Second, with the second player (government) treated as the dominant player, we consider policy evaluation and optimization by the government under the assumption of rational expectations.

This paper is concerned with further developments of Chow (1979), entitled "Estimation of Rational Expectations Models" [see chap. 19 above], where I have proposed two methods for the estimation of the parameters of a linear model

$$y_t = Ay_{t-1} + Cx_t + b_t + u_t \qquad (1)$$

which describes the environment of a set of economic decision makers, and the parameters of a quadratic objective function

$$-E_0 \sum_{t=1}^{T} (y_t - a_t)'K_t(y_t - a_t) \qquad (2)$$

which the decision makers are assumed to maximize. Resulting from this maximization is a linear behavioral equation (feedback control equation) for the decision makers who control x_t, written as

$$x_t = G_t y_{t-1} + g_t. \qquad (3)$$

The parameters G_t and g_t in (3) are derived from the parameters of (1) and (2). The econometrician observes the data on x_t and y_t, and wishes to

I would like to acknowledge financial support from the National Science Foundation through grant no. SOC77-07677.

estimate the parameters of (1) and (2). The two methods proposed in Chow (1979) are maximum likelihood and a consistent method corresponding to two-stage least squares. Detailed knowledge of these methods is not required for the reader of this paper, who is asked only to keep in mind that the methods exist for the estimation problem just described.

The present paper is concerned with two extensions of the above estimation problem. First, there are two sets of economic decision makers, so that the model becomes

$$y_t = Ay_{t-1} + C_1 x_{1t} + C_2 x_{2t} + b_t + u_t. \tag{4}$$

Each set i of decision makers chooses its control variables x_{it} to maximize an objective function

$$-E_0 \sum_{t=1}^{T} (y_t - a_{it})' K_{it} (y_t - a_{it}) \qquad (i = 1, 2) \tag{5}$$

and derives its optimal behavioral equation

$$x_{it} = G_{it} y_{t-1} + g_{it} \qquad (i = 1, 2). \tag{6}$$

The econometric problem is to estimate the parameters of (4) and (5). Second, when one decision maker is the government, we are concerned with the evaluation of the effects of government policy changes and the choice of an optimum policy for the government.

To illustrate the application of this model, let x_{1t} be the variables subject to the control of some group of decision makers of the private sector and x_{2t} be the variables subject to the control of the government. If the government adheres to a policy rule—that is, if G_2 and g_{2t} are given—the environment facing the private decision makers is

$$\begin{aligned} y_t &= (A + C_2 G_2) y_{t-1} + C_1 x_{1t} + (b_t + C_2 g_{2t}) + u_t \\ &\equiv A_{12} y_{t-1} + C_1 x_{1t} + b_{12,t} + u_t. \end{aligned} \tag{7}$$

They would maximize their objective function to derive their behavioral equation. As Lucas (1976) has stressed, if the policy rule of the government changes, the behavioral equation of the private decision makers will also change. Therefore, an econometrician should not rely on a stable relation (3) to evaluate the effects of government policy. A correct procedure is to estimate (1) and (2), rather than (1) and (3), and then derive the changes in (3) due to changes in (1). Lucas (1976, p. 20) reminded the reader that this point had been made by the proponents of structural estimation for simultaneous-equation models, and cited Marschak (1953) for having pointed out the change in the reduced-form equations due to a policy change. Another manifestation of this problem occurs when the behavioral equations of the private sector contain expectations variables which are explained by some distributed lag relationships. As government policy changes, the model (1) or (7) will change, and these expectations will also change under rational expectations, thus making the historical distributed lag relationships unstable. The solution again is to rederive the expectations using the new structure (1) or (7), but this topic will not be treated in the present paper, since the estimation and control problems associated with it are discussed in Taylor (1979), Wallis (1980), and Chow (1980).

The first extension of this paper is to allow for two sets of decision makers whose actions affect the environment of each other. In the above example, while the government policy rule $x_{2t} = G_2 y_{t-1} + g_{2t}$ affects the optimal policy of the private sector, the latter's optimal behavioral relation $x_{1t} = G_1 y_{t-1} + g_{1t}$ will also affect the policy rule of the government if it is also assumed to maximize its objective function. We will study this dynamic game model in this paper. Section II deals with the estimation of the parameters of this model under the assumption that player 2 (the government) is the dominant player. Section III treats the estimation problem when the two players are assumed to be in a noncooperative Nash equilibrium. Section I sets the stage by treating the topic of government policy evaluation and optimization under the assumption that the government is the dominant player. In this paper, we assume that the optimal reaction coefficient G_{it} in (6) for both players will reach a steady state G_i, that is, the rational expectations equilibrium. Otherwise, no stable relationships can be estimated.

I. Policy Evaluation and Optimization under Rational Expectations

The critique by Lucas (1976) of econometric policy evaluation is essentially that when the policy of player 2 (the government) is being evaluated, the econometrician should not take the behavioral equation $x_{1t} = G_1 y_{t-1} + g_{1t}$ for the private sector as given. To evaluate the consequences of any government policy rule (G_2, g_{2t}), proper account has to be taken of the optimizing reaction of the private sector since its environment consists of (4) and $x_{2t} = G_2 y_{t-1} + g_{2t}$. The private sector derives its optimum behavioral equation $x_{1t} = G_1 y_{t-1} + g_{1t}$ by maximizing its objective function subject to this environment. Linear-quadratic optimal control theory as found in Chow (1975) can be used to find this optimal feedback control equation. The problem of policy evaluation is thus solved.

Turning to policy optimization by the government, we observe that its optimal policy is the strategy of the dominant player in a two-person dynamic game. We will derive a pair of optimal steady-state strategies (G_1, g_1) and (G_2, g_2) for the two players when the system is in a covariance-stationary equilibrium, assuming that b_t, a_{1t}, K_{1t}, a_{2t}, and K_{2t} are all time-invariant, the time subscript t for these variables being omitted in the remainder of this section.

If the dominant player adheres to a feedback control policy $x_{2t} =$

$G_2 y_{t-1} + g_2$, player 1 will face (7) as its environment and adopt the optimal equilibrium strategy $x_{1t} = G_1 y_{t-1} + g_1$ where (see Chow 1975, pp. 170–71)

$$C_1' H_1 C_1 G_1 + C_1' H_1 (A + C_2 G_2) = 0 \tag{8}$$

$$H_1 - K_1 - (A + C_2 G_2 + C_1 G_1)' H_1 (A + C_2 G_2 + C_1 G_1) = 0 \tag{9}$$

$$C_1' H_1 C_1 g_1 + C_1' [H_1 (b + C_2 g_2) - h_1] = 0 \tag{10}$$

$$[I - (A + C_2 G_2 + C_1 G_1)'] h_1 - K_1 a_1$$
$$- (A + C_2 G_2 + C_1 G_1)' H_1 (b + C_2 g_2) = 0. \tag{11}$$

Given G_2, equations (8) and (9) can be solved to obtain G_1 and H_1. Given g_2 in addition, equations (10) and (11) can be solved to obtain g_1 and h_1. In a covariance-stationary equilibrium, the system will have a mean vector $\bar{y}$ and a covariance matrix $\Gamma = E(y_t - \bar{y})(y_t - \bar{y})'$ which satisfy (see Chow 1975, pp. 51–52)

$$(I - A - C_1 G_1 - C_2 G_2)\bar{y} - b - C_1 g_1 - C_2 g_2 = 0 \tag{12}$$

$$\Gamma - (A + C_1 G_1 + C_2 G_2)\Gamma(A + C_1 G_1 + C_2 G_2)' - E u_t u_t' = 0. \tag{13}$$

Player 2's problem is to minimize

$$\frac{1}{2} E(y_t - a_2)' K_2 (y_t - a_2) = \frac{1}{2} \operatorname{tr}(K_2 \Gamma) + \frac{1}{2} (\bar{y} - a_2)' K_2 (\bar{y} - a_2)$$

with respect to G_2 and g_2 in its feedback control equation, subject to the constraints (8)–(13). This problem can be solved by forming the Lagrangian expression

$$L = \frac{1}{2} \operatorname{tr}(K_2 \Gamma) + \frac{1}{2} (\bar{y} - a_2)' K_2 (\bar{y} - a_2) - \omega'(10) - \phi'(11) - \lambda'(12)$$

$$- \operatorname{tr}\{\Omega(8)\} - \frac{1}{2} \operatorname{tr}\{\Phi(9)\} - \frac{1}{2} \operatorname{tr}\{\Psi(13)\},$$

where ω, ϕ, λ, Ω, $\Phi = \Phi'$, and $\Psi = \Psi'$ are vectors and matrices of Lagrangian multipliers and, for brevity, the equation number in parentheses denotes the corresponding constraint.

Using the differentiation rule $\partial \operatorname{tr}(AB)/\partial A = B'$, we obtain the following equations, with R denoting $A + C_1 G_1 + C_2 G_2$,

$$\frac{\partial L}{\partial g_1} = -C_1' H_1 C_1 \omega + C_1' \lambda = 0 \tag{14}$$

$$\frac{\partial L}{\partial h_1} = C_1 \omega - (I - R)\phi = 0 \tag{15}$$

$$\frac{\partial L}{\partial g_2} = -C_2' H_1 C_1 \omega + C_2' H_1 R \phi + C_2' \lambda = 0 \tag{16}$$

$$\frac{\partial L}{\partial \bar{y}} = K_2(\bar{y} - a_2) - (I - R')\lambda = 0 \tag{17}$$

$$\frac{\partial L}{\partial G_1} = C_1'[H_1C_1\Omega' + H_1R\Phi + \Psi R\Gamma + h_1\phi' + H_1(b + C_2g_2)\phi' + \lambda\bar{y}']$$
$$= 0 \tag{18}$$

$$\frac{\partial L}{\partial G_2} = C_2'[H_1C_1\Omega' + H_1R\Phi + \Psi R\Gamma + h_1\phi' + H_1(b + C_2g_2)\phi' + \lambda\bar{y}']$$
$$= 0 \tag{19}$$

$$\frac{\partial L}{\partial H_1} = -\Phi + R\Phi R' - C_1g_1\omega'C_1' - C_1\omega g_1'C_1' - (b + C_2g_2)\omega'C_1'$$
$$- C_1\omega(b + C_2g_2)' + (b + C_2g_2)\phi'R + R'\phi(b + C_2g_2)' = 0 \tag{20}$$

$$\frac{\partial L}{\partial \Gamma} = K_2 - \Psi + R'\Psi R = 0. \tag{21}$$

To solve these equations, we first consider an approximate solution for G_2, G_1, and H_1 in a simpler problem. The problem is the minimization of $\operatorname{tr}(K_2\Gamma)$ when $b = 0$, $a_1 = 0$, and $a_2 = 0$. The optimal strategies are $x_{1t} = G_1y_{t-1}$ and $x_{2t} = G_2y_{t-1}$; the constraints (10), (11), and (12) are no longer relevant. One only needs to solve equations (18)–(21), with $\omega = 0$, $\phi = 0, \lambda = 0, \bar{y} = 0$, and $g_2 = 0$. Equation (20) would become $\Phi = R\Phi R'$, which has a solution $\Phi = 0$. Equation (18) would imply $\Omega' = -(C_1'H_1C_1)^{-1}(\Psi R\Gamma)$, which, when substituted into (19), would yield

$$C_2'[I - H_1C_1(C_1'H_1C_1)^{-1}]\Psi(A + C_1G_1 + C_2G_2)\Gamma = 0. \tag{22}$$

Starting with an initial guess for G_2, we solve (8) and (9) for G_1 and H_1. Given G_1, we solve (21) for Ψ. Equation (22), postmultiplied by Γ^{-1}, can be used to compute a new G_2.

$$G_2 = \{C_2'[I - H_1C_1(C_1'H_1C_1)^{-1}]\Psi C_2\}^{-1}C_2'$$
$$[I - H_1C_1(C_1'H_1C_1)^{-1}]\Psi(A + C_1G_1).$$

This iterative process can be continued to find G_2, G_1, and H_1 for the simpler problem.

To solve the original problem, we start with the above approximate solution for G_2, G_1, and H_1. Equations (14), (15), (16), and (17) imply, respectively, with $P_1 = C_1(C_1'H_1C_1)^{-1}C_1'$,

$$\omega = (C_1'H_1C_1)^{-1}C_1'\lambda \tag{14a}$$

$$\phi = (I - R)^{-1}P_1\lambda \tag{15a}$$

$$C_2'\{I - H_1[I - R(I - R)^{-1}]P_1\}\lambda = 0 \tag{16a}$$

$$\lambda = (I - R')^{-1}K_2(\bar{y} - a_2). \tag{17a}$$

Equations (17a) and (12) give

$$\lambda = (I - R')^{-1}K_2[(I - R)^{-1}(b + C_1g_1 + C_2g_2) - a_2]. \quad (23)$$

Combining (23) with (16a), we get

$$C_2'\{I - H_1[I - R(I - R)^{-1}]P_1\}(I - R')^{-1}K_2$$
$$[(I - R)^{-1}(b + C_1g_1 + C_2g_2) - a_2] = 0. \quad (24)$$

With G_2, G_1, and H_1 given, equations (24), (10), and (11) can be solved for g_2, g_1, and h_1. Equation (24) is used to express g_2 as a linear function of g_1; equations (10) and (11) become two linear equations in g_1 and h_1. Equations (23), (14a), and (15a) are then used to find λ, ω, and ϕ, while equation (12) is used to compute $\bar{y}$.

We now follow the steps of the simpler problem to solve equations (18)–(21). Equation (20) is used to solve for Φ iteratively, that is, $\Phi^{(i+1)} = R\Phi^{(i)}R' +$ known matrix. Equations (18) and (19) imply

$$\Omega' = -(C_1'H_1C_1)^{-1}C_1'[H_1R\Phi + \Psi R\Gamma + \cdots] \quad (18a)$$

$$C_2'[I - H_1P_1][H_1R\Phi + \Psi R\Gamma + h_1\phi' +$$
$$H_1(b + C_2g_2)\phi' + \lambda\bar{y}'] = 0. \quad (19a)$$

Since (13) and (21) can be used to compute Γ and Ψ, respectively, (19a) after being postmultiplied by Γ^{-1} can be solved for G_2 iteratively, that is

$$C_2'[I - H_1P_1]\Psi C_2G_2 = C_2'[I - H_1P_1][H_1R\Phi\Gamma^{-1} +$$
$$\Psi(A + C_1G_1) + \cdots] \quad (22a)$$

where we have recalled $R = (A + C_1G_1 + C_2G_2)$. Having thus obtained a new matrix G_2, we can continue with the iterative process by returning to the beginning of the preceding paragraph.

Mathematically, the solution to the two-person dynamic game formulated above under a Nash (or Cournot) equilibrium is simpler, for each player would treat the other's strategy as given, without being affected by his own strategy. Given (G_2, g_2), player 1 would find (G_1, g_1) by equations (8)–(10) as before. Symmetrically, given (G_1, g_1), player 2 would find (G_2, g_2) by solving an identical set of equations with subscripts 1 and 2 interchanged. A Nash equilibrium is found by solving these two sets of equations.

II. Estimation of Dynamic Game Model with a Dominant Player

When x_{2t} in (4) represents the policy instruments of the government and the government is treated as the dominant player, we will study the estimation problem in two stages. First, assuming that the government adheres to a policy rule $x_{2t} = G_2y_{t-1} + g_{2t}$, which is decided upon by whatever means, we will consider the estimation of the parameters of (4) and

(5) for $i = 1$ under the assumption that the private sector behaves optimally. Second, from the above framework we take the next step by assuming that the government is also trying to maximize (5) for $i = 2$ and consider the estimation of the parameters of its objective function as well.

For the first problem, the stochastic environment facing the private sector consists of two equations, (4) and

$$x_{2t} = G_2 y_{t-1} + g_{2t} \tag{6a}$$

These two equations comprise the model (1) in the framework of Chow (1979). In that paper, two methods were provided to estimate the parameters of (1), now consisting of (4) and (6a), and of (2), now represented by (5) with $i = 1$. The methods are maximum likelihood and a consistent method analogous to two-stage least squares. The latter method requires consistent estimates of the parameters of (1) and (3); and, using them, solves for the parameters of (2) in the second stage of two-stage least squares.

We now incorporate the assumption that the government also maximizes to obtain its behavioral equation (6a). If we are not interested in estimating the objective function of the government, and are willing to assume that the parameters of (4) and (5) remained unchanged for the sample observations, then (6a) is a stable equation and the methods of Chow (1979) would suffice, as pointed out in the last paragraph. The new problem is to estimate the objective function of the government as well. From the viewpoint of the maximizing government, the stochastic environment consists of (4) and (5) with $i = 1$, which, together with its own policy (G_2, g_{2t}), determine G_1 and g_{1t} in (6) as a result of the private sector's maximizing behavior.

Maximum-likelihood estimation of the parameters of (4) and (5) under the assumption that player 2 (the government) is the dominant player can proceed as follows. Adding a residual v_{it} to (6) and assuming a joint normal distribution of u_t, v_{1t}, and v_{2t}, one can easily write down the likelihood function which has the parameters of (4) and (6) as arguments. As a first step, we postpone the estimation of K_{2t} and a_{2t}, and assume some given values for G_2 and g_{2t} (which could be the coefficients of a least-squares regression of x_{2t} on y_{t-1} and appropriate trend terms). Given G_2 and g_{2t}, we can express G_1 and g_{1t} as functions of the parameters of (4) and K_{1t} and a_{1t} in (5) through the maximization of the private sector. K_{1t} and a_{1t} thus replace G_1 and g_{1t} as arguments in the likelihood function. To reduce the number of parameters, we assume here as in Chow (1979) that $K_{1t} = \beta_1^t K_{10}$ and $a_{1t} = \phi_1^t a_{10}$, β_1 being the discount factor for the private sector and ϕ_1 being a diagonal matrix with some elements known to be one if the targets in a_t are constant through time. Given G_2 and g_{2t}, then, we can maximize the likelihood function with respect to the parameters of (1) and K_{10}, β_1, a_{10}, and ϕ_1. This problem was solved in Chow (1979).

In order to solve the more difficult problem of estimating K_{2t} and a_{2t}, we treat a more restrictive case by introducing the assumption of Section I that b_t, K_{1t}, a_{1t}, K_{2t}, and a_{2t} are all time-invariant. Given K_1, a_1, K_2, a_2, and the parameters of (4) we can apply the method of Section I to find (G_1, g_1) and (G_2, g_2); thus the likelihood function can be evaluated. A gradient method can in principle be applied to maximize the likelihood with respect to these parameters, but this numerical maximization problem requires further investigation.

III. Estimation of Dynamic Game Model under Nash Equilibrium

The estimation problem for a dynamic game model under a Nash equilibrium is simpler. We can apply iterative techniques by considering this estimation problem in two stages. First, assuming tentatively that the government adheres to a policy rule (G_2, g_{2t}), we will consider the estimation of the parameters of (4) and $K_{1t} = \beta_1^t K_{10}$ and $a_{1t} = \phi_1^t a_{10}$ under the assumption that the private sector behaves optimally. Our estimation procedure assumes optimal behavior (G_1, g_{1t}) of the private sector, with (G_2, g_{2t}) taken as given. Second, assuming that the private sector adheres to the policy (G_1, g_{1t}) as determined above, we consider the estimation of the parameters of (4) and $K_{2t} = \beta_2^t K_{20}$ and $a_{2t} = \phi_2^t a_{20}$ under the assumption that the government behaves optimally. Similarly, this estimation procedure assumes optimal behavior (G_2, g_{2t}) of the government, with (G_1, g_{1t}) taken as given. We now go back to step one, and iterate back and forth until convergence.

As pointed out previously, given (G_2, g_{2t}), the methods of Chow (1979) can be used to estimate the parameters of (4), K_{10}, β_1, a_{10}, ϕ_1, and, accordingly, G_1 and g_{1t}. Similarly, given (G_1, g_{1t}), the same methods can be used to estimate the parameters of (4), K_{20}, β_2, a_{20}, ϕ_2, and, accordingly, G_2 and g_{2t}. If the method of maximum likelihood is used, we start with some consistent estimates of G_2 and g_{2t} (as obtained by regressing x_{2t} on y_{t-1} and appropriate trends), and maximize the likelihood function with respect to the parameters of (4), K_{10}, β_1, a_{10}, and ϕ_1, yielding maximum likelihood estimates of G_1 and g_{1t} as well. Using these estimates of G_1 and g_{1t}, we again maximize the likelihood function with respect to the parameters of (4), K_{20}, β_2, a_{20}, and ϕ_2, and so forth until convergence. This procedure amounts to maximizing the likelihood function with respect to two sets of parameters iteratively, that is, to one set while holding the other set fixed and alternatively.

To propose a simpler and yet consistent method, we start with consistent estimates of the parameters of (4), and of (G_2, g_{2t}) and (G_1, g_{1t}), by the method of least squares, for instance. The parameters of (4) and (G_i, g_{it}) can be employed to solve for K_{i0}, β_i, a_{i0}, and ϕ_i for $i = 1, 2$ by the method analogous to two-stage least squares as given in Section 4 of Chow (1979).

Given the parameters of (4) and K_{i0}, β_i, a_{i0}, and ϕ_i ($i = 1, 2$), one can then find the Nash equilibrium solution for (G_1, g_{1t}) and (G_2, g_{2t}) iteratively, to improve upon the initial, consistent estimates of these parameters.[1] The situation is exactly analogous to the estimation of the reduced-form parameters Π in linear simultaneous stochastic equations. Consistent estimate $\hat{\Pi}$ of Π by least squares can be used to estimate the parameters $(B\Gamma)$ of the structure using the method of two-stage least squares. Given these estimates of $(B\Gamma)$, denoted by $(\widehat{B\Gamma})$, we can obtain a new estimate of Π as $\hat{B}^{-1}\hat{\Gamma}$, to improve upon the initial estimate $\hat{\Pi}$.

This section has treated the estimation of rational expectations models under the assumption of Nash equilibrium. If player 2 represents the government, the solution concept of having a dominant player as expounded in Section II may be more appropriate. Given their likelihoods, these two solution concepts can be tested statistically, but this topic is not pursued here.

References

Chow, G. C. *Analysis and Control of Dynamic Economic Systems.* New York: Wiley, 1975.
——. "Estimation of Rational Expectations Models," Research Memorandum no. 252, Econometric Research Program, Princeton Univ., 1979.
——. "Econometric Policy Evaluation and Optimization under Rational Expectations." *J. Econ. Dynamics and Control* 2 (1980): 1–13.
Cruz, J. B., Jr. "Survey of Nash and Stackelberg Equilibrium Strategies in Dynamic Games." *Ann. Econ. and Soc. Measurement* 4, no. 2 (1975): 339–44.
Lucas, R. E., Jr. "Econometric Policy Evaluation: A Critique." *J. Monetary Econ.*, 1, suppl. (1976): 19–46.
Kydland, F. "Noncooperative and Dominant Player Solutions in Discrete Dynamic Games." *Internat. Econ. Rev.* 16 (1975): 321–35.
Marschak, J. "Economic Measurements for Policy and Prediction." In *Studies in Econometric Method,* edited by Wm. C. Hood and T. C. Koopmans. Cowles Commission Monograph 14. New York: Wiley, 1953.
Taylor, J. B. "Estimation and Control of a Macroeconomic Model with Rational Expectations." *Econometrica* 47, no. 5 (1979): 1267–86.
Wallis, K. F. "Econometric Implications of the Rational Expectations Hypothesis." *Econometrica* 48, no. 1 (January 1980): 49–73.

[1] An algebraic expression for the Nash equilibrium can be found in Kydland (1975, pp. 323–26), e.g., but here we need only a numerical solution by iterations, i.e., by solving a standard optimal control problem to get G_1 and g_{1t} for the first player, given G_2 and g_{2t}, and then solving a standard optimal control problem to find G_2 and g_{2t} given the above G_1 and g_{1t}, and so forth. For more references on dynamic games, see Cruz (1975).

Robert E. Lucas, Jr., is John Dewey Distinguished Service Professor of Economics at the University of Chicago and author of *Studies in Business-Cycle Theory*.

Thomas J. Sargent is professor of economics at the University of Minnesota and advisor to the Federal Reserve Bank of Minneapolis. He is the author of *Macroeconomic Theory*.